STRANGE ENTHUSIASM
A Life of
Thomas Wentworth Higginson

Thomas Wentworth Higginson, 1903
Photo courtesy Library of Congress

STRANGE ENTHUSIASM

A Life of

Thomas Wentworth Higginson

by Tilden G. Edelstein

New Haven and London, Yale University Press, 1968

Copyright © 1968 by Yale University.

All rights reserved. This book may not be
reproduced, in whole or in part, in any form
(except by reviewers for the public press),
without written permission from the publishers.

Library of Congress catalog card number: 68–27752

Designed by Marvin Howard Simmons,
set in Janson type,
and printed in the United States of America by
The Colonial Press Inc., Clinton, Massachusetts.
Distributed in Great Britain, Europe, Asia, and
Africa by Yale University Press Ltd., London; in
Canada by McGill University Press, Montreal; and
in Latin America by Centro Interamericano de Libros
Académicos, Mexico City.

Excerpts from the poems of Emily Dickinson
are reprinted by permission of the publishers
and the Trustees of Amherst College
from Thomas H. Johnson, Editor,
The Poems of Emily Dickinson, Cambridge, Mass.:
The Belknap Press of Harvard University Press,
Copyright, 1951, 1955, by
The President and Fellows of Harvard College.

Published with assistance from
The Louis Stern Memorial Fund

To my father, Theodore Edelstein
In memory of my mother, Nettie Edelstein

Preface

Graduate students in C. Vann Woodward's seminar at The Johns Hopkins University, during the mid-1950s, could not fail to appreciate the role that irony played in his view of the American past. *Reunion and Reaction* and *Origins of the New South*, which recently had been published, treated the rise and fall of reform in a manner that left a marked impression upon us. But Professor Woodward's first book, *Tom Watson, Agrarian Rebel*, had additional relevance to me for the discussions we were having about the relationship of history to the social sciences. Newly published were the Social Science Research Council's *The Social Sciences in Historical Study, Bulletin 64*, David Donald's "Toward a Reconsideration of Abolitionists," and Richard Hofstadter's *The Age of Reform: From Bryan to F.D.R.* I believed then, and it has since been convincingly stated in Martin Duberman's "The Abolitionists and Psychology," that psychosocial accounts of individuals would be necessary to aid historians to generalize ultimately about the motives and behavior of members of a reform movement with a greater precision than Professors Donald and Hofstadter could achieve in their important syntheses.

Thomas Wentworth Higginson seemed well suited for the kind of biography that I planned to write. He had been the most renowned disciple of Theodore Parker and (except for John Brown) the most militant Abolitionist. During the Civil War he had commanded the first freed slave regiment and then successively became a radical Republican, a mugwump, an anti-imperialist, and a Progressive.

The sources for a study of Higginson were plentiful and diverse. Like a dutiful nineteenth-century Cambridge citizen—with seventeenth-century ancestors—he had kept either a diary or a journal since he was twelve years old; these were preserved with family correspondence (including letters and diaries written by his parents before his birth and during his childhood), undergraduate and divinity school essays and examinations, and scrapbooks of newspaper clippings. He also left bound volumes of many of the magazines for which he had written, with notations identifying many of his essays, and systematic listings of the titles and locations of other articles. (Higginson had published more articles in the *Atlantic Monthly* than any other contributor except Lowell and Holmes.) Manuscripts pertaining to his reform and literary activities were available. He had published some thirty books, including *Army Life in a Black Regiment* and a novel called *Malbone*. His autobiography, *Cheerful Yesterdays,* was only the most extensive account of his life among the many that he published.

The nature and extent of the Higginson material has enabled me to devote more than the customary attention to parental influences, to essential biographical details of his youth, and to his emerging ideas, personal traits, and behavioral patterns. Viewed prior to the time he becomes historically significant provides understanding of the meaning and motives of his adult actions and ideas. During his adult years I have sought to avoid presenting either the force of historical context or the force of childhood as exclusive determinants—history and personality, it is hoped, can be seen interacting.

I have assumed that personality and historical context help shape the boundaries for an individual's thought and action. In recent years there has been a growing reaction, especially among younger historians, against the psychological explanations that several revisionist historians have applied to the Abolitionists. Perhaps only when our historians seek to describe the nonrational motives and pathological behavior of moderates and conservatives, more than they have done thus far, will there be some assurance that psychology is a useful tool for helping to understand all historical figures. Surely it is worth heeding Karen Horney's warning that in times of social injustice it may be the inactive individual, not the reformer, who is mentally disturbed. The biography of a reformer can be written with sympathy and understanding, I believe, if one recognizes that it is a rare man, reformer or not, who shows no

evidence of some pathological behavior, and that human heroism
need not rely upon impersonal devotion to ideals.

During the preparation of this book I have received much in-
valuable help. C. Vann Woodward generously gave his direction,
criticism, and encouragement. Charles A. Barker read and criticized the manuscript with special attention to my treatment of
American intellectual history. And I owe special thanks to Willie
Lee Rose and Aileen S. Kraditor for their suggestions and kind
encouragement. Hugh Hawkins repeatedly exceeded all obligations
of friendship by offering suggestions and criticism when I needed
them most.

Ira Klein, Daniel H. Calhoun, James M. McPherson, Richard
H. Sewell, Otto H. Olsen, Charles E. L'Homme, Richard C.
Sterne, Frederick M. Anderson, and Donald Dunbar read portions
of the manuscript and shared with me their respective expertness.
Martin Duberman and Frank O. Gatell provided me with Higginson material that they discovered in their work. Among the
many things for which I am grateful to Peter Kussi is his continuing ability to be intellectually stimulating. Former students of mine
who provided perceptive comments and useful information were
Ann Jackowitz, Janet Sharistanian, and Terri Stargardter.

I am especially indebted to the following librarians for their
help: Carolyn Jakeman, Kimball Elkins, Katherine Kuechle, Ann
Berry, Alma Brown, Margaret Davis, and Stephen Folts. A generous fellowship from the Samuel S. Fels Fund enabled me to do a
year of research uninterrupted by teaching responsibilities. A grant
from the Shell Oil Company helped defray the cost of typing

At every stage in the preparation of this book, my wife Marjorie
Edelstein has given immeasurable aid and understanding.

T.G.E.

Princeton, New Jersey
January 1968

Contents

Prologue

As a postgraduate student at Harvard in 1845, twenty-one-year-old Wentworth Higginson carefully decorated his dormitory room: on one side he placed a bust of Hebe, the Greek goddess of youth, on the other a bust of the only slightly less godlike Daniel Webster. Hebe was to remind him of what was already his, Webster of what he hoped to attain. He had taken time from studying Locke and Kant to purchase the Webster head, which he described as "the personification of intellectual powers," explaining that he was not "superstitious—but mystical enough to believe that by hanging it before me I shall gain something of its strength—enough to be worth more than the two dollars it cost." A few months earlier Higginson had exuberantly reported: "I had a great honor—being introduced to Daniel Webster! . . . If it had been Queen Victoria I shouldn't have cared half so much." [1]

But seven years later when Webster died, Higginson publicly assailed the Massachusetts senator for having supported the Compromise of 1850. Webster's renowned oratory, he added, had never reached the heights of an Emerson, whose pages remained "starry with statements of absolute truth." [2]

Why Massachusetts men like Higginson, Whittier, and Emerson ultimately had to walk backward with averted gaze when once they had idolized Webster can best be understood by recalling what their Senator said on March 7, 1850. His unwillingness to support the Wilmot Proviso to prevent the extension of slavery, and his support of a strict fugitive slave law were of course most disturbing to antislavery men who had applauded his earlier opposition to the annexation of Texas and to the extension of slavery. But it was what

1. Thomas Wentworth Higginson to Louisa Higginson, Mar. 11, 1845, TWH to Mary Elizabeth Channing, July 6, 1844, Higginson MSS.
2. "Elegy Without Fiction," Oct. 31, 1852, Worcester *Spy*, Nov. 5, 1852.

Webster said in that address about ways of thinking and acting that separated him from many New England intellectuals. Said Webster: "There are men who . . . are of opinion that human duties may be ascertained with the exactness of mathematics. They deal with morals as with mathematics and they think what is right may be distinguished from what is wrong with the precision of an algebraic equation." Not only was Webster critical of these moralists, he also showed contempt for the zealous reformers by saying: "If their perspicacious vision enables them to detect a spot on the face of the sun, they think that a good reason why the sun should be struck down from heaven."[3]

In his compromise speech Webster uncompromisingly stated that he had clear notions and opinions about Abolitionists. "I do not think them useful. I think their operations for the last twenty years have produced nothing good or valuable." The only result of their agitation was to bind the slaves in the South more firmly. In short, the moralist, the zealous reformer, and the Abolitionist exhibited a "strange enthusiasm." According to Webster, this strange enthusiasm, this dogmatic attachment to a cause endangering the Union, deserved the contempt of all who revered their fathers and grandfathers.[4]

Forty miles north of Boston, in the coastal town of Newburyport, Wentworth Higginson read the 7th of March speech in the local Whig paper which recommended the address as a welcome contrast to the beliefs of "clergymen, closet thinkers . . . and people of contemplative habit." Higginson had been all of these. He had approvingly read the *Dial* wherein transcendentalism was defined as a doctrine which held "that moral and religious truths can be proved . . . with the same degree of certainty that attends mathematical demonstration . . . because they can be shown to conform to certain fundamental truths, axioms." And in the *Dial*, enthusiasm was judged and defined differently from the way Webster had evaluated it:

3. Newburyport *Herald*, Mar. 13–18, 1850.
4. Harold D. Foster, "Webster's 7th of March Speech and the Secession Movement," *American Historical Review*, 27 (1922), 245; Tremaine McDowell, "Webster's Words on Abolitionists," *New England Quarterly*, 7 (1934), 315. McDowell notes that the "strange enthusiasm" section of the speech was removed from later editions.

Let the flame of enthusiasm fire alway your bosom. Enthusiasm is the glory and hope for the world. It is the life of sanctity and genius; it has wrought all miracles since the beginning of time.[5]

Higginson had always looked to Emerson, who, though mocking many of the preachers and protesters at the sabbatarian Chardon Street convention, had praised the zeal and enthusiasm of the best reformers. He had thrilled at the antislavery oratory of Wendell Phillips, who now reviled Webster's speech for its impartiality between right and wrong and for treating the sin of slavery as a "cold, tame, passionless political commodity."[6] For Higginson and for so many New England intellectuals and reformers, Daniel Webster had abdicated as an intellectual and statesman; he had attacked not only abolitionism but also major New England intellectual beliefs.

Wentworth Higginson was filled with that strange enthusiasm which Webster found so reprehensible. Unlike Webster he viewed the New England past as rich with leaders of moral absolutism and uncompromising enthusiasm. Higginson thought of his most distinguished ancestors in this manner, convinced that they had shunned expedience and embraced what was right.[7]

The first Higginson in America had arrived in Salem harbor June 29, 1629. At the Massachusetts Bay Company's invitation the Reverend Francis Higginson had transported his wife and eight children across the ocean, not to separate them from the Church of England, he noted, but only from its corruption. In America, however, Higginson, like others, indeed became a separatist. Finding New England's climate good for working, preaching and diligent catechizing, he concluded that a draught of New England air was better than a flagon of Old English ale. The Indians appeared friendly but did nothing but hunt and fish. This lack of diligence Higginson vowed to remedy forthwith. "We propose to learn their language as soon as we can, which will be a means to do them good." As for any subsequent dangers, he asserted, "we doubt not

5. Charles M. Ellis, "An Essay on Transcendentalism" in *The American Trancendentalists,* ed. Perry Miller (New York, 1957), p. 31; Bronson Alcott, "Orphic Sayings," *Dial, 1* (1840), 85.

6. *Liberator,* Mar. 27, 1850.

7. TWH, *Larger History of the United States* (New York, 1885), p. 197.

but God will be with us, and *if God be with us, who can be against us*." [8]

Francis Higginson's eldest son John lived ninety-two years, became a ranking colonial minister, and earned the title of "Nestor of the New England clergy." In a tract, "The Cause of God and his People in New England," he castigated the increasingly numerous and powerful merchants for lacking humility and for their failure to see that it was not their rational calculations but the hand of God that accounted for the success of the Massachusetts plantation. Also, by supporting Samuel Sewall's antislavery tract, "The Selling of Joseph," he condemned the New England merchants' participation in the African slave trade.[9]

Tolerance was not one of John Higginson's characteristics. Devotion to God, he argued, must not include "toleration of all Religions, or of the Heresies and Idolatries of the age we live in," for what contravenes the Gospel "hath no right, and therefore should have no liberty. . . . Your nontoleration of that which is contrary thereunto . . . will be . . . a glory to New England so long as the Sun and Moon endure." John succinctly characterized the Quakers' inner-light doctrine as "a stinking vapor from hell." [10]

Modern scholarship has suggested a high degree of compromise in Puritan society; Wentworth Higginson reflected an idealized nineteenth-century conception that Puritan clergymen "sometimes lost their temper, and sometimes their parishes, but never their independence." He concluded that "there was such an absolute righteousness about them, that to this day every man of New England descent lives partly on the fund of virtuousness habit they accumulated." [11]

Although a recent historian of puritanism has said: "Indeed, of all the governments in the Western world at the time, that of early

8. *Proceedings of the Massachusetts Historical Society*, 2d series, *16* (Boston, 1902), 48; TWH, *Life and Times of Francis Higginson* (New York, 1890), pp. 106–08 (hereafter cited as *Francis Higginson*).

9. Ibid., p. 128.

10. Perry Miller, *The New England Mind: From Colony to Province* (Cambridge, Mass., 1953), p. 132; *Francis Higginson*, p. 143.

11. Edmund S. Morgan, *The Puritan Dilemma* (Boston, 1958); TWH, "The Puritan Minister," *The Writings of Thomas Wentworth Higginson*, 7 (Cambridge, Mass., 1900), pp. 127–28.

Massachusetts gave the clergy least authority," this was not Wentworth Higginson's view. He shared the belief with many of his
contemporaries that Puritans and their secular magistrates deferred
to people of higher education and authority, especially the clergy.[12]
Higginsons of the eighteenth century he pictured as less religious,
but neither less zealous in their beliefs nor less important as public
leaders. They had in fact turned from the ministry to combine
commerce with civic activity. Wentworth Higginson's paternal
grandfather Stephen, whose awesomeness he remembered from
boyhood visits, used his wealth and prestige as a powerful shipowner to become politically influential. Although chosen in 1783
to the Continental Congress, Stephen Higginson had little sympathy for the loosely structured Confederation. He helped raise
money for and joined the field forces to suppress Shays' Rebellion.
The crisis, he realized, could be turned into a political blessing by
dramatizing the need for a strong federal government.[13]

During the administrations of Washington and Adams, Stephen
Higginson was considered the practical merchant of the Essex
Junto, one of that group of lawyers and merchants including
George Cabot and John Lowell, Jr., which issued its commands
about the new nation's financial and foreign policy. For a short time
he served in the Navy Department in the Adams government. His
popularity seldom equaled his determination, and one opponent
noted: "I saw Stephen . . . grinning ghastly, a horrible smile; his
eyes darting at once triumph, terror and treachery. . . . He ought
to be burnt for sedition, treason, stratagem and spoils." [14]

His belief in a strong central government favoring foreign commerce moved him to brand as Jacobin all those opposed to the Jay

12. Morgan, *Puritan Dilemma*, p. 96; TWH, "Puritan Minister," p. 127.
13. Bernard C. Steiner, "Two New England Rulers of Madras," *South Atlantic Quarterly*, 1 (1902), 215–23; *Francis Higginson*, p. 149; TWH, *Life and Times of Stephen Higginson* (New York, 1907), pp. 272–73; Boston *Advertiser*, Nov. 25, 1828. Also see Stephen Higginson to Henry Knox, Nov. 12, 1786, Feb. 8, 13, 1787, Knox MSS; Robert A. East, "The Massachusetts Conservatives in the Critical Period," in *Era of the American Revolution*, ed. Robert Morris (New York, 1939), pp. 382–89.
14. Samuel Eliot Morison, *Maritime History of the Massachusetts, 1780–1860* (Boston, 1921) p. 167; quoted in Anson E. Morse, *The Federalist Party to the Year 1800* (Princeton, 1939), p. 147.

Treaty, which promised fiscal stability and increased trading rights.[15] The Louisiana Purchase he judged as a conspiracy by Virginia to exploit the new "democratic mania" in order to subdue New England. The Federalist party, he said, was fighting "a contest of Vice against Virtue." [16]

In his family life Stephen Higginson was no less formidable. He produced nine children (including Wentworth's father) by his first wife, Susan Cleveland; after her death he married Elizabeth Perkins and had another child. When his second wife died he married her younger sister. Outliving his third wife, he died in 1828 at 85. Besides bequeathing a small fortune in real estate and securities, Stephen Higginson left behind 62 bottles of old Madeira and 316 bottles of excellent port wine.[17]

Daniel Webster in his attack on absolute truth and the zealous spirit of some of his contemporaries was implicitly criticizing much of that kind of heritage represented by the Higginson family, a heritage of both fact and myth. Relativism and compromise were "corpse-cold" to many of the Senator's intellectual constituents, who disagreed with him in the way public leaders should view phrases like "New England tradition" and "Puritan heritage." [18]

15. Boston *Advertiser*, Nov. 25, 1828.

16. Morse, *Federalist Party*, p. 151; S. Higginson to Timothy Pinkney, Nov. 23, 1803, Pinkney MSS.

17. TWH, *Descendants of the Reverend Francis Higginson* (Boston, 1910), pp. 21, 22 (hereafter cited as *Descendants*); Will of Stephen Higginson, 1828, MS, Suffolk County Probate Office.

18. Perry Miller, "From Edwards to Emerson," *Errand into the Wilderness* (Williamsburg, 1952), p. 199.

1

A Cambridge Boyhood

The first sounds of life were familiar to thirty-seven-year-old Louisa Higginson. Thomas Wentworth Higginson, born December 23, 1823, was her tenth and last child (Stephen Higginson, Jr., had fathered an additional five children during a previous marriage). A granddaughter of Anne Appleton and a descendant of the aristocratic Appletons and Wentworths of seveteenth-century New Hampshire, Louisa Higginson was nine years old when her father died and eleven at her mother's death. She was taken into the fashionable Beacon Hill home of Stephen Higginson, Jr., like his Federalist father a wealthy shipping merchant, to care for his two young daughters and his invalid wife Martha Salisbury Higginson. In 1805, a year and half after Martha's death, the nineteen-year-old girl married her guardian, who was thirty-five. One of their children died before the birth of Wentworth; two others died before he was three. Both of the boys who had died had been named Edward Cabot in lingering memory of Louisa Higginson's first love, lost at sea more than twenty years before.[1]

Life for the Higginsons was filled with eighteenth-century elegance. The young and pretty Mrs. Higginson was the hostess at many Mt. Vernon Street parties where the Adamses, Lowells, Salisburys, and Cabots dined. George Cabot, a social lion in Boston society, reported that no one received company more graciously than the petite Mrs. Higginson, even when she judged excessive the number of invitations issued by her overly generous husband.[2]

1. *Descendants*, pp. 28, 29; Louisa Higginson to TWH, Dec 17, 1861, "Field Book, 1860–1862," MS, Higginson MSS; TWH, *Cheerful Yesterdays* (Boston, 1898), p. 9 (hereafter cited as *Yesterdays*); Mary Thacher Higginson, *Thomas Wentworth Higginson* (Boston, 1914), p. 3.

2. *Yesterdays*, p. 10; L. Higginson diary, Feb. 22, 1827, Higginson MSS; Anne Cabot to Anne Grant, Mar. 18, 1809, in *Proceedings of the Massachusetts Historical Society*, 2d Series, *18* (Boston, 1905), 311; S. Higginson, Jr. to L. Higginson, May 26, 1810, Misc. MSS, Houghton Library.

Stephen Higginson, Jr., enjoyed being an affluent merchant and charitable gentleman. He owned three fine horses, stressed polished manners, and collected a tasteful private library containing books bound to his order. He freely gave money to educational and religious institutions, and though unquestionably a Unitarian he was still one of the largest contributors toward the construction of Boston's first Catholic Church.[3]

Stephen Higginson, Jr., however, was to be ruined financially by the War of 1812 for, despite his father's advice he had taken excessive commercial risks. His cautious father's wealth remained intact, but the son was forced to retire to a more modest existence on a nearby sheep farm. Much of his property, including his library, was sold. Leaving Boston caused great anguish for the Higginson family because it meant failure, the loss of old friends and relatives, and surrendering the amenities of culture.[4]

Stephen now looked more toward noncommercial activities; he expressed increased concern with unitarianism and the lack of zeal among its theologians. The difficulty in filling vacant pulpits disturbed him, as did the establishment of the Andover Theological School to counter Harvard unitarianism. He was appointed Steward at Harvard in 1818, and helped establish the Harvard Divinity School and the American Unitarian Association.[5]

A three-story colonial house was built on Harvard land near the Yard for Steward Higginson and his family. He was primarily responsible for collecting student rents for the college's living quarters and for procuring supplies (books as well as firewood). Receiving in trust the spending money from the parents of out-of-town stu-

3. S. Higginson, Jr. to L. Higginson, Oct. 31, 1805, Nov. 3, 1810, Higginson MSS; "Subscription List, Mar. 31, 1802," "Subscription List, 1803," Harvard Corporation Papers, 1802–03; receipt from Josiah Quincy, Mar. 30, 1805, Harvard College Papers.

4. *Yesterdays*, pp. 5, 14; S. Higginson to Henry Higginson, July 6, 1813, Misc. MSS, Houghton Library; L. Higginson diary, Apr. 8, 1815; Ann Storrow to Jared Sparks, Apr. 10, 1815, Sparks MSS.

5. S. Higginson, Jr. to J. Sparks, Nov. 17, 1816, Dec. 23, 1817, May 19, Oct. 10, 1819, Jan. 2, 1820, Sparks MSS; J. Sparks to A. Storrow, L. and S. Higginson, Jr., May 17, 1819, Higginson MSS; Herbert Baxter Adams, *Life and Writings of Jared Sparks*, 1 (Boston, 1899), 6, 164; George E. Cooke, *Unitarianism in America* (Boston, 1902), pp. 129–30.

dents, he was expected to dole it prudently to the boys. All his work took no more than five hours a day.[6]

Stephen Higginson's administrative status and an annual salary of $1,250 enabled him to mix socially with the faculty. But this opportunity, even after ten years in Cambridge and despite her social grace, filled his wife with "dread." She was sure of the correctness of serving wine, fruit, and cake to the Harvard scholars, but less sure of the correctness of her husband's behavior in this company. Despite her repeated pleas, he embarrassed her by reading aloud personal letters from relatives. She believed that he was perfectly willing to show "these letters to everybody in Boston. . . . I never saw anybody who has such a desire to make all things common— I think sometimes he will offer his wife and children to somebody who has not got any." No more comforting was the memory of her husband's complaint to President John Kirkland that a Hebrew edition of the Old Testament received by Harvard was incorrectly printed, for the text began on the back page and the print ran from right to left.[7] One observer noted that Stephen Higginson "frequently defeats his own object by the injudicious expressions of his feeling." But he was among those men "who may say what they please; for everybody *believes* his intention is good." [8]

It was in this Harvard atmosphere that Thomas Wentworth Higginson was born. The arrival of another child apparently was not received with joy. Louisa's sister Anne, still living in the Higginson home, expressed the collective hope that this "would only be the last blessing of this sort which was to fall to our happy lot. Surely we ought to be resigned—even if our hard fate should condemn us to count only eleven children." The new baby's mother, slightly built and worry-prone, found little solace in the birth of a sickly child. Mrs. Higginson would remember Wentworth as that "poor half dead baby that I had for so long walked about in my arms and

6. Andrew Peabody, "Stephen Higginson," *Harvard Reminiscences* (Boston, 1888), p. 18; Samuel A. Eliot, *History of Cambridge, Massachusetts* (Cambridge, 1913), p. 105; S. Higginson, Jr. to (?), Nov. 3, 1818, S. Higginson, Jr. to John Kirkland, May 14, 1825, Harvard College Papers; L. Higginson diary, Feb. 27, 1827.

7. "Estimate of Expenditures of Harvard College, Year 1824," MS, Harvard College Papers; L. Higginson diary, Dec. 17, 18, 1827; L. Higginson to Harriet Jackson [1823], Higginson MSS; *Yesterdays*, p. 6.

8. A. Storrow to J. Sparks, Nov. 6, 1822, Sparks MSS.

fed religiously . . . bearing hope in my heart, when there seemed no hope, & even the most experienced doctors gave him up." [9]

Although the boy slowly grew stronger, his mother continued to be weak and apprehensive about her health. Before she had a chance to recuperate, Edward Cabot Higginson, her two-and-a-half-year-old son died. "We live in a land of shadows," noted Mrs. Higginson's sister "where our dearest pleasures and our heart felt enjoyment are held by a tenure so very uncertain." Wentworth was five months old when his brother died; three years later his six-year-old sister succumbed to dysentery. Although early death was common in nineteenth-century families, Mary's death still was "like a flash of lightning" to her mother, who "was exceedingly overwhelmed" for a long while.[10]

Louisa had always been solicitous about her children; her daughter's death now caused constant concern for Wentworth's health. When he sniffled or coughed she used greater precautions with him than with any of her other children. She conceded to her diary: "It is bad to have such anxiety on one's mind for I never feel safe." This child, Louisa began to believe, was provided "as a sweet solace in the anguish of bereavement— . . . a source of consolation and hope and joy in the dark hours of affliction." [11]

To serve as a solace could be a heavy burden for a young boy, especially when his mother's fears and needs changed to concrete demands. After the deaths of Edward and Mary, her next youngest children, Wentworth was even more clearly the baby of the family. Next in age was Thacher, who was six years older and, unlike Wentworth, always a robust child. Louisa, years later, would still call Wentworth "the Star of my life," and they remained exceedingly close to each other.[12] His life would reflect the force of her presence.

Stephen Higginson, Jr., recognized that his wife supervised the children's moral training. Although regularly listening to the ser-

9. A. Storrow to Harriet Stowe, Mar. 16, 1824, L. Higginson to TWH, Dec. 27, 1861, Higginson MSS.

10. A. Storrow to J. Sparks, May 9, 1824, Oct. 15, 1826, Sparks MSS.

11. TWH, "Women that Have Influenced My Life," *Ladies Home Journal, 12* (1895), 8; L. Higginson diary, Nov. 22, 1827.

12. *Descendants*, p. 29; L. Higginson diary, Oct. 23, 1827; L. Higginson to TWH, Dec. 26, 1861, Higginson MSS.

mons of the Reverend Henry Ware, Convers Francis, and Caleb Stetson, Mrs. Higginson admitted that she was less interested in understanding than in feeling "the influence of His Spirit" animating her conduct. Her own experiences made terribly personal the prevailing belief that death must not be looked upon as evil but as an entrance into divine life.[13]

In the evenings, surrounded by her children, Mrs. Higginson was fond of reading aloud. As in many other American homes Sir Walter Scott's novels were chosen for their moral and religious observations. She felt that reading Scott lifted people to "a higher and better being and left one more vigorous in faith and happier." She conducted family prayers and read to her youngsters those reprinted sermons which held the necessary instruction, in her opinion, for this life as well as for the next. Young Higginson was taken to church for the first time before he was four years old. Henry Ware delivered a sermon about retribution in this world. The boy, however, appeared not even to fear parental retribution, for Mrs. Higginson patiently reported: "Wentworth went to church . . . but behaved so bad that I think I shall not let him go again for the present."[14]

Religion struck no fear into his heart. Since the Higginsons were Unitarians the tenets of strict Calvinism were avoided. Wentworth never had to listen to the old New England theology which frightened little boys and humbled adults. Never did he experience that sense of sin that plagued the more orthodox. But throughout his adult life, he, like his mother, would be outspoken in expressing a belief in life after death.[15]

At age four Wentworth was sent to a Cambridge dame-school kept at home by the daughter of the very proper Dr. Timothy Lindall Jennison, a local physician who attended his patients adorned in a wig and knee-breeches. Both the sons and daughters of the "best families" were there to learn the rudiments of reading and spelling.[16]

13. S. Higginson, Jr. to L. Higginson, Oct. 3, 1810, Higginson MSS, L. Higginson diary, Oct. 16, 27, Nov. 11, Dec. 2, 1827.

14. *Yesterdays*, pp. 14, 15; L. Higginson diary, Oct. 29, Nov. 8, 11, 1827.

15. *Yesterdays*, p. 35.

16. L. Higginson diary, Nov. 19, 1827; *Yesterdays*, p. 19; Eliot, *Cambridge*, p. 140.

Mrs. Higginson was certain that her son would be able to read before he was five. When Wentworth tired and Louisa excused him from his reading lessons, she happily reported that he exclaimed, "Oh I must read . . . because it is right." In her view the boy displayed a "combination of quickness and perseverance, with a power of attention and abstraction" unusual in so young a child. She noted that he was a docile little thing, so much so that a child two years his junior was able to dominate over him. His ten-year-old brother, Thacher, could easily frighten him by roaring like a lion.[17]

The years 1827 and 1828, before Wentworth was five, were also trying for Mrs. Higginson partly because her nineteen-year-old son Stephen was on a commercial sea voyage to Rio de Janeiro. She dreamed such horrible things about his fate in such a sink of iniquity that she recorded her thoughts in a diary in the form of imaginary letters to her absent son. There she expressed the wish that she could look in upon him to learn exactly how he was situated; she was not overly confident in the power of a youth to withstand evil, once he was away from his mother.[18]

Another important strain during these years was her husband's difficulties at Harvard. When first appointed steward in 1818 he had been among friends in the administration, and the manner in which the strong-handed president, John Kirkland, administered the college meant that with his support one need not fear opposition. But the way in which President Kirkland and Treasurer John Davis allowed Higginson to keep his account books eventually produced a crisis. With no annual audit, the hastily scribbled notes between Higginson and Davis indicating money received and spent, plus those innumerable messages they passed between them which cryptically indicated that an accounting error had been "just discovered," had added up to elephantine financial disorder.[19] Higginson appeared to be acting less like the meticulous steward than the capricious lord of the Harvard estate.

The turning point in the rather loose means of financial administration occurred in 1823 when the Republicans carried the Massachusetts elections largely on the issue of Harvard's "infidelity" and

17. L. Higginson diary, Nov. 11, 1827, Oct. 20, Mar. 20, Feb. 15, 1828.
18. Ibid., Oct. 22, 1827; Feb. 25, 1828.
19. Jan., July 1, 1819, Oct. 18, 1818, Harvard College Papers.

the consequent need to grant a state charter to Amherst College. What followed was the loss of the state subsidy for Harvard. By the end of 1824 it was noted that only $360 for the college library could be spent without the state grant.[20]

But reform did not become very vigorous until 1826 when Nathaniel Bowditch was elected to the Corporation. Bowditch, author of *America's Practical Navigator*, a guide for shipmasters, had risen without a formal education from a ship-chandler's apprentice to a prominent businessman. Neither tact nor hesitancy was among his characteristics. Bowditch's efforts at retrenchment not only meant the loss of President Kirkland's own student secretary and a $200 salary reduction for all the faculty, it also brought about a financial investigation which disclosed that the accounts of Treasurer Davis and Steward Higginson were in terrible confusion. As Josiah Quincy, the man who soon succeeded John Kirkland as president, observed: "Order, method, punctuality, and exactness" were to Bowditch "cardinal virtues, the want of which, in men of official station he regarded not so much a fault as a crime." [21] Higginson soon was "harassed and perplexed." It was discovered that he had spent close to $30,000 for which he had no receipts; $7,890.40 was cited as the amount disbursed for scholarships to divinity students in excess of the approved amount. Furthermore, at least $6,000 in loans had been accrued as "bad debts." [22] The college accepted Higginson's resignation as his penalty for lacking receipts. Nathaniel Bowditch even tried holding him liable for the amount disbursed for divinity scholarships, and the Corporation continued to insist that Higginson should remain personally responsible for the $6,000 in "bad debts." A year after his job terminated Higginson was still trying to collect some of this amount for the college and continued to do so until he finally was absolved of the responsibility. At no point was his "honest intent" impugned. The most critical judgment was recorded by his successor, who promised to revert to the

20. Samuel Eliot Morison, *Three Centuries of Harvard, 1836–1936* (Cambridge, 1936), p. 217; "Estimate . . . 1824," Harvard College Papers.

21. Morison, *Harvard*, p. 220; Josiah Quincy, *Harvard University*, 2 (Boston, 1840), 439.

22. L. Higginson diary, Oct. 29, 1827; Benjamin R. Nichols to (?), July, 1827, N. Bowditch, F. C. Grey to President and Fellows of Harvard College 1828, S. Higginson, Jr. to E. Frances, Mar. 20, 1828, Harvard College Papers.

accounting methods of Higginson's "intelligent and accurate" predecessor.[23]

Stephen Higginson, who had always shown a marked nervous energy, was determined to maintain his equilibrium despite these personal reverses. But one observer noted that "his words . . . seemed to trip one another up in their haste to find utterance." Like his wife, Higginson resolved to remain in Cambridge; with financial aid from his eldest son Francis, who was now a doctor, the Higginsons moved from Professors' Row to a modest red brick house across the street from the Cambridge Common. He stayed active and interested in the Society for Promoting Theological Education in Harvard College and remained a member of the Board of Directors of the Divinity School.[24]

Like her husband, Mrs. Higginson was much disturbed about the charges of incompetency and the pressure for his resignation. The atmosphere of her home would surely be affected, but she was prepared to economize to remain in Cambridge. There was a small "family fund" to draw upon; boarders would be taken in; her son Waldo would get a job as a tutor in a Cambridge preparatory school; and the death of her husband's father meant a modest inheritance. Within six years, however, her husband had accumulated over $32,000 in personal debts. Louisa Higginson wrote in her diary: "I am tired to death and long for the rest to mind and body." [25]

Living in Cambridge, despite such adversity, could be comforting. Visitors were frequent. Wentworth's sister Susan Louisa played the piano and at times the sounds of Beethoven trios filled the house. Mrs. Higginson especially enjoyed Sunday afternoons of promenading with her husband on the Cambridge Common, where Washington had taken command of the Continental Army.[26]

23. P. Smith to S. Higginson, Jr. [1828], S. Higginsn, Jr. to E. Frances, May 30. 1828, Harvard College Papers; Quincy, *Harvard University*, 2, 363–64; Charles Sanders to E. Frances, Jan. 15, 1828, Harvard College Papers.

24. Peabody, *Harvard Reminiscences*, p. 19; *Yesterdays*, p. 106; Richard Sullivan to J. Quincy, Jan. 12, 1831, J. G. Palfrey to R. Sullivan, Jan. 6, 1831, Harvard College Papers.

25. L. Higginson diary, Nov. 10, 1827, March 20, 1828; Will of Stephen Higginson, 1828; Will of Stephen Higginson, Jr., 1834, MS, Middlesex County Probate Office.

26. *Yesterdays*, p. 18; L. Higginson diary, March 22, 1828, Dec. 2, 1827; TWH, *Old Cambridge* (Boston, 1899), p. 78.

Young Wentworth Higginson also imbibed Cambridge's historic past. At home—now a place of shabby gentility—oil portraits of his ancestors, posing with their wigs or powdered hair, hung from the walls. Brattle Street, once called Tory Row, still had its spacious colonial houses and its giant elms to evoke thoughts of the American Revolution. There was a strange fascination for Wentworth in kneeling down and peering closely at the flat tombstones in the Old Cambridge cemetery. Latin inscriptions made the stones even more mysterious for a boy who had just learned to read English. The hollows in the tombstones where the leaden coats of arms had been pried out to make bullets for the Continental Army further stirred his imagination.[27]

On rainy days Wentworth and his childhood friend Charles Parsons, son of Dr. Usher Parsons, distinguished anatomist and nephew of Dr. Oliver Wendell Holmes, would seek the warmth of Holmes' library. For a while the two boys might look through some of the books. Then the heavy encyclopedias might be stacked on top of each other to provide an excellent barricade against volleys of "cannon shot." Winter apples served as the ammunition which the boys lobbed across the room for their own American Revolution.[28]

There were more lethal battles from which Wentworth for a time was protected. Upon completing dame-school at eight years of age, he was enrolled in the Cambridge preparatory school of William Wells, a former bookdealer, who after having his bookshop destroyed by fire turned to training boys for entrance to Harvard. Adults judged Wells to be courteous and kind, but in the classroom students knew that he was a terror with the rattan. "There was never a half-day without a good deal of flogging," reported one of Higginson's classmates. Wentworth was a good student, however, and learned his Latin, Greek, and mathematics quickly, thereby avoiding the force of Mr. Wells' blows. Also the slight boy could escape at sundown since he was not boarding at the school.[29]

To supplement the academic lessons learned at Wells' school

27. *Yesterdays*, pp. 32, 33.

28. Ibid., p. 13; *Old Cambridge*, p. 80.

29. Eliot, *Cambridge*, p. 103; Richard Henry Dana, Jr., *An Autobiographical Sketch*, ed. Robert F. Metzdorf (Connecticut, 1953), p. 52; *Yesterdays*, p. 20.

Wentworth attended Sunday School. Here, among other moral
lessons, he was lectured on stealing, and he noted that those who
have committed crimes were forced to live in stone buildings and
forced, though adults, to take orders. The rigors of academic and
moral training were tempered by dancing lessons. Wentworth, along
with other Cambridge children, learned the proper waltz steps necessary for future adult "refinement." [30]

There were other kinds of lessons to be learned and remembered.
On an August day in 1834 Wentworth stood next to his mother on
the front steps of the Higginson home and watched the rising
smoke from the direction of Boston. The Ursuline Convent, a target for the rage of anti-Catholic feeling, had been set afire by a
furious mob. The school had been attended by the daughters of
many parents who were Unitarian friends of the Higginsons and
had believed that the public schools were too much controlled by
a strict congregationalism. Hatred had been nurtured by the fear
that strict Congregationalists felt from this alliance of Unitarians
and Catholics. Dislike of upper-class Unitarians and lower-class
Irish Catholics provided the impetus for the attack; and doubtless
the harangues of Lyman Beecher from his Boston pulpit about this
threatening association of "irreligion" helped goad the mob to action. To the Higginsons the fire once again illustrated the barbarism
of "hell-fire religion." Prominent citizens (many from among the
Higginsons' Cambridge friends) called a protest meeting and unequivocally condemned the attack. Wentworth was well aware of
his mother's feelings at this time.[31]

Between the ages of eleven and thirteen the boy read voraciously.
Scott's *Waverly Novels* were favorite fare, and he found Jane
Austen's *Pride and Prejudice* entertaining. The *Select British
Poets* provided poetry in "great big book." At age nine Higginson
had helped inaugurate a juvenile book club, evidently emulating
the adult clubs so popular before the advent of the public library.
Indicative of his commitment to books was an effort to solicit
Arthur Fuller, younger brother of Margaret Fuller, to join this

30. Sunday School Notebook Sept. 14, 1834, Higginson MSS; *Yesterdays,* p. 37.
    31. Ibid., pp. 34–35; *Report of the Committee Relating to the Destruction of the
Ursuline Convent, Aug. 11, 1834* (Boston, 1834), p. 16; Ray A. Billington, "The
Burning of the Charlestown Convent," *New England Quarterly, 10* (1937), 6, 7.

club: Wentworth noted that his brother Thacher owned a book 920 pages long and that it had been said that one book was 1180 pages.[32]

Soon his reading would become more meaningful, for at the age of thirteen Wentworth Higginson took his entrance examinations for Harvard College. The fragile baby was now a tall and thin candidate for admission into "the College."

Had he lived, Wentworth's father would have been pleased by his son's college plans: But Stephen Higginson, Jr., had died in early 1834 at age sixty-four. With unintentional irony, an obituary in the *Christian Examiner* stressed his charity and disinterested benevolence. While he left to his family an estate of $26,000, his $32,000 in debts canceled any inheritance. A public sale of his house, lot, and furnishings was necessary to meet the $6,000 deficit.[33]

Ten years old at the time, Wentworth, who much later in life could vividly remember the burning of the convent, seems to have been unable to recall anything about his father's death, or indeed much about his father. Some four years after the event he could write in his diary: "My father died Feb'y 20th 1834. I was unfortunately too young at that time to feel my loss very much." In subsequent years, when he wrote biographies about his grandfather Stephen Higginson and his first American ancestor Francis Higginson, and would frequently write about his mother, his father—as if he had never existed—remained relatively absent from his public statements. He did allude to his father's public charitableness by calling him "a man of boundless and somewhat impetuous kindness." [34] It was a characterization quite close to his mother's view that Stephen would have offered his wife and children to anyone.

With Stephen Higginson's death Wentworth's development more than ever fell to the willing hands of his mother. The only people living with him now were women—his mother, his aunt, and his two older sisters.

32. Loans from Cambridge Book Club, 1832–36, Higginson MSS; *Yesterdays,* p. 14; TWH to Arthur Fuller, May 14, 1833, Fuller Family MSS; Jan 2, 1833, Harvard College Faculty Records.

33. *Christian Examiner, 16* (1834), 270; Will of Stephen Higginson, Jr., 1834.

34. Journal of Thomas Wentworth Higginson, MS, Higginson MSS (hereafter cited as TWH journal); *Yesterdays,* pp. 7, 6.

2

An Adolescent Cantab

Wentworth Higginson stood on the steps of University Hall with the other candidates applying for entrance into Harvard College. It was just before 6:00 A.M. on August 26, 1837. Soon doors were opened and the boys filed into the hall to begin two days of entrance examinations. By late afternoon of the second day Wentworth was summoned before the faculty: President Josiah Quincy formally announced his admission to Harvard College. Two days later the boy acknowledged the fact in his own way by saying: "Wore my coat for the first time." That coat was black with black buttons, required dress for all Harvard students on the Sabbath and on public occasions.[1]

Harvard had changed since 1818 when Higginson's father had been steward. In the earlier period the college had still resembled an "unkempt sheep-commons"—few trees, a brewhouse, a woodyard, and numerous privies lent little dignity to the Yard. Probably the most conspicuous college property had been a pigpen, scene of battles between rats and pigs for the common garbage, which had provided a clamor that echoed into the halls of learning. But President Kirkland with zealous cooperation from Steward Higginson had made large gains over all this blight so that by 1828 when Josiah Quincy had become president, and by the time young Higginson had entered the school, trees bloomed, paths were distinguishable, and the only squeals came from the less than four hundred boisterous students.[2]

Other changes were occurring at Harvard which were less visible but certainly more subject to criticism. By 1837 the intellectual forces that earlier had moved men to look to Germany for

1. *Harvard College Catalogue, 1837* (Cambridge, 1837), p. 22; TWH journal, Aug. 28, 29, 31, Sept. 2, 1837; Entrance Certificate, Aug. 28, 1837, Higginson MSS.
2. Morison, *Harvard*, p. 216.

the best examples of learning were bringing strange and often unwanted returns. Those who had received both their learning and their unitarianism from Harvard seemed to turn their learning against this theology. Even undergraduates by 1837 were talking about the new transcendental philosophy which found fault with the accepted unitarianism.[3]

Just before Higginson's entrance examinations Ralph Waldo Emerson had delivered his address, "The American Scholar," to the Harvard Phi Beta Kappa Society. This alumnus had told his audience that "the first importance of the influences upon the mind is that of nature. . . . Books are for the scholar's idle times. When he can read God directly, the hour is too precious to be wasted in other man's transcripts of their readings." Emerson's words left their mark. The Reverend John Pierce judged them to be "in the misty, dreamy, unintelligible style of Swedenborg, Coleridge, and Carlyle." James Russell Lowell, on the contrary, pronounced the address "an event without any former parallels in our literary annals . . . for its picturesqueness and its inspiration." Both Pierce and Lowell, the old and the new generation, the minister and the poet, understood that lines of battle were being drawn. Emerson might not push into the confines of Harvard the real Trojan horse until his Divinity School address the following year, but the Phi Beta Kappa speech indicated that differences, however distasteful to the Harvard Unitarians, would be publicly aired.[4]

For young Higginson these currents had no immediate personal meaning. His family training had given him a nominal preference for the conservative unitarianism of Andrews Norton, but he had not had a significant religious commitment before entering Harvard, and daily compulsory chapel or Sunday sermons in the First Parish Church in Cambridge did not stimulate his religious interest. Although Harvard preachers seldom discussed social issues—instead they considered themselves moral philosophers primarily interested in explicating Christian principles—a conscientious undergraduate, it might be thought, would be moved to compare the

3. Miller, *Transcendentalists*, p. ix; see Edgeley W. Todd, "Philosophical Ideas at Harvard College, 1817–1837," *New England Quarterly*, *16* (1943), 6, 9.
4. *Emerson's Complete Works*, *1* (Boston, 1885), 86, 92; Morison, *Harvard*, pp. 248–49.

society about him with these religious principles. Higginson heard the sermons of John Gorham Palfrey, Henry Ware, Jr., and James Walker, all prominent Unitarian ministers, but made no such comparisons. During one service in the Harvard chapel, with Palfrey preaching, the student noticed the presence of "some deuced pretty girls," and on another day was given a demerit for "half lying down in my seat . . . so as to tempt sleep, if not actually going to sleep." [5] He was sufficiently attentive later in college to James Walker's sermons to note that Faith and Temptation were the minister's topics, and another time expressed the opinion that Walker "preached two good sermons, but *Lockeish*." Here at least the boy echoed the Transcendentalists' criticism of Unitarian adherence to Lockeian sensationalism. Walker's ability to arouse his interest, however, was not absolute since he had soporific powers over him more potent than Ware's or Palfrey's. Said Higginson: "Dr. Walker preached all day. Went to sleep in the aft'n & when I woke-up, rose with a dim idea that they [the students] were at prayers but found I had slept through the sermon, prayers, hymn, readings, proclamation and blessings." [6]

His notoriety among classmates for dozing in chapel caused him no shame. In short: "*Snoozed* through it all comfortably," well reflected his undergraduate religiosity. But he was conscientious about other things. Wentworth usually arose at 5 A.M. to drill himself in Greek, Latin, mathematics, or history. He never complained about studying, even to his diary.[7]

To room and board at home was unusual even for Cambridge and Boston students, but economy necessitated this as it had earlier for his brothers, Francis and Waldo. With Wentworth still so tied to his home, Louisa Higginson remained ever present in the boy's life. On nights when he was out of the house she would sit in the parlor until he returned. Quite often she would spend evenings with him playing backgammon.[8]

5. Wilson Smith, *Professors and Public Ethics* (Ithaca, 1956), pp. 149–85; TWH journal, Jan. 5, 1838, Mar. 29, 31, Sept. 29, 1839.

6. Ibid., Nov. 10, Nov. 24, 1839, July 5, 1840.

7. Ibid., May 8, July 5, 28, 1840.

8. *Harvard Student Directory* (Cambridge, 1837–41); TWH Term Bills, S. F. McCleary Term Bills, Harvard Secretary File; TWH journal, Nov. 15, 24, 29, Dec. 11, 1839.

He was generally looked upon by his classmates as a pariah who attended classes with them but was not really one of them. Neither getting drunk nor blowing up a college outhouse was part of his college life. As a senior he did venture to join his classmates in a defiant dance around Harvard's "Rebellion Tree." A tutor of Greek, Charles Stearns Wheeler, friend of Thoreau and Emerson, was the object of a rebel proclamation declaring that "the students of Harvard University . . . are now in a state of disaffection to the Government of the University." Six students were expelled, but Higginson justly escaped any punishment as he took no major part in the riot. He had merely participated, he noted, in the "excited orgies round that monument of folly." More often Higginson deplored student riots and once signed a petition against them.[9] His acts of rebellion, though no less overt, were mostly for more personal reasons.

Academic involvement was more important than fighting for student justice. As early as his freshman year he was befriended by his Greek tutor, Jones Very. Very, soon to become the poet of the Transcendentalists but at this time studying at the Divinity School, was known to scribble occasionally old mystic religious sonnets on the back of student examination books before returning them. Higginson quickly grasped his teacher's views and responded accordingly. To Very's Greek examination question: "Since we know better than to make war, and those before us have fought that we might have peace, what ought we to be doing in it?" Wentworth answered: "We should be engaged in performing those duties towards our fellow men, which the giver of peace has imposed upon us." Very not only helped the boy translate Herodotus but also invited Higginson to join a group which met in his room on Sundays to read the Greek Testament. The twenty-four-year-old teacher, tall and thin, with a head of thick hair and a mouth too sensitive for his angular face, could be seen on the Cambridge Common with fourteen-year-old Higginson earnestly kicking a football.[10]

9. *Class Book, 1841,* Harvard College Papers; TWH journal, Oct. 18, 1837, Feb. 5, 1838, Oct. 17, 1839, June, 1841; "Draft of Rebel Proclamation 1841," *Class Book, 1841,* Harvard College Papers; "Thomas C. Smith Account of Rebellion," 1841, Harvard Secretary File.

10. William I. Bartlett, *Jones Very, Emerson's Brave Saint* (Durham, 1942),

During the student's freshman year, Very also was a welcome visitor in the Higginson home where Mrs. Higginson happily served dinner to this deeply religious man. But a year later, Very began warning people: "Flee to the mountains for the end of all things is at hand." Religious zeal soon drove him temporarily insane, and he was committed to McLean Asylum for a time. Emerson pronounced Very profoundly sane and wished that the whole world was as mad as he, and Higginson called him a "man of genius," but neither the prospect of translating Greek nor kicking a football reunited the teacher and his student. The poet, Higginson subsequently concluded, was after all "not deep." [11]

Higginson would remember Benjamin Peirce as his most stimulating college teacher. The country's foremost mathematician often got so enthralled by his subject that he would momentarily forget he was in front of a class and would concentrate on the solution of some problem in his own research. When Wentworth could not understand what Peirce was doing he still experienced a joyful feeling, and this seemed most important. He reacted similarly to other things he did not fully comprehend.[12]

Another stimulating teacher was Henry Wadsworth Longfellow. From him Higginson learned French literature and language, which he elected during his second year. Wentworth several times read the teacher's poem, *Hyperion*, and was fond of quoting it. Longfellow also impressed him with his good manners and propriety. He became most important to Higginson during his senior year by encouraging him to read nineteenth-century German authors.[13]

Edward Tyrell Channing, who had come to Harvard as the Boylston Professor of Rhetoric and Oratory in 1819, was still a most potent force in forming his students' ideas and style for oral

---

pp. 25, 35; Undergraduate Notes and Exercises, Feb. 5, 1838, Higginson-Student MSS; TWH journal, Sept. 5, 16, 1837, Feb. 6, 11, 1838.

11. Ibid., Nov. 12, Dec. 17, 1837, Oct. 10, 1843; John O. Edson, "Charles Stearns Wheeler: Emerson's Good Grecian," *New England Quarterly*, 27 (1944), 472; Miller, *Transcendentalists*, p. 279.

12. TWH, "Obituary for Benjamin Peirce," *Woman's Journal*, Oct. 22, 1888; *Yesterdays*, pp. 50–51; TWH journal, Sept. 11, 1837.

13. TWH, *Henry Wadsworth Longfellow* (Boston, 1902), pp. 176–77; TWH journal, Mar. 29, 1839, Feb. 29, 1841.

and written expression. Higginson was required to write a theme every two weeks and prepare once a week for forensics. Not only did Channing assign the topic but he appears to have graded his students' views. Higginson received a lower grade when he attacked cosmopolitanism and defended an uncritical patriotism; when in his easy, "Solitude," he equated solitude with misanthropical behavior the grade remained low. When Higginson wrote that public opinion often failed to recognize a distinguished man, Channing graded the essay higher; and when he criticized Alexander the Great for having little strength of principle, the teacher commented, "very much to the purpose." [14]

For oratory, Channing stressed measured, dignified speech with careful enunciation and a precise choice of words. Higginson gave his first public address during his sophomore year at the annual Harvard Exhibition. But his debut was inconclusive since he recited in iambic Greek verse. When he later spoke on "American Political Influences," he concentrated so fiercely on looking up at his audience that he was forced to admit that he did not know what he was saying, made mistakes, hesitated, and omitted. He sought to reverse what he had said in the past about patriotism for he now defined it as excessive nationalism. Equating it with conceit and vanity, he criticized those who ridiculed immigrants for departing from any American customs. [15]

A more successful address was "Poetry in an Unpoetical Age," which he believed he spoke calmly and very well. It looked to the day when America would cease copying European literature and turn to the uniqueness of the American environment for inspiration. One critic agreed it was well delivered, but pronounced the content flighty. [16]

If Higginson, while at Harvard, never achieved the oratorical

14. TWH journal, May 11, 1839; "Solitude," April 13, 1839, "Alexander," April 27, 1839, "Public Opinion," Dec. 14, 1838, "Self-Knowledge," March 15, 1838, Higginson-Student MSS.

15. Morison, *Harvard*, p. 216; "A Greek Version in Iambic Verse: Soliloquy of Henry V," July 17, 1839, Exhibition and Commencement Performances, 1839, "American Political Influence," Oct. 20, 1840, Harvard-Student MSS; TWH journal, Oct. 23, 1840.

16. TWH journal, Aug. 25, 1841; Commencement Program Exercises, Aug. 25, 1840, Harvard-Student MSS.

ideal set by Channing, clarity and decorum later would characterize his platform style. And style itself would remain a central concern. At the numerous student debates he attended, a witty speech
or a splendid debate appeared more important to him than the
subject matter. He commented on the score of a debate or on the
speaker's delivery but never on the matter of such controversial
subjects as "Rebellion vs. Passive Submission," "The Justifiability
of War," "The Abolition of Capital Punishment," The White
Man's Treatment of the Indians as Compared to the Negro,"
"The Expediency of Abolishing the D.C. Slave Trade," or "The
Correctness of Encouraging Immigration." [17]

A lack of interest in subject matter was also evident in his grasp
of current events. During a visit to Washington, D.C., as late as
his senior year, Higginson's observations about the Supreme Court
and Congress lacked political acumen or interest. All he had to say
about John Quincy Adams, who was arguing a case before the
Court, was that he was rather undignified and decidedly dull.
Adams in this brief on the *Amistad* case sought freedom for the
slaves who had successfully mutinied aboard a Spanish ship, but
had been later captured by an American warship.[18]

Higginson decided that the House of Representatives was inferior to the Senate because it was vehement and noisy and lacked
oratorical grace. The exception was the Speaker of the House,
Henry Wise of Virginia, who possessed a "splendid voice and decided manner. . . . He is a young man & something about his appearance interested me much." [19]

For Higginson, high class rank assumed an importance that far
exceeded devotion to subject matter. Being the youngest member
of his class and the baby of his family encouraged this emphasis.
Aided by the stimulus to prove himself and by his mother's concern, Higginson placed among the first eight students in a freshman class of forty-five. It was essential to him that he get higher
grades than his classmates. Mentioning in his journal the prospect
of being ranked third in his sophomore year, he added three excla-

17. TWH journal, Feb. 27, Jan. 22, Feb. 22, Mar. 4, May 31, Oct. 31, 1838, Sept.
25, 1837.
18. Ibid., March 1, 1841.
19. Ibid., March 2, 1841.

mation points. When he knew he would beat a classmate in rank he wrote: "I don't feel afraid of him." [20]

His concern for status through high grades knew few bounds. Sometimes he would surreptitiously open a book upon which the class was currently being questioned. Or he might copy his arguments for an essay from the pages of the *North American Review, Edinburgh Review*, or other magazines that were received at home. Certainly his boldest deed, and no arbitrary college prank, was to enter President Quincy's office when this official was at dinner. Without acknowledging guilt, Higginson declared: "Executed a daring design conceived yesterday morning in church, of carrying off one book of marks from the President's room after seeing him . . . at supper—selected the book by the light of the fire though I had a lighting apparatus in my pocket. Spent all evening putting together the account." On the following day the boy concluded "I am going to study more for *rank*. Yet it seems as if I ought to be satisfied, looking at the book and seeing how immensely I'm above most of them!" Higginson was elected Phi Beta Kappa in his junior year and graduated second in his class.[21]

His confidence was hindered by his appearance: he was now six feet tall, very thin, and moved with self-conscious clumsiness. After a particularly uncomfortable evening, he plaintively expressed in his journal a desire to be "handsomer—shorter, straiter, less awkward—with black hair & small hands." [22] Strongly desiring to prove his physical prowess, Higginson kicked a football on the Common or played ice hockey at Fresh Pond for more than just amusement. Swimming was not simply recreation for it also provided some proof of masculine strength. His long walks with his boyhood friend Charles Parsons or with his college friend Frank Parker became statistical sources, minutely recorded in his diary, to document physical accomplishments.[23]

Throughout Higginson's life, physical feats and the sanctioning of them in others were far more vital than to the majority of his

20. Ibid., Jan. 20, Feb. 24, 1838, March 1, May 22, 31, 1839.

21. Ibid., Nov. 6, 1837, Oct. 18, 1839, Dec. 14, 15, Aug. 27, 1840.

22. Ibid., Jan. 25, 1837, Apr. 4, 1841, Feb. 8, 1840.

23. Ibid., May 3, July 17, 1841, Feb. 8, 1840, July 11, May 29, Feb. 28, Nov. 16, 1839; TWH to Charles Parsons, July 9, 1838, Higginson MSS.

contemporaries. Later, his physical action could be given a variety of theoretical justifications. The issue of manliness would be very close to many of the social causes he would champion.[24]

In choosing companions at Harvard, Higginson also revealed the effects of his childhood problems. Charles Parsons had continued to be his friend during freshman year at college. Parsons, though only two months older, was in the sophomore class and for a time served as Wentworth's mentor. The two friends, both conscious of their respectable family backgrounds, would visit old houses, take excursions on the Nahant steamer, or walk to the railroad tracks to watch passing trains.[25]

But childhood experiences proved insufficient to keep their friendship alive. By the middle of Higginson's sophomore year he and Parsons saw less and less of each other. Soon Higginson complained, "Parsons used up the rest of my afternoon." [26] Parsons was not a sufficiently conscientious student nor did he have a strong enough personality to continue to interest one so committed to competing for academic excellence and so desirous of attaining strength. Such strength for a fatherless adolescent would be sought from a more mature male companion.

Higginson found a replacement for Parsons in a boy who not only was two years older but also possessed a cynicism that passed for maturity, and a popularity that made him president of the Hasty Pudding Club. Francis Parker shared some important similarities in family background with Higginson. They were descendants of seventeenth-century New England ministers, and in adolescence had lost fathers who had left their families without an inheritance. In college, Parker was remembered as one who had "an attraction for younger men, as they had for him, and a great facility in impressing and influencing them." Academically he was the top student in Higginson's class, a handsome boy whose fluency and aggressive manner made him a leader. A far more popular figure than Jones Very had been, Parker possessed much that Higginson admired.[27]

24. For a discussion of "manliness" in nineteenth-century England see Walter E. Houghton, *The Victorian Frame of Mind* (New Haven, 1957), pp. 198–216.

25. TWH journal, Sept. 1, 16, 29, 30, Nov. 17, 1837.

26. Ibid., May 28, 1839.

27. *Class Book, 1841*, pp. 55–57, Harvard College Papers; *Tribute of Massachu-*

He first acknowledged his friendship with Parker in this way: "I came across something in his room in his absence which increased my opinion of him a good deal. He speaks of me thus in his journal: 'I like Wentworth quite well. He is now young but a good scholar—tolerable looking—awkward. He is rather to my mind—I like him!!!'" After examining Parker's private journal, Higginson concluded: "Parker is I think the finest fellow in the class, moral, honourable and gentlemanly. He is a noble fellow—my most intimate friend."[28]

But Higginson did not look at his "most intimate friend" as an equal. Soon after he wrote: "I have been at Parker's room and have been reading his journal. . . . Am I worthy of such a friend? No. . . . He will make a great man." To Parker and to Parker's journal Higginson increasingly turned for paternal assurance and guidance. This was especially true after he read the diary of another classmate twelve years his senior, who was qualified in age to lead but failed to win Higginson's allegiance because he expressed no liking for him. One evening when Wentworth was depressed at being rejected for membership in the college Natural History Society, he wandered down to the Cambridge graveyard where he sought his father's tombstone. Finding it, he read his father's epitaph: "In works of love he found his happiness." It was Parker who provided the consolation the epitaph could not. "He talked very kindly to me indeed," said Higginson later that night.[29]

With Parker he could talk of "love and novel reading." From Parker he could directly learn what other students said about him. When Higginson learned of a compliment from another classmate he called the talk pleasant conversation. He felt rewarded when Parker reported that his forensic was thought the best. When Parker left Cambridge during vacation Higginson admitted feeling "lonely as usual & . . . I shall continue to be until Parker returns—for alas! he is my only friend!"[30] The direct reports from this only friend also disclosed negative things. Telling Wentworth that he had become more unpopular than ever, Parker re-

---

setts Historical Society to Francis E. Parker (Boston, 1880), p. 20; *Yesterdays,* pp. 53, 63.

28. TWH journal, May 22, 1839.
29. Ibid., June 26, Sept. 21, Oct. 5, 1839.
30. Ibid., July 5, 1839, Feb. 8, 28, 1840.

vealed that the Higginson character had been discussed disparagingly by faculty and students, and word had been spread that Higginson often copied his themes out of literary magazines. Parker charged Wentworth with using their friendship for a mere convenience. Higginson denied only that convenience characterized their friendship. He was hurt that, while criticizing him, Parker extolled Wickham Hoffman, a classmate and rival for both class rank and Parker's friendship. Later, during his senior year, when Parker roomed with Samuel Longfellow, Higginson upon seeing them together wrote that he "felt constrained and awkward" and also "morbid." [31]

Worried about losing Parker, Higginson again read the older boy's journal, hoping for some positive assurance of his loyalty to him. After this foray Wentworth concluded: "He seems to like me, yet with a kind of doubt and jealousy." Higginson returned to Parker's room and his journal for more information, and was evidently satisfied with compliments to his looks from three members of his class. Either directly or once again through reading his friend's journals the boy learned that Parker considered "Language, Caution, Benevolence and *Amativeness, particularly the latter*" to be Higginson's strongest traits. He seemed pleased with this characterization and for a time he ceased peering into Parker's journal and continued to consider Parker his only friend. Able to tolerate Parker's coldness, taciturnity, or sullenness, Higginson enjoyed those evenings together of "reading Locke, & fighting!" [32]

But this unequal rather tense relationship became more and more aggravated by Parker's prodding evaluation of Higginson's "artfulness of character"; Wentworth "was less trusted than imagined." According to Parker, even Professor James Walker was perplexed by his character. While Parker's criticism had often been accepted by Higginson as evidence of a loyal paternalism, less and less could he countenance Parker's dominance. Wentworth finally concluded that the friendship had done him more harm than good.[33]

Another relationship during his college days was revealing in itself and also for the future. Wentworth first met Phebe Adam,

31. Ibid., Nov. 17, 24, 1839, July 19, 30, 1841.
32. Ibid., Nov. 4, Dec. 16, 1839.
33. Ibid., Dec. 16, 1840, Jan. 7–16, Aug. 21, 1841; *Tribute to Parker*, p. 17.

daughter of William Adam, Harvard Professor of oriental languages, at dancing school when the two were ten years old. At that time Phebe had been given the sobriquet "spitfire" by the young male students of the waltz. During the summer of 1839, shortly after he had turned to Frank Parker, Higginson confided to his journal: "Saw Phebe Adam . . . now a fine looking girl of sweet sixteen. Think I'll fall in love with her in vacation." But it was not until some six months later at a party given at the Higginson house, attended by young Quincys, Storys, and Longfellows, that the boy found something worth recording. While the tables laden with ham, oysters, ginger, and charlotte russe doubtless enhanced the elegance and gaiety of the party, for Wentworth the presence of Phebe and her sister Hannah was far more entrancing. He reported a glorious flirtation with both of them. Since Phebe could not dance because of a temporary lameness, Higginson played checkers and backgammon with her. The highlight of the evening arrived when Phebe and two of the young gentlemen splashed cologne at each other until the bottle was nearly empty. This bothered Higginson far less than the fact that William Wetmore Story, the judge's son, was too attentive to Phebe.[34]

The Adam girls, especially Phebe, became increasingly important in Higginson's undergraduate life. First he found it difficult to choose between the two sisters; he evidently enjoyed the idea of being "decidedly in love with both of them!" On one side he saw Hannah Adam "more beautiful" with "manners . . . more like those of a girl" and "like a beautiful subject"; on the other, Phebe, who was "*Handsome*," looked "like a princess," with manners "those of a woman more experienced & formed." The choice for his admiration lay between Hannah the less mature and Phebe the more mature. Just as he had chosen the dominating Frank Parker, he would turn to Phebe Adam who possessed a "strong mind." [35]

But unlike his temporary success in making Parker his confident, his admiration for the Adam girl was from a distance. His difficulty in making contact was disclosed to his diary: "I hate to have girls

34. TWH journal, July 11, 1839, Jan. 31, 1840; Ann Storrow, *A Poem of the Olden Times* (Boston, 1909).
35. TWH journal, Feb. 6, Mar. 6, July 11, 21, 1840.

intimate—I always feel as if they discussed me. . . . I always feel they think me a fool. I always feel so different, and suspicious & jealous." He was determined nevertheless to win Phebe's attention.[36]

Admitting that he was not as agreeable, gay, graceful, handsome, or elegant in dress as her other beaux, he imagined attracting her by winning the Bowdoin prize or leading the Phi Beta Kappa procession. "I feel that the recitation not the ballroom is my element," he concluded.[37]

But Higginson soon sought a more immediate and bolder form of public display. He wrote an unsigned letter to the Editor of the Boston *Post*,[38] which the newspaper published. "It is not usual," began the letter, "to make a newspaper the *confidante* of a love affair, but . . . this is a case which calls for the interference of the main pillar of democracy in the Bay State." What followed was a revealing description of a rather ambiguous pursuit.

> Wherever I go, I see her—there! there she is now passing by my window—I must fly and take refuge behind the book-case. . . . At a party . . . the first object that meets my eye is that lovely form . . . now smiling with such angelic sweetness on her partner. . . . Would I were in his place—yet why do I say so, for I could not long survive it—alas I hardly know what I am saying. Now the music has changed to a waltz, but there she goes whirling about the room, encircled by the arm of that coxcomb.

Before the sounds of the waltz drowned out Higginson's alleged purpose for this effusion to the editor, he asked for some advice, adding "I thought it possible, moreover, that it might meet her eye and impress on her a due sense of the enormity of her conduct, for her father takes your paper, and is like myself, a CANTAB."

To appear literary, witty, indeed brilliant, for Phebe and the *Post* readers was Higginson's intent. But his subsequent reference to "that d——d piece of mine in the Friday Post" revealed its embarrassing failure. When Frank Parker correctly guessed the iden-

36. Ibid., Feb. 7, 8, 1840.
37. Ibid., Feb. 8, 1840.
38. Boston *Post*, Feb. 28, 1840.

tity of the "Cantab," Wentworth acted indignant and attributed authorship to someone else. He felt sure that Parker told others that he had written that "ridiculous letter." [39]

Having written the letter to the *Post*, however, gave him courage to seek new ways of making the relationship meaningful—at least to his imagination. Dressing in an "abbreviated study gown" Higginson would pass by the Adam house "to receive an angelic smile from the enchantress." Instead of just waiting for a glance during the day Wentworth stationed himself outside the Adam house at night and "spied on Phebe." [40] Rather pleased that he had renamed the Adam house "Eden," he often noted, "Evening Edenized," to identify these silent vigils. Parker, who had a "curiosity" but never an admiration for females, tried to stop these frequent excursions. They exchanged notes about Phebe in Cicero recitation, but Higginson noted that Parker's view made him indignant—that the Adams left the shutters open at night, according to Parker, was an immodest act known through town. Higginson admitted being troubled by this but persisted in his evenings of "Edenizing." While longing for something which could reach her, like "athletic exercises, swimming in particular, literary exercises," he still found being "Down by Eden" the most effective way to see Phebe without the fear of being rejected. [41]

Higginson's forwardness increased as he began to sneak to the side windows of the Adams' house to peer inside; he became convinced that Phebe was far more charming in the privacy of domestic life than in the excitement of a party. Domesticity was not his only concern. "Came about X by Eden . . . & afterward watched them going to bed until XI—saw P[hebe] in night gown." The next day he feared that the Adam girls lacked the necessary religious feeling. Later he noted seeing "H[annah] sitting with her legs crossed ungraciously, not to say improperly." His aggressiveness culminated with the following: "Watched long & at last growing bolder—rushed up on the piazza—in at the long window and seized for a trophy, a white handkerchief I'd seen on the table, and rushed off with the treasure." But Higginson was not to be wel-

---

39. TWH journal, Mar. 3, 27, 1840.
40. Ibid., Mar. 16, 17, 1840.
41. *Tribute to Parker*, p. 31, TWH journal, April 6, July 1, 1840.

comed into his Eden. Instead, the Adam family, for scholarly reasons, left for Europe.[42] In his future relationships with women he
also seldom emerged from his "refuge behind the bookcase."

During the last year at Harvard he noticeably changed, which
probably contributed to the end of his friendship with Parker.
Economic difficulties at home forced him to seek lodging—not
board—in a private home so that Mrs. Higginson could offer
room and board to students. At first he felt unhappy about having
to sleep and study away from hime. That he would have to share
a room with Charles Perkins (son of the wealthy merchant, James
Perkins), who was younger than himself, was a discomforting
prospect. From being the youngest son of his mother, a fatherless
adolescent, a younger and subordinate companion to Frank Parker,
and a young admirer of the womanly Phebe Adam, Higginson
understood that he was being forced to assume an unaccustomed
degree of independence and dominance.[43]

Much to his surprise and satisfaction, the new arrangements
provided the setting for new ways of behavior. Once settled with
Perkins in the new room he discovered that he enjoyed the late
hours, the independence, and his younger roommate. Very soon
he turned to cigars to provide some visible symbol of this new
feeling of manhood. He became ill from smoking, but neither
Parker's nor his mother's admonitions moved him to seek different
ways to appear adult. Before the end of the first month of classes
he proudly reported on his attendance at morning prayers: "this
the fifth I've missed already!" Or shortly after: "Said 'not prepared' to Dr. Walker Friday and Saturday for effect, & produced
it." And when President Quincy personally admonished him for
cutting seventeen chapel sessions in less than three months Higginson commented to his journal that Quincy's warning was "rather
a bore, for I shall have to cut some more for skating." [44]

Mrs. Higginson was suddenly confronted by a son who was
becoming critical of her authority. Wentworth for the first time

42. TWH journal, July 18, 20, 21, Aug. 21, 22, 27, 30, 1840.
43. Ibid., Aug. 29, 1840, Feb. 1, 12, July 8, 1840.
44. TWH to L. Higginson Aug. 1840, Higginson MSS; TWH journal, July 30,
Aug. 20, Sept. 3, 7, 11, Nov. 5–14, 22–26, 1840.

reported a blowup at home. During mid-semester vacation, when he went South to visit his stepsister's family, the harshness of the exchange of letters disclosed further friction. With more than a little sarcasm, Louisa told her son, "I should like when it is *quite convenient* to have some letter of how these places and cities strike your young mind . . . and shall depend on your saying a *good deal* about every member of the Farley family." Wentworth countered with a sarcasm that went to the very roots of their relationship: "I suppose some new plans you have formed for me, without communicating them, will continually astonish me all along my journey." He hoped that his failure to visit a fourteenth cousin would not prove him an unworthy Higginson descendant.[45]

Mrs. Higginson did not take such filial insubordination passively. "When you are more acquainted with the fair sex," she noted, "you will understand the force & fervor of their imaginations, and perhaps the superior wisdom of the *stronger vessel* may condescend to temper its [imagination] by allowing less food for it than *one* of the Lords of creation now thinks fit to do." Three days later she grew calmer and explained her previous excited letter in terms of the "anxiety" felt toward her children, "one that prevents me from feeling *quite* easy unless I know they are doing well." She then turned to complimenting her son, but did so by indicating her plans for his future.[46] Mrs. Higginson's hold on Wentworth was not to be loosened, of course, by his first real attempt to establish his independence.

With girls closer to his age, change also was noticeable. Determined to captivate them, to make them all admire him rather than be admired, he looked less for girls like Phebe Adam with her "strong mind and character." He turned rather to people whom he considered weaker than himself and who appeared to need his care. The sight of tall, awkward, country-looking girls seemed worth noting in his journal. He became convinced that if only he had had someone weaker, like a younger sister, to watch over, he would have been a better person. "Don't be shocked," he wrote Parker,

45. Ibid., Sept. 22, 1840; L. Higginson to TWH, Jan. 28, 1841, TWH to L. Higginson, Jan. 29, Feb. 17, 20, 1841, Higginson MSS.
46. L. Higginson to TWH, Feb. 17, 20, 1841, Higginson MSS.

"you know I've always wished for one a little younger than my-self." [47]

This desire for respect or recognition from someone younger, weaker, or dependent was not confined to girls. "All know me!" he happily exclaimed about a group of young boys who remembered him though he had not recognized them. For his landlady, a Mrs. Dix, he had special warmth; she had a high opinion of his worth. "I act autocratic with the Dixes," he boasted.[48]

Although he insisted that he no longer felt like an awkward lout and had acquired entire confidence, he still was compelled to make resolutions about being confident. Exulting in his new ability to win the admiration of others, he sadly admitted: "There's still the horrid thing at the root!" [49]

It would take some time before Higginson could find a role that would allow him to soothe that intense feeling of inadequacy and insufficiency. In an age when paternalism was a common attitude in public and private life, the long Higginson family tradition of public stewardship and the personal needs growing out of his childhood and adolescence would make the paternal role especially central in his life. As an adolescent he could condescendingly say: "Gave my old black friend 50 cts." And in the back of a notebook, as if to establish the degree and reason for his interest, he wrote the word "African" nine times; he surpassed this by writing his own name thirteen times.[50]

47. TWH journal, Jan. 23, 31, 1841; TWH to Frank Parker, Feb. 17, 1841, Higginson MSS.

48. TWH journal, Mar. 2, 3, Aug. 22, 1841.

49. Ibid., May 5, 9, 1841.

50. Ibid., Jan. 26, 1841; "Latin Exercise Book," 1839 Undergraduate Notes, Higginson-Student MSS.

3

"Launched Upon the World"

Not yet eighteen years old and not quite one hundred and fifty pounds, Wentworth Higginson received his Harvard degree in August 1841. "Launched upon the world," he exclaimed, "at last alone! Tragic!" For Higginson, as for New England, the forties would be a time of doubt, experiment, and finally of shaky affirmation. The decade, conditioning the soil on which "The New England Renaissance" would grow in the fifties, also would be an intellectually formative period for him.[1]

Just prior to the final semester of his senior year, Mrs. Higginson had advised Wentworth to continue studying and begin to support himself. Urging him to do justice to his talents and opportunities and to "persevere steadily in a course which will lead to perfection," she suggested that he either study for a profession or give himself to "Science & Literature in a University Life." Money could be earned by teaching school, tutoring in a private family, or perhaps by working on a railroad for a year. The latter would be "an excellent place for your *Physical* Man." [2]

To accept his mother's direction again was not difficult as there was little alternative for a boy undesirous to enter the commercial world and unsure about a specific profession. The analysis of the contours of his head during his senior year by the renowned phrenologist Orsin Fowler had not helped. "He told my character," said Higginson, "far better than anyone else ever did—said I had had splendid talents but no application." [3]

When hopes for a Greek tutorship at Exeter and a position as a mathematics and natural philosophy teacher both failed to materialize, he accepted a job in suburban Boston as an assistant in a

1. TWH journal, Sept. 20, 23, 1841.
2. L. Higginson to TWH, Feb. 8, 20, 1841, Higginson MSS.
3. TWH journal, April 30, 1841.

private school at Jamaica Plain. With room and board at $4 a week
and an annual salary of $600, he contemplated a surplus. But all
did not go smoothly. A love for children, he judged, made him too
familiar with his students, who soon ignored his authority. Lacking permission to punish them, he saw his classroom become the
scene of "spitballing" and general rowdyism. The loneliness that
moved him to befriend some students multiplied disciplinary problems and brought charges of partiality against him.[4]

To assuage his loneliness he took long walks with some of his
boys or strolled through the woods alone and tried to lift his
spirits "by warbling some twenty songs." During weekend trips
to Cambridge he visited Levi Thaxter, a Harvard undergraduate
aspiring to become a poet, or he attended a Saturday night party
with familiar company. Hopefully reporting that he was in the
process of "changing my timidity and awkwardness to boldness,
self-possession & agreeableness," he noted that it had become
unnecessary to prepare conversation in advance of a social gathering. The more unhappy teaching made him, however, the more
he turned to such practices as renting a carriage to be conspicuous,
or curling his hair to look elegant, or promenading after church
"to display the beautiful combination of gaiters & high heels." Such
behavior helped temporarily to submerge a "listless" feeling.[5]
Symptomatic of his unhappiness was his zest in unexpected adven-
tures, he reported his participation in a fire-bucket brigade:

> With others I rushed to the pump . . . and was . . . up on
> the 2nd ladder. . . . I got excited directly & burned to distin-
> guish myself which I did—staid on the ladder . . . then in-
> side the house, working like a horse, distinguishing myself still
> more. . . . I worked furiously all the time & my excitement
> supported me through fatigue . . . tremendous labor . . .
> this thorough soaking and the violent blows from empty
> buckets. Oh it was glorious. I revelled in it & felt & thought
> nothing but enthusiasm till it was 2:30 a. m.

After another fire, which he battled while dressed in his velvet
coat and new black trousers, there was less satisfaction: he was

4. Ibid., April 1-11, 23, 30, Aug. 6, Sept. 22, 24, Oct. 13, 14, 17, Nov. 11, 1841.
5. Ibid., Sept. 27, 29, Oct. 3, 5, 9, Feb. 14, 18, 1842.

accused of vain display besides "having ruined a pair of gloves if not my best pants." [6]

Admitting a strong desire for distinction and conquests, Wentworth indexed in his journal descriptions of parties attended. He devoted a full four pages to a specific Boston social affair which he titled his debut. Expecting it to be a very important event, he was "in a tremor all day." At the party his sense of success was enhanced by "7 delicious dances." A few months later he was uncertain about future success in Boston society. [7]

There was always the daily teaching chore. To show superiority by surreptitiously tutoring his young students in boxing, or by distinguishing himself on ice skates was temporarily reassuring, but continual failure as a teacher left him "deeply homesick" and "dismal" or "almost in tears." "My daily labor disgusts me," he groaned, "how I detest it." [8]

Teaching every day and evening plus half a day on both Saturday and Sunday made leisure too scarce for a boy who had always had it in abundance. And at this time, leisure for reading and writing seemed especially vital. The *Dial* first attracted his attention during his initial months of teaching. The magazine had been published since July 1840, but not until a year and a half later did Higginson indicate interest. After teaching all day, he began to stay awake until the early hours of morning to indulge in "sprees of poetry." During one such spree he wrote something called "The Song of the Night Wind in November" which he claimed was entirely unconscious and written as fast as he could put down the lines. The poem, tracing the wind around his window pane with its "moaning, moaning . . . groaning, groaning," ends with the wind making its rounds of the graveyard and then fading away scornfully "Singing Ha! Ha! Ha!" This effort was not published, but Wentworth thought the poem showed promise. More conventional were the sonnets written to Longfellow and Tennyson. [9]

It was probably the *Dial*'s frequent references to romantic literature which led him to read Madame de Staël's novel *Corinne*.

6. Ibid., Mar. 23, 1842, Oct. 8, 1841.

7. Ibid., Aug. 22, Nov. 20, Dec. 1, 1841, Feb. 10, 1842.

8. Ibid., Nov. 7, Dec. 11, 17, 1841, Jan. 7, 1842.

9. Ibid., Oct. 21, Nov. 14, 21, 1841; Poems of T. W. Higginson, MS, Higginson MSS.

Corinne was a heroine who could "declaim melodiously in verse."
If Margaret Fuller played the American Corinne, as some said,
Higginson also could find a part in the novel. There was a guilt-
ridden hero, ill from the "most intimate of griefs, the loss of a
father." The heart, de Staël wrote, by a "mysterious enthusiasm"
combined poetry, heroism and religion. Reading this book marked
an era in his life, Higginson proclaimed. Soon after he also reported: "usual dose of Emerson & to bed." Reading Emerson, as
he said in later years would be for any young person "a great event
in life, but in the comparative conventionalism of the [American]
literature of that period it had the effect of a revelation." [10]

After four months of teaching, life at Jamaica Plain seemed
unbearable. Without his mother's knowledge he planned to become
a tutor of the three children of his Brookline cousin, Stephen
Higginson Perkins. When Mrs. Higginson learned of the change
she disapproved, for Perkins in her opinion was "very visionary
and somewhat radical." She could not happily contemplate having
her son transformed into a social reformer. But Wentworth persisted. [11]

Perkins, now thirty-eight years old, had been schooled in Germany under Edward Everett's guidance and was sent to the East
and West Indies as a supercargo. He subsequently became a Boston
merchant. A widower with three children, he fashioned his household into a center of taste and culture while leading a public life
characterized by social awareness and patrician benevolence. Each
afternoon sherry and madeira were served in the parlor with pears,
peaches, grapes, or strawberries, and rich sweet cream. His home
was graced by a Sir Joshua Reynolds, a Willem van de Velde, and
a large copy of the *Sistine Madonna*. Wentworth was invited to
partake of the fruit, the sweet cream, and the conversation. To the
Raphael painting he composed a poem, his first to be published. [12]

Perkins exemplified a reformer who could envision a class struggle if the classes were delineated morally, rather than economically.

10. Quoted in J. Christopher Herold, *Madame de Staël: Mistress to an Age*
(New York, 1958), pp. 213, 305, 155; TWH journal, Dec. 17, 1841, Jan. 7, 1842;
TWH, *Contemporaries* (Boston, 1899), p. 10.

11. L. Higginson diary, Mar. 18, 1841.

12. *Yesterdays*, pp. 70, 82; TWH, "La Madonna di San Sisto," *Present*, 1
(1843), 165.

In answer to Victor Considerant's blanket attack on all business-men, he insisted that honesty could be the business ethic, that it was the most practical way of gaining wealth and indeed was more important than any monetary reward. Perkins was vitally concerned about two dramatic phenomena that marked the Boston of his day: the irresponsible success-conscious businessman and the irresponsible, impoverished immigrant.[13]

Opposing entrance restrictions for immigrants who arrived in America as paupers, Perkins wanted the city government to pro-vide them with western land for which it would later be reim-bursed. For Boston's immigrants, he advocated a large housing development financed by private capital: in this way slums would disappear, the poor would benefit, and private capitalists would receive a profit. Not only would there be material gain for all, but the horrendous tendency—"the separation of rich and poor" —would be reversed.[14]

Somewhat shy and slightly deaf, Perkins showed a gentle affec-tion for the new tutor. He provided the boy's first directly personal exposure to ideas of social protest and reform, which would have a lasting influence. Now that Mrs. Higginson with her sister and daughters had moved from Cambridge to Brattleboro, Vermont, to live near her son Francis, who opened a medical practice there, Higginson was drawn to the frequent and prominent visitors at the Perkins household. Among them was Perkins' niece and Higgin-son's second cousin, Miss Mary Channing, twenty-two years old, three years older than Higginson. She was the daughter of Dr. Walter Channing, dean of the Harvard Medical School and the leading American specialist in obstetrics. Miss Channing, mother-less from the age of two, had developed some of the forcefulness of personality that characterized Louisa Higginson. While lacking Mrs. Higginson's physical health, she possessed a strength in her knowledge and articulation about the work of reform and re-formers. She was the first girl with whom Higginson had ever felt comfortable. At the outset he found her less fascinating than

13. Stephen H. Perkins, "The Tradesman's Sermon," *Present*, 1 (1843), 125–29.

14. Victor Considerant, "The Vices of Commerce," *Present*, 1 (1843), 129–33; Perkins, "Tradesman's Sermon," p. 126; Perkins in Boston *Advertiser*, June 11, 1847; Stephen H. Perkins, Walter Channing, et al., *Report of the Committee on the Expediency of Providing Better Tenements for the Poor* (Boston, 1846).

another more feminine girl that he had recently met: "Mary is less perfect but has fine points of character—a seeming want of softness, but a fine heart—very independent in her opinions & a love for the beautiful and strong. . . . She has great comic powers which of course affected her character but I like her better as I know her more." Higginson appreciated Mary's high spirits and shared her intellectual interests; her "fresh smile" lifted his morale and he obviously enjoyed doing such things as touring the Boston Atheneum with her. "Whatever be her faults of manner," he observed, "I do like her very much indeed, & think she has substantially a fine mind & a fine character." [15]

Mary's brother Ellery, who already had published a volume of verse, interested Higginson not because of his personality, which Wentworth considered disagreeable, but because he was a poet. From Ellery, who recently had married Margaret Fuller's youngest sister Ellen, he learned about the great financial difficulties facing American writers.[16]

A more important person to Higginson was the most prominent of all the Brookline circle, Mary's father, Dr. Walter Channing. His brothers were Professor Edward Tyrell Channing, who had taught Higginson at Harvard, and the renowned Unitarian leader the Reverend William Ellery Channing. Dr. Walter Channing was not known just for his medical work or his famous relatives; he was deeply concerned with social issues and spoke for abolition, pacifism, and temperance and was as concerned as Stephen Perkins about the plight of the poor. Pauperism, he argued, resulted from "our present modes of industry and division of profits . . . which irrevocably doom a class of our fellow beings . . . while conscience is lulled to sleep by the lie that pauperism is a self-inflicted woe." [17] Neither Perkins nor Channing felt much rapport with Emerson. Channing admitted that listening to Emerson's generalizations and abstractions gave him a headache. Immersed in imme-

15. TWH journal, April 23, 1842, May 10, 1842; TWH to A. Storrow, July 24, 1842, Levi Thaxter to TWH, Mar. 24, 1842, Higginson MSS.

16. M. T. Higginson, *Higginson*, p. 51; TWH journal, Oct. 12, 1842.

17. Henry R. Viets, "Walter Channing," *Dictionary of American Biography,* 55 (New York, 1930), 3–4; Walter Channing, *Thoughts on Peace and War, May 27, 1844* (Boston, 1844); Stephen H. Perkins, Walter Channing, *Tenements for the Poor;* Walter Channing, "Pauperism," *Present,* 1 (1843), 143.

diate social problems, neither Channing nor Perkins could say, as Emerson did: "Are they *my* poor?" [18]

At Mary Channing's urging, Higginson began attending the liberal Unitarian sermons of James Freeman Clarke and became interested in the reform views of another Channing relative, the radical Unitarian minister William Henry Channing. He and Mary also visited the nearby communitarian experiment at Brook Farm. In the *Dial*, Elizabeth Peabody had extolled this life near the "healthy earth," and suggested that the "perfume of clover lingers about it. The lowing of cattle is the natural bass to the melody of human voices." But Nathaniel Hawthorne, who enlisted in the community, wrote his betrothed, Miss Peabody's sister Sophia, that "a man's soul may be buried and perish under a dung-heap or in a furrow of the field, just as well as under a pile of money. Dost thou think it a praiseworthy matter that I spent five golden months in providing food for cows and horses?" [19]

Lacking Hawthorne's repugnance for exercise, Higginson was attuned to the harmony depicted by Elizabeth Peabody. At first he was attracted by the "combination of gentlemen and laborers," but he soon concluded that Brook Farm encouraged affection and impracticality. The unkemptness of some participants convinced him that there were only "one or two clean ones" at the West Roxbury utopia.[20] Despite his enjoyment of the outdoors, Higginson preferred a more urban life. His Brook Farm impressions revealed his lifelong ambivalence toward isolation from general society: as a source of personal fulfillment or as a resignation from directly influencing others.

Mary Channing had no immediate success in changing Higginson's view toward the South and toward the fugitive slave's plight. During the visit to some Virginia cousins in his senior year at Harvard, Higginson had chided Frank Parker for accepting the

18. Ralph L. Rusk, *The Life of Ralph Waldo Emerson* (New York, 1949), p. 248; Henry S. Commager, *Theodore Parker* (Boston, 1936), p. 150.

19. TWH, *Margaret Fuller Ossoli* (Boston, 1884), p. 133, TWH journal, May 9–11, 14, 31, July 20, 1842; Elizabeth Peabody, "Plan of West Roxbury Community," *Dial*, 3 (1842), 14; Hawthorne to Sophia Peabody, June 1, Aug. 12, 1841, in *Autobiography of Brook Farm*, ed. Henry W. Sams (Englewood Cliffs, 1958), p. 21, 30.

20. Nathaniel Hawthorne, *The Blithedale Romance* (Cambridge, 1833), p. 394; TWH journal, May 14, 31, July 20, 1842.

prejudices against the South of their predominantly New England classmates. The South, Higginson had reported, was not filled with "indolent luxury—[people] reclining on couches of feathers, or with people conversing languidly with languid Southern ladies, or lulled to a siesta by vast quantities of fans agitated . . . by the hands . . . of sable hue. . . . But for the color of the few visible domestics . . . I see nothing . . . to remind me that I am south of the Potomac. I never saw a more industrious or more religious household." Even his Virginia cousin Farley Storrow, whom Higgonson disliked, showed no signs of dissipation. And "as for young negresses, I haven't seen one since I came here." To Higginson the abject status of Negroes in Philadelphia was almost as striking as that of those slaves he saw sold at auction in Baltimore. The sight of Negroes bought and sold was associated more with the general wretchedness of Baltimore than with the prettier and more genteel sites farther south. This lack of sympathy for anti-South opinion in the North declined, however, as he imbibed Brookline's reform spirit. Soon he would proudly shake hands with John Greenleaf Whittier, the author of "Massachusetts to Virginia," the antislavery poem inspired by the Latimer fugitive slave case.[21]

The Reverend James Freeman Clarke preached sermons devoid of the soporific effect of Higginson's undergraduate days. Clarke, one of the original members of the transcendentalist circle, had recently returned North from a Kentucky pastorate. Antislavery views, he concluded, were harder to express in the Boston of the forties than they had been in the South. Clarke had condemned slavery but opposed its immediate abolition; the mildness of his position appealed to Higginson and helped make him sympathetic to antislavery agitation. Higginson also was impressed by Clarke's success in establishing the Church of the Disciples in Brookline. Anyone could worship there without buying a pew, and Clarke introduced regular group discussions for what he deemed the intellectual part of the mind, prayer for the spiritual part, and community reform activity for the moral faculty.[22] His willingness to

21. TWH to F. Parker, Feb. 17, 1841, Higginson MSS; TWH journal, Jan. 27, 1841; TWH, *John Greenleaf Whittier* (New York, 1902), p. 95.
22. TWH journal, Sept. 25, Oct. 9, 1842, TWH to L. Higginson, June 2, 1844, Higginson MSS; William R. Hutchison, *The Transcendental Ministers* (New Haven, 1959), pp. 145–46; Van Wyck Brooks, *The Flowering of New*

invite Theodore Parker to speak from his pulpit, at a time when other ministers shunned Parker, would continue to ally Higginson to Clarke well after his own antislavery position had gone beyond Clarke's.

The most radical public figure introduced to Higginson was the Reverend William Henry Channing. He dimly remembered that Channing, whose mother was the sister of Higginson's father, had visited the Higginson house in the thirties bringing stories about the local "come-outer" religions. Subsequently he had preached in Cincinnati and replaced Clarke as editor of the *Western Messenger*, a magazine devoted to "the spread of a rational and liberal religion." During Clarke's editorship the magazine's views had been distinctly Unitarian and its contributors mostly New Englanders. Serving as a testing ground for those who would later write for the *Dial*, it included among its writers Emerson, Fuller, Peabody, F. H. Hedge, Very, and Parker. Editor Channing, who had become an advocate of a new universal religion that sought to combine the best from all religions, removed all allegiance to unitarianism from the *Messenger*. Instead he suggested that all "sectarianism is heresy." His religious eclecticism, paralleling the philosophic eclecticism of the Transcendentalists, led a critic to allege that Channing believed that "Christ did not understand his own religion." Despite such criticism, Channing returned East undaunted and established a "free religious society" (pews were not sold); he displayed a belief in the priesthood of all men by removing the pulpit and inviting the discussion of the sermon at each church service. More mystical in his religious conception than Clarke and more radical in his commitment to social reform, Channing vigorously supported Brook Farm and preached Christian Socialism. His antislavery views were far closer to Garrison's than were Clarke's.[23]

Teaching less than five hours a day in Brookline, Higginson had time to discuss transcendentalism, free religion, and social reform with Perkins, Clarke, and the Channings. Settled in a room

England (New York, 1936), p. 230; James F. Clarke, *Autobiography, Diary and Correspondence* (Boston, 1899), pp. 98, 314, 214.

23. TWH journal, Mar. 8, 1838; Frank L. Mott, *History of American Magazines, 1740–1850* (Cambridge, 1950), pp. 659, 661, 663, 669; Brooks, *New England*, pp. 271, 249; Hutchison, *Ministers*, p. 174

which he pronounced "not Nicholas Nicklebyish," he lived quite
differently from Dickens' genteel teacher. If the Jamaica Plain job
had reminded him of the squalid life of an English boarding school
like Dotheboys, the good living with Perkins was as nourishing as
the fruit and sweet cream. Higginson's reading continued to shift
from the more accepted Anglo-American authors—Dickens, Sedge-
wick, Martineau, Irving, Cooper, and Hawthorne—to those romantic writers heralded in the *Western Messenger* and the *Dial*:
Carlyle, Goethe, Coleridge, Fouqué, and Richter. But in J. P.
Bailey's poem *Festus* and Mrs. Elizabeth Buckminster Lee's *Life
of Richter*, he found more personal meaning.[24]

Margaret Fuller equated *Festus* with Goethe's *Faust* and lauded
it for emphasizing a higher faculty than reason. Its praise of youth,
beauty, and truth well suited the romantic ideals of transcendentalism. Bailey had sought to achieve a spontaneity for which Higginson had striven in "The Song of the Night Wind in November."
He proclaimed that *Festus* had risen from "one burning illumina-
tion" and that thereafter his writing would forever cease. Like
Margaret Fuller, Higginson was enthralled by Bailey's intuitive
power.[25]

Thomas Carlyle and Margaret Fuller agreed on Jean Paul
Richter's artistic genius. Brookline's Elizabeth Buckminster Lee,
who published a biography of Richter in 1842 and translated portions of his autobiography, heightened the interest in this German
romantic. Mrs. Lee told about Richter's poor but clean home and
the plain and simple people of his childhood. In his autobiography,
Richter noted being born "in the same month that the golden wag-
tail, the robin-redbreast, the crane, and the red-hammer appeared."
To cite this correspondence of man and nature, and to refer to
"thirsting soul," "idyllic joys," and the "deep folds of the heart,"
confirmed the antimaterialist outlook attracting Higginson. If
Emerson could find Richter's prose filled with "excessive efflor-
rescence and German superlative," he sufficiently esteemed it to
give a German edition as a prenuptial gift to his fiancée. Long-

24. TWH to L. Higginson, April, 1842; TWH journal, June 18, 19, 25, Sept.
8–20, 1842; Books Read, 1842, MS, Higginson MSS.

25. Margaret Fuller, "Festus," *Dial*, 2 (1841), 231–61; TWH to L. Higginson,
Aug. 20, 1842, Higginson MSS; TWH journal, Aug. 12, 13, 16, 1842, Sept. 8, 1842;
TWH, "The Passing of Festus," *Nation*, 75 (1902), 241.

fellow perhaps best expressed Richter's appeal to the more effusive New England romantics when he claimed that "to read his writings is like climbing a high mountain in merry company to see the sun rise." [26]

At the time Higginson was reading *The Life of Richter* a decision was necessary about his own future. Being a tutor at Brookline, while pleasant and edifying, provided no clear path to a permanent occupation. He was sure, however, that he did not want to become a lawyer: "The legal study itself, whatever general bursts of eloquence man may make out of it, cultivates no powers but those of acuteness—the analytical faculties— . . . which are certainly far from being our most noble powers. . . . Law could never make a Channing!" [27]

To his journal he reported that he had read Richter and resolved to make that day a milestone in his life by vowing not to study for a profession, but instead to strive as mightily as Richter did, labor as intensely, and suffer as much. The success of this spiritual duty could only be measured in one's soul, not by the opinion of others. He further ascertained that for him there was an

> inevitable & indivisible connection . . . between *determination* & action—the impossibility of a state of vacillating performance. . . . I know myself thoroughly . . . I cannot doubt my actions. This sounds presumptuous and arrogant— I am sorry if it seems so—but it is *true*—I *know* it. These are my fundamental principles and by them I shall live. . . . They are certain—& time will confirm them.[28]

His decision was to relinquish Brookline's comforts for the spare life of a nonmatriculated scholar at Harvard, hoping to study there for the next five years and eventually become a writer. Unlike Emerson, Lowell, and Everett, who had enrolled in either divinity school or law school before turning to writing, Higginson planned to study independently. Although encouraged by a letter from

26. Edward B. Brewer, "The New England Interest in J. P. Richter," *Publication in Modern Philology* (Los Angeles, 1945), pp. 11–13, 6; Elizabeth Buckminster Lee, *Life of J. P. F. Richter with His Autobiography* (Boston, 1842), *1*, 5, 8, 11; *2*, 305; Rusk, *Emerson*, p. 236.

27. TWH to L. Higginson, Jan. 31, 1843, Higginson MSS.

28. TWH journal, Oct. 16, Sept. 6, 1842.

William Henry Channing supporting his decision, leaving Brook-line was difficult even for one determined to be "independent of the opinion of the world." He granted that the Perkins household had taught him that to be loved was as "delicious" as receiving esteem, appreciation, and sympathy. But he earnestly reported: "I feel overflowing with mental energies—I will be Great if I can." [29]

Settled in College House at Harvard by September 1843, Higginson reported that he was thriving on bread and milk, exercise, excitement, and Hebrew roots. His room befitted his promise to forsake gaiters, pantaloons, French boots and a fashionable life. A washstand, pale white curtains, a print of a Titian portrait, a copper relief of the Alhambra, plus a white bust of Hebe surrounded by fresh flowers were the highlights of the low-ceilinged, closetless room. "I am quite as happy as I expected—I enjoy the independence very much as I knew I should, & do not feel lonely. . . . I have no one here whom I shall see much of. . . . Some of the first days I passed the whole day without talking five minutes to anybody." [30]

His first important acquaintance was William Bachelder Greene, a contributor to the *Dial* and the author of a new book, *Doctrine of Life,* which combined Unitarian theology with an advocacy of social reform. At present Greene was auditing divinity lectures at Harvard and arguing his views with divinity students. After reading Greene's book, Higginson concluded that its author was a great man. Comparing himself to Greene, he judged him to be dogmatic, "while I am a seeker & entirely unsettled by moods of thought . . . far more poetical or ideal than his. I go by impressions very much. . . . He is a person with whom nothing vague or ambitious will be sown." [31]

Greene's very self-confidence disturbed him. First he tried to rationalize Greene's invulnerability by suggesting that if this man "were less wise it might be dangerous for me." Obviously pressed,

29. TWH to L. Higginson, Aug. 11, Oct. 24, 1842, Jan. 31, 1843, TWH to A. Storrow, Oct. 20, 1842, Higginson MSS; TWH journal, Nov. 5, 1846.

30. TWH to L. Higginson Sept., 1843, TWH to Mary Channing, Aug. 13, 1843, Higginson MSS; TWH journal, Sept. 22, 1843.

31. TWH to M. Channing, Sept. 8, 1843, Higginson MSS; William B. Greene, *Doctrine of Life* (Boston, 1843).

he inaccurately stated, "submission was never in my vocabulary before." And soon Higginson conceded that Greene's superiority had caused the end of their relationship.[32] Once more Higginson was repulsed by the threat of a dominant male personality.

A few weeks later, he reported: "I continue to be a sort of pariah, an outcast of the world—but then I bear it patiently & humbly." He experienced moods of depression and found no relief in solitary walks in the countryside. He was quickly dissatisfied with the results of his efforts to write poetry and anxious to know whether he really had it in him to become a poet, or whether he deceived himself and possessed only a mediocre talent. He admitted that he was too social-hearted to enjoy solitude. Emerson's self-reliance, for him, led not to heroic independence and self-fulfillment but to painful loneliness and a debilitating indirection. Yet, where should he turn? Of course there were the examples of Clarke and W. H. Channing in the ministry, but Higginson reflected: "I don't myself think I shall ever become a minister. . . . I value my time too much to spend 2 hours a day on a study I don't care for. . . . I don't relish any restraint imposed by others. . . . There's something I can do well, there must be. I shall look for that till I find it." [33]

Insisting that he had no time to spend with people, he nevertheless occasionally saw Frank Parker and Jones Very. Parker he now judged his inferior. Very was "not very deep, but . . . always happy & bright & I feel at liberty to say just what I please to him which is a satisfaction." Very also agreed that Divinity School was unsuited for Higginson. Those enrolled, Higginson concluded, were uninspiring, and there were one or two forlorn youths who thought they were transcendental but who probably could not "understand the Orphic sayings of Bronson Alcott." [34]

The absence of compatible male companionship and the presence of the *Dial* led Higginson to assail all his countrymen: "they are not aesthetic—there's some mistake about American young men,

32. TWH to M. Channing, Oct. 6, 1843, TWH to L. Higginson, Nov. 1843, Higginson MSS.

33. TWH to L. Higginson, Jan. 31, 1843, TWH to M. Channing, Aug. [1843], Higginson MSS.

34. TWH to L. Higginson, Oct. 10, 12, 15, 1843, Higginson MSS.

. . . they are good & sensible & bright & agreeable & perhaps even brilliant—but they aren't enthusiastic about anything . . . —they don't recognize the existence of the trees, the flowers, the sky & the stars & the sea and music (a little) & Shakespeare." Lonely and uncertain about his future, he came to a decision. With admitted suddenness he announced his engagement to Mary Channing.[35]

Although having known Mary for a year and a half, he recognized that his announcement would surprise both his mother and Mary's father; it was necessary to inform Mrs. Higginson that his fiancée was Dr. Walter Channing's daughter and that Channing, upon hearing about the engagement, "behaved better than could have been expected under such trying circumstances." [36] Both parents apparently were comforted by the realization that the couple had set no marriage date and that Higginson, now twenty years old, still intended studying independently rather than training for an occupation.

Eager to increase his knowledge, Higginson began to read some German philosophy—especially Kant, Fichte, and Schleiermacher. "Playing" with philosophical idealism by noting that "outdoors the stars are shining lustrously, under the apparent impression that I am looking at them," he concluded that intuition in philosophy, as in literature, was superior to reason. More appealing than the difficult texts of German philosophy was the popular book, *Proverbial Philosophy*. Written by an Englishman, Martin Tupper, in a style described as "the English of an erudite German," it contained effusive chapters about rest, recreation, and joy, and sought to reduce formal philosophy to aphoristic slogans about the validity of intense feelings.[37]

Also to his taste was *Letters from New York* written by Mrs. Lydia Maria Child. Higginson said she adored everything that he did—"music, clouds, stars, water, flowers, trees, birds, moons & little children," and her words were tinged with romance and

35. Ibid., Oct. 15, 1843.
36. Ibid. [Nov. 1843].
37. TWH to L. Higginson, Sept. 22, Oct. 10, 12, 15, 1843, Higginson MSS; Martin F. Tupper, *Proverbial Philosophy: Thoughts and Arguments Originally Treated* (Boston, 1840) pp. 3, 4; "Tea Table Literature—Martin Farquhar Tupper's Works," *Fraser's Magazine*, 46 (1852), 420; "Martin F. Tupper," *Dictionary of National Biography, 19* (Oxford, 1951), 1246.

mysticism. He failed to note, however, that Mrs. Child revealed more than this characteristic list of romantic affinities.[38]

First published in the *National Anti-Slavery Standard,* which Mrs. Child edited with her husband, *Letters from New York* contained detailed accounts of the horrors of the city's slums. Yet it simultaneously expressed confidence that though "Mammon as usual coolly calculates his chance of extracting a penny from war, pestilence and famine, . . . and though the practical tries to snuff out the ideal, the ideal is immortal and cannot die." Advocating temperance, the cause of the slave, the abolition of capital punishment, woman's rights, tolerance toward Catholics—all dramatized with relevant scenes from city life—Mrs. Child thus directed her romantic empathy to social problems. Sometimes sentimental preconceptions undermined her humanitarianism and her intelligence. At a New York synagogue she felt cheated that so many of the Jews were fair-haired and blue-eyed. From a Negro Baptist church meeting she was happier to report that tears rolled down her cheeks.[39]

William Henry Channing asked Higginson to review *Letters from New York* in the *Present,* a new magazine dedicated to "advance the Reign of Heaven on Earth" and with the didactic slogan to "Act, act in the living present." Higginson's piece, his first published prose, was rapturous. He claimed that Mrs. Child, like the author of *Festus,* was teaching lessons of beauty and truth, and understood the importance of "the inward experience, the real life of any one person, . . . [the] childlike honesty [to express] how he feels and how he thinks when the stars wink at him." She displayed sincerity, earnestness, simplicity, and independence. Above all, said this beginning reader of German philosophy, "she is no metaphysician; she does not argue nor demonstrate; but she *knows*—she has the higher gift, . . . an intuitive perception, seeing at once . . . judging with a single piercing glance the Right from the Wrong." [40]

38. TWH to L. Higginson, Oct. 15, 1843, Higginson MSS; Lydia Maria Child, *Letters from New York* (Boston, 1843).

39. Ethel K. Ware, "Lydia Maria Child and Anti-slavery," *Boston Public Library Bulletin,* 3 (1951), 254; Child, *Letters,* pp. 1, 5, 31, 67.

40. TWH to L. Higginson, October, 1843, Higginson MSS; *Present 1* (1843), 1; TWH, review of *Letters from New York,* in *Present, 1* (1843), 45.

He especially appreciated her moral perceptivity. "It was some time ago discovered," he lectured his mother, "that the *legal* line was not the right one—now people were disposed to go somewhat farther & inquire whether the line drawn by society, though certainly nearer, is really the right one—Mrs. Child says no. . . . What *law authorizes* is constantly found to be in the wrong, what society authorizes is often wrong. There can be no true satisfactory line drawn until the law of Love is established in society & of this Mrs. C. is an apostle." [41]

While Higginson again omitted mentioning even one specific social issue that concerned Mrs. Child, he qualified his sympathy with romanticism when it was divorced from moral right and wrong. Here he echoed American Transcendentalists. But he was soon prepared to go further. Commenting upon Goethe's *Sorrows of Young Werther*, he noted that the hero's all-consuming and unrequited love for Lotte does "not do in these days of Fourierism & Reform trumpets; we are too much in earnest not to sit & let sentimentality addle our brains a while & finally conduce itself to a pistol bullet & blow them all to pieces." At about this time Higginson began subscribing to Garrison's *Liberator*.[42]

Later in life he would maintain that reading Mrs. Child's *Letters* had caused a longing "to put myself on more equal terms with that vast army of handworkers who were ignorant of much that I knew, yet could do much that I could not." It appears more likely that instead of such an equality Higginson was beginning to envision a more elevated social role for himself. At Boston's Amory Hall, listening to William Henry Channing's lecture on Fourierism, he felt that "the best part was the breathless attention with which he was listened to by the people, many of them *real workingmen*." Afterward, when Higginson mingled with some of the audience and gave his views "with emphasis & success," he felt as if he could have stepped up & followed W. H. C. with perfect facility & great eclat—it was a very exciting scene." [43]

Higginson also began attending antislavery meetings but, of

41. Ibid.; TWH to L. Higginson, Nov. 24, 25, 1843, Higginson MSS.
42. TWH to L. Higginson, Mar. 23, 1844, Higginson MSS; TWH, Account Book, 1843–44, MS, Higginson MSS.
43. *Yesterdays*, p. 77; TWH to L. Higginson, October, 1843, Higginson MSS.

course, no one was summoning him to the platform to follow
Channing or Garrison. Still, reform meetings relieved some of
his isolation and loneliness and fostered a new degree of personal
involvement. "I have pretty much concluded," he noted, "that a
consistent abolitionist (which at last any person who thinks &
feels must be, whether nominally or not) must choose between
the Liberty Party and the Disunion Party. . . . I don't like the
dilemma at all, but I fear that I must come to it." Meanwhile, his
failure as a solitary scholar and an aspiring poet caused him to
accept again the position of tutor in the hospitable Perkins household. By the spring of 1844 he was back in Brookline, more interested in learning about reform than literature.[44]

It was probably at this time that he read Lydia Maria Child's
Appeal in Favor of That Class of Americans Called Africans. Published in 1833, six years prior to Theodore Weld's *Slavery As It Is*,
the book was more influential with New England intellectuals
than any other volume on the subject. Not only Higginson but
William Ellery Channing, John Gorham Palfrey, and Charles
Sumner claimed that it first convinced them to speak against slavery.
More moderate in tone than Weld's book, *Appeal* confronted
questions about post-emancipation problems, while Weld primarily
catalogued atrocities against the slave. Mrs. Child, though emotional in her way, was no evangelical revivalist; *Slavery As It Is*
provided dramatic facts especially useful to the heightened antislavery oratory of the 1850's, but *Appeal* was better suited to ease
men into antislavery agitation. Discussing the widespread northern
fear about emancipating illiterate slaves, Mrs. Child said: "We trust
the civil power to keep in order the great mass of ignorant and
vicious foreigners continually pouring into the country; and if
the laws are strong enough for this, may not they be trusted to
restrain the free blacks?" Such assurance would be less comforting
in the fifties to those men who combined their antislavery with
nativism. Moreover, Mrs. Child asked northerners to examine their
own race prejudice and the manner in which they treated northern
Negroes.[45]

44. TWH to L. Higginson, Nov. 19, 1843, TWH to M. Channing, July 6, 28,
1844, Higginson MSS.
45. TWH journal, May 4, 1844; Account Book; *Yesterdays*, p. 125; Lydia

Much later in life, Higginson claimed that this book had made him an Abolitionist. What appears more accurate is that it reflected his abandonment of a purely literary life and strengthened his new interest in reform. He now reported that his Virginia of 1841 had proven to him that the South was filled with "temptation to indolence . . . [and] full of vaporized laziness. But at the North, in the busy action life . . . where all are governed by one Yankee principle—push yourself ahead by your own energy," one could better fulfill oneself. When he heard Emerson call for a more vital religion, he was not only impressed by the lecturer's voice, manner, and looks but could envision himself speaking from a northern public platform. The American Unitarian Association's annual meetings in Boston excited him: after a heated four-day discussion it was resolved that slavery "subverts the fundamental principles of Christian Brotherhood." [46]

Although still fearful of restricting his independence, Higginson in the summer of 1844 enrolled in the Harvard Divinity School. "One thing is plain," he warned Mary Channing, "my ever being a minister is far from certain." Comparing himself to Festus, he claimed that with all his doubts he did not doubt God. A commitment to religion might "settle a person," [47] and the ministerial role might lift him to that position of leadership which he once had hoped to attain as a writer. His decision, by providing the future promise of a regular salary, might also bring closer his marriage to Mary.

Maria Child, *Appeal* (Boston, 1833), pp. 99, 189–93; Benjamin P. Thomas, *Theodore Weld* (New Brunswick, 1950), pp. 169–72; David Donald, *Charles Sumner and the Coming of the Civil War* (New York, 1960), p. 131; Helene Baer, *The Heart Is Like Heaven* (Philadelphia, 1964), pp. 65–71.

46. TWH to L. Higginson, April 1844, Higginson MSS; *Christian World*, quoted in *Liberator*, June 14, 1844.

47. TWH to M. Channing, July 6, and 28, 1844, Higginson MSS.

4

The Divinity Student

The Harvard Divinity School was no sanctuary for the insecure, nor for a young man leaning toward liberal unitarianism and social reform. Conservative unitarianism seemed thoroughly entrenched; after Emerson had rocked the school with his address advocating individual intuition rather than theological tradition, a sharp reaction was reflected in the choice of speakers in subsequent years. Ezra Stiles Gannett, Andrews Norton, and Andrew Peabody assailed the new strains of unitarianism. Peabody, with Theodore Parker in mind, suggested that any minister who denied the authenticity of Christian miracles should not be recognized as a Christian leader. For these three men biblical exegesis directed by "right reason" was properly the core of the Divinity School curriculum.[1]

Unitarianism of the forties was thoroughly dispirited. Such a theological contradiction as rejecting the fall of man and yet accepting redemption was only one of the weaknesses in rational Unitarian doctrine. Still committed to a doctrinal dogmatism, it also professed a desire to de-emphasize sectarian differences. Natural theology was taught in the Divinity School and reason viewed as harmonious with revelation, but Gospel truth still remained most important. While there had been efforts to subordinate strictly theological questions to ethical ones, they had been hampered by the danger of moral questions being turned into controversial social issues about slavery, woman's rights, and the treatment of the poor.[2]

Furthermore, the administration of the school was at its nadir.

1. Divinity Student History, July 1843, MS, Andover-Harvard Theology Library.
2. Sydney Ahlstrom, "The Middle Period (1840–1880)," *The Harvard Divinity School*, ed. George H. Williams (Boston, 1954), pp. 38, 104; "Phillip Harwood," *Present*, 1 (1843), 122–25; Hutchison, *Ministers*, pp. 18–20.

Only two professorial posts were filled, a condition which meant heavy teaching schedules for both Convers Francis and George Rappall Noyes. The number of graduates had been declining so sharply that some Unitarian pulpits remained empty. In Higginson's class of thirty-eight members, the largest ever to be enrolled, most of the students would not accept a pastoral position.[3]

Both Francis and Noyes, however, were highly competent. Francis, appointed in 1842, had attended meetings of Transcendentalists, was versed in German biblical criticism, and disagreed with little of Emerson's Divinity School address. Noyes, despite a fundamental belief in scriptural truth, accepted biblical criticism of portions of the Old Testament. But Higginson, having imbibed the views of radical Unitarian theologians, was intolerant of Unitarian contradictions. He agreed with Theodore Parker, who acidly observed that "it took Egyptian embalmers only seventy days to make a mummy out of a dead man, while Unitarian embalmers were three years in making mummies out of the living." [4]

Unitarian epistemological problems stimulated Higginson's reading in philosophy and helped articulate his assumptions. He now aspired to master "all the wisdom of the ages & sum it all up in a deep wisdom—to renounce action & be wholly thought." Admitting a "strong mystical tendency to seek the secretest parts of these ideas," Higginson repeatedly judged reason useless in religious matters. Individual revelation, not scriptural revelation, he argued, was necessary for religious knowledge: "Religion . . . is a feeling obviously—exists as a feeling in our mind. Reason can do nothing itself but . . . accept revelation." [5]

In contrast, Andrews Norton, the leading Unitarian theologian, had said: "The human mind has no inherent faculty of perception in the sphere of facts which transcends the cognizance of the senses. . . . Intuition can inform us of nothing but what exists in our own minds; it is therefore a mere absurdity to maintain that we have an intuitive knowledge of the truths of religion." Higginson correctly associated Norton with Locke, of whom he said scornfully, "[he]

3. Ahlstrom, "Middle Period," pp. 104–07; Divinity Student History, p. 140.
4. Ahlstrom, "Middle Period," pp. 104–07, 127.
5. TWH to M. Channing, Oct. 6, 1844, Higginson MSS; TWH Divinity School Notes, 1844–45, Higginson-Student MSS.

must of course materialize; and explain away all our highest ideas." With some accuracy he noted that "we must go back for the origin of the difficulty to the middle ages when Abelard & Nominalism triumphed over William of Champeaux & Realism"; and that even Kant, who attacked English empiricism, did not grasp the *absolute* validity of the human mind's spontaneous ideas. On the other hand, Emersonian transcendentalism, with its stress on the infinitude of man, was criticized by Higginson for its excessive optimism and its failure to acknowledge the essential mystery of man's existence. Here he accepted W. H. Channing's objection (previously stated by William Ellery Channing) that transcendentalism frequently exhibited an "ego-theism" by exaggerating self-reliance in assuming man's natural goodness. But like the Transcendentalists, Higginson saw both reason and material verification as subservient to the flash of insight. He agreed with Frederic Hedge, a leading Transcendentalist, that when the material facts differed from the truth—"so much the worse for the facts." [6]

This philosophic realism, this revolt against the finality of particulars, which was integral with the revolt against both Enlightenment rationalism and the nominalism of English empiricism, was readily incorporated by Higginson. His position, so heavily reliant on personal feelings, was now given an intellectual formulation. He had acquired a personal philosophy which had some intellectual respectability.

Intuitive religion hardly harmonized with the Unitarian belief in the primacy of reason and scriptural truth; Higginson was contemptuous of his fellow divinity students for justifying reason's function, and he also criticized his teachers. Convers Francis, though more liberal than Noyes, was assailed with apparent justification for continually "amalgamating the most opposite views into a tasteless transcendental mush." One class discussion was "unsatisfactory, more so than any we have had. Nothing new brought out . . . words—words—words." As for his own essay on the existence of God: "Nothing could be more wholly original." Confronting the problem of how to deal with an unbeliever, Higginson stressed the need to influence his heart, to appeal to his impulses, and to bring tears to his eyes. Only then could one admit the doubt

6. Ibid.; quoted in Miller, *Transcendentalists*, p. 65.

that Higginson now had: "There is no certainty, no sure knowledge of God's existence." [7]

It was not only theological dissent that alienated him from Divinity School. During those first pivotal months he noted:

> Daydreams are my passion & always I am for the time being the character I think of & all else seems apart and away from me. I read history—& as I am borne along in its tide & live again the times gone by—and see everywhere the same story of the power of the individual soul, the one great man—& when I look to the present & see how never was this man more needed, never was there a time a leader of men more wanted —& know from the past how glorious the power of such a leader: then I feel called to the work [by] the energetic & earnest powers within me. . . . I long to be . . . guiding, governing, pointing out the true course to those who cannot find it unaided—& adding to this the moral force of a disinterested philanthropy.

And the worst of it, he concluded, was that no such leaders looked forward to the ministerial profession.[8]

Sustained studying was impossible. He confessed: "I always enjoy thoroughly intellectual men who go on so regularly with neither passions nor feelings to interrupt them—I shall never be so I fear, for every now and then comes something & upsets me. Either a cloud that will pursue me—or a sunbeam that I must pursue & in either case philosophy & theology must suffer for a day or two till I get right again; I sometimes sigh to see that I do not become calmer as I grow older." [9]

He still wished for some vocation that would provide "the will & the power always to pitch right into people & show 'em how foolishly they are thinking and acting." His own nature, he hoped, inevitably would reveal the way. One thing was certain: all the existing denominations exhibited "everlasting dogma, talk, talk,

7. Divinity School Notes, Higginson–Student MSS; TWH to L. Higginson Nov., 1844, Higginson MSS.
8. TWH to L. Higginson, Nov. 1844, Higginson MSS.
9. Ibid.

talk, but no cooperation in good works." Talk was meaningful, however, if directed to action. In January 1845, at a meeting at Faneuil Hall, a resolution denouncing the future admission of Texas to the Union was supported by Daniel Webster. Charles Sumner predicted that the Senator's position would "lift our public sentiment to a new platform for Anti-Slavery," and W. H. Channing linked "Texas and DISUNION." Higginson hoped Massachusetts would be unwilling to be bound by any annexation act. It was then that Higginson bought the bust of Webster.[10]

The more incensed some Massachusetts citizens grew over Texas, the more Divinity School seemed meaningless. Since Higginson's family no longer lived in Cambridge it was also a lonely place. He made attempts to revive the Cambridge of his childhood when his mother had looked over him and taken command of his future. But wandering for hours in Mt. Auburn cemetery where his father was buried, or visiting the grounds of the William Wells School where he had learned Latin and Greek, or walking along Professors' Row where he had been born, only depressed him further. This depression he labeled a weakness, something his mother would urge him to overcome. He was right. "My precious boy," Mrs. Higginson counseled, "action is the only balance to those natural feelings which if indulged might weaken the nature and make life a harder struggle. I rejoice to think of the healthful structure of your mind which will save you from anything morbid & of course injurious. . . . God will help those who look to him and everywhere there is diffused a tone of joyousness from him." By action Mrs. Higginson meant that her son should preach Christian Union. "People have preached dissension long enough, let them try Union & for such you may prepare yourself."[11] To her such a mission was not synonymous with preaching the reforms of the day.

Higginson's answer was soon in coming.

10. TWH journal, Dec. 1844; Sumner to William Story, Feb. 5, 1845, in Edward L. Pierce, *Memoir, and Letters of Charles Sumner, 3* (Boston, 1877–93), 33; Donald, *Sumner,* p. 136; TWH to L. Higginson, Dec. 13, 1845, Higginson MSS; *Present, 2* (1844), 430; *1* (1843), 143; Frank O. Gatell, *John Gorham Palfrey and the New Conscience* (Cambridge, 1964), pp. 123–25.

11. TWH to L. Higginson, Mar. 15, 1845, L. Higginson to TWH, Mar. [1], 22, 1845, Higginson MSS.

Entirely apart from the fact that instructors, companions &
courses of study have failed to interest me or satisfy—I am
now convinced . . . that I cannot obtain equilibrium & peace
of mind . . . [as] a member of Divinity School. . . . I am
finally driven to the course which seems best calculated to
promote the mental calmness that in the present unsettled state
of my mind I cannot yet hope to attain. . . . Each year
weakens my control not over my actions, but my internal
states. . . . My faith in God is unshaken . . . but God gives
to some people a temperament much harder to deal with than
others. . . . I was never very dependent on sympathy & the
help that comes from it—I have always expected to give without receiving & this feeling grows more & more. . . . It is
now as impossible to tell what the course of my life will be as
when I was a baby. . . . If I could by any act of will settle it
tomorrow I would do so—but I know I cannot. . . . I have
known repeatedly within the last two years states of mental
depression with no direct cause and utterly beyond [com-
prehension] that if continued a month would have produced
insanity.

His conclusion indicated his decision: "I write to say what probably will not be agreeable to you to hear, that I have finally made
up my mind that I must leave Divinity School." [12]

When Higginson likened his feelings to early childhood, his
mother responded: "How lamentable there are so few ministers.
Oh I hope you will find yourself strenghtened to preach the everlasting Gospel—what occupation can be so ennobling as to show
the blessed tidings of Peace on earth good will to Man! and you
can & may preach *Christian Love*. I trust you will be called to do
so." [13]

But Higginson viewed differently the minister's role and the
meaning of Christian love. Attending Divinity School graduation
exercises in July 1845 he witnessed the influence that the radical
theology of Theodore Parker had upon all the speakers, including
those opposed to Parker. Although thinking himself permanently

12. TWH to L. Higginson, April 1845, Higginson MSS.
13. L. Higginson to TWH, May (?), 1845, Higginson MSS.

separated from ministerial training, Higginson admired the few courageous clergymen, especially among Unitarians, who were vocally antislavery. Pleasing also was an antislavery meeting where the majority of the Protestant ministry was assailed by Garrison, Phillips, and Dr. Walter Channing for acquiescing to slavery. The spirited tone of the meeting and the resolution that abolitionism was a strictly moral movement—opposed to insurrection and bloodshed—struck a sympathetic chord within him. Higginson found Wendell Phillips' eloquence "truly magnificent . . . with a calm graceful dignity so different from the normal" platform histrionics. When the aristocratic Phillips showed "such calm mild firmness in his quiet blue eyes," Higginson glimpsed the power and restraint he hoped some day would be his own.[14]

He began to see a tie between Christian union and Garrisonian disunion. His sonnet to the editor of the *Liberator* expressed this link. It suggested that men should look beyond Garrison's ardent phrases to the stern devotion of his heart, which atoned for his language. After major revisions, the poem was printed in the *Liberty Bell*, an antislavery annual edited by Maria Weston Chapman. Higginson's new lines contained no misgivings about Garrison's harsh language:

> I yet would thank thee for thy manly life,
> Thou rugged Luther of these latter days.
> Oh when will men look through thy devoted heart
> Where selfish hope or fear had never part
> To swerve thee with the crowd, from Truth's plain ways!

Whittier, some thirteen years before, also had written a poem to Garrison urging him to wait his sure reward. Longfellow and Lowell were treating reform in poetry: the possibility of becoming a poet of reform beckoned.[15]

Higginson, in September 1845, once again settled in Cambridge

14. TWH to L. Higginson, June (?), July 19, 1845, Higginson MSS; *Liberator*, June 6, 1845.

15. "To William Lloyd Garrison," Early Verse of TWH, MS, Higginson MSS; TWH to Maria Chapman, September 15, 1845, Weston MSS; "Sonnet to William Lloyd Garrison," *Liberty Bell* (Boston, 1846), p. 192; "William Lloyd Garrison," *Poetical Works of John Greenleaf Whittier, 3* (Cambridge, 1888), 9, 10.

for independent study, professing no desire to return to Divinity School. He judged its new group of students far inferior to those of the 1825–36 era when George Ripley, Frederic Hedge, William Henry Channing, James Clarke, and Theodore Parker had attended. Bemoaning the fact that of the last two Harvard classes no graduating student had chosen to go into the Divinity School, Higginson concluded that that school "grows deader and deader every year of Mr. Francis' administration & must continue to—a man who never has been known to express a positive opinion himself or encourage such in another, cannot do much for the students. . . . Any man with some Yes in him would be a blessing. . . . The once synonymous names of Unitarianism & Liberal Christianity" had been severed. What was needed were more ministers of the Theodore Parker variety.[16]

In spite of his mother's desire for him to turn to the ministry and her explicit opposition to his literary ambitions, Higginson retained some hope. He was encouraged when Lowell assured him that poetry was beginning to pay, and his own poetic efforts temporarily increased during the year in Cambridge. In a volume of unpublished poems, he wrote a "Fugitive's Hymn," extolling New England as "the Country of the Free." In W. H. Channing's *Harbinger*, a Fourieristic periodical announcing itself champion of the injured masses, he wrote of the mockery of calling America free "While, with calm eyes beholding slavery's horror, we dare to read of Sodom and Gomorrah!" In another poem, "From Broadway," he spoke of "the cities' sin and crime," of how "our fellow men have fallen from their place." But unlike Hawthorne in "The Celestial Railroad" and Thoreau in the poem "What's the Railroad," Higginson hailed incursions into nature, whether city or railroad, as "part of progress, part of the march forward."[17]

He no longer aspired, however, to be a *major* poet. "The idea of poetic genius," he noted, "is now utterly foreign to me and I cannot conceive at all the feeling that underlay my whole life two years ago. I must be content to enjoy instead of creating poetry."

16. TWH to L. Higginson, Sept. 20, Oct. 20, 1845, Mar. 20, 1846, Higginson MSS.

17. L. Higginson to Waldo Higginson, Jan. 1845, cited in TWH journal, Nov. 1849; Early Verse of TWH, MS, Higginson MSS; *Harbinger*, 1 (1845).

The conclusion he came to by June 1846 was illustrated by his poems in the *Harbinger*: he might once again seek the ministry. In "Holiness Unto the Lord," he wrote of "sin's horrid strife" and urged men to "Speak for a holier life in accents loud,/And show this atheist world that truth and virtue live!" Then again in "Hymn of Humanity," he wrote that the "Past is dark with sin and shame . . . 'Tis dark around, 'tis dark above,/But through the shadow streams the sun;/We cannot doubt Thy certain love,/And yet man's aim shall yet be won!" [18]

During this time he became friendly with two senior divinity students. One was Samuel Longfellow, the twenty-six-year-old brother of the poet and a writer of hymns; the other was Samuel Johnson, a mystically oriented, intense young man who also expressed poetic inclinations by writing hymns. Both men revered Theodore Parker and William Henry Channing and, like Higginson, had begun to see the Reverend John Weiss of Watertown (a graduate of the Divinity School) as a vital force among young ministers. Accompanied by Longfellow, Higginson occasionally would visit Weiss, a boyish, exuberant scholar, twenty-six years old, who was the son of a Jewish barber. Weiss had recently translated and edited portions of Schiller and Fichte and, as an admirer of Theodore Parker, would subsequently become his biographer. Known as a "passionate believer in the immortal life," he combined, Higginson thought, earnestness with verve and charm, and was "so male too." With Johnson and Longfellow showing that there was a place in the Divinity School for those with poetic inclinations, and with Weiss representing the strength and attraction of the ministry, Higginson filled with hope. He now believed that the pulpit, unlike teaching or the legal profession, promised a position of leadership which would allow him to "go by impressions," unencumbered by material details.[19]

Attending the Visitation Day ceremony for the graduating divinity class of Longfellow and Johnson, Higginson wrote, "I feel

18. M. T. Higginson, *Higginson*, pp. 64–65; *Harbinger*, 3 (1846), 28, 40.
19. Samuel B. Stuart, "Samuel Johnson," John White Chadwick, "Samuel Longfellow," Minot F. Savage, "John Weiss," *Heralds of a Liberal Faith*, ed. Samuel Eliot (Boston, 1910), pp. 185, 216, 376–80; TWH to M. Channing, July 13, 19, 1846, Higginson MSS; Samuel Longfellow to Samuel Johnson, October 8, 1846, Johnson MSS.

a strong wish for the next Visitation Day when I may speak of the Relation of the Clergy to Reform." Here was a theme expressed by Johnson in his, "The Duty of the Christian Teacher." It was also a theme forcibly stated a year previously by Theodore Parker.[20]

By now, with the outbreak of the Mexican War, Parker was beginning to speak from the Faneuil Hall antislavery platform, where he denounced the war, prophesying that "the superior Anglo-Saxon race" would in fifty years *peacefully* spread itself over Mexico. W. H. Channing told the same audience that Americans were living under a "usurped oligarchy" and suggested that a moral person would prefer to enlist under the Mexican banner. Channing called for a peaceful revolution by means of a convention of towns and counties to form a new government. Even more to the point for Higginson was Wendell Phillips, who urged marshaling "the religious element in the nature of man" against the forces of slavery. "The chances of radicalism," Higginson observed, "are looking up." [21]

After an abolitionist meeting, Higginson revealed how his personal needs had fused with the religious, romantic, and reform elements. He described the scene when an old Negro woman:

> burst out into a most ardent, eloquent & beautiful tribute of gratitude from her self & her race to Garrison. . . . Her style was . . . tinctured strongly with methodistical expressions & scriptural allusions, but her voice was clear & her language fluent & easy; if ever a speech came straight from the heart of the speaker & went straight for the heart of the hearers that was the one. . . . Tears came to many eyes. . . . It was a truly beautiful & noble scene, one which opens to one's view the prospect of a Future where Human Brotherhood shall be a reality of daily life & honor & respect be given where they are truly due.[22]

20. TWH to M. Channing, July 19, 1846, Higginson MSS.
21. Ibid.; *Liberator*, June 5, 1846; Phillips quoted in Leo Stoller, *After Walden: Thoreau's Changing Views on Economic Man* (Stanford, 1957), p. 43; TWH to L. Higginson, July 10, 1846, Higginson MSS.
22. TWH to L. Higginson, May 31, 1846, Higginson MSS.

Here was the "mysterious enthusiasm" he had found in Madame de Staël's *Corinne*, a kind that united poetry, heroism, and religion.

At an antislavery picnic with Mary Channing, on July 4th, 1846, he disclosed his desire to write and preach sermons and to have followers so that he could "take hold and shake them up a little." She approved, understanding that if he once again entered Harvard Divinity School the chances would increase for her fiancé finally becoming both a minister and her husband.[23]

Having decided to recommence his ministerial training he looked back, reflecting: "Everything I have ever felt or done well has grown up silently and burst out in this unexpected way & I have always expected more from such impulsive notions than from any regular progress." His application for readmission suggested that he had finally found peace of mind and the knowledge that love and spiritual trust were "the only basis of Christian Life within, or Christian Union without." He felt that he now had a gospel to preach and was prepared to preach it. But he reserved his gospel for a published essay: the desire to awaken the moral sentiment of the community. "There are times when the *assertion of greater principles* is the best service a man can render society," he noted. To progressively rid the world of evil would be his goal. And he wrote in verse:

> And so the race moves on; this upward yearning
> From age to age shall work itself more clear,
> Till God's redeemed ones, the Evil spurning
> Shall walk again in Eden-gardens here.[24]

Re-entering Divinity School and taking his meals at the College Common with classmates, Higginson told Mary that he felt "calm & contented so far & I do not see what I may not remain so—certainly I pray the continuance of this feeling." Professors Noyes and Francis were sympathetic, and the presence of Samuel Longfellow, who was serving a Cambridge parish, was helpful. Also comforting was

23. TWH to L. Higginson, July 10, 1846, Higginson MSS.
24. TWH to M. Channing, Sept. 14, 1844, TWH to Faculty of Theology, Sept. 19, 1846, Higginson MSS; TWH, "A Word of Hope," Boston *Chronotype*, Sept. 10, 1846.

the development of a friendship with William Hurlbut, a Harvard undergraduate from Charleston, South Carolina. He described Hurlbut as "a true Southerner, the best sort—slender, graceful, dark, with raven eyes and hair"—adding: "But what sort of soldiers can such make?" And later he recalled his relationship with Hurlbut: "I never loved but one male friend with passion—and for him my love had no bounds—all that my natural fastidiousness and cautious reserve kept from others I poured on him; to say that I would have died for him was nothing." [25]

Higginson now discovered in the Divinity School an atmosphere of spiritual vitality, intellectual vigor, and a new liberal tone. Evidence of the change was the selection of William Henry Furness, Unitarian minister from Philadelphia who was both antisectarian and antislavery, to deliver the annual Dudleian Lecture. Furness, unlike Noyes and Francis, stressed the Christ of history rather than the Christ of theology. An even greater change occurred during Higginson's term when the Reverend Samuel J. May of Syracuse, representing the liberal transcendental side of unitarianism, was chosen to address the third-year divinity class. May, the most radical figure to appear since Emerson in 1838, was elected by the senior class on the eleventh ballot by a vote of seven to six.[26]

Although there was equivocation implied in the closeness of the vote that invited May, the speaker was unequivocal. He praised those who spoke against slavery: "It will no longer answer the demands upon the ministers of religion for them to preach . . . for or against Original sin, or sin in the abstract. They must preach . . . against the actual transgressions of our own times." Not since Puritan days, May declared, had the spirit of religious reform been so promising. But he also warned that Jesus exemplified what must not be forgotten even in the most righteous reform crusade. This lesson was that "wrong may be corrected without doing other

25. TWH to L. Higginson, Sept. 20, 1845, Higginson MSS; quoted in M. T. Higginson, *Higginson*, p. 126.

26. TWH to M. Channing, Sept. 14, 1844, Higginson MSS; TWH, Divinity School Notes, MS, Higginson–Student MSS; Samuel Eliot, "William Henry Furness," *Heralds*, pp. 136, 137; W. H. Furness, "Nature and Christianity," *Christian Examiner*, 43 (1847), 31–52; Class Secretary to Samuel May, April 2, 1847, MS copy in Divinity Student History, Andover–Harvard.

wrong; . . . *evil may be overcome with good*. The great lesson of his life, the doctrine of the cross, was, Never Retaliate." [27]

To Higginson, May's sermon was both "brave and noble." Afterward at tea, May told him that when he had his own pulpit he would find that he must and could speak out. Higginson vowed to do so.[28]

He delivered his first public sermon in January 1847 to Samuel Longfellow's West Cambridge congregation, reporting to Samuel Johnson:

> I pleased the audience I hear & did something towards satisfying myself that the pulpit is my vocation. And I never felt the true importance of it before. . . . Oh Sam, we can do something to help this poor world along, if we can keep true to ourselves—but to do this we must take the right means. I felt at W[est] C[ambridge] that I should much prefer a larger centre of influence. The people were so quiet, moral-looking, dully attentive. I'm afraid I couldn't preach to a handful—but to a congregation like Theodore Parker['s] I should feel as if every sermon were as good as a miracle.[29]

A month later, he was more pleased by his pulpit efforts. At Walpole, Massachusetts, one listener commented that he had given "a real Parker sermon." Admitting that his first success at preaching was inconclusive, Higginson still believed that it gave him an excellent opportunity to judge his chances "of really obtaining a position & influence as a preacher which may make it worthwhile for me to devote my life to it. . . . I know myself this would not lead me to manserving." On two successive Sundays he preached at Newburyport, Massachusetts. Here it was clear that a new minister was being sought and Higginson correctly thought well of his chance. He was sure that he had said nothing that might scare the congregation.[30]

27. *Jesus the Best Teacher of His Religion, July, 1847* (Boston, 1847).
28. TWH to L. Higginson, July 12, 1847, Higginson MSS.
29. TWH to Samuel Johnson, Jan. 13, 1847, Higginson MSS.
30. TWH to M. Channing, Feb. 14, 1847, TWH to L. Higginson, Feb. 22, Mar. 5, 19, 1847, Higginson MSS.

"Tranquilly & fast slide away the weeks of my last term," he wrote. Yet as ministerial and marriage responsibilities drew closer he confessed to his mother: "I have felt all this term a kind of restlessness which tells me how near I am drawing to the time where the gate will fly open & the full roar of life strike suddenly on my half stunned ears. I find I can lay no plans for the future—I know not how to look at it—my moods are more variable than ever. At times I am intensely impatient—& at times I shrink terribly & feel as if in leaving this beloved Cambridge I shall leave all that is ideal & beautiful in life behind me." [31]

Visitation Day arrived on July 16, 1847; guests included the Reverend Messrs. Weiss, Parker, W. H. Channing, May, and Hale. Higginson spoke on "The Clergy and Reform." [32] Arguing that antagonism toward American clergymen was justified because they held power on the basis of status, not on accomplishments, he assailed them for not guiding reform and regenerating the world. "A secular reformer, therefore, had an absolute duty when discovering deceit to proclaim it & instantly do his utmost to annul the influence of the clergy." Ministers wrongly exhibited a comparative standard, and upheld the status quo while true reformers "refer . . . to an *absolute* standard, point to a possible future and condemn the present. . . . Neither appreciated the other's view . . . so the one is driven into a position more antagonistic than in any way necessary—while the other slides back into conservatism." Social evils required only the Christlike spirit of love and moral indignation to put them down and yet ministers had not only left them untouched and even unmentioned but had actually opposed these reform movements. "For they have said, 'Our business is to conduct public worship & to preach the abstract gospel, not to excite men's minds by a specific application of it'—in other words 'our Priesthood is built on Form & Doctrine, not on practical Life!'"

Higginson also spoke of the inevitable future, insisting that a new religious movement was taking possession of men's minds— the simple religion of Christ's two great commandments, the love of God and the love of man. And these doctrines would inaugurate

31. TWH to L. Higginson, July 12, 1847, Higginson MSS.
32. TWH to L. Higginson, July 16, 1847, Waldo Higginson diary, Dec. 30, 1854, "The Clergy and Reform," MS, Higginson MSS.

a universal movement for freedom within the existing churches everywhere, which would unite with universal philanthropic movements in society.

The response to Higginson's address was gratifying. He was told that it was in the best Higginson tradition. Parker was especially complimentary. George Channing, Higginson's uncle, volunteered to reprint it in the ecumenical *Christian World* because it was forthright without giving offense. John Weiss found the address "discriminate and irresistible." It had reached the hearts and best impulses of its listeners, Higginson concluded. After having struggled for so long, he was ecstatic over the acclaim: "Like Byron I have waked up & found myself famous—it bewilders me—& yet I take it composedly. I feel if I can stand this I can stand anything in the way of applause, for I shall never have anything more sudden & intoxicating." He also assured his mother that his success had not overwhelmed him. "My head doesn't swim in *that* way yet. My inner life has been too intense for anything outward to weigh much in the balance." [33]

Enhancing his triumph was the publication, in the Visitation Day program, of a hymn that he had written.[34] But the future issue, as he had said in his address, was whether reformers could unite "the Christlike spirit of love & moral indignation." For Higginson's generation of "transcendental ministers," neither the teachings of Christ nor of Emerson could be separated from social action. Living in a country unwilling to support its writers, and in a time of moral crisis, these new aesthetic men turned their literary skills to sermon writing and reform.

33. TWH to L. Higginson, July 16, 1847, TWH to M. Channing, July 17, 1847, Higginson MSS.
34. *Program of the Annual Visitation of the Divinity School*, July 6, 1847, Higginson MSS.

5

The First Church

Higginson, during his final semester in Divinity School, had taken the forty-mile trip along Massachusetts' North Shore to deliver a sermon in Newburyport. Ten years had elasped since the night when the members of the Essex County Anti-Slavery Society had been evicted from two different meeting halls. The barrage of sticks and rotten eggs tossed to the dissonant sounds of fish horns, tin pans, and angry shouts, which the citizenry had directed against the antislavery conventioneers, had then made further abolitionist exhortation imprudent. John Greenleaf Whittier, among those scheduled to speak but instead forced to flee, found verse too restrictive for expressing his indignation. Said the poet in pointed prose: "As for Newburyport we shall remember it. We shall place it, as the Sandwich Islanders say, under *taboo*, until it comes to its senses." It is doubtful whether Whittier, from his nearby home at Amesbury, believed that Newburyport by 1847 had come to its senses.[1]

In 1847, before any word that the taboo had been lifted, a son of Newburyport displayed pride that this town had been his birthplace. Suggesting that his former townsmen should likewise be pleased that he, William Lloyd Garrison, was of Newburyport birth, the Abolitionist did find rhyme the proper vehicle to say:

> My labors shall not sully thy fair fame;
> But they shall be to thee a fountain-source
> Of joyfulness hereafter—when my name
> Shall e'en from tyrants a just tribute force.[2]

1. TWH to L. Higginson, Feb. 22, 1847, Higginson MSS; John A. Pollard, *John Greenleaf Whittier: Friend of Man* (Boston, 1949), pp. 152–53.
2. "To My Birthplace," *Liberty Bell* (1847), p. 304.

Newburyport, however, withheld any burst of joy for having sired him. Garrison, who had spent the first two decades of his life here and been a compositor and writer for the Newburyport *Herald*, had not caused much concern among his townsmen. His anonymity rested upon the fact that before the thirties he had not been much of an Abolitionist, and abolition had not been much of a cause.[3]

Not until 1829 did he attract notice. While writing in Baltimore for Benjamin Lundy's newspaper *The Genius of Universal Emancipation*, he assailed shipowner Francis Todd, a leading Newburyport citizen, for engaging in intercoastal slave trade and for voluntarily surrendering stowaway slaves to southern authorities. Though relatively inexperienced at this time in antislavery vituperation, Garrison had already published an equation of Todd's morality with the deeds of highway robbers and murderers. Todd sued Garrison for libel. The immediate result was Garrison's conviction and the famous internment for forty-nine days in a Baltimore jail. By the time Higginson first appeared in Newburyport, Francis Todd was a large shipowner and a vice-president of a local insurance company, and was reputed to be among the town's richest men. He remained influential in the Unitarian church for whose pulpit Wentworth Higginson was asked to be a candidate.[4] Initially, the disunion abolitionism of Garrison and the political antislavery of Whittier seemed to represent the primary alternatives open to the young minister. Soon Higginson, however, would take a stand significantly different from these two men. His own position would lead more directly to Sumter, Bull Run, Gettysburg, and Appomattox.

Newburyport crowds would still sporadically gather to harass antislavery meetings in 1847, but they were far more energetic in showing their love for the torchlight parades that preceded and followed successive Whig victories. Their political partisanship was not tempered by any noticeable sympathy for the new group of "conscience Whigs" who were concerned about slavery. New-

3. John Thomas, *The Liberator: William Lloyd Garrison* (Boston, 1963), pp. 27–53.

4. Ibid., pp. 109–10; John Albree, *Whittier Correspondence from the Oak Knoll Collection* (Salem, 1911), p. 104; *The Rich Men of Massachusetts* (Boston, 1852), p. 90; *Yesterdays*, p. 127; *Newburyport Directory, 1849.*

buryport's loyalty to the party of Webster expressed a political conservatism that was deeply rooted in the town's past. From the decaying wharves at the mouth of the Merrimack to the solidly built homes on High Street, the Whigs were considered the rightful heirs to the old Federalist party. Even Caleb Cushing, Newburyport's favorite son, though still maintaining his conservative views, lost electoral support when he turned Democrat. That Whig party which had raucously defeated Van Buren in 1840 was linked in many minds to the more dignified Federalist party reigning during the prosperous days when the town was the third largest in Massachusetts. The Essex Junto, once having led the Federalist party, symbolized the past importance of Essex County and Newburyport to the United States. It was also the Federalist party that had opposed the great terror and bogey of port towns—Jefferson's Embargo.[5]

The embargo, together with a devastating fire that swept through the town in 1811, the decline in shipbuilding during the War of 1812, and the loss of trade to inland towns resulting from the completion in the 1820s of the Middlesex Canal, had all contributed to continuous economic deterioration. Finally, the accumulation of harbor sandbars in the 1830s had assured the end of Newburyport as a major shipping port.[6]

Although John Currier kept his shipyards active, the great day of Newburyport shipbuilding had clearly passed. By 1847 only the cod and mackerel fisheries maintained the town's economic contact with the sea. No longer did India cottons, English woollens, Russian canvas and duck, and Baltic iron arrive in port. The stately houses of High Street, built by skilled shipwrights and once the property of sea captains and shipowners, remained as an impressive reminder of Newburyport's prosperous past and of Federal architecture and Federal government at its best.[7]

When repeated economic setbacks and marked emigration made

5. Claude M. Fuess, "Essex County Politics a Century Ago," *Essex Institute Historical Collection*, 95 (1959), 105, 109; Works Progress Administration, *Massachusetts: A Guide to its Places and People* (Boston, 1937), p. 292.

6. E. Vale Smith, *History of Newburyport* (Newburyport, 1954), p. 223.

7. John J. Currier, *History of Newburyport*, 2 (Newburyport, 1909), 72; *Hunt's Merchants' Magazine*, 21 (1849), 320; a graphic description of the town is in Oliver W. Holmes, *Elsie Venner* (Cambridge, 1891), pp. 14-15; Robert C.

Newburyport seem "especially distasteful to Providence," it became evident to men with foresight and capital that bold action was necessary. The small merchant of State Street replaced his little curtained windows with large plate glass and brilliantly colored displays. More important, available Newburyport capital, and money from Boston, were invested in the construction of textile steam mills. The first one began operating in 1834. By the time of Higginson's arrival, five such steam mills had their spindles whirling from dawn to dusk. The largest establishment, the four-story James Mill, was reputed to be the finest in the country, and Newburyport to be the nation's leader in steam mills. Since 1840, population had increased by about a third and some 600 new houses had appeared. Economic optimism replaced despair as Newburyport moved for its support from wharf to spindle. The successful bid for improved railroads obviated the town's fear of sandbars; the production of fine shirting replaced the manufacture of fine sails. Approximately 1,500 of a population of 8,500 were employed in the five mills—the majority of the workers were American-born women. The town's capitalists rejected the Lowell plan of mixing the agrarian ideal with industrial success; they did not seek unmarried rural girls for factory labor, nor force them into a regimented and paternal community life, nor expect their eventual return to agricultural pursuits and family life. Embracing the new industrial order, Newburyport's leaders rejected an agrarian nostalgia and a paternal responsibility toward laborers.[8]

The Whig party with its interest in expanding economic horizons through governmental support, and specifically with its advocacy of a protective tariff, assumed an importance to the citizenry that now went beyond merely traditional or sentimental attachment to the Federalist party. With Polk and the Democrats in office after 1844, passage of the low Walker tariff of 1846 portended danger to those new industries.

The proprietors of the First Religious Society of Newburyport were almost all directly connected with either the town's steam

---

Albion, "From Sail to Spindle: Essex County in Transition," *Essex Institute Historical Collections*, 95 (1959), 115–36.

8. Smith, *Newburyport*, p. 228; Stephan Thernstrom, *Poverty and Progress* (Cambridge, 1964), pp. 14–15, 60.

mills or its banks and were outspoken in their support of conservative Whiggery. Most influential was John Porter, once a shipowner and now having banking and insurance interests. He served as treasurer for the newest of Newburyport's steam mills. William Lunt, active in Unitarian affairs, was this group's political spokesman, and Francis Todd could be depended upon for Whig support. The Newburyport *Herald*, whose editor belonged to this church, served as the local organ for their Whig views.[9]

From the outset Higginson well understood how desperate the Unitarian church was to hire a permanent minister. A year had already passed since the previous minister, Thomas Fox, had moved to a Boston pulpit. Fox had been a popular minister, but his love for church picnics made more orthodox churchgoers believe that their minister had forgotten the solemnity of religion in his zeal for repeatedly leading "Fox's caravan" to the woods for another box lunch. Among Unitarians, Fox was not considered a radical. Although his social consciousness had moved him to help start in Newburyport one of the first high schools in the country for girls, he, like most clergymen, largely avoided the day's most controversial issues.[10]

The pressing need for a minister in 1847 was forcing the conservative proprietors to be less discriminating about the views of the man to be chosen for their pulpit. Painfully evident were the many empty Unitarian pulpits and the dearth of ministers produced by the Divinity School. Higginson was so pleased by his hospitable reception during the initial visits to Newburyport that he minimized the possibilities of conflict between minister and congregation. He was, nevertheless, cautious at the outset about expressing controversial views to his future congregation. He confined such talk to his hosts, John Porter and Henry Frothingham, both receptive to his opposition to the Mexican War and his criticism of the Polk administration. With the Democrat Caleb Cushing in Mexico using his own money to lead the only regiment Massachusetts had

9. Currier, *Newburyport*, 2, 70, 138, 154, 162; *Newburyport Directory, 1850.*
10. TWH to L. Higginson, Mar. 5, 1847, Higginson MSS; Minnie Atkinson, *A History of the First Religious Society in Newburyport* (Newburyport, 1937), pp. 63, 67; Dec. 1, 1846, Feb. 25, 1847, MS, Parish Records.

recruited, Higginson's views were not particularly controversial to the Whig-minded.[11]

To Higginson, Newburyport indeed seemed like a good place to have a parish. Being away from Boston, the center of Unitarian orthodoxy, promised a chance for minimizing traditional forms and doctrines. Only veteran Unitarian ministers like Parker and Clarke had thrived in the Boston area while simultaneously defying the Unitarian orthodoxy. Not only was the practice of religious reform possible away from Boston but there was also evidence that Newburyport would prove a fertile site for social reform. Long hours and illiteracy for laborers was an accepted corollary to the necessary growth of manufacturing. And symbolizing the moral threat of industrialism was the fact that the first steam mill stood in Newburyport's business district only a few yards away from Higginson's church. Also, the sweet smell of boiling molasses coming from John Caldwell's half-century-old rum distillery was especially distinct to a minister interested in temperance. With rum selling as cheaply as three gallons for a dollar, local consumption of this famous Newburyport brew was brisk and drunkenness evident.[12] In the midst of the Mexican War, to preach in a town that had chased Whittier and shunned Garrison was a special challenge.

Higginson judged the Unitarian leaders to be "simple people"; after tea in the homes of some of the leaders he vowed to "aesthetize these people and reform their parlors that ought to be pretty, but always just miss it." Higginson was confident that it would continue to be "easy to make myself acceptable to those over whom my education & position give me a preliminary advantage."[13]

By the beginning of August it appeared certain that he would be called to the Unitarian church. Now Higginson preached what he termed his "worst thunder." Stressing the dichotomy between private and public Christian ethics evidenced by the Mexican War, he attacked Polk and the Democrats for involving the United States

11. TWH to L. Higginson, July 20, 1847, Higginson MSS; *Liberator*, June 7, 1850.

12. Thernstrom, *Poverty*, p. 13.

13. TWH to L. Higginson, July 20, 1847, TWH to Mary Channing, July 26, 1847, Higginson MSS.

in the "slaveholders war." But he went farther: he denounced those Whigs who suggested that the hero of Buena Vista, General Zachary Taylor, was qualified to be the next Whig presidential nominee.[14] Here was a sensitive point, for it seemed likely that the Whigs, remembering their previous success with Old Tippecanoe, would choose a candidate from among the Whig generals in Mexico.

Higginson's willingness to treat social issues from the pulpit, even controversial ones, should have forewarned the conservative proprietors. One woman parishioner remarked afterward, "Well, I am thankful for this sermon even if we lose you in consequence." Knowing how desperately the church needed a minister and remembering his warm reception earlier, he concluded: "All will go well." Such "plain dealing" from the pulpit would not hurt his popularity. "Hereafter," he told himself, "I shall feel free as Theo. Parker or J.[ames] F.[reeman] C[larke] in their churches." Two days after his Mexican War sermon, the proprietors voted unanimously to "call" him to the Newburyport pulpit at the annual salary of $1,000. A week later, Higginson accepted with the stipulations that he be guaranteed freedom of speech in the pulpit, freedom to exchange pulpits with other ministers, and freedom to have the contract terminated by either party with six months' notice. Looking toward his ordination, he stressed freedom to choose laymen or fellow clergymen for the initiation ceremonies instead of being ordained by a formal council.[15] By this latter demand he hoped to assure liberty from Unitarian orthodoxy; but it had been a request also made fifteen years earlier by the Reverend Thomas Fox, which had been accepted by the church proprietors.

His terms met, Higginson laid plans to make his ordination memorable. In asking William Henry Channing to deliver the ordination sermon, he invited one of the most radical Unitarian ministers. Channing, even more than Parker, represented social and religious radicalism. While Emerson, in his "Ode to William Henry Chan-

14. TWH to L. Higginson, Aug. 2, 1847, Higginson MSS; Samuel Johnson to TWH [Oct.] 1847, Johnson MSS; TWH, "Not by Bread Alone," *Advertiser*, Nov. 12, 1848.

15. TWH to S. Johnson, Aug. 18, 1847, Higginson MSS; TWH to Committee of First Religious Society in Newburyport, Aug. 11, 1847, Committee . . . to TWH, Aug. 18, 1847, Parish Records.

ning," had called the minister "The evil times sole patriot," others found him "the most extreme embodiment among the Church reformers, of the misty ill-defined Transcendentalism." [16] If Higginson desired to have an ordination sermon preached as controversial as Parker's famous "Transient and Permanent in Christianity," Channing was capable of doing it.

A few minutes before noon on Wednesday, September 15, 1847, the church organ began the ceremony with the voluntary. The white wooden Federalist-style church, a handsome replica of McIntire's Old South Church in Salem, with its gallery and double row of high windows, was filled. Before Channing rose to speak the choir sang a hymn written by Higginson's friend Sam Johnson, which called upon men to join saints and "speed Reform." [17]

Channing's sermon aptly recalled that one hundred years ago, just a few blocks away from where they were presently assembled, "the heads of the vast multitudes rose and fell beneath and waves" of exhortation unleashed by that "mighty preacher" George Whitefield. Just as Whitefield had preached a religious revival in 1740, and had caused a split in Newburyport Congregational ranks resulting in the establishment of the Old South Presbyterian Church, so was Channing prepared in 1847 to disrupt the unitarianism of the First Religious Society.[18]

All men, said Channing, were capable of having a direct religious experience; it was the minister who must help man understand the meaning of the world God created and who must lead his congregation into "the grand cooperative army of reform." Charity to the poor, education for the unlettered, and, most important, freedom for the slave were campaigns worthy of such an army. Only then could each Christian society become a holy brotherhood and not "a congregation of worldly Ishmaelites."

He said that men were "wearied and perplexed . . . beyond endurance by the tumultous rush of anarchic individualism. . . . They long for cooperation." It was necessary to eliminate the re-

16. TWH to L. Higginson, Aug. 2, 1847, Higginson MSS; "Ode Inscribed to W. H. Channing," George Whicher, *Poetry of the New England Renaissance,* *1790–1890* (New York, 1959), p. 66; Hutchison, *Ministers,* p. 169.

17. Newburyport *Herald,* Sept. 9, 1847; *Ordination of Thomas Wentworth Higginson* (Boston, 1847).

18. Ibid., p. 5.

maining vestiges of free competition and bring about a redistribu-
tion of landed property, and a new sliding scale of wages, graduated according to labor and skill as well as to the needs of capital,
and above all, a system of equitable commerce whereby the go
between would not absorb both the worker's gains and the con-
sumer's means, while adulterating the merchandise. Religion must
be integrated with society. "Yes! the final word of Political Economy, is that the law of 'Supply and Demand' is a delusive guide,
even a devilish incantation, unless fulfilled and interpreted by the
two central laws of Humanity and Heaven,—Thou shalt love thy
neighbor as thyself—Thou shalt love the Lord thy God with all
thy heart, mind and strength."

God's word then was cooperation in religion as in all life, but a
cooperation that would allow for individual responsibility without
bringing a leveling equality. The life of Jesus, Channing concluded,
is an inexplicable enigma except as it pointed toward the goal of
Heaven on Earth. The diversity of the historical past and the opposing forces of the present must converge to one end—"Perfect
Society." [19]

These words were familiar to Channing's regular followers, but
there were few, if any of them, in the Newburyport congregation.
It was hard to imagine that Parker or Emerson could have been
more radical. No marked relief was in sight when James Freeman
Clarke came forward to deliver the "charge" to the new minister.
He advised Higginson to avoid ultraism, but nevertheless urged him
to speak regardless of "who is offended by that honesty." For
"while the nation . . . plants its feet on the necks of millions of
slaves . . . while the nation sends out its armies to pollute with the
abominations of war the homes of innocent brethren . . . thou
shalt surely answer it to God if thou hold thy peace." Then turning
to Higginson, Clarke said: "You cannot please everybody,—perhaps not anybody; still you may please your own conscience and
God." [20]

Clarke was followed by the Reverend Thomas T. Stone of
Salem, who offered the traditional Right Hand of Fellowship. A
contributor to the first issue of the *Dial* with an essay criticizing

19. Ibid., pp. 41–44.
20. Ibid.

American society's love of material wealth, Stone remained closely associated with the transcendental ministers. Having previously assailed the murder of his friend Elijah Lovejoy, he would soon lose his pulpit because of further antislavery preaching. At Higginson's ordination he said that the new minister was following the tradition of "saintly ancestors," the Reverend Francis Higginson and grandfather Stephen Higginson. Stone also urged him to speak God's word.[21]

The only ordination message not urging Higginson forward was delivered by Thomas Fox, the former pastor. While advising the congregation to allow the new minister to speak his views, he cautioned that if these views "are not Christian, tell him so kindly, and ask him to resign his office." Unlike the other speakers, Fox suggested that Higginson was subject to human fallibility.[22]

But the final words were not Fox's. They were the hymnal lyrics written by Higginson's Cambridge friend William Hurlbut, which well represented the ceremony's temper:

Lift up the poor, borne down by weary anguish,—
Renew the hearts consumed by crime and sin,
Strengthen their souls who fear, and doubt and languish,—
Commence the works men tremble to begin.[23]

On the day following the ordination, the Newburyport *Herald* voiced what many of the Whig proprietors of the First Religious Society had felt as they listened to Channing, Clarke, and Stone, and sang of uplifting the poor and speeding reform. While the *Herald* granted that "Mr. Higginson is a young man of much intellectual and moral power," it warned that "he seems tinctured with those radical and imaginative notions . . . which would fain seek to govern society at large more wisely than God has seen fit to guide it ever since the dawn of creation." [24]

Soon after the ordination, the woman who had led him to some of these "radical and imaginative notions" became his wife. Mary

21. Thomas T. Stone, "Man in the Ages," *Dial*, 1 (1840), 1–41; George A. Cooke, *The Dial* (New York, 1885), p. 457; *Ordination*, p. 47.
22. Ibid., pp. 5–55.
23. Ibid., p. 9.
24. *Herald*, Sept. 16, 1847.

Channing was married to Higginson in Clarke's Brookline church. The couple had known each other for five years and had been engaged for three and a half years. She was now twenty-seven years old, he was twenty-four. They settled in a house on narrow Essex Street, a block from the Pleasant Street Church. A maid was hired so as not to strain Mary's delicate health, but her proneness to fatigue continued throughout the couple's Newburyport days. Initially their marriage seemed satisfactory, but Mary's health remained an ever-present threat. Even in the midst of these early days, Higginson felt anxious about their ability to sustain happiness together and found it remarkable that "nothing has yet gone wrong." "It seems strangely beautiful," he commented, "that one who has had so little outward sunshine as she has, so much inward darkness as I, should now have such childlike merriment as we at times do." Perhaps he was also worried about his recent promise to Mary to be more tolerant of her faults and less intent on reforming them.[25]

Together they attended the welcoming teas. The ugliness of Newburyport parlors offended Mary's taste also. Too many of the parishioners were without charm or were "unfascinating," she decided, though she appreciated that "good people" showed their simple friendliness to the Higginsons.[26] For her the town's social life would never attain the satisfying level reached in Brookline society. Newburyport merchants, bankers, and manufacturers were different people from the ministers, reformers, and literary people who had frequented the homes of her father and her uncle, Stephen Perkins.

Afternoon tea in Newburyport was more to her husband's taste than to Mary's. He enjoyed social gatherings, and many of his new parishioners showed him warmth and respect. "The prestige of influence" seemed to be a fact. It even moved him to vow at this early date that he would never leave Newburyport. As the new

25. TWH to L. Higginson, Oct. 24, Nov. 16, 24, 1847, TWH to Waldo Higginson, Nov. 30, 1847, Mary Higginson to Louisa Higginson, Nov. 23, 1847, Higginson MSS.

26. M. Higginson to L. Higginson, Oct. 27, 1847, TWH to L. Higginson, Oct. 10, 1847, Higginson MSS.

minister, one of his first duties was to officiate at the funeral of a child of one of his congregation. He revealed that he liked having "an access to the souls of one's people at the most impressible moment"; he believed that he had acquired "a permanent hold" on the bereaved parents. The sense of power over others seemed to have quieted his doubts about the ministerial profession and about himself. Only when he could see himself as a strong leader, as a man in control, was he at ease. This characteristic, of course, served both to stimulate and limit his effectiveness as a reformer. After a month in the pulpit he saw that his flock had not in the past "been awakened to reforms. But they seem willing to be; & ready in particular to be led by me," he reported. "I began, by exhorting them to resist me & stand for their own independence, & so I hope they will do, but I have had all just as I wished it so far. I shall have a fair opportunity of trying how much may be done for a place by one man thinking & speaking freely." [27]

The first test of his leadership came before he desired it. The Essex County Anti-Slavery Society announced a meeting in Newburyport for early October 1847. Despite qualms about taking a public position on abolitionist meetings before he had gained more of his congregation's confidence, Higginson committed himself. His Sunday sermon, an attack on the North's apathy to the evils of slavery, was climaxed by noting the forthcoming meeting and his suggestion that the congregation attend it.[28]

Given Newburyport's antipathy toward even moderate antislavery views and the radical reputation of the speakers, a lively meeting was anticipated. The major addresses were delivered by Parker Pillsbury, the New Hampshire Abolitionist renowned for scourging proslavery churches, and by Samuel May, one of the founders of the Garrisonian Massachusetts Anti-Slavery Society and a frequent contributor to the *Liberator*. The audience's hostility reached its peak when the speakers assailed the Whig party. Then hecklers grew more vociferous and more numerous; shouts of "throw him

27. TWH to L. Higginson, Nov. 16, 1847, TWH to a Storrow, Sept. 6, 1847, TWH to Waldo Higginson, Nov. 30, 1847, Higginson MSS.
28. TWH to Samuel Johnson, Oct. 7, 1847, Higginson MSS; *Advertiser*, Sept. 8, 1847.

out," and worse, soon drowned the words from the platform. This time neither eggs nor sticks were thrown.[29]

The following day the local Democratic paper noted that nothing worthwhile was ever said at abolitionist meetings, but cautioned that hostile demonstrations provided sufficient recognition to "keep these ranters alive." Higginson became uncertain about the effect of having advertised the meeting and wondered if he had offended his parishioners. They will be frightened "at the bugbear of Disunion," Sam Johnson advised him, but the fright *will very soon pass over.*" Higginson concluded: "At all events I have defined my position." [30]

From the Pleasant Street Church, in a pulpit "as high as an observatory" (it was two stories above the seated congregation), Higginson further defined his position. Determined not to argue traditional theological doctrine nor indulge in Biblical exegesis, he dealt with local and national problems. He talked of the long hours and low wages in Newburyport factories, of crime, and of the "share society has in creating the evils it punishes," of the rum producer and the rum retailer. Unlike the Whig *Herald* which claimed that the indolence and imbecility of the poor caused their poverty, the minister cited social causes for drunkenness, crime, and poverty.[31]

While his congregation, numbering about five hundred, still attended his sermons regularly, within a few months this Sunday attendance became its only contact with him. Traditional hospitality sharply faded; invitations to tea or to dinner diminished. So eager to instruct his parishioners, he uncomprehendingly found this change "queer." Higginson believed that he was following "the Right" not only "strenuously & fearlessly—but also gently & lovingly." When the discontent was articulated he found little consolation. Some of the congregation charged that his sermons were too much like lyceum lectures—they were not religious enough. In Higginson's view the sermons simply were too much in contrast to the accompanying traditional services.[32] And there was still

29. Ibid., Sept. 12, 1847; TWH to L. Higginson [Nov. 1847], Higginson MSS.
30. *Advertiser*, Sept. 12, 1847; S. Johnson to TWH, Oct. 8, 1847, Johnson MSS; TWH to L. Higginson [Nov. 1847], Higginson MSS.
31. *Advertiser*, Sept. 12, 1847; S. Johnson to TWH, Jan. 17, 1848, L. Higginson to TWH, Dec. 16, 1847, Higginson MSS; *Herald*, July 31, 1847.
32. TWH to L. Higginson, Feb. 9, Dec., 1847, TWH to A. Storrow, June 26,

much that had to be said: "As regards *preaching* proper, I have no sort of doubt of its being my mission—in some form or other—that is speaking to men, in the pulpit or elsewhere." But the disaffection troubled him. It became difficult to prepare sermons, and his friend Hurlbut observed that "he seemed to pity himself beyond measure." [33]

Striving to find bonds with people of similar views, Higginson visited Theodore Parker at his Boston home. Parker seemed "strong and sufficing . . . [and] needed so little from any other person," which made the visit "rather disappointing." Higginson also traveled to nearby Amesbury to speak with Whittier, but the meeting left him feeling isolated. Whittier showed a "tinge of narrowness" in criticizing other Abolitionists, and lacked "profound, all embracing views." With a touch of pride but with a certain sadness, he noted finding no "body of reformers which satisfies me. For the present at least I am compelled to stand alone." [34]

Sam Johnson and William Hurlbut, both lacking the stature of Parker and Whittier, were the only men with whom he found rapport. Johnson he described as "so much less a complex character than I, that I feel about him as we do about children." Hurlbut, who was "like some fascinating girl," he had been "able to help a good deal." Higginson happily declared: "he is most truly attached to me." The letters between Higginson and Hurlbut were "more like those between man and woman than between two men," recalled one observer. But a friendship with Johnson and Hurlbut had to be largely affirmed by correspondence. There was little they could do to make him feel fellowship and strength in his day-to-day work in Newburyport. And working on behalf of the town's poor provided no satisfaction either. "It is to me very painful work," he claimed. "This necessity of entering into the concerns of so many families (in sympathy if not in fact)" too often required a giving of

1848, Higginson MSS; "Social Benevolent Society of First Religious Society of Newburyport, 1822–1851," MS, Parish Records.

33. TWH to L. Higginson, Nov. 16, 1847, Higginson MSS; William Hurlbut to S. Johnson, Nov. 9, 1847, Johnson MSS.

34. TWH to L. Higginson, Nov. 24, 1847, TWH to W. Higginson, Nov. 30, 1847, Higginson MSS; TWH to Maria Chapman, Nov. 9, 1847, Weston MSS; TWH, *Contemporaries,* pp. 34–35.

oneself without either immediate results or the compensating appreciation from the poor or his fellow townsmen.[35]

Nor did Higginson find solace at the annual Unitarian Convention of June 1848. Speaking against his elders for not encouraging young ministers to think and speak freely, he argued, as did W. H. Channing, that catholicity must replace the sectarianism which characterized unitarianism. And there was no encouragement in Newburyport where the proliferation of churches and denominations, not Christian unity, was most pronounced. In a letter to Sam Johnson Higginson revealed hope for a "dawning age of Faith . . . this great period of commencing reconstruction to be embodied in a new social organization, to *include* Christianity rather than to *be* Christianity." This new social organization he believed would solve the grand problem of both religious and social sectarianism. It would "unite all tendencies religious and social, and set the race a distinct step farther on." [36]

This quest for some kind of unity appealed to groups ranging from radical to conservative. What was to be the basis of this unity, however, remained a crucial and unsolved problem. Should it be a social issue like slavery as the Abolitionists said, or should it be preservation of the Union? All might agree that unity and cooperation of some sort were necessary, but few could agree on what could *not* be compromised. In an era which Channing had called one of "anarchic individualism," men sought other men in the numerous organizations that blossomed everywhere for varied causes. But each new organization insisted upon its uniqueness while simultaneously calling for further unity and the end of sectarianism. None found a means of agreement that would include many Americans. Not even the desirability of citizenship was something all Americans could agree upon. In the end, a dogmatic fervor was the only thing common to all factions. Unity remained the unfulfilled goal of the forties and fifties.

By exchanging pulpits at times with the local Universalist minister, Higginson took a step toward religious catholicity. He further

35. TWH to L. Higginson, Nov. 16, 1847, April 3, 1848, Higginson MSS; S. Johnson to TWH [June] 1848, Johnson MSS; M. T. Higginson, *Higginson*, p. 125.
36. Thernstrom, *Poverty*, p. 46; TWH to L. Higginson, June 6, 1848, TWH to Johnson, Mar. 16, 1848, Higginson MSS

broke precedent by inviting the fugitive slave, William Wells
Brown, to speak at his church, and followed Brown's address with
his own attack on slavery and a sympathetic account of a fugitive
slave's plight. Gratified that his congregation would listen, if not
explicitly agree with antislavery views,[37] Higginson's boldness
would be further tested by the political events beginning in June
1848.

37. Thernstrom, *Poverty*, p. 46; TWH to L. Higginson, May 18, 1848, Higginson MSS.

6

The Christian Minister as Reformer

The split within the Massachusetts Whig party by 1846, over the admission of Texas and the propriety of the Mexican War, was widened by the impending nomination of General Zachary Taylor. At the 1848 National Whig Convention, Charles Allen of Worcester called for the party's dissolution for failing to endorse the Wilmot Proviso and for supporting Taylor. Higginson understood that Allen was speaking for an independent political movement in Massachusetts. While acknowledging interest, Higginson appeared unready to support the dissident Whigs. Even in July 1848, when Richard Henry Dana, Jr., led a "conscience Whig" convention at Boston's Tremont Temple, he remained silent.[1] When Whittier, just prior to the Buffalo Convention in August, invited Higginson to join the third-party movement, he wavered. "My position," he explained with understatement, "is rather a difficult one just now for my good friends here, though ready to allow me any amount of liberty in the pulpit, have yet prejudices which make it a hard trial to them to have their minister take the stump in a Presidential election particularly on what they think the wrong side." Ultimately he promised to support the Free Soil party if the Buffalo Convention nominated Martin Van Buren and Charles Francis Adams on a platform advocating the Wilmot Proviso and free homesteads. By early September, Higginson was writing articles to the local Whig paper attacking Taylor as a slaveholder and was stumping the county for the new party.[2]

1. Frank O. Gatell, "Conscience and Judgment: The Bolt of the Massachusetts Conscience Whigs," *The Historian*, 21 (1958), 26; D. Hamilton Hurd, *History of Worcester*, 2 (Philadelphia, 1889), 1662; TWH to L. Higginson, June 20, July 27, 1848, Higginson MSS; Charles F. Adams, *Richard Henry Dana, Jr.*, 1 (Boston, 1900), 122.

2. TWH to J. G. Whittier, Aug. 3, 1848, in Albree, *Whittier*, pp. 105–06; *Herald*, Sept. 20, Nov. 2, 1848.

Deciding to support the Free Soil party openly was a turning point for Higginson. Here was a political organization which included a body of sufficiently diverse reformers to provide allies. Most important of these initially was Whittier, who combined abolitionist sentiment and political action. Higginson's decision gave his ministerial post a greater political partisanship than ever. His radical friends were uneasy, however, about the wisdom of his choice. Sam Johnson cautioned that the Free Soil stance was inadequate because it merely sought to limit the extension of slavery.[3] Higginson, on the other hand, hoped to combine action for Free Soil with sympathy for the more thoroughgoing Garrisonian abolitionism.

While pledged to Free Soil, he also invited political Abolitionists to speak from his pulpit where he too attacked slavery. He was chosen in October 1848 as a delegate to the Essex County Free Soil Convention, where Charles Sumner was a keynote speaker. During the ensuing campaign, Whittier, who began to win his confidence, arranged Higginson's speaking engagements. After an address in Amesbury, which Higginson thought weak, Whittier wrote: "Thy address was liked well, notwithstanding thy misgivings. Courage. Go on and prosper." His Whig parishioners were less satisfied. Led by John Porter, the proprietors ruled that the church was not to be used for antislavery meetings. They probably also would have liked to say that their minister could not be used in Free Soil politics. Higginson refused to accept their admonitions. After publicly chiding them for their decree, he decided that they bore his exhortation with Christian meekness. "The truth is," he decided, "they are so much more dependent on me than me on them that I am in no danger of offending them by anything." [4]

Mary encouraged her husband to teach Newburyport all the lessons it deserved. But she objected to being hostess to a variety of visiting lecturers who preferred staying at the Higginson home to a room over the Old Wolfe Tavern. Mary's critical eye made her intolerant of some of the personal foibles of visiting reformers. When Charles Sumner visited she noted that "he has not very good

3. S. Johnson to TWH, Oct. [1848], Johnson MSS.
4. *Herald*, Sept. 11, 13, 1848; J. G. Whittier to TWH [n.d.], Higginson-Huntington MSS; TWH to L. Higginson, Sept. 19, 1848, Higginson MSS.

manners—he always sits in the rocking chair, gapes almost constantly without any attempt at concealment, &—picks his teeth! But he is a true moral reformer which is a good thing." Frederic Hedge seemed unbearably pompous and egotistical. Higginson, on the other hand, concluded that most reformers were far more appealing around a fireside than they were during speeches from the lecture platform.[5]

One Sunday morning in November 1848, Higginson chose a special guest preacher. Without any previous announcement he exchanged pulpits with Theodore Parker, self-styled "the most hated man in America." The *Herald*, only a few months before, had indicated its fears. At a time when conservatives worried about the 1848 revolution in France and about English Chartism, the paper likened Parker to those "thoroughgoing radicals who have eliminated the Bible to suit their theories, and, in imitation of some of the French and English infidels, changed Jesus Christ from the meek and lowly Messiah . . . into a great democratic reformer . . . [thus pleasing] the wildest of the Parisian populace." [6]

Parker preached an uncontroversial sermon, but his mere presence disturbed the congregation. Meanwhile, Higginson spoke from Parker's pulpit in Boston's great Melodeon Hall to an audience of two thousand. He was elated by the attentiveness of the highly diverse congregation.[7]

No words of Parker, Higginson, Sumner, or any of the visiting reformers could make Newburyport forsake its Whig sympathies to vote Free Soil. The election results showed that Van Buren, Stephen C. Phillips, and Charles L. Knapp, the Free Soil candidates for President, Governor and Congress respectively, each polled no more than 73 votes (3 per cent of the town's total vote). The Whig candidates had almost a two-to-one edge over the Democrats. In the total Essex County vote (primarily rural) it was significant, however, that the new party ran second to the victorious Whigs, though losing three to one. Newburyport's Caleb Cushing, the Democratic candidate for governor, ran 10,000 votes behind Phil-

5. M. Higginson to L. Higginson Sept. 23, 1848, Feb. 5, 1849, TWH to Samuel Johnson, Jan. 2, 1848, TWH to L. Higginson, Mar. 5, 1849, Higginson MSS.
6. Parker to TWH, Aug., Sept. 22, 1848, Higginson-Huntington MSS; M. Higginson to L. Higginson, Nov. 14, 1848, Higginson MSS; *Herald*, Sept. 26, 1848.
7. TWH to L. Higginson, Nov. 14, 1848, Higginson MSS.

lips. Likewise, in the statewide returns, Van Buren ran ahead of the Democratic Cass.[8] Higginson grudgingly conceded that in spite of hard work little had been accomplished that showed in Newburyport election returns, but he noted that the "Democrats talk already of coming over" to the Free Soilers. "I am on the whole better satisfied with Taylor's election than if it had been Cass—since the Democratic party had much more affinity with an antislavery movement than the hopeless Conservatism of the Whigs. And the Whig party of the North will be condemned to a Southern policy for four years & never regain the prestige of conscience and respectability which had alone sustained it in the state so long." [9]

Far less satisfied, of course, were Newburyport's Democrats. To win a war and still lose an election made the defeat especially distasteful. Since it appeared that most of the Massachusetts Free Soil vote had come from those who had previously voted Democratic, the results were bitterly received. The local Democratic daily, which had previously avoided the slavery issue, in keeping with the party's platform, depicted the Taylor triumph: "Three hundred slaves will be under the supervision of competent overseers. While the General is administering free government, they will administer the cat-o-nine tails,—while huzzas are going up to his honor at the North, yells from his scared 'niggers' in the South, will intermingle. Hurrah for Van Buren and Free Soil—the author of this result!" [10]

The real Taylor hurrahs that sounded in Newburyport grated on Higginson's ears. The Whig victory celebration, with exploding firecrackers and a boisterous torchlight parade, made the statewide moral victory of the Free Soilers less comforting. Defeat became "quite painful" to Higginson upon learning that those Whig festivities were financed by some of the leading members of his own church. John Porter, the major power in the church, and Charles Brockway, a proprietor and superintendent of the church's Sunday School, had financed the parade, and other familiar parishioners had joined in the revelry. Higginson concluded that his congregation shamelessly "had succumbed to Baal." Amidst the brightness of their triumph, he acridly noted that "torches might turn night into

8. *Advertiser*, Nov. 19, 1848; *Herald*, Nov. 14, 1848.
9. TWH to L. Higginson, Nov. 14, 1848, Higginson MSS.
10. *Advertiser*, Nov. 17, 1848.

day, but not moral darkness into light, or a triumph of Slavery into a triumph of freedom." Mary was less ideological: "The extreme littleness and want of enlightenment of these people has been very much forced upon us during the whole Taylor affair." [11]

A few days after the parade, Higginson heard Frederick Douglass talk with persuasive earnestness of the wrongs done to the Negro race, underscoring "the hypocritical religion of this slave-holding nation." His words helped remind the minister of his post-election role. Higginson warned his congregation: "I felt after hearing Douglass, as if I were a recreant to humanity, to let one Sunday pass in the professed preaching of Christianity, and leave the name of SLAVERY unmentioned. . . . And so help me God I never will again." [12]

On Thanksgiving morning, 1848, Higginson delivered a sermon that did considerably more than mention slavery. From his high pulpit he hurled a holiday jeremiad upon the heads of his congregation.[13] He began with a familiar theme: "Money getting . . . is our peculiar sin, it comes so close to our Thanksgiving . . . to counterfeit it." Like W. H. Channing he charged that the ideal man in America was unfortunately "a respectable man, a substantial man, a solid man, . . . a man of independent property." Americans believed that "it is wise and good to compromise principle a *little* in order to succeed in life. It is *not* considered wise and good to live . . . for the sake of an uncompromising abstraction." Linking moral compromise to political expediency he criticized his congregation's role in the nomination and election of Zachary Taylor: "By your *expressions of delight* at the results of the election, you have voluntarily foregone all the defense you had when you candidly lamented for the 'necessary evil.' " Higginson charged that all knew that Taylor's nomination "was first brought forward by ultra-slavery men, avowedly as the ultra-slavery candidate; that ultra-slavery men carried him through the convention, in opposition to the demands of the North, and then threw the Wilmot Proviso on the floor. . . . You knew all this . . . and yet when the

11. John Lord diary, Nov. 15, 1848, MS, Newburyport Public Library; *Herald*, Nov. 15, 1848; TWH to L. Higginson, Nov. 23, 1848, M. C. Higginson to L. Higginson, Nov. 23, 1848, Higginson MSS.

12. "Not by Bread Alone," *Advertiser*, Nov. 12, 1848.

13. Ibid.

time came that this so humiliating stroke of the Slave Power triumphed, you accepted it as your triumph."

But why did his congregation feel joy? "This one great reason stood, and forever will stand in history, underlying all, overtopping all—this—that slavery or no slavery, consistency or no consistency, honor or dishonor, that spirit in the Northern people, which lives 'by bread alone' has secured its PROTECTIVE TARIFF!"

> There is no intrinsic harm in Protection, as there is nothing intrinsically wrong in Bread. But when protection means compromise; when protection means help to me, gained by the sacrifice of honor, the sacrifice of pledges, the sacrifice of Freedom and the slave; when it means, my dividends increased by my consent being given to the proportionate increase of slave territory, when *this* is the meaning of that omnipotent word, then I say, *from such Protection God protect us!*

Of his own antislavery stand and his participation in the recent election he said: "I do not wish to *be* a fanatic,—but I have no fear of being called so. There are times and places where Human Feeling is fanaticism,—times and places where it seems that a man can only escape the charge of fanaticism by being a moral iceberg."

Denying the charges of political partisanship, he insisted that the duty of every preacher who was a man was to grapple with sin in high places, sin in the majority, sin that is popular, and sin that is politically bipartisan. The great hope against the sin of slavery was the Free Soil movement, which was destined ultimately to triumph. In conclusion, he insisted that because of the state of society and his parishioners' selfishness, Thanksgiving in 1848 must be "mingled with repentance."

These words were clearly the most censorious he had ever spoken. A sermon that made Whiggism synonymous with selfishness, materialism, and slavery could hardly have served as a digestible appetizer for the holiday dinner. If the parishioners did not believe the truth of his words, they also could not quite believe that they had chosen a minister who could so publicly flagellate them for their political beliefs while simultaneously supporting a maverick political party. The *Herald*'s earlier evaluation of the minister being "a little tinctured with radicalism" had surely missed the degree of saturation by more than a drop or two. The sermon was subsequently printed in the local Democratic paper and as a pamphlet. A Garrisonian noted: "The best piece of thunder I have late read or *heard* is a sermon from Higginson, a Unitarian minister." Other radicals wrote Higginson to praise it. He acknowledged that in Newburyport it had caused "quite a little commotion." [14]

Some empty seats the following Sunday and talk that the congregation finally had had enough of unitarianism Higginson style were immediate reactions to his discourse. These symptoms of discontent were nothing serious, the minister diagnosed. But that he really thought a full-scale revolt possible was suggested by his promise to "resign at once, in case of any serious disaffection." Choosing to ignore the antagonisms he had raised, he assumed that the congregation "will see on reflection that I could not well have done other than I did; and they know in their souls that I could spare them better than they me." Although granting that it must have been trying for his congregation to sit and hear what was the certain truth, he was sure that the personal alienation and lack of understanding he felt because of their opposition was far more painful. Yet he did not intend to let things cool; instead he ignored the *presence* of ill-feeling.[15]

Within a week after the sermon, Ralph Waldo Emerson made his first appearance at the Newburyport Lyceum. It appeared at first that the town's clergymen were publicly united against his speaking. It was believed that once Emerson spoke, swarms of varied radicals would regularly descend and cause trouble. Emerson, said the *Herald*, was a "professed pantheist, . . . the dividing line between Pantheism and Atheism is so fine as to be visible only to the microscopic eye." [16] The conspiratorial intent of Emerson and his sympathizers seemed subsequently proven by the disclosure that he had been invited despite a negative majority vote by the Lyceum committee. Also ominous was the nonscientific topic Emerson chose, thus violating the agreement to make science the theme of the lecture series. Into this storm of mounting opposition stepped

14. TWH to L. Higginson, Dec. 3, 1848, Higginson MSS; Richard D. Webb to Maria W. Chapman, Feb. 7, 1849, Weston MSS; TWH to A. W. Weston, Jan. 29, 1850, Chapman MSS.

15. TWH to L. Higginson, Dec. 3, 1848, Higginson MSS.

16. *Herald*, Dec. 8, 1848.

Higginson. In print he suggested that his fellow clergymen and all self-appointed keepers of Newburyport morality could surely find more constructive ways of showing concern for the corruption of the town's youth. As a member of the Lyceum committee, Higginson categorically denied that Emerson had been invited against the will of the committee's majority. The committee's vote, thanks to his own efforts, he asserted, was three to one for the speaker. He neglected to indicate that four of the eight members—all opposed to Emerson—were not present during the voting. In spite of the furor, Emerson came and lectured, and the content of his talk caused less of a stir than Oliver Wendell Holmes' attack, a few weeks later, on homeopathic medicine.[17]

Higginson in the Emerson affair had once again shown a forthrightness undiminished by the inevitably negative effect on his popularity. To Emerson, however, he did not express the confidence of a self-sufficient crusader but instead confided an emptiness at being "lonely and unsupported." He also wondered if there would ever again be a magazine like the *Dial*.[18] Parker's new *Massachusetts Quarterly*, though strong on reform and especially abolition, had little of experimental interest in philosophy, poetry, or literature. Now that the ministry seemed less promising, Higginson began again to wonder about being a writer. Perhaps there he could receive a sympathetic audience.

Within a few months after Emerson's visit, Higginson looked outside Newburyport for fellowship to the new Town and Country Club. Bringing together leading New England intellectuals, many of whom had been part of the original transcendental circle, it had Bronson Alcott as chairman; Emerson, Hedge, and John Dwight were among the club members. Liberal unitarianism was represented by Parker, Channing, and Stone. Sumner, Palfrey, and E. Rockwood Hoar were the political antislavery men, while Garrison represented the disunionists. Longfellow and Lowell, frequently present, were the leading literary members. The club's view of itself was best drawn by Lowell. It consisted, he said, of "all the eccentric particles of the world's orbit, and had come to-

17. *Herald*, Dec. 15, 21, 1848; TWH to *Herald*, Dec. 16, 1848; *Advertiser*, Dec. 12, 19, 1848.

18. Emerson journal, Dec. 10, 1848, *Heart of Emerson's Journal*, ed. Bliss Perry (Boston, 1914), p. 241.

gether to make a planet of their own." [19] Soon Higginson discovered that this new planet had some of the distasteful features of the old one. Lowell, he thought, "never appears the least dependent on any one or to care to hear the opinion or feeling of another." Furthermore, the club's discrimination against admitting women (Emerson argued they would be fatal to the club's survival) and the unlikelihood that a Negro would be admitted soon sapped Higginson's interest. The battlefield continued to be Newburyport, where he still hoped to "do a great deal of good." [20]

Opposition to capital punishment and a belief in the environmental cause of crime served as an impetus in the spring of 1849 for Higginson's involvement with the fate of an illiterate northern Negro. George Hannewell, convicted in Massachusetts for murder and sentenced to be executed, had already spent half his life in prison and the other half in a home of drunken and quarreling parents. Hannewell, claimed Higginson, had burned his parents' home hoping to terrify rather than kill them. Composing a Newburyport petition that asked for clemency, Higginson tried to enlist others in Hannewell's cause by a letter to the Newburyport *Advertiser*. The paper sympathetically said: the " 'poor nigger' is selected as an example to deter genteel white men from the commission of the crime of murder." But neither the cause of capital punishment nor the plight of the free Negro received enough sympathy to marshal public opinion behind Hannewell and save him from execution.[21]

Even a quiet New England summer with Higginson away on vacation was not sufficient balm for his critics. By September 1849, after two years in the pulpit, he conceded the real possibility of being ordered to resign. He described the situation this way: "the discontented in the parish created last winter, slumbering through the summer, but not as I hoped *dead*, have been blown into flame again by the necessity I was under to speak my mind." It now seemed certain that his few supporters had been unable to gain addi-

19. "Town and Country Club," Broadside, Higginson MSS; TWH journal, Mar. 27, May 2, 1849; Lowell quoted in TWH, *Old Cambridge*, p. 166.
20. TWH to L. Higginson, Jan. 26, 1859, Higginson MSS; TWH to James R. Lowell, July 5, 1849, Lowell MSS; TWH to J. R. Lowell, May 19, 1849, Higginson MSS; Emerson to TWH, May 16, 1849, Higginson-Huntington MSS.
21. TWH to J. R. Lowell, Jan. 28, 1849, Lowell MSS; *Advertiser*, March 27, April 6, 8, May 28, 1849.

tional allies. "Even my friends feel grave," he reported, "when they look for and fancy a gradual procession of staunch members retiring one by one, leaving at last a dozen come-outers in the gallery and one more in the pulpit." To his mother, the primary advocate of his choosing the ministry, Higginson wrote, "I have not sufficient sympathy and stimulus to call my whole heart to the discharge of its duties." He decided to resign before the flames of opposition consumed either the size of his congregation or himself. Self-doubt and his doubts about the ministry being his proper vocation now again came forward. He did not acknowledge, however, that he had misjudged Newburyport. Granting "this experiment has failed," he added, "the only wonder is it failed no sooner all things considered." [22]

In keeping with the dramatic and didactic way he usually dealt with his parishioners, Higginson planned to keep his resignation secret until the second anniversary of his Pleasant Street church ordination. Vowing to make this day notable, a town event, he envisioned his powerful words being read in a widely circulated pamphlet. He further vowed to remain a public figure despite the end of his ministerial duties.[23]

But on that Sunday morning of September 16, 1849, his words showed a low degree of exhortative heat. A desire to modify the antagonism felt toward him, and the unexpressed hope that he would not have to resign after all, tempered his address. By forcing resignation, he assured his listeners, wrong had not been done to him personally but rather "against truth and light." Instead of once again flailing them for their Whig sympathies or their antagonism to abolition, he talked unspecifically of his own inability to refrain from preaching "on a certain topic of practical morality." [24]

His success with this approach brought a favorable reaction. Tears appeared in the eyes of some of his congregation. Even the editor of the *Herald*, "the thinker general for Newburyport," seemed moved. Most taken was Higginson, who touchingly disclosed, "I did not realize before how much they care for me." He now came to feel he had always had the support of "the young

22. TWH to L. Higginson, Sept. 6, 1849, Higginson MSS.
23. Ibid.; TWH to Waldo Higginson, Sept. 19, 1849, Higginson MSS.
24. TWH to L. Higginson, Sept. 18, 1849, Higginson MSS.

women, the young men, the poor men, the Democrats and the Come-outers." He even harbored some hope that his congregation would not let him resign, feeling that he never had realized before how strong a hold he had upon the people. Very soon, however, it became evident that those who were sympathetic or friendly were not going to fight for his retention. Although a parish meeting voted to request that Higginson reconsider his resignation, a more forceful request was not forthcoming. The proprietors were under no real pressure from the parishioners to change their attitude. "Honest and conscientious differences of views and opinions," they explained as the reason for accepting the minister's resignation. Unlike Higginson, the proprietors made no mention of differences being a matter of truth and right.[25]

Only the Democratic newspaper openly reprimanded the Whig proprietors. The First Religious Society of Newburyport, it suggested, "would do well after the appointment of a new pastor, to select a committee of the most opulent pew owners in the congregation whose office it should be, to read each sermon in advance of its delivery and alter it to suit their pleasure." [26]

As for Higginson, with the unhappy contract obligation ahead to continue in the pulpit for another six months, he revised once again the nature and size of his opposition, concluding that "not a dozen can really be opposed to me, but they have all the *wealth*." The closer the termination of his duties became the more he diminished the amount of opposition against him. But one member of the church, a carpenter by trade, who attended his final sermon in March 1850, more accurately summarized the situation. The trouble, he noted, was that the minister was "too much of a reformer. . . . This has always been a very pro-slavery society, and it was always strange to me how a man so strongly imbued with anti-slavery sentiments and others of a similar kind, should be permitted to settle there at all." On the other hand, Higginson, who with some justification saw the moneyed interests the cause of his undoing, judged the entire affair as a failure of institutional religion. "O Christian Church," he now lamented to Sam Johnson, to whom he earlier had prophesied a dawning age of faith. His assertion that

25. Ibid.; "Resolution of Proprietors, Sept., 1849," Parish Records.
26. Newburyport *Union*, Sept. 17, 1849.

it was better to be alone than with those whom "there is no tie of spirit," indicated not any misanthropy but rather how deeply he felt the failure to make that tie.[27]

The belief so prevalent among liberal New England ministers that the old religious ways were disintegrating helped to keep Higginson from immediately seeking another pulpit. "It is plainer & plainer that this age is about to try the utterly novel experiment of living without faith in ritual or mythology. . . . Never since the world began were men so near this as now. Nothing justifies Hope but the certainty that there never was such a vigor of moral & spiritual life before." Here was intellectual justification for participating in this novel experiment without commitment to a regular pulpit. Still relevant was the earlier and more personal appraisal: "I like to have full swing for my impulses. . . . I do not feel that I gain anything by any system not self-imposed." [28]

A new life followed these hectic Newburyport days. The Higginsons moved to nearby Artichoke Mills, into the rural home of a distant relative, Mrs. Mary Curzon. She was receiving $5,000 annually from the estate of Henry Higginson (the brother of Wentworth Higginson's father) and now provided free lodgings to the displaced couple. Artichoke Mills had other compensations too. Surrounded by elms, oaks, and rolling hills, the house provided a view of the Merrimack River. There was time to enjoy the river whose allure grew once Higginson read the book written by that man "who lived alone in the woods for 23 cents a week in a shanty of his own building." At a time when few agreed, he found Henry Thoreau's *Week on the Merrimack and Concord Rivers*, "rich in thought and beauty, . . . a rare and delicious thing." Although he judged Thoreau's religious view, with its appreciation of the primitive in nature and man, to be touched with some "wild speculations," he concluded that "in these unsettled days it is perilous for a writer to commit himself to a course of systematic thought, . . . better to fall back upon nature. Shelter oneself behind her & shoot random shots [in] a kind of bush fighting. This I felt before read-

27. TWH to Samuel Johnson, Sept. 26, 1849, Higginson MSS; John Lord diary, March 10, 1850, MS, Newburyport Public Library.

28. TWH journal, Sept. 22, 1849; TWH to M. Channing, Jan. [1845], Higginson MSS.

ing Thoreau's book—how much more now. I cannot describe the
delight I took in the book." [29]

Some of the empathy he felt for the *Week* also came from its
stress on solitude. "It is a great pleasure," Thoreau had written, "to
escape sometimes from the restless class of Reformers. What if
these grievances exist? So do you and I." Or meaningful at this
time was Thoreau's statement that "Generally speaking the political
news, whether domestic or foreign, might be written today for the
next ten years with sufficient accuracy." [30]

Convinced that Thoreau knew more of nature than any man in
America, Higginson also endeavored to learn. Nature, he hoped,
would increase his power to observe and ability to write. After active Newburyport days "we are quite bewildered by the calm that
succeeds the storm. . . . We feel no hurry but that of Nature, who
is slowly and surely harvesting every leaf, so that for her gold as
the poorer of California one must look soon or it will be gone."
Like Thoreau, he saw in the winter that the blanket of snow cover-
ing the river "cast long black shadows, shadows which made the
subterranean fire of nature" seem very close to the surface. Then
during spring, blue waves skimming the river's surface made "the
world seem very young, & all evil short lived." Warm weather's
arrival made him glory in the "ecstasy of June," a feeling that gave
him courage to pay an unannounced visit to Concord and to
Thoreau.[31]

When Higginson arrived, Henry Thoreau, alongside his father,
was indoors making pencils. Thoreau, now thirty-two years old, a
"little bronzed square man," stopped working to talk with his tall,
thin visitor, seven years his junior. Since Emerson had previously
spoken to his Concord friend about Higginson, Thoreau was especially cordial. Conversation, by Higginson's direction, soon gravi-
tated to a discussion of the *Week*, and he spoke in sincere praise for

29. TWH to L. Higginson, Nov. 20, 1849, Higginson MS; M. T. Higginson,
Higginson, p. 106; Will of Henry Higginson, 1838, Suffolk County Probate
Office. While there appears to be no evidence during the antebellum years as to
the total dividends Higginson received from his grandfather's legacy, his "fixed
income" from this source was at least $500 annually from 1865. TWH journal,
June 8, 1850; *A Week on the Concord and Merrimack Rivers* (Boston 1893)
p. 162.
30. Ibid., pp. 166–67.
31. TWH to L. Higginson, June 5, 6, 1850, Higginson MSS.

the book that was such a publishing failure. They also talked about how a man could survive without steady employment in a world of expedience and materialism. Higginson concluded with satisfaction that Thoreau "surveys land, both mathematically and meditatively; lays out house lots in Haverhill & in the moon." White Thoreau's undoubted uniqueness and reputation impressed the visitor, Higginson still found him "the most unvaryingly facsimilie of Mr. Emerson." Paradoxically, two years later, after Thoreau heard Higginson lecture, he noted in his journal a resemblance to Emerson, facetiously adding, "and I could not afford to be reminded of Christ himself." [32]

Although they met occasionally in the fifties, Thoreau and Higginson never came closer to each other than on that first warm summer day in Concord. To Thoreau, Higginson was not simple enough in manner. While granting importance to the ex-minister's ideas, he judged that his style "choked off and stifled . . . the matter." Thoreau's growing dislike of Emerson's formal platform appearance was gradually alienating him from his more famous Concord friend. A Higginson lecture, during which the speaker displayed charm and erudition, moved Thoreau to remark about his waning attraction for Emerson: "I never realized so distinctly as this moment that I am peacefully parting company with the best friend I ever had." [33]

Higginson preferred Emerson to Thoreau. While admiring Thoreau's nonconformity, the more sociable and gregarious Higginson found him too rustic and isolated. With all the feeling Higginson professed for nature and solitude, he was far more comfortable in a city home with company readily accessible.

While out of the pulpit, Higginson supplemented the income he received from the bequest of his grandfather Stephen Higginson by lecturing in New England. Not yet well known on the Lyceum circuit, he initially received about fifteen dollars for each talk, not the twenty-five dollars Parker or Emerson could command. At least one lecture, "Nature and Religion," echoed Emerson's discussion in *Nature*. Like Emerson, he found that nature's facts reveal "de-

---

32. Ibid., June 5, 1850; Thoreau journal, Jan. 21, 1852, *The Journal of Henry David Thoreau*, ed. Bradford Torrey (Cambridge, 1906), *3*, 213.
33. Ibid., 214.

tails so vast . . . laws so profound" that the "most enlightened naturalist is most conscious of ignorance." He too felt that man could come closer to God when surrendering to nature.[34]

But Higginson was far more suspicious of nature than either Thoreau or Emerson. Emerson, for example, was so taken with Horatio Greenough's belief that in nature form follows function and should do so in man's creations, that he thought the idea contained "more useful truth than anything in America I can readily remember." This unmodified praise Emerson conveyed when Higginson visited Concord. Higginson, on the contrary, argued that nature also exhibited "a love of luxury, a voluptuousness," and an arbitrariness that defied a theory that form follows function. Ornament for its own sake was justified, he maintained, whether it be the wallpaper of a room or the color of a growing pansy. Emerson so adamantly dissented—Greenough's idea was indeed an essential corollary to much that Emerson had written—that Higginson grew angry. As Emerson relentlessly argued for functionalism, Higginson "felt like stopping his ears." [35]

Contact with nature, while aesthetically pleasing, had fewer moral qualities to Higginson than to Emerson or Thoreau. He was far less sure of correspondences: "she [nature] does not give us inductions nor deductions but only piles fact on fact, of whose connections . . . we only have, at best, glimpses." He granted that one might find rest and comfort in nature "to lay aside our human responsibility, and become part of the unconscious universe." But to do this could be deadly. The soporific effects of man getting so close to nature, so far away from the society of men, might result in a paralysis that would end the desire and ability to act.[36]

In the course of his life Higginson characteristically turned to nature after having been rejected by men. Once he did so, however, he found himself becoming uncomfortable in her presence. Even using nature to write about would be insufficient: "to merely con-

34. Carl Bode, *The American Lyceum: Town Meeting of the Mind* (Oxford, 1956), p. 138; TWH, "Man and Nature," *Christian Examiner*, *51* (1852), 116; TWH to L. Higginson, Feb. 1, 1850, Higginson MSS.

35. TWH to (?), Sept. 1852, Higginson MSS; R. W. Emerson to Horatio Greenough, Sept. 6, 25, 1852, in William J. Griffin, "Thoreau's Reaction to Horatio Greenough," *New England Quarterly*, *30* (1957), 510, 511.

36. "Man and Nature," 124.

template nature is to become her slave at the expense of the most earnest though." Soon, he made the attraction and isolation of nature the theme of a poem that looked back on "the spells of the Merrimack Valley," where the gorgeousness of nature intoxicated him almost to the point of a deathlike inertness. Later, after a similar period of intimate contact with nature during the first year after Sumter, he would write a semi-autobiographical short story of a man so entranced by beautiful dreams that he no longer was able to act, and was left entangled in the embrace of his reverie while the troop train headed South to meet the storm of civil war.[37]

At Artichoke Mills Higginson experienced the old "inward darkness." He wrote in his journal: "I often feel suffocated inwardly—and want to push away the side of the house & scream in the open air, but instead sit in silence and apparent coldness to conceal my sighs and tears." This same feeling of intense suffocation would later occur when he was confined to a real house—a house whose windows would be tightly shut because of Mary's insistence that her health required it. Foremost in his Newburyport days had been the belief that it was not his wife but his mother who always held him back; yet he apparently understood the personal relevancy of a quotation from Margaret Fuller for he found it pertinent to record: "Man may escape from every foe & every difficulty, except what are within himself." For here were walls that would not for long stay pushed away. Still he might try to reach the open air by preaching, exhorting, rebelling, and inciting other men to tear down society's legal walls. That restrained desire to scream in the open air had found partial expression in Higginson's belief that he "knew his mission—in some form or other . . . is speaking to men, in the pulpit or elsewhere." [38] His inward darkness could only be abated when his voice could be heard by other men.

37. TWH journal, July 1850; TWH, "Odensee," *Putnam's Monthly Magazine*, 3 (1853), 469; TWH to L. Higginson, Feb. 1, 1850, Higginson MSS; "The Monarch of Dreams," *The Writings of Thomas Wentworth Higginson*, 5 (Boston, 1900), 259.
38. TWH journal, Nov. 7, Jan. 7, 1849; TWH diary, April 18, 1873, Higginson MSS.

7

The Free Soil Candidate

Higginson's new-found solitude and leisure were short-lived. Lyceum lecturing provided varied audiences but no regular forum, no familiar listeners enabling him to feel a sense of leadership. And Daniel Webster's plea for compromise, which was delivered just prior to the termination of Higginson's contract with the Newburyport church, emphasized the need for new leadership. Further dramatizing the problem was the subsequent passage, in the summer of 1850, of the Compromise Acts with their fugitive slave law.

But if slavery was being strengthened through politics, as the critics of the new legislation argued, perhaps the antislavery cause could also utilize politics for its own ends. The Liberty party, and its successor the Free Soil party, indeed had had this aim—now the need seemed greater. To Higginson and others, the best way to revive the Massachusetts Free Soil party was to unite various political factions opposing the new law. An uncompromisingly antislavery tone was necessary. It must not be so rigidly uncompromising, however, that a conservative element would be frightened away. If the Garrisonian doctrine of immediate abolition could be avoided, conservatives might support antislavery politics.[1]

Higginson found a forum for his antislavery views by beginning a daily column in October 1850 for the Newburyport *Union*. At the outset he promised opinions "of value to all . . . because they are intrinsically true and important." The cruel and immoral fugitive slave laws necessitated doing over the "old business of Runnymede and Magna Carta" to prevent the return of Negroes to the South, "compared to which a Turkish harem is a cradle of virgin purity." [2]

1. TWH to Waldo Higginson, June 4, July (?), 1850, TWH to L. Higginson, Aug. 7, 1850, Higginson MSS.
2. *Union*, Oct. 7, 11, 1850.

As a delegate to the Essex County Free Soil Convention in October, he found that his newspaper pronouncements were received quite literally. Just prior to the convention he had said that antislavery principle was the primary issue and vowed that "upon it . . . we are willing to stand, if need be, alone . . . in political action." Whittier, having declined the party's nomination to represent the third district in Congress, urged the delegates to nominate Higginson. The convention unanimously approved Whittier's choice. With characteristic bravado Higginson accepted by saying, "If you want somebody to *elect*, you had better look elsewhere—but if you want someone to stand and be shot at, let it be so." [3] The prospect of stumping the county in behalf of political antislavery now appealed to the same man who had so recently embraced Thoreau's political nihilism. The campaigning candidate warned, "We don't believe in half way measures. Anything that is worth doing is worth doing thoroughly." But what he specifically endorsed was less radical than his exuberance indicated. Ending the expansion of slavery, abolishing slavery in the District of Columbia, repealing the Compromise Bill, and repealing the three-fifth clause of the Constitution were the measures he suggested. Never in the campaign did he call for the abolition of slavery in the existing states. Here was the Free Soil concession to the "conservative element." But he did declare that in many Massachusetts towns "it would be impossible or difficult to reclaim a fugitive publicly" since men rightly understood that the fugitive slave law "must . . . yield to a higher law." [4]

This higher law doctrine was sufficiently repugnant to alienate most Democratic support. The *Union* charged that its columnist "openly advocates the nullification of the laws of the land, when they do not correspond with his individual opinions." The newspaper wanted a coalition of Democrats with the Free Soil ticket of state senators; this it claimed was possible without conceding the primacy of legislation and the Constitution. Coalition, it insisted, meant compromising about candidates but not about different principles. This general willingness of Massachusetts Democrats to co-

3. Ibid., Oct. 8, 11, 1850; J. G. Whittier to Editor, *Essex County Freeman*, Oct. 19, 1850; TWH to Waldo Higginson, Oct. 13, 1850, Higginson MSS.
4. *Union*, Oct. 10, 1850.

operate with the Free Soil party was stimulated by the devastating electoral defeat suffered in 1848. Many men besides those who supported the Compromise Bill would learn in 1850 about the taste of political compromise. But some politicians, men like Palfrey, Dana, and Charles Francis Adams, all "conscience Whigs" and conservatives turned Free Soil, did not wish to ally with the national party of Cass, Cushing, and Douglas, nor to shop for votes in the company of a Democratic state party which had loco-foco propensities. To these men, compromising in order to share the spoils of victory was "mere trade," and undermined their criticism of the major parties for ignoring principle for the sake of popularity. Understanding the vulnerability of antislavery men contemplating coalition, a loyal Whig paper said: "The Democratic party will never do any more for the slaves than it did in behalf of the Cherokees of Georgia." [5]

As for coalition-minded Free Soilers, the good prospects of getting their man chosen to the United States Senate by the state legislature promised a very concrete answer to Webster's 7th of March speech and the compromise acts. Henry Wilson of Natick, as early as June 1850, had been the leader of coalition. Webster's subsequent appointment as Secretary of State and Charles Sumner's defeat for Congress in August had whetted Wilson's desire for Whig defeat. Those "conscience Whigs" led by Palfrey still refused coalition, and the state Free Soil Convention agreed only to allow each of its members to act independently. Wilson, still hoping for electoral success, wrote Higginson: "If we carry Essex [County] we are sure of the State." Sumner, however, understood what the campaign meant to Higginson. Looking past 1850, Sumner envisioned an antislavery political party which would include a wide spectrum of opinion: if the antislavery faction of the Democrats and the Whigs could unite, "there would be a party which would give a new tone to public affairs." [6]

During the compaign Higginson utilized his daily column and spoke widely. Distributing 4,000 copies of his "Address to the Vot-

5. Ibid., Oct. 11, 15, 23, 1850; *Herald*, Nov. 8, 1850.

6. Henry Wilson, *Rise and Fall of the Slave Power in America*, 2 (Boston, 1872–77), 341–43; Wilson to TWH, Oct. 28, 1850, Higginson-Barney MSS; Charles Sumner to John Bigelow, Oct. 4, 1850, in Pierce, *Sumner*, 3, 218; Donald, *Sumner*, p. 188.

ers," he privately noted: "it quite tickles me to look at the big letters of the title page." Just prior to his nomination he had assailed both parties for not confronting the slavery question; now as the candidate partly allied with the Democrats he mainly criticized the Whigs. In his district, the Whig incumbent James Duncan, also a Harvard graduate but thirty years his senior, was favored for re-election. Duncan had been one of the few Massachusetts congressmen who had voted for the annexation of Texas. While he had abstained from voting on the fugitive slave law, he was the only renominated Massachusetts Whig who had voted for other sections of the compromise acts. Although granting "there is no chance of my being elected," Higginson expected that his efforts would mean the defeat of that "small man" Duncan. In neither his private correspondence nor his public statements did he mention his Democratic opponent A. R. Brown.[7]

The Compromise Acts, specifically the fugitive slave law, provided the focus for Higginson's campaign. To dramatize the plight of the runaway he quoted advertisements from southern newspapers in his column: "fiendish details of that catalogue of brandings, maimings, scars, cuts, bruises, mutilations." He also reported "dead or alive" advertisements including one offering to lease a pack of dogs for hunting the runaway, and appended some of his own experiences below the Mason-Dixon line. Sharply contrasting with his description of southern conditions in 1840, he now noted, without having been South again: "Our own abolitionism, at least, dates chiefly from this writer's visit to Virginia ten years ago and though slavery there appeared in its mildest form, yet when we find our conscience growing dull on the subject, we have only to revert to that visit, and gain the needed stimulus."[8]

Higginson's "Address to the Voters"[9] is the most comprehensive statement of his position. "The intrinsic sin and wrong of Slavery," and "the intrinsic peril to Freedom from the Slave Power," he pre-

7. TWH journal, Sept. 28, 1850; *Essex County Freeman*, Oct. 26, 1850; William G. Bean, "Party Transformation in Massachusetts with Special Reference to the Antecedents of Republicanism, 1848–1860," Unpublished doctoral dissertation, Harvard University, 1922, pp. 29–32; *Union*, Oct. 9, 1850; *Herald*, Oct. 10, 1850; TWH, "James H. Duncan," *Essex County Freeman*, Sept. 21, 1850.

8. *Union*, Nov. 23, 1850.

9. *Address to the Voters of the Third Congressional District* (Newburyport, 1850).

sented as the basic issues. Momentous evidence of the South's un-
satiated boldness and the North's continued cowardliness were the
Missouri Compromise, the acquisition of West Florida, the annexation of Texas, the Mexican War, and the imprisonment in southern
ports of free northern Negroes. "Texas bonds were more dangerous than Texas bayonets. . . . Those millions of scrip" were the
real reason for bowing to Texas' demands. "Oh spirits of Adams
and Warren. . . . Where would this country have been had you
thus made danger paramount to duty! Or had your brave soul, O
Andrew Jackson, met the threats of South Carolina with gold instead of iron." At last it had been understood, his address continued,
that the Democratic and Whig parties had been so subservient to
southern desires that the Free Soil party had begun *"political* agitation . . . to induce Congress to settle the question on the side
of freedom; and . . . moral agitation to induce the inhabitants
of the new territory to settle it themselves." But political agitation, Higginson granted, had thus far failed. For on Capitol Hill
and Beacon Hill, "There are always compromisers. There are always men . . . who if anyone claims that two and two make six,
will find it absolutely necessary to go half way, and admit that two
and two make five."

By far the worst bit of southern aggression and northern compliance was the new Compromise of 1850: "Of the six measures proposed, four were repugnant to freedom, to justice, and to the
North. . . . And of the others, the one (the admission of California) was a tardy act of the plainest justice, and the other (the abolition of the slave trade in Washington) was expressly urged on
the ground that it would do slavery no harm. Such was the 'compromise'; such have been all compromises with slavery." There
was also the possibility, Higginson warned, that Cuba with 325,000
slaves would come into the Union.

Northern men, therefore, had to cease being cowed by southern
threats. Blocking the enforcement of the fugitive slave law through
state legislation should be done simultaneously with other action.
Men must agitate for repeal of this law and the passage of a federal
law to protect the runaway slave; they must also amend the Constitution to prevent future proslavery legislation. But legal reform
was not enough. To men faced with bowing to the fugitive slave

law, Higginson counseled: "DISOBEY IT . . . and show our good citizenship by taking the legal consequences!" He asked his fellow Christians: "Shall wild Indians and Arab tribes whom no bribe or penalty would allure to the surrender of a guest—shall these haunt us and proclaim that their barbarism is honor and love compared with ours?" His answer was unequivocal: "The duty is so plain that it hides from view the thought of consequences. I cannot tell what may happen; but I can tell what is right. . . . If Massachusetts is not free, I know at least of one house that shall be. . . . And when I close my door against a hunted guiltless man, or open it to his pursuers, then may the door of God's infinite mercy be closed forever against me." Such disobedience to the law was compatible with serving in Congress for "the first duty of representatives is to represent Truth and Right; the second, to represent his constituents." Finally, in answer to antislavery men who found weaknesses in the Free Soil platform, Higginson promised that if he found a political party truer to freedom he would join it.

Two days after the initial delivery of his address, began the first major test in Massachusetts of the fugitive slave law. Warrants were issued in Boston on October 15, 1850, for the arrest of William and Ellen Craft, a Negro couple who had been there since 1848. In an article, "The Crisis Coming Now," written while the search for the Crafts was in progress, Higginson applied his "DISOBEY IT" dictum to their case. There was, of course, the possibility that he would suggest that the couple flee to Canada and freedom, as fugitive slaves before them had done. Instead he urged that they calmly "remain and then throw themselves on the sympathies of the people. . . . Better test the question at once—test it as peacefully as it is possible to do—and see whether the law of God or man is to prevail." As for the legality of disobeying the fugitive slave law, he asked, "Is it not a crime to permit a fellow being carried into slavery? . . . Can there be any moral obligation to commit a crime?" To those who hesitated to answer these portentous questions correctly, he advised: "We should in all cases disobey the law and show our good citizenship by taking the penalty." Soon after, Higginson was even more explicit: "We abhor bloodshed, and they are terrible times when it becomes necessary to speak of bloodshed; yet when it comes to the actual case, it is hard to say where a man must stop in defending his inalienable rights." [10] Here was Thoreau's civil disobedience garbed in the mail of physical defiance rather than in the robes of nonviolence.

The Craft affair was not to be the real test of violence. After the southern agents hired to return the fugitives had been arrested, first for having slandered the couple by calling them slaves and then arrested again for having conspired to kidnap them, Theodore Parker whipped Boston crowds into such frenzy that the agents were informed that local authorities could no longer guarantee their personal safety. Although one of the agents allegedly declared that "It isn't the niggers I care about, but it is the principle of the thing," he and his cohort chose to forsake principle and chilly New England to return South empty-handed. Meanwhile, Parker gave the Crafts a legal marriage and instead of further testing Boston sent them hurrying off to England. "I thank God," he said, "that Old England, with all her sins and shames, allows no Slave-Hunter to set foot on her soil." [11]

This partial victory in defiance of the fugitive slave law was to be paralleled by a partial political victory in 1850. In both instances compromise was necessary. For Higginson, the Free Soil candidate for Congress, it became increasingly difficult to avoid discussion of what a coalition compromise meant, especially when the electoral hopes of the Free Soil party—though not his own—depended upon coalition. He chided the critics of coalition by saying, "It does seem rather hard that so long as anti-slavery men stand alone, they must be denounced as unpracticables, and as soon as they cooperate with anybody, be denounced yet more as compromisers." A week before the election, he explained that the Free Soil party was interested in national, not state issues. "The Democrats want certain State reforms; we as a Free Soil party are indifferent to those, but we want a United States Senator. . . . If we can get it by Democratic aid, it is worth considering." He succinctly put the choice to "conscience Whigs" while himself scrupulously avoiding a judgment about the state Democratic platform: any Free Soiler concerned more about local Whig measures than about Free Soil national measures could not vote for coalition. Here the conscience Whig

10. *Union*, Nov. 4, 12, 20, 1850.
11. *Union*, Nov. 8, 1850; Commager, *Parker*, p. 216; Theodore Parker to James Martineau, Nov. 11, 1850, Parker MSS.

Free Soiler was being asked to decide whether slavery was indeed the most important political issue. To aid those who vacillated, he further suggested that the Democrats had "made fewest pro-slavery professions." [12] This was the best he could say for the Democrats before the election.

In Higginson's congressional district the election results were disappointing. His vote was 2,487, or 21 per cent of the votes cast in Essex County's third district. Duncan, the Whig incumbent, polled 6,086 votes against the Democratic challenger's 3,750—though Duncan's margin was short of the required majority. Duncan polled 47 per cent of the vote compared to the 54 per cent he had recived in 1848. Those third district votes which now left the Whig column went largely to Brown, the Democrat, who with 31 per cent of the total vote ran better than George Boutwell, his party's candidate in 1848. In this year of statewide Democratic success, Higginson ran 3 per cent lower than Charles Knapp's Free Soil vote two years earlier.[13]

After primarily attacking Duncan, Higginson could be pleased that in Newburyport, Duncan's overwhelming 64 per cent in 1848 had been shaved to 52, while his own vote was 7 per cent higher than Knapp's had been. In Georgetown he ran ahead of Duncan, and in Salisbury a close second. Higginson, hoping to see Duncan defeated in the runoff election, now privately offered to withdraw his candidacy in favor of a coalitionist, Josiah Abbot, if his Democratic opponent also would withdraw. George Boutwell, who headed the Democratic state ticket, refused, however, to accept this compromise. Duncan subsequently received a majority in the runoff. Still, the statewide Democratic victory in 1850, with Free Soil help, was significant for the future of antislavery politics. Although disappointed by not unseating Duncan, Higginson judged the Whig defeat to be as revolutionary as Jefferson's first victory over the entrenched Federalists. At least it showed that in Massachusetts the Whigs did not rule by divine right.[14]

With the election over, Higginson made his first specific statement about desired reform legislation for the coming session of the new state legislature. Echoing the Democratic platform, he advo-

12. *Union,* Oct. 24, Nov. 9, 1850.
13. Ibid., Jan. 21, 1851; *Commonwealth,* Jan. 23, 1851; *Herald,* Nov. 14, 15, 1850.
14. Ibid.; TWH to George Boutwell, Nov. 22, 1850, Washburn MSS.

cated a ten-hour labor bill, homestead exemptions, and election by
simple plurality. A law to abolish capital punishment was his own
suggestion.[15]

The most pressing issue to Higginson and the Free Soilers who
had joined the coalition was the forthcoming election in the state
legislature of governor and United States senator. Here was the
crucial test of compromise. The Free Soil caucus agreed to vote for
Democrat George Boutwell for governor in return for a six-year
Senate seat. But no written agreement was made.[16] The *Commonwealth*, the new newspaper of the Free Soilers, sought to assure its
uneasy readers that Boutwell was no Hunker. Boutwell was elected,
but the State Senate, on the first ballot gave Charles Sumner only
186 votes—far short of the necessary majority—while the Webster
Whig Robert Winthrop received 168. The national Democratic
leaders were pressing the state party to keep clear of an antislavery taint. In the face of this, the *Commonwealth* cried, "They have
taken and used the goods; and it no longer lies with them to decline
paying the consideration." [17]

Aggravating matters, Governor-elect Boutwell chose his first
state message to support the fugitive slave law. Free Soilers conceded they would swallow such statements if the bargain was completed. And when a portion of Democrats, led by the Hunker
leader Caleb Cushing, and the Hunker paper, the Boston *Post*, became more aggressive, the Free Soilers heightened their defensive-
ness. In answer to irresponsible Hunker charges, coalitionists felt
compelled to circulate Sumner's statement: "I am a constitutional-
ist and a unionist, and have always been." Sumner thought the
Union a "blessed bond," they told those who wavered.[18] Even
Higginson hesitated, though he tried to hide the symptoms. Said
he: "We do not demand a nullifier, but we would not help to place
for one hour in Congress a senator who might vote within that
hour for the fugitive slave bill as it is." He had earlier labeled Boutwell a Wilmot Proviso man, then remained silent about the views
of the man the Free Soil party had helped elect. Whittier, like other

15. *Union,* Nov. 7, 15, 1850.
16. Ibid., Jan. 13, 1851; *Commonwealth,* Jan. 17, 1851; Donald, *Sumner,* p. 189.
17. *Commonwealth,* Jan. 14, 15, 17, 1851; Donald, *Sumner,* pp. 193–95.
18. *Commonwealth,* Jan. 20, 1851; Donald, *Sumner,* p. 192; C. Sumner to John
Bigelow, Jan. 21, 1851, in Pierce, *Sumner,* 3, 240.

Free Soilers who experienced the guilt of having aided in choosing Boutwell, moaned, "May God forgive us for permitting his election." The poet suggested that the Free Soilers concede their fight to elect Sumner and elect the best Whig available.[19]

A hard core of coalitionist Free Soilers led by Henry Wilson would not accede to the Democratic about-face. Higginson warned the state Democrats that if they expected to carry their campaign promises into legislation, *"not one of them can be carried until Charles Sumner is elected. . . .* You cannot complain if we refuse any more credit." [20]

When balloting continued through January with no sign of a Sumner victory, the *Commonwealth's* disclosure that the party originally had planned to send the names of a governor and a senator to the legislature simultaneously, made the Free Soil plight seem more pitiful. At this news Higginson registered shock over the political naïveté in abandoning such a plan: "The conduct of the crow towards the fox in the fable is a piece of deep dyed political chicanery compared to this transaction on the part of the Free Soilers." Wilson remained determined, however, and his relentlessness was decisive. A successful vote allowing for a secret ballot finally served as the interparty sedative. Three months and twenty-five ballots after the first vote, Charles Sumner was elected by a bare majority to the United States Senate.[21]

Sumner still looked to the day of "consolidating a permanent party in Massachusetts—not by coalition, but by fusion of all who are truly liberal, humane, and democratic. . . . We can get along very well without the Hunkers." [22] This, however, was for the uncertain future. More directly apparent to Higginson was having been successively rejected in the pulpit and at the polls. The present contained other harsh realities which became evident during the first four months of 1851 while Sumner was waiting to be elected.

19. *Union,* Jan. 10, 15, 1851; J. G. Whittier to C. Sumner, Feb. 1851, in Samuel L. Pickard, *Life and Letters of John Greenleaf Whittier* (Boston, 1907), *1,* 352.
20. *Union,* Jan. 8, 1851.
21. Ibid., Jan. 31, 1851; *Commonwealth,* April 23, 1851; Donald, *Sumner,* p. 202.
22. C. Sumner to John Bigelow, May 2, 1851, in Pierce, *Sumner, 3,* 247.

8

Slaves and Laborers

William and Ellen Craft had hardly arrived in England when in mid-February 1851 another Negro was arrested in Boston and brought before Federal Commissioner George T. Curtis. Fred Wilkins, who had assumed the name Shadrach after fleeing the "fiery furnace" of southern slavery, had been working as a waiter in a Boston coffee house. He was the first man brought into a Massachusetts court under the new fugitive slave law. Just as the courtroom was emptying after the preliminary hearing, a muscular Boston Negro, Lewis Hayden, suddenly led a group of colored sympathizers toward Shadrach. They lifed the surprised prisoner from a chair and fled the courtroom with him. Shadrach, reported his lawyer Richard Henry Dana, Jr., was carried away "with his clothes half off, and so stupefied by the sudden rescue and the violence of the dragging off that he sat almost dumb, and I thought had fainted; but the men seized him and being powerful fellows hurried him through the square . . . where he found the use of his feet, and they went off to Cambridge, like a black squall, the crowds driving along with them and cheering as they went." The official pursuers kept his trail only as far as Concord. Shadrach went to Sudbury, and eventually reached Canada. Safe there, the former waiter opened a barber shop.[1]

Theodore Parker was ecstatic. The rescue, he said, was "the noblest deed done in Boston since the destruction of tea in 1773." Garrison's *Liberator*, however, committed to nonviolence, emphasized that no blood had been spilled and that in the rush for freedom a few officers had been merely jostled: "It was as peaceable a

1. Dana journal, Feb. 15, 1851, Dana MSS; Harold Schwartz, "Fugitive Slave Days in Boston," *New England Quarterly*, 27 (1954), 195; Richard H. Sewell, *John P. Hale and the Politics of Abolition* (Cambridge, 1965), pp. 140–42, 266.

rescue as has ever been in any case of forcible rescue." Higginson suggested that "in these matters, the heart is the best logician." [2]

"We seriously believe," he told the citizens of Newburyport, "that there is not a man in this town of any real manliness who does not in his secret soul respect these colored men of Boston." He agreed, however, that it was commendable that the rescue on this occasion took place peaceably and without bloodshed. To those who assailed the lawlessness of the act—and most of the local press did—he lectured about representative government. "It is hard to see how any inhuman statute becomes the less inhuman because we have, through our ancestors or our representatives, part of the responsibility of making it. Is it inhuman or sinful seems the only question." [3]

Knowing the direction of the "secret soul" as Higginson claimed, or knowing the "real sentiment of the Commonwealth" as her senator-elect would assert, was the kind of thinking that gave antislavery men hope for the future. Even the three thousand prominent men who signed a petition supporting the Union and the fugitive slave law were judged to harbor abolitionism in their secret souls. [4] This optimistic faith in man's potential goodness and in mankind's progress sustained men in what seemed a hopeless cause. Frederic Hedge's transcendental view "so much the worse for the facts," indeed served the antislavery cause. And to pursue truth apart from institutional restrictions—guided by an "invisible hand"—would inevitably benefit the community. For Higginson and many other reformers of his era, this assumption underlay the separation of means from ends, and gave cogency to the idea that action could be taken without "the thought of consequences."

While Higginson's articles about the Craft and Shadrach rescues had relied upon accounts from Boston newspapers, the seizure of Thomas Sims, before dawn on April 3, 1851, provided a firsthand experience with the fugitive slave law. Soon after Sims' forcible arrest (he had drawn a knife on his captors) by federal Deputy Marshal Asa Butman, the Boston Vigilance Committee learned of the Negro's incarceration. Before noon on the same day, Higgin-

2. Commager, *Parker*, p. 219; *Liberator*, Feb. 21, 1851; *Union*, Feb. 18, 1851.
3. *Union*, Feb. 18, 1851.
4. Ibid., Nov. 30, Dec. 7, 1850.

son, in Newburyport, was informed by a messenger that another fugitive slave had been arrested in Boston, and they wished him to come. By midafternoon he was attending a meeting in the *Liberator*'s Boston office. The convened group included nonresistors like Garrison, who were more interested in using moral suasion for total and immediate abolition than in planning the freeing of Sims. Also present were political antislavery advocates who opposed extralegal action, as well as others who believed in militant action. Higginson, determined on action, was disturbed by the Boston scene. It seemed even worse than Newburyport, for "there is neither organization, resolution, plan nor popular sentiment—the negroes are cowed, the abolitionists irresolute & hopeless with nothing better to do on Saturday than to send off circulars to clergymen!" Even Lewis Hayden admitted that Negro support would be hard to muster because the government's vigilance after the Shadrach case had scattered militant colored men. But Hayden was ready.[5] Yet what was to be done?

Sims, a slim twenty-three-year-old Georgia mulatto, who had furiously resisted arrest, was now thoroughly cowed and imprisoned in the custody of United States Marshal Charles A. Devens. Like Shadrach, Sims was confined in the United States Court House because he could not be legally put into a state jail, and the federal government had no jail in Boston. On the first day of his incarceration, the Court House steps were lined with policemen with riot clubs. Though still few in number, they seemed "enough to keep the whole city in awe," reported Higginson. The federal officials, with memories of the Shadrach escape still fresh, were determined to decide unequivocally the question Senator Henry Clay posed after that escape: "whether the government of white men is to be yielded to a government of blacks?" About 150 policemen were soon stationed in and around the Court House. Only authorized persons could come within ten feet of the building. Six men guarded the courtroom door and seven more surrounded the prisoner. Most dramatically, three or four feet from the ground, and completely surrounding the building hung a great chain. For those

5. *Commonwealth*, April 5, 1851; Leonard Levy, "Sims Case: The Fugitive Slave Law in Boston," *Journal of Negro History*, 35 (1950), 49–74; TWH to Mary [Curzon], April 6, 1851, Higginson MSS; *Yesterdays*, pp. 139–40.

sympathetic with Sims, the chain readily symbolized the manacled status of Massachusetts justice.[6]

While Dana and Sumner (the latter despite his then undecided senatorial election) sought to secure Sims' release by appealing for various legal writs, Robert Rantoul, Jr., Charles Loring, and Samuel Sewall served as Sims' counsel in Commissioner Curtis' court. Any legal defense had to be prepared quickly because Curtis, following to the letter the fugitive slave law's provisions that cases be handled in a "summary manner," ruled that proceedings begin nine hours after Sims' capture. Affidavit or testimony by the slave's owner was admitted as sufficient proof for identification in accordance with the law. Curtis, not a jury, would decide upon extradition. Sims' affidavit that he was free was disallowed since the law said: "In no trial or hearing under this Act shall the testimony of such alleged Fugitive be admitted as evidence." [7]

Simultaneously with the proceedings before Curtis, Dana and Sumner appealed to State Supreme Court Justice Lemuel Shaw for a writ of habeas corpus, claiming Sims' illegal determent. But the judge denied jurisdiction and also refused to hear argument concerning the law's unconstitutionality. Other legal attempts to circumvent the proceeding against Sims were equally unavailing. Suffolk County's Justice of the Peace even tried to arrest Sims for the knife assault on his captors to remove him from federal jurisdiction. Appeals to the United States District Court and to the itinerant Federal Supreme Court Justice Levi Woodbury were also fruitless.[8]

Higginson remained little interested in what a recent historian of constitutional law has called "a bewildering number of legal actions." The closest he came to contributing to the legal side was by suggesting that lawyer Loring rest his court argument for a time and abscond with a document received from a southern court. The document lay invitingly among the lawyer's papers on a table in the court. Such audacity seemed too much like shoplifting for Loring; he preferred to try to persuade the court to admit more

6. TWH to Mary [Curzon], April 6, 1851, Higginson MSS; *Liberator*, April 4, 1851; *Commonwealth*, April 5, 1851; Dana journal, April 13, 1851, Dana MSS.

7. *Union*, April 5, 1851; *Commonwealth*, April 7, 1851; Levy, "Sims Case," p. 49.

8. Boston *Advertiser*, April 12, 1851; *Liberator*, April 11, 18, 1851; Levy, "Sims Case," pp. 53, 54; *Union*, April 8, 12, 1851.

evidence rather than to cause some to disappear. His final court plea denied that customary extradition proceedings were applicable. Sims, Loring argued, would be sent to Georgia "with no security for a trial, and no relief even if he be another person than that intended to be arrested." [9]

On April 11 Curtis rendered his decision. Expressing regret that duty obliged him to act, he promised not to accept the $10 fee given to commissioners for rendition of a fugitive slave. The case he judged mere extradition, as defined in the law; Sims, Curtis declared, must be returned to slavery.[10]

The Vigilance Committee during all these legal proceedings was not silent. Meetings were held, speeches delivered, broadsides circulated, and extralegal action planned. For use in Boston churches, the *Liberator* printed a statement signed with an "X" and alleged to be written by Sims, which read: "The undersigned freeman, in peril, desires the prayers of this congregation that God may deliver him from the oppressor." On Tuesday, April 10, a mass meeting convened in Tremont Temple to protest the incarceration. The proceedings began at ten in the morning and, like some evangelical camp meeting, lasted through the day and into the night. Samuel Gridley Howe called the convention to order, Congressman Horace Mann presided, and John G. Palfrey was made an officer of the meeting. Coalitionists Henry Wilson, Elizur Wright, Jr., and Anson Burlingame spoke, as did the disunionist Wendell Phillips. Higginson, warming to battle, also spoke. Burlingame reported that the speech "held the audience spellbound. It was more remarkable for it kept back & hinted. . . . There was a fire in the eye" that made the assembly "tremble." Phillips felt sure that "we were on the eve of revolution with that speech." Charles M. Ellis, the man who once had defined transcendentalism in a *Dial* essay, now a Free Soiler by belief and lawyer by profession, followed Higginson on the rostrum with a plea against the use of force. "The 'law & order' men" prevailed, reported Dana.[11]

Higginson and a few followers were undaunted by Ellis' success

9. Levy, "Sims Case," p. 61; *Yesterdays*, p. 141; *The Trial of Sims* (Boston, 1851), pp. 33, 36.

10. Ibid., p. 37; *Union*, April 11, 1851.

11. *Liberator*, April 11, 1851; *Commonwealth*, April 9, 1851; *Yesterdays*, pp. 141–42; Dana journal, April 9, 1851, Dana MSS.

at calming the crowd. Enjoying his momentary effectiveness, Higginson only half jestingly claimed that he now understood what Napoleon meant by saying a leader could most easily excite men to action by infrequent appearances. He subsequently attended the secret meetings of the Vigilance Committee, "meetings where everyone present had to be identified & every window closed." At one such meeting Higginson, with a dozen followers, formulated a plan for Sims' escape. A Negro clergyman of Boston, the Reverend Mr. Grimes, who had been permitted to visit Sims, was asked to be the liaison between the conspirators and the prisoner. Grimes accepted.[12]

Under cover of darkness a thick mattress would be placed under the third-floor window where the prisoner was confined. At a prearranged hour Sims would be expected to jump onto the mattress and be picked up by a rented carriage and whisked to Canada.[13]

The liaison was made, the mattress procured, and the carriage readied. But iron bars were installed, just prior to the planned escape, in the window from which Sims was to jump.[14] Now the only alternative was the direct use of force.

In the impressive atmosphere of Theodore Parker's study, with its collection of books containing the "wisdom of the ages," a plan was discussed. It was not complicated. First, a vessel chartered for the occasion would be placed under the command of a Cape Cod sea captain, Austin Bearse. Then the brig *Acorn*—the ship in which Sims would be transported South—could be boarded in pirate fashion with the forthright goal of kidnaping the prisoner. Even Charles Sumner agreed with this extralegal plan, suggesting that Captain Bearse take Sims to Halifax. This time it was indecision that blocked boldness. For as Higginson reported: "The Vigilance Committee meetings were a disorderly convention, each man having his own plan or theory, perhaps stopping even for anecdote or disquisition, when the occasion required the utmost promptness of decision and the most unflinching unity in action." Time ran out, and Higginson left the meeting disgusted. He reported to his journal: "It left me with the strongest impressions of the great want of preparation on our part for this revolutionary work. . . . Espe-

12. Ibid.; TWH journal, April 13, 1851; *Yesterdays*, p. 143.
13. Ibid.
14. Ibid.

cially this is true among reformers, who are not accustomed to act according to fixed rules and observances, but to strive to do what seems to themselves best without reference to others." [15] Higginson was growing aware of a unique revolutionary role for himself as a militant leader.

A final meeting of the Vigilance Committee agreed to urge Boston men to demonstrate their protest at the time Sims would be marched to the wharf and placed aboard the Georgia-bound *Acorn*. The *Commonwealth*, the Boston voice of the Free Soil party, assured all that "we countenance no resistance to law," but also said: "Our wish is *that the largest number possible of the good people of the Commonwealth may be present to witness this infamous mockery of the law, and this crowning disgrace to the soil of Massachusetts, GOD SAVE THE COMMONWEALTH.*" It printed the names of Marshal Charles Devens, Commissioner George T. Curtis, and the attorney for Sims' master, Seth Thomas, and enclosed them within a thick black line.[16]

On the evening of the 11th, the day of Curtis' decision to return Sims to Georgia, Higginson with others kept a vigil outside the Court House. There they saw the police drilling, as the military had been ordered to do earlier in the week, to show the dissenters that no Shadrach-like rescue would succeed. Higginson graphically described the spectacle:

> They marched & countermarched, drew their cutlasses & went through various evolutions. Lastly they formed a hollow square & marched a little up Court Street. It was a horrible thing, that hollow square. . . . Massachusetts ceased to exist & we seemed to stand in Vienna. . . . Yet I do not believe they will dare to carry out this plan; I do not think the blood even of Boston merchants could bear it.[17]

Just before sunrise on April 13, Thomas Sims, accompanied by Boston policemen with sabers bared, was marched within that hol-

15. Ibid., p. 144; *Commonwealth*, April 28, 1851; Austin Bearse, *Reminiscences of Fugitive Slave Days in Boston* (Boston, 1880), pp. 24, 25, 34; TWH to S. J. May, Jr., April 6, 1851, Higginson MSS; TWH journal, April 13, 1851.

16. *Commonwealth*, April 9, 1851.

17. TWH to Editor, *Union*, April 14, 1851.

low square to the wharf. Only a hundred witnesses, most of them members of the Vigilance Committee, followed the procession, calling "shame, shame." At the wharf, they sang the hymn "From many a Southern river/And field of sugar cane/They call us to deliver/Their land from slavery's chain." [18]

When the *Acorn* left its dock, escorted by a revenue cutter, the group slowly moved away chanting to the tune of Auld Lang Syne, "Repeal, repeal." Higginson, with the chance of action gone, was not among those men who sadly stood in the morning light to witness the return of the first fugitive slave from Boston. Six days later, in Savannah, Sims was publicly whipped.[19]

Theodore Parker, a year later, delivered his sermon. "The Boston Kidnapping," before two thousand people at the Melodeon. Higginson, who preceded the sermon with a reading from the scriptures and a prayer, sat on the platform as Parker gave one of his most scathing speeches. Sims, Parker charged, was baptized by the "Trinity of Money. . . . Said the New England church of commerce, 'Thy name is Slave.' I baptize thee in the name of the gold eagle, and of the silver dollar, and of the copper cent.' " Always ready to allude to the American Revolution to make a point, Parker noted that April 19, the day Sims arrived back in Savannah, was the day in 1775 when the shot heard around the world was fired.

> Some of you, I think, keep trophies . . . won at Concord or at Lexington, . . . powderhorns, shoe-buckles, and other things, from the nineteenth of April, 1775. Here is a Boston trophy from April nineteenth, 1851. This is the coat of Thomas Sims. He wore it on the third of April last. Look at it. You see he did not give up with alacrity, nor easily "conquer" his "prejudices" for liberty. . . . His coat was torn to tatters. And this is Massachusetts Liberty. Pardon me my country, that I rated you too high! Pardon me, town of Boston, that I thought your citizens all men! Pardon me, lawyers, that I thought you had all been born of mothers! . . . Where are the children of the patriots of old? . . . Adams and Han-

18. Boston *Advertiser*, April 14, 1851.
19. Ibid.; Irving H. Bartlett, *Wendell Phillips* (Boston, 1961), p. 157.

cock died without a child. Has nature grown sterile of men? Is there male and manly virtue left? [20]

With Sims returned South, the Richmond *Republican*, unlike Parker, found manliness wanting only in New England Abolitionists. It too referred to the past: "Boston owes itself to dress up these pretenders in petticoats and put them in pillories, where they may pay the penalty due to humbugs and impostors." The *Liberator* reprinted this southern insult.[21]

Boston antislavery men did not seek to purchase Sims' freedom. His reputation, prior to his arrest, for allegedly having spent money on drink and loose women, diminished concern about him once he was returned. Also some people opposed paying ransom to slave owners. For others, the cause rather than the man was important. But in 1860, Sims' freedom was purchased for $1,800. The amount was paid by U.S. Marshal Charles Devens, who had sent the fugitive back to slavery in 1851. When Devens later became Attorney General under President Grant, he employed Sims in the Department of Justice.[22]

The Sims affair, especially the extralegal plans, tremendously impressed Higginson. "In fact I walked in a dream all that week," he wrote. "It is strange to find one's self outside of established institutions; to be obliged to lower one's voice and conceal one's purpose; to see law and order, police and military, on the wrong side, and find good citizenship a sin and bad citizenship a duty." He also learned that "it takes time to prepare one to act coolly and wisely, as well as courageously, in such an emergency." [23] For such personal preparations he would have three years before the next attempt to return a fugitive slave from Boston.

His appetite for militancy was growing. Before 1851 passed, he advocated the end of the United States' nonintervention policy toward Louis Kossuth's crusade for Hungarian independence. Granting that "it will be bad to arouse the war spirit in any cause,"

20. *The Boston Kidnapping: A Discourse to Commemorate the Rendition of Thomas Sims, April 12, 1852* (Boston, 1852).

21. *Liberator*, May 9, 1851.

22. *Advertiser*, April 18, 1851; Lydia Maria Child to TWH, Mar. 26, 1866, Galatea MSS.

23. "TWH Memo on Sims Case," Higginson-Burns MSS.

Higginson argued "we cannot keep free from that & it is a great thing to get the popular sympathy enlisted in the right direction." [24] For Higginson and his generation of moralists, however, a war against the alien South eventually would seem far more splendid than any war fought across the Atlantic. A victory in Richmond or Charleston was more relevant than one in Vienna or Innsbruck—though the causes to them seemed similar.

The talk about revolution affected Higginson's political attitude. He had to decide, late in 1851, whether to support another Free Soil–Democratic coalition for state offices: he now argued that anti-Whig sentiment, which had been stimulated by Webster's actions, had produced an overeagerness to accede to the conservative Hunker wing of the Democratic party. There had been much justified criticism of Webster and Winthrop, but far too little of Cushing and Hallett. Garrison, quickly recognizing the anticompromise implications of this Higginson speech, printed it in the *Liberator*. Senator Sumner, on the other hand, believing that such a compromise was needed for political survival, wrote to Higginson: "I feel that our aims are so nearly identical, my sympathy with your earnestness is so complete, that I do not think we could differ substantially as to the true course to be pursued if we could see each other and fully exchange opinions." Sumner asserted: "I covet the entire absorption of the Democratic party by our force, yet I am willing to *use them*, and also to cooperate with them, on the best terms, we can get." But no meeting took place. Higginson maintained with much reason that Free Soilers conceded more in 1851 than in 1850, and got less in return. He granted that coalition had some plausibility since there were areas of agreement, but the Free Soil party must not relinquish its antislavery position as it had done in the past year. Questioning the sincerity of the 1851 state Democratic campaign promise to oppose slavery, he predicted that if a Democratic president were to be elected in 1852, that party would be as proslavery as the Whigs now were. "The only thing we can do is to keep not only our organization but our principles intact." Free Soilers should not sanction coalition in 1851 unless the Democrats opposed enforcing the fugitive slave

24. TWH to L. Higginson, Dec. 28 [1851], Higginson MSS; TWH to R. W. Emerson, Nov. 17, 1851, Misc. MSS, Houghton Library.

law.[25] This stipulation, of course, was too radical for Democratic endorsement.

Yet despite this, Sumner hoped both Whittier and Higginson would support coalition and join men like Palfrey, who had been opposed to it in 1850. "Will not Higginson see the matter in a practical light?" Sumner asked Whittier. "I am pained to differ from him; but I do feel that we must not neglect the opportunity by alliance." Both Higginson and Whittier remained opposed. As for Palfrey's advocacy of coalition, Higginson noted, "The Dr. P. & I are like the Christian & Mohammedan lovers who mutually converted each other & were then as far apart as ever." [26]

This was the last time the Free Soil and Democratic parties would ally; such an alliance would be unacceptable to either side in the following year when the national election of 1852 would necessitate the reconciliation of the slavery issue with a national platform. Although eschewing coalition, Higginson desired to bring reform through political channels, whether it be labor reform or temperance reform. But 1850, the time when he both ran for office and supported coalition with the Democrats, would remain the high point of his antebellum political activity. His response to the extralegal aspects of the Craft, Shadrach, and Sims affairs, and his refusal to support coalition in 1851 indicated a diminishing faith in the viability of political antislavery. More frequently his articles and speeches would be printed or reported in the anti-political *Liberator*.

Higginson remained close to various controversial issues, but he usually tried to avoid following in the wake of other reformers. "I hate to go out of my way to see great people and always decline being introduced to them," he confessed. One friend noted that Higginson was "remarkably fastidious . . . in respect to people." [27] His leadership was thwarted even when he sought the establishment of a public library in Newburyport, for his reputa-

25. "The Prospect Before Us," *Liberator*, Oct. 2, 1851; C. Sumner to J. G. Whittier, Oct. 7, 1851, Whittier MSS; Sumner to TWH, Sept. 5, 1851, in Pierce, *Sumner, 3,* 254; TWH to L. Higginson, Oct. 30, 1851, Higginson MSS.

26. Sumner to Whittier, Sept. 11, 1851, Whittier MSS; TWH to James Kimball, Oct. 15, 1851, Misc. MSS, Essex Institute; TWH to L. Higginson, Oct. 30, 1851, Higginson MSS.

27. Ibid.; Ellis G. Loring to Anna Loring, Dec. 22, 1851, Loring MSS, Houghton Library.

tion as the town's critic caused unpopularity. As a member of the Merrimack Temperance Society, for example, he did not merely condemn the inexpensive rum produced in John Caldwell's distillery—he characterized the entire town as "stained by intemperance (and its inevitable companions, licentiousness and gambling . . .), [where] wealth is not considered dishonorable though gained by the profits of the rents of rum selling," where no effort had been made "to restore a better standard of morality." Now, at the library meeting he was punished. From the time the chairman recognized him he was accosted by shouts of "I'll be damned if he shall speak," and other less intelligible but vociferous sounds that accompanied fist-shaking. Not only was he prevented from being heard but one quiet observer noted that "there came near being a fight." [28]

When Higginson championed Newburyport's poor he received another public cuffing. In this instance, however, he was heard. The dispute began when the *Herald* discussed a very sensitive subject: Abolitionists' unconcern about northern conditions. It suggested that they should stop antagonizing the South with antislavery verbiage and instead crusade against charity squandered upon the poor, a charity which only encouraged poverty's great cause—mismanagement. Higginson forcefully responded. He knew that wages were low (the 1850 census returns reported $1.33 as the typical daily wage for unskilled labor) and that few men could find employment for more than eight months of the year. He advised the editor to "spare an hour from cutting pro-slavery scraps for his exchange column and instead visit those local poor where economic support was dependent upon the income of children eight to fourteen years of age"; or visit places where fathers "walk the streets all day looking for work (after applying in vain at the door of every factory) and find perhaps once a fortnight a chance to saw a cord of wood." The twelve-hour cotton-mill day worked by young children "is wretched for soul and body— . . . yet what else can parents do when they cannot live without the children's wages?" "Philanthropy," he told the *Herald*, "is not a vice so prev-

28. *Union*, Nov. 11, 1850; Caleb Cushing, TWH, et al., *Address to Citizens in Behalf of a Public Library, Sept. 13, 1850* (Newburyport, 1850); TWH, "The Public Library," *Union*, Mar. 1, 1851; John Lord diary, Mar. 1851, Newburyport Public Library.

alent in Newburyport that a special crusade is necessary against
it." [29] But the paper persisted: "We will maintain against a world
in arms that where there is no sickness, there need be little suffering
if there is industry and right management in the household." Having shown remarkable restraint during the course of Higginson's
ministry, during his '48 election campaigning, and even during his
Free Soil candidacy, it could no longer withhold its true feelings.
Higginson, it declared, displayed both a "disagreeable dogmatism"
and a failure to realize that he had "no monopoly of truth and
righteousness," about charity to the poor or anything else. "We
should judge from the writings of Mr. H.," it added, "that the
possibility of this never entered his head." Higginson demurred.
Feigning magnanimity, he promised not to sue the *Herald* for libel,
and defended the freedom of the press to criticize public leaders.[30]

Higginson's dual concern for the businessman's failure to trans-
cend the values of the marketplace, as well as for the plight of the
poor and uneducated, was similar to his antislavery position. The
antislavery cause was linked with a paternalistic humanitarianism
that must strive to override the great concern for economic profit.
Southern paternalism he either ignored or attributed to the selfish
economic motives and brutality of slave-owning masters. Both the
northern poor and the southern slave needed help from the more
fortunate, and from those less blinded by the myopia of economic
self-interest. While logically a man sympathetic with the plight
of the slave would also be concerned with northern unfortunates,
many Abolitionists ignored northern social injustice because they
were not thoroughgoing reformers. Often sectional pride, especially the New England variety, thrived upon the actual and imagined horrors occurring under the live oaks and magnolias, while
heedless of the ugliness beneath the northern pines. An antislavery
man might ignore the condition of the northern debtor, the northern poor, or the northern laborer because, as one paper noted,
"Alas! he was a white man." [31] But Higginson, introduced to reform by men like Stephen Perkins, and Walter and William Henry

29. Thernstrom, *Poverty*, p. 20; TWH, "Charity Begins at Home," *Union*, Dec.
21, 1850.

30. *Herald*, Dec. 24, 1850; *Union*, Dec. 30, 1850.

31. Boston *Christian Observer*, quoted in *Liberator*, April 25, 1851.

Channing refused to confine his own moralistic gaze to sights below the Potomac.

In one of his Sunday evening lectures (which he gave in addition to his Lyceum lectures), he specifically dealt with the role of northern merchants. To his Newburyport audience he presented a view he had expressed privately in June 1847. Then, like his cousin Stephen Perkins, Higginson hoped a way would be found to find work and land in the West for indigent Boston immigrants. "If some capitalists would take it up," he had suggested, "it might save us." Now he echoed his words and those spoken by Perkins, the Channings, and Theodore Parker. For it was in Newburyport that the Whig *Herald* had applauded Webster's 7th of March address by noting, "It is necessary to bear in mind that our government was formed for business purposes." Higginson of course recalled other purposes. He argued that the economic contributions of those involved in commerce were overvalued since they served as mere carriers, not as producers of goods. And business became especially antisocial when merchants—as he felt was often the case —put profit foremost and ignored honesty. This lust for profits, frequently sought by speculative means, was a moral danger to the nation inasmuch as even "the sober mechanic, tired of steady work day in and day out," was being enticed to seek these ill-gotten gains. Finally, the tie that bound the slaveholder, merchant, and manufacturer threatened to strangle the promise of American life.[32]

To townsmen struggling for industrial growth, to countrymen seeking economic expansion, Higginson exhorted, "Live in your occupation so as to ennoble it while you stay in it; when the nobleness ceases, let the occupation cease. . . . It is well to be independent; but it is a sham independence which is bought with money. It is well to show what good can be done with wealth, but it is better to show what can be done without it." Of most importance: those with wealth must meet their social responsibilities. By this he did not mean emulation of the paternalism of English Tories, for theirs was a kind of proprietorship based on the assumption that the masses preferred subjection, an "astounding and shocking" no-

32. TWH to S. Johnson, June 18, 1847, Higginson MSS; *Herald*, March 15, 1850; *Union*, Mar. 3, 1851.

tion to Higginson. Describing the American problem, he wrote:

> That there is at times improvidence among the poor (as well as among the rich) is a thing too sadly apparent to all who visit them. . . . The great difficulty is not that the fortunate classes do not see the improvidence, but they do not see anything else, fence themselves round with a general distrust, and will invest nothing in charity without a far more ample security against loss than they obtain in any other investment.[33]

Higginson sought to help the lower class strive toward achieving some of its human potential by alleviating the most pressing problems of illiteracy and poverty. He had led a campaign in October 1850 to begin a Newburyport free evening school for illiterate adults. As originally planned, the school, in a room above a dry-goods store, was to give instruction two evenings a week to fifty young men and women. In practice, classes convened every day an hour after the mills closed. At eight each evening and at seven on Saturday, factory laborers, foreign-born (mostly in their teens), and any others seeking literacy or desirous to avoid becoming "dissipated from not having other things to do in the evening," climbed the flight of stairs to the makeshift classroom. The fifty students originally anticipated proved to be never fewer than one hundred and fifty, and sometimes attendance was as high as four hundred. Higginson subsequently advocated the admission of children who were "employed, to the injury of themselves and of the community, in the factories." With fifteen women teachers under him, he directed the school's female department. Funds came from private donations and occasional small grants from the School Committee.[34]

Teaching matter was largely elementary, since only about half could read and even fewer could write; the more advanced students were taught the rules of grammar. But something more was taught. "Wholesome maxims which the pupils are accustomed to repeat night after night," reported Higginson, "are not unmeaning

---

33. *Merchants* (Newburyport, 1851), p. 30; Quarry [ca. 1847], MS, Higginson MSS; *Union*, Dec. 30, 1850.
34. *Union*, Jan. 19, 21, Nov. 25, 30, Dec. 5, 1850, Mar. 11, 1851; TWH, *Report of the Evening School* (Newburyport, 1851); Thernstrom, *Poverty*, p. 51.

and useless formulas, but become impressed upon the mind and exert a refining and salutary influence." Lack of refinement seemed especially noticeable in those who had been inside a cotton mill. In compiling a collection of "Maxims for Maidens," presented to girls leaving Newburyport to attend normal school, he was continuing an interest shown in 1848 when he had been an advisor to *The Mirror and the Casket of Female Industry*, a monthly Newburyport magazine fashioned after the *Lowell Offering*, but with a more distinctive name. The *Mirror* had promised to be "a welcome, instructive, interesting and chaste visitor to all who may become its readers . . . and to dignify the character of female laborers, by inducing them to pay attention to the culture of the mind." He had previously taught poetry to some young Newburyport ladies (the future poet Harriet Prescott Spofford among them) and was becoming interested in woman's rights, but of the evening school project he was especially proud. For despite the state law requiring children under fifteen who were employed in factories to attend school for eleven weeks, nearly half the children had rarely been in a classroom before. And for the rising number of immigrants in the town's labor force, the evening school was their first experience with American education. Continuing to teach there for two years, Higginson became involved in more than grammar and refinement.[35]

To the famous Amesbury–Salisbury labor dispute of 1852, Higginson brought almost none of the attitudes toward labor held by his intellectual contemporaries. In the forties when some had praised working conditions in Lowell, and others had extolled the promise of Brook Farm, he had found them both an unsatisfactory response to industrial problems.[36] Not even the idyllic reports about Lowell by his favorite English commentators, Charles Dickens and Harriet Martineau, had convinced him. Unlike these foreign observers who found Lowell superior to the squalid English in-

35. *Union*, Oct. 30, 1850; TWH to L. Higginson, Mar. 19, May 19, Aug. 3, 1852, Higginson MSS; Newburyport *Advertiser*, Feb. 11, 1848; Harriet Prescott Spofford to TWH [1909], Higginson-Barney MSS; Elizabeth K. Halversen, *Harriet Prescott Spofford* (Philadelphia, 1935), pp. 40, 43.

36. Massachusetts Bureau of Statistics of Labor, *Eleventh Annual Report* (Boston, 1880), p. 9; TWH to S. Johnson, Sept. 4, 1846, Higginson MSS; Norman Ware, *The Industrial Worker, 1840–1860* (Boston, 1922), pp. 175–79.

dustrial towns, Higginson used American domestic and rural standards as the basis for his judgments.

Despite his earlier criticism of Brook Farm, now that he had seen
both Lowell and Newburyport, he denied that Fourierism destroyed individual self-expression and traditional family bonds.
This kind of socialism, Higginson argued, sought a greater degree
of individual development than was possible under laissez-faire
capitalism. He criticized English Chartism for its exclusive concern for amelioration through political legislation.[37] Yet his sympathy for Fourieristic socialism was a matter of toleration rather
than outright advocacy. And, unlike many supporters of Brook
Farm, he was also concerned for wages and hours.

The Amesbury–Salisbury strike had its roots in the appointment
of a new agent to manage the Salisbury Manufacturing Company.
The agent posted notices announcing a half-hour increase in the
5 A.M. to 7 P.M workday by eliminating the midmorning and midafternoon recesses. Defying this order the men recessed as usual,
but upon their return they were dismissed. The company hired
new help and continued operating. In response, a gathering of
Amesbury and Salisbury citizens convened under the direction of
John Greenleaf Whittier. Drafting a series of resolutions (one expressed pride in having the mills in their town), they noted that
since so many of the employees were from the oldest local families,
it would be regretted by all citizens if "present workers are driven
elsewhere for labor, and their places supplied by a vagrant and
unsettled class." Only earnest negotiations, suggested the citizens'
committee, could prevent such doleful change. The company,
however, less fearful of the influx of immigrant laborers and more
interested in an anticipated drop in labor costs, announced that it
would not allow any outside dictation in the management of the
mills. None of the strikers, it insisted, would be rehired.[38]

Higginson, interested in the strike by Whittier, understood that
its importance went beyond the specific controversy. Some labor
leaders had advocated the ten-hour day since the forties. By mid-
century, new efforts were initiated to organize unions and press

37. TWH, review of *Alton Locke* by Charles Kingsley, in *Union*, Dec. 5, 1850;
Caroline Ware, *Early Cotton Manufacture* (Boston, 1931), pp. 294–95.
38. *Union*, Dec. 19, 1850; Thomas F. Currier, "Whittier and the Amesbury-
Salisbury Strike," *New England Quarterly, 8* (1935), 105–12.

for a shorter day. New Jersey, Pennsylvania, and New Hampshire by 1851 had passed ten-hour laws. Higginson soon became active in collecting money, food, and clothing for the locked-out workers, and allowed Whittier to publish a letter disclosing his views on the strike. Read at a town meeting, printed in the Amesbury *Villager,* and put into pamphlet form, it reminded all employers that their action toward strikers would renew

> that conflict between capital and labor which capitalists have hitherto deprecated as both unnecessary and dangerous. We have been assured that the interests of capital and labor are identical. But if it turns out that this is an error, and that the interests are distinct, then there is no question which of the two is most important. *Labor must be protected first.*

The basis for this choice was not, as he said in his "Merchants" lecture, that laborers were the producers of wealth, but rather that "there are thousands of laborers who are not, and cannot become capitalists." [39] Higginson was displaying a skepticism about economic mobility that was virtually unique among his contemporaries.

Although desiring "peaceful and lawful means" in settling labor–management differences (he sanctioned strikes), he noted: "If the time has come when capital does *not* meet labor as an equal—refuses to conciliate, and it aims only to command—then it is quite time for the community to know it and act accordingly. I am anxious to see the result." [40]

This strike's result was the influx of Irish millworkers and the departure of native employees. The lockout had succeeded, but before the year ended, advocacy of ten-hour legislation appeared in the state platform of the Massachusetts Free Soil party, largely the result of the strike. Whittier and Higginson, in the midst of the strike, had vowed to press this. Not until 1874, however, did a ten-hour bill become law in Massachusetts.[41]

39. Whittier to TWH, July 13, 1852, Higginson-Huntington MSS; N. Ware, *Worker,* p. 158; *A Succinct Account of the Late Difficulties of the Salisbury Corporation* (Salisbury, 1852); TWH to Whittier, July 8, 1852, in *A Succinct Account . . . ,* pp. 19–20.
40. Ibid.
41. Whittier to TWH, July 13, 1852, Higginson-Huntington MSS; N. Ware, *Worker,* p. 158.

Despite his ouster as minister and his criticism of the sectarian nature of institutional religion, Higginson still hoped that religion would force the end of slavery. While telling Sam Johnson in June 1851 that he would never again accept a parish, he conceded that on antislavery the "game of Puss-in-the-Corner" had become "harder and hotter." Unitarians were beginning to be heard. "It shows the clergy," concluded Higginson, "to be a grade above politicians after all, that the capitalists have less power to muzzle the Reverends than the Honorables." Six months later he advised a ministerial acquaintance to try to reform the church by staying in it.[42]

42. TWH to S. Johnson, June 29, 1851, Higginson MSS; TWH journal, July, 1851; TWH to David Wasson, Nov. 17, 1851, Higginson MSS.

9

Worcester Agitator

Higginson accepted an invitation to speak at Worcester, Massachusetts, during late March 1852. It had been sent by men seeking to inaugurate a Free Church like Parker's in the "heart of the Commonwealth." Ironically, it arrived the day before his mother had entreated him to heed the Unitarian orthodoxy of Ezra Stiles Gannett and beware of the reformist views of Theodore Parker. "The gifted Theodore," warned Louisa Higginson, was "giving people the idea that they can do as well without Christianity." But upon learning about Higginson's Worcester offer, she welcomed his chance for enlarged opportunity. "I would not want you," she cautioned, "to go to a set of radicals or Buddhists or Mohammedans, but a Christian society . . . desiring *earnestly* your services." Also Mary would find a more congenial social life there than in Newburyport. With a rare reference to Stephen Higginson she assured him that the energy, ability, and desire to help others were attributes he had inherited from his father.[1] She did not know that one of the Worcester men most desirous of attracting Higginson to the Free Church was radical Martin Stowell, a leader of the forcible rescue in Syracuse of the fugitive slave Jerry in 1851.

Despite bleak Newburyport prospects, Higginson was adamantly against accepting the Worcester position. Granting that Newburyport's deep conservatism would thwart his reform efforts, he insisted that he did not wish to devote much time to "immediate action." Action was important, he admitted, but activity at Worcester would submerge his contemplative side, and emerging from contemplation to go into action was far easier than reversing this process. At this juncture, however, the only concrete literary result of contemplating nature had been the preparation of a poetry

1. TWH to Mary Curzon, April 16, 1852, L. Higginson to TWH, Mar. 19, 23, April 16, 22, 1852, Higginson MSS.

anthology, *Thalatta,* which he had edited with Samuel Long-fellow.[2]

When officially informed that he had been unanimously chosen to head the Free Church, Higginson relented. "Rather to my own surprise," he confessed, "I find myself likely to assume the charge of a new Free Church." Hesitatingly he noted: "I feel a sort of duty toward it," adding: "because I see clearly the need and possibility of infusing more *reverence* and *piety* into this come-outerism of New England, to which I belong by nature." Higginson emphasized that the congregation was very large and they desire very much that he should come.[3]

Shortly before deciding, he had attended a spiritual seance at 50 Lowell Street, Boston, to seek advice. At Newburyport, Higginson, who like many of his contemporaries believed in spiritualism, had assailed the town government for forbidding a "medium" to practice there, and in 1857 he would attack Harvard for expelling one from the Divinity School. Now, seated in a dimly lit room with two others seeking to communicate with a departed spirit, he first tried to reach his brother, Thacher Higginson, who had been lost at sea when Higginson was eighteen. Other spirits, however, seemed to block communication, he reported. His father was then summoned. Stephen Higginson's spirit reached his son. "I need hardly say," Higginson reported, "that these experiences . . . could not have been produced by chance or jugglery; but I can say no more." [4]

He consulted personally with the very concrete Theodore Parker, who also urged him on to Worcester. After deciding to settle there he enthusiastically stressed the town's material, intellectual, and moral vitality. Radicalism appeared to be flourishing and the Free Church movement very strong.[5]

Once again, just as he had relinquished privacy to return to

2. TWH journal, April 25, 1852; *Thalatta* (Boston, 1853).

3. Perry Thayer, Martin Stowell, et al. to TWH, May 3, 1852, TWH to L. Higginson, May 17, 1852, Higginson MSS; TWH to Alfred Roe, Nov. 12, 1903, Misc. MSS, American Antiquarian Society.

4. TWH journal, April 29, 1852; *Union,* Feb. 1, 1851; TWH to L. Higginson, Nov. 19, 1851, Higginson MSS; TWH to (?), April 15, 1857, Harvard College Papers; *The Rationale of Spiritualism, Dec. 5, 1858* (New York, 1859).

5. TWH to L. Higginson, June 19, 1852, Higginson MSS; TWH to Parker, June 24, 1852, Parker to TWH, June 25, 1852, Higginson-Huntington MSS.

Divinity School after expressing unwillingness to shed solitude, Higginson became committed to public action. Only by being continually sought and acknowledged by others did he feel his own strength. Upon leaving Newburyport he could write the poem about Odensee, a bewitching Danish valley (described by Hans Christian Andersen) in which a man had died from being unable to disengage himself from nature's beauty.

> Ah! sadly I heard the story,
> For my full heart answered me,
> There were spells in Merrimack valleys
> As strong as in Odensee.[6]

In Worcester's Horticultural Hall, to parishioners characterized by one newspaper as being seven-eighths Free Soil, and whom Higginson assessed as a religious amalgam of orthodox Congregationalists and Methodists who hardly knew what they wanted, the new minister preached his installation sermon, Sunday morning, September 15, 1852. For the opening text he turned to his seventeenth-century ancestor, the Reverend Francis Higginson, who, upon leaving England had proclaimed: "We go to practice the positive part of church reformation and propagate the gospel in America." Wentworth Higginson promised his six hundred listeners that he too would practice church reformation, but founded upon the belief that "man and his institutions can only follow the great Law of Nature." Unlike his Puritan forebear, he denied the literal truth of the Bible; instead he stressed the Inner Light and the simple humanity of Jesus. Religion must be based upon a belief in the individual relation of the soul with God. For men who rejected all religion, he preached: "Without the religious spirit, practical reform becomes intemperate and vindictive. . . . We need more radicalism in our religion and more religion in our radicalism." But it was not the religion of the majority of professing Christians, who believe that most men had been damned to Hell. "For rather would I disbelieve in God," he exclaimed, "[for] God's power . . . without His love is only infernal."[7]

---

6. *Putnam's Monthly Magazine, 3* (1853), 469.

7. Newspaper clipping in TWH journal, Sept. 1852; TWH to S. Johnson, Sept. 9, 1852, Higginson MSS; *Things New and Old: An Installation Sermon* (Worcester, 1852).

The moral minister must not be a mere weathercock: "The theme of the pulpit sermon every summer should predict the matter of next winter's legislation." Support was needed for temperance enforcement, woman's rights, land reform, a ten-hour bill, and penal reform. The minister must also publicly examine "the manufacturing system which fills our towns with stout Irishmen who live helplessly on the labor of their children ten years old, working thirteen hours a day—the whole problem of Associated Labor which we must inevitably meet and settle—and above all the great cloud of slavery, the one immediate storm." [8]

Although song and prayer at Horticultural Hall would still be part of public worship, he promised to make them as informal as the use of the free pews. Sermons would be delivered by both visiting clergymen and by itinerant laity in efforts to emphasize all-embracing Christian love rather than narrow Christian sectarianism. With a new zest and renewed determination, Higginson had returned to the pulpit. After printing and circulating thirteen hundred copies of his installation sermon, he was assailed by a Worcester clergyman for preaching atheism. And while pleased that her son now seemed a settled divine, Mrs. Higginson sadly noted that their views were so different. She sought consolation in "the religious spirit which I know to breathe in all your actions, thoughts and feelings." [9]

The political scene in the fall of 1852 provided Higginson's first chance in Worcester to demonstrate the bond between the religious and secular life. His support of the Free Soil party in 1848 from his Newburyport pulpit was an important reason for his forced resignation. But Worcester, and especially his new congregation, had voted overwhelmingly Free Soil. Since the shaky Free Soil–Democratic coalition of the last two years was crumbling under the impact of Democratic unity in a presidential year, Higginson found the Free Democracy party of 1852 (it had changed its name from Free Soil to indicate it represented more than just one idea) far more appealing than a year earlier. He was pleased that those coalition opportunists, who in his view had sacrificed principle for victory in the 1851 election and then had accomplished little

8. Ibid.
9. Ibid.

in the state legislature, were now abandoned by their Democratic cohorts. Free Soil failure became apparent when the much-desired liquor law, the only reform legislation passed in 1852, had to be bought by agreeing to a judgeship for the hated Hunker Democrat, Caleb Cushing. Since both the national platforms of the Whigs and Democrats now explicitly supported the fugitive slave law, it had become painfully obvious that the Free Soil party had been overtly snubbed.[10]

In the 1852 election, with coalition admittedly dead even to some of its staunchest supporters, a return to principle seemed a necessary and welcome alternative. Higginson in a sermon, "Elegy without Fiction," attacked the high praise rendered to Webster after his recent death, noting that political success requires "an amount of compromise to which a man of the highest order cannot consent." The candidates and platform of the Free Democracy, however, had both the noble ring as well as the reconciliation to inevitable electoral defeat which had characterized James G. Birney's Liberty party. With New Hampshire Senator John P. Hale as their presidential candidate (he had stepped aside in 1848 to allow Barnburner and "conscience Whig" to unite behind Van Buren), and George W. Julian of Indiana as his running mate, the party presented two men who had proved in Congress their antislavery position. For the top state offices, Horace Mann and Amasa Walker not only represented the old Free Soil view but also were vigorous activists for temperance and educational reform. Mann, nevertheless, appeared more interested in his impending trip to Ohio to assume the presidency of Antioch College than in stumping Massachusetts for Free Democracy. Higginson was pleased that the gubernatorial candidate was a remarkable man and in awe that "such eloquence should flower from that old whiteheaded stick of a body"; he did not expect electoral victory. Here was a campaign enabling him to support men of the highest order.[11]

Higginson helped organize the Worcester Freedom Club, a group committed to the end of fugitive slave laws and to "pro-

10. Dean Burnham, *Presidential Ballots, 1836–1892* (Baltimore, 1955), pp. 212, 213; Bean, "Party Transformation," pp. 128, 114–25.
11. TWH, "Elegy Without Fiction," Oct. 31, 1852, Worcester *Spy*, Nov. 5, 1852; Theodore C. Smith, *The Liberty and Free Soil Party in the Northwest* (New York, 1897), p. 244; TWH to L. Higginson Sept., 1852, Higginson MSS.

tecting the rights of the men of toil." A constitutional convention
to redistrict the state, a strict personal liberty law, shorter hours
for labor, and support for the enforcement of the new temperance
law completed the platform. Sumner and Wilson provided support
in Worcester, and Higginson composed the text of a handbill "To
the Young Men of Worcester County." [12] Said the Free Church
minister:

> The old parties are undeniably languid. . . . There is no
> essential difference in their policy. Both make it their chief
> aim to please the Slave Power. But as it will not do to say
> this in Massachusetts, they have gone back to the details of
> a war that had better be forgotten. . . . The Whigs narrate
> the distinguished deed of a distinguished General; the Demo-
> crats the rather obscure deed of a rather obscure one.
>   Are we Indians, to elect a chief by counting only the scalps
> he has taken?

The third party, asserted Higginson, had an issue. That issue
was "Liberty." Appealing to a northern pride and hope, he struck
a new patriotic note in his own thinking when he said, "We see
but one obstacle in the way of this nation's greatness. That obstacle
is the influence of slavery. When that is removed, other evils will
quickly fall." He declared: "All history has shown that it is the
third parties which have done the work of the world." [13]

To men observing the national election returns, it seemed as if
the Whig party had been annihilated. It carried only four states
for Winfield Scott, who was defeated by the greatest plurality since
popular votes had been recorded. The party decisively lost control
of Congress to the Democrats. While carrying Massachusetts and
gaining a ten-vote majority in the legislature, Whig ranks were
torn. Neither could Free Democracy be jubilant, since its recent
Democratic allies had polled 9,000 votes more than four years
previously, while Free Democracy was 10,000 short of its own
1848 total. Even in Worcester County, a Free Soil stronghold in
1848, Free Democracy received some thousand votes less while

12. *Commonwealth*, Sept. 14, 1852; *Spy*, Sept. 15 Nov. 3, 1852; *To the Young
Men in Worcester County* (Worcester, 1852).
    13. Ibid.

Democrats and Whigs each gained. One consolation for the third party was that Whig factional strife made plausible some future national alliance on an antislavery basis with portions of that party.[14]

Higginson had fulfilled his wish of the previous year that the third party's efforts be brought back to "self-control & consistency from the more fascinating paths of coalition and conquest." Now was the time for moral agitation. To be able to write the handbill for the Freedom Club, and to be enthusiastically called upon to speak at a Free Democracy caucus was more satisfying to him than any partial third-party victory. Most important, he was suddenly caught up in both a dynamic congregation and an exciting city. From the stimulation of a responsive congregation, and recognition from some clergymen, he was quickly losing his feeling of aversion for the pulpit.[15]

Higginson reported that his congregation was composed mostly of "intelligent mechanics, a special breed . . . with keen eyes for machinery & reforms." They reflected the great changes in Worcester. In less than a decade its population ceased to be mostly farmers; by 1850, manufacturing had become the principal business. To the boot and shoe factories and to the agricultural implements factories flocked thousands of new laborers, many of them Irish immigrants. From 1840 to 1850 Worcester's population had more than doubled. During the next five years the rate of increase would be even greater, making a city of 25,000.[16]

Higginson took a distinct liking to rugged Elijah Thayer, a Worcester carpenter, who for comfort would stretch prone on one of Horticultural Hall's wooden benches to hear him preach. Thayer, he noted with pride, was a devout Catholic. Martin Stowell, less conspicuous, also listened. Some of the ladies attending Free Church were adorned in the new bloomer costume of ad-

14. Bean, "Party Transformation," p. 115; Burnham, *Ballots*, pp. 512, 510; William W. Rice, "Worcester County in the Free Soil Movement," in Hurd, *Worcester*, pp. 1658–69.

15. TWH to S. Longfellow, Oct. 25, 1851, Higginson MSS; TWH to George Ellis, Dec. 7, 1852, Ellis MSS; TWH to Parker, Oct. 17, 1852, Higginson-Huntington MSS.

16. TWH to Mary Curzon, Nov. 9, 1852, Higginson MSS; William B. Hersey, *Worcester in 1850* (Worcester, 1898), pp. 64, 27.

vanced women, and even the "respectable" sometimes appeared. The sight of the busy main street filled with farmers in their buckboards coming to view the annual cattle show enhanced Higginson's feeling of being in the very center of American life.[17]

As a minister and a Free Soiler, Higginson received no sympathy from Worcester's two most radical Abolitionists, Stephen and Abby Kelley Foster. They owned a 39-acre farm on the town's outskirts which occasionally served as a haven for fugitive slaves en route to Canada. The Fosters spoke against slavery to a variety of Protestant congregations, many of which forcibly ejected them. Abby, the daughter of an Irish Quaker farmer and a graduate of Oberlin College, adhered to her motto: "Go where least wanted, there you are most needed." Although less zealous than his wife, Stephen had branded the churches as "combinations of thieves, robbers, adulterers, pirates, and murderers, and as such . . . the bulwark of American slavery." The Fosters were Garrisonians (Stephen had provided the type for the first issue of the *Liberator*), but even Garrison worried about the way they ignored the effect produced by their three-hour speeches. He told Abby that it was no longer necessary for Abolitionists to prove themselves courageous and mob-proof.[18]

Higginson was astonished by the support for his clerical radicalism in Worcester. The entire atmosphere of the city and congregation invigorated him. To his journal he revealed:

> I am almost terrified when I consider the sudden expansion
> & inspiration since I came to Worcester. Every thought, look
> & action seems to belong not to me, but to some new being
> which I am. It opens whole new vistas of destiny. . . . All
> my previous life seems to have been merely maturing within

17. TWH to L. Higginson, Aug. 16, 1852, Higginson MSS; TWH journal, Nov. 21, 1852.

18. Daniel MacGilvray, "Stephan Symond Foster," MS, Worcester Historical Society; Robert Riegal, *American Feminists* (Lawrence, 1963), pp. 35–38; Garrison to A. K. Foster, Aug. 12, 1851, Mar. 25, 1851, Foster MSS.

Higginson later admitted there was no organization that deserved the name Underground Railroad: TWH to William H. Siebert, July 24, 1896, Siebert MSS. Also see William Siebert, "Underground Railroad in Massachusetts," *Proceedings of the American Antiquarian Society*, 56 (1935), 25–100; Larry Gara, *The Liberty Line* (Kentucky, 1961), *passim.*

me this flower. . . . I was not aware of my store of accumulated ammunition . . . & I have learned of Napoleon never to spare it. But this is nothing compared with the strange freshness & vigor I feel. May the body only have strength to sustain me.[19]

Higginson had mentioned Napoleon during the Sims case to indicate that like the Emperor he would limit, for effect, the number of his public appearances. Now he transformed Napoleon into a symbol of one possessing a superior and vast store of ammunition. Higginson's exhilaration was in public evidence with the sudden flowering of an ability for extemporaneous speech. He no longer feared that he had passed his "culminating point of radicalism," and that his radical Worcester congregation would leave him far behind.[20]

A visit to New York City and Brooklyn, in November 1852, reflected his confidence. He accepted an invitation to the home of Freeman Hunt, editor of *Hunt's Merchants' Magazine.* Hunt, ever concerned with the level of business morality (he soon published a book titled *Worth and Wealth*), once again asked Higginson to write some articles. His last essay had been partly cut by Hunt because it was too critical of the merchants' role in perpetuating slavery. But now Higginson did not oppose merchants per se and was anxious to restate his views in this influential business magazine.[21]

While in New York he also visited some of the former members of Brook Farm and appeared pleased to find them disappointing. Charles Dana seemed as dogmatic as ever, while George Ripley was fat and uninteresting. Later he traveled to Brooklyn, and though acknowledging that Henry Ward Beecher was charming at home, he seemed far more impressed with the immensity of Beecher's Brooklyn church, with its overflow congregation of about 3,000, than with the minister himself. Granting Beecher's

19. TWH to William Hurlbut, Nov. 26, 1852, Higginson MSS; TWH journal, Nov. 1, 1852.
20. Ibid.; TWH to S. Johnson, Aug. 9, 1852, Higginson MSS.
21. *Worth and Wealth* (New York, 1856); TWH to M. Higginson, Nov. 20, 1852, TWH to L. Higginson, Oct. 12, 1851, Higginson MSS; "Merchants," *Hunt's Merchants' Magazine,* 25 (1851), 403–13.

eloquence of feeling and his intense, simple earnestness, Higginson judged him as having "no grace, no moderation or taste in delivery; and [he said] very little to remember." He considered Beecher far less impressive intellectually than Parker. One would go to hear him often, he believed, only because of the "magnetism of the congregation." The visit to New York confirmed Worcester's superiority: "New York strikes me as being a little less provincial than Boston, & more cockeyish & far more conceited." [22]

Theodore Parker preached in the Worcester Free Church in December 1852 and was afterward entertained in the Higginson home. More secure now than he had been in Newburyport during Parker's last visit, Higginson could grant that the Boston minister "is the most eloquent talker living. . . . Some are more *original*, . . . but he knows everything. . . . [For] popularizing information and thought . . . he has no equal." [23]

President Millard Fillmore's last annual message, the last of any Whig President, reminded Higginson that there were many men not listening to Parker. The President lavishly praised the deceased Webster, certain that he deserved a lasting place in our history. Gratified that sectional strife had been "so happily compromised," he warned the nation against those who mistake change for progress and who were constantly agitating for some change in the organic law, or urging new and untried theories of human rights. Higginson carried a copy of Fillmore's message in his pocket. He found it pleasant to reread it, he noted, "like taking a bit of salt junk to renew one's thirst." [24]

Higginson's happiness in Worcester was suddenly threatened on New Year's Day 1853. His wife, who had been a chronic victim of colds and minor aches and pains, suffered an attack of "violent rheumatism" that was severely crippling. Higginson said that rheumatism was a sort of epidemic at that time. Her rheumatism, a catchall nineteenth-century term for crippling diseases, resembled arthritis or a slowly developing form of muscular dys-

22. TWH to M. Higginson, Nov. 20, 1852, TWH to Hurlbut, Nov. 26, 1852, Higginson MSS.
23. TWH to L. Higginson, Nov. 30, 1852, Higginson MSS.
24. James D. Richardson, ed., *Compilation of the Messages and Papers of the Presidents, 1789–1897*, 5 (Washington, 1907), 163, 166, 181; TWH journal, Dec. 7, 1852.

trophy. Treatment was first given by two homeopaths; then an allopath was summoned who prescribed wrapping her body in wet sheets. By May, pain had subsided in all but her knee joints which remained stiff and, according to Higginson, still made her very dependent on him. During the summer Mary could scarcely walk along the shore at Rockport. Higginson reported: "the rocks are just beyond Mary's walking distance, so she rides part-way in a wheelbarrow," adding, "the bathing (which Mary doesn't do) is delightful." [25] But rather than restrict his activities as a reformer (including overnight trips to other cities), he became more involved.

At the height of Mary's invalidism he attended a meeting early in 1853 in the Worcester Police Court to form a municipal antislavery society. Higginson was elected president; his neighbor, Theophilus Brown, a tailor by trade and country philosopher by inclination, was made one of the directors. Because of the society's efforts, the leading men of the New England Anti-Slavery Society were soon speaking more frequently in Worcester. This was the first time Higginson had ever been so committed to a nonpolitical antislavery organization. Now he had an excellent chance to talk with Phillips, Douglass, and Garrison. With the Massachusetts Free Soil party extinct as a political force and mainly justifying its existence by being a moral force, Higginson came to a greater appreciation of Garrison's faith in moral suasion. On one evening when Frederick Douglass failed to meet a speaking engagement at the Worcester Anti-Slavery Society, Higginson instead read to the audience from the speeches of Wendell Phillips.[26]

Higginson consented to address the Massachusetts Anti-Slavery Society in the last week of January 1853. On the platform of Boston's Melodeon Hall along with Garrison, Edmund Quincy,

25. TWH to L. Higginson, Jan. 4, 30, May 15, 1853, Higginson MSS. I. Bernard Weinstein, Assistant Professor of Medicine at Columbia University (College of Physicians and Surgeons), and Ann Elizabeth Lord, Assistant Professor of Nursing at Simmons College, note that in the absence of modern medical tests one can only speculate among several possible diagnoses. Whether the cause of Mrs. Higginson's invalidism was psychosomatic or physical is even more difficult to determine. They both agree, and manuscript evidence confirms, she would likely have been a difficult person to live with.

26. *Liberator*, Jan. 28, 1853; TWH to M. Higginson, Feb. 18, 1853, Higginson MSS; TWH to (?), April 18, 1853, Misc. MSS, American Antiquarian Society.

Pillsbury, Abby and Stephen Foster, and Lucy Stone, he grandly began his maiden speech: "There had never been a time or place . . . in all history, when the intellect and hearts of young men were so deeply imbued with a moral purpose." Taking a position well known to a Boston abolitionist audience he attributed the success of southern aggression to the selfishness of those who "now sit enthroned in State Street." [27]

Higginson contrasted Boston with Worcester, the "new cradle of liberty," a city which would prevent the American eagle from being devoured by "the obscene and rapacious bird of Southern clime." Moral agitation would keep the American eagle strong: "We fight no longer with bayonets and bullets. We have melted all our lead into types for 'Uncle Tom's Cabin.'" [28]

Before this meeting of nonvoting Garrisonians he defended political Abolitionists, "strong in purpose, though not perhaps conforming to your stand in all their plans, since they, like myself believe in voting." He hopefully concluded: "This anti-slavery movement is doing more than any influence . . . in reconciling sectarian animosities and clearing narrow prejudices away. Men who work side by side for the slave, cannot long condemn each other to everlasting fire for errors in theology. I think we should regard the anti-slavery agitation as a kind of solemn sacrament." [29]

To support a principled Free Democracy and speak from a Garrisonian platform combined two types of moral agitation, Here Higginson channeled his earlier opposition to anarchic individualism and dogmatic sectarianism, religious or secular, into an "ecumenical" antislavery course. Although somewhat sympathetic, he shared little of the anti-institutional attitudes which characterized reformers who had come to prominence in the thirties, nor was he attuned to the perfectionism and utopianism of reform in the forties.

Now he criticized only Boston's bankers (his "Merchants" lecture of February 1851 had assailed all merchants and the whole competitive profit system). In an article printed in the same month of his Boston speech before the Garrisonian society, he defended

27. *Liberator,* Feb. 11, 1853.
28. Ibid.
29. Ibid.

the merchant. "Conscience in the Counting Room," appearing in *Hunt's Merchants' Magazine*, argued that the merchant was no more subject to moral temptation than men in any other professions—a statement contradicting the one he had made two years previously. At a time when southerners increasingly defended slavery as part of the natural order, Higginson held that "trade has its fixed place among the providential laws of the universe. It is part of nature." The excesses of northern materialism had been exaggerated, he argued, for a greater esteem was given to scientific, literary, artistic, professional, and political distinction than in any other nation.[30]

A few months later Freeman Hunt printed another Higginson article: "Moral Results of Slavery." Here, like Harriet Beecher Stowe in *Uncle Tom's Cabin*, he defended the northern way of life. Both praised northern industriousness while criticizing those northern businessmen with no moral conscience about slavery. Higginson, like many northerners, found Mrs. Stowe's book extraordinary. He thought the picture of southern life was wonderful. It reminded him, he said, of his visit to Virginia, which in his memory was increasingly recollected as a visit to an immoral and decadent South. Not only did he believe the novel accurate but he found its literary quality another indication of the aesthetic heights to which a northerner could ascend.[31]

Higginson judged *Uncle Tom's Cabin* "unequalled in American fiction & would still be if the characters were all snow white." It was not the "cheap potion" that Herman Melville brewed for his readers.[32] Melville, in Higginson's view, either wrote mere adventure stories or was critical of the wrong things. Higginson's transcendental outlook made him see Melville as too unsympathetic with reform-minded optimists and too insistent upon the world's ambiguities.

Along with most readers of his era, Higginson remained silent about the racial values Mrs. Stowe propounded in her novel. Such statements as that the African race was "not naturally daring and

30. *Hunt's Merchants' Magazine, 28* (1853), 19–26.

31. *Hunt's Merchants' Magazine, 28* (1853), 706-09; TWH to L. Higginson, 1852, Higginson MSS.

32. TWH to Mary Curzon [1852], TWH to L. Higginson [April, 1851], Higginson MSS.

enterprising, but home-loving and affectionate . . . and naturally patient, timid and unenterprising," were digested without dissent by him and most friends of the Negro. Also not criticized were her words about the Negroes' "gentleness, their lowly docility of heart, their aptitude to repose on a superior mind, and rest on a higher power." He accepted Mrs. Stowe's famous preface in which she refers to the Negro as a member of "an exotic race" with "a character so essentially unlike the hard and dominant Anglo-Saxon race." And he accepted her judgment that the "Negro is naturally more impressible to religious sentiment than the white." Here was a romanticism, shared by North and South, that was at best ambivalent about the effect of environment on Negro temperament. Nor did Higginson balk at Mrs. Stowe's concluding chapter which advocated African colonization. A few years later, he would admit having once believed in the docility of the Negro. But he would never believe that the Negro could exhibit the cold deceit and wanton brutality portrayed by Melville in *Benito Cereno*.[33]

His only antebellum criticism of *Uncle Tom's Cabin* was that Mrs. Stowe had "softened down the actual evil. . . . Her woman's fear shrank from it. . . . She has not described the choice of a mother having to choose of being burnt at stake or have her virgin daughter taken & dropt into the hell of slavery." [34]

In a lecture which he sardonically called the "Romance of Slavery," Higginson claimed that no one can ever have visited the South without being impressed by the medieval aspect of things. He halfheartedly exempted Charleston from this charge, but noted that it too had its armed patrol and curfew, its stocks and whipping post. Branding the South feudal, he cited the medieval chronicler William of Malmesbury, who had noted that the gay and the gallant treated their servants like hordes of swine. "Such a spectacle," charged Higginson, could be "seen nowhere in Christendom but in Russia & America & described nowhere on earth except in the

33. *Uncle Tom's Cabin* (Boston, 1852), *1*, v, 112, 113, 213, 315, 2, 22, 318.

Rollin G. Osterweis, *Romanticism and Nationalism in the Old South* (New Haven, 1949), p. vii, argues that romanticism "differentiated Southern States from the rest of the Union."

34. TWH, "Romance of Slavery or American Feudalism," Oct. 9, 1853, MS, Higginson MSS.

advertisements of runaway slaves in Southern newspapers." Slavery, moreover, lacked the one thing which made feudalism endurable, its cathedrals and its religion. Unlike "picturesque" and "chivalric" feudalism, the South maintained itself "not under the white plume of Navarre, but under the whip of Legree." [35]

Higginson, one of the few Abolitionists concerned with northern labor conditions, also spoke of the danger to northern labor from the South's peculiar institution. Slavery stressed the superiority of a leisure class. It thus stressed the inferiority of the black race as well as the inferiority of any laboring class.[36]

As to the possibility of revolution, Higginson argued: "Gentlemen who expect to be republicans & slaveholders at the same time must invest more money in whips & chains than if they lived in . . . consistent, despotic Russia." Only by force could slavery be maintained, and had the South allowed Negroes a choice, a large portion of the mulatto and quadroon slaves would come to freedom. For Higginson (and Mrs. Stowe) believed that white blood in the veins stimulated a yearning for freedom not found in black Uncle Tom. Higginson's quadroon and mulatto were innately the same people as George and Eliza of *Uncle Tom's Cabin*. And like Mrs. Stowe, Higginson at this time refrained from advocating a slave revolt.[37]

He preferred to remind the North of the inferiority of southern civilization by noting southern illiteracy. Admittedly the South had once produced a line of distinguished statesmen, but now it depended upon compromising northern politicians. Higginson warned that such "Northern tools are apt to slip in the hand that uses them, & cut the wrong way at last. . . . Those who are tools in the hands of one are as ready to be so in another." [38]

As for his own antislavery handiwork, it was absurd to say that moral and political agitation on the subject of slavery would hurt the slave. The solution was to

> let man only *find truth* & tell it, God will find the consequences. For myself, let there be a plain truth to be told . . .

35. Ibid.
36. Ibid.
37. Ibid.
38. Ibid.

& I must speak it though ten thousand Unions be shattered, nay even though harm seem to follow to the very men I would serve—I must still speak it. . . . I have no doubt that angry things have been said . . . but anger & opposition are often the first steps toward conviction. To stop effort because there is resistance would be like refraining from the attack of a city in war-time, because the prospect of attack made the city fortify itself more strongly." [39]

As to earlier southern efforts at abolition, he asked,

What kind of Abolitionism? A moral one? No, no—a pecuniary one. Slavery was growing unprofitable, the land was exhausted. *Abolish slavery* said the humane & the timid. Never, said the selfish & far-seeing. . . . The cotton crop is about to expand enormously—let us breed slaves instead of working them, & we will save our prosperity yet. It was said & done. . . . One piece of shrewdness was added—Virginia statesmen, after pocketing the profit, turned & charged the result on Abolitionism.

Such southern duplicity had to be met with increased moral suasion. "Political action is only valuable in connection with moral power. . . . No tactics can enable an anti-slavery party, for years to come, to control national parties. The moral power is not yet built up firm enough for them to stand on. . . . I may not see how moral power will overthrow slavery, but I know that it must overthrow it." [40] This was as close as Higginson would come to the Garrisonian dependence upon moral agitation. To declare repeatedly to northern audiences that slavery was sinful would prove insufficient, partly because sinfulness was less personal to him than to Garrison, Phillips, or Weld. If political action now appeared futile, other means to attack slavery eventually would have to be found. Meanwhile, moral suasion seemed important.

Since Higginson considered the church's role essential in moral agitation, he castigated the American Unitarian Association after its Worcester convention in late 1853. The meeting, concerned

39. Ibid.
40. Ibid.

with formalizing a Unitarian creed, drafted eight articles, with emphasis on church liturgy. This was like trying to revive a faltering army with a new drill step, Higginson commented. Pronouncing an epitaph for unitarianism he compared it to the falling autumn leaves, "because their beauty and their work is over, and so are the organization and name of Unitarianism. Brave men worked to build it up—my own father among them. It was well done, *then*. Now thirty years have passed—the times are transformed—and the organization appears to me aimless, hopless, powerless, and dead." [41]

Other organizations seemed better suited for the times. Higginsons had been concerned about temperance since Colonial days. In the seventeenth century, the Reverend John Higginson had opposed the sale of liquor, but stressed individual responsibility rather than proscriptive legislation. He had joined Increase Mather in publishing a tract, "Woe to Drunkards," which suggested that habitual drunkards be banished from the colonies. In the 1830's Higginson's father-in-law, Dr. Walter Channing, informed the public that liquor did *not* prevent disease or relieve fatigue. He spearheaded a petition campaign to make illegal the sale of intoxicating liquors in less than 15-gallon amounts (if enacted it would have allowed the rich to stock their cellars and prevented the poor from buying liquor). For a time it appeared that proscriptive legislation either could not be enforced or was too unpopular to remain in Massachusetts law. This was the era when Worcester's John B. Gough, who took the pledge in 1842, presented his personal case of what it was like to be an ex-drunkard. But in the late forties, reformers once again desired proscriptive legislation[42] in their general reaction against laissez-faire, exemplified by the advocacy of congressional prohibition of slavery in the territories. Higginson participated in this movement for legislative action.

He had become a lecturer and agent for the Massachusetts Temperance Committee in Newburyport. When Neal Dow led a successful campaign in Maine for strict temperance legislation, the

41. Hutchison, *Ministers*, pp. 128–36; *Unitarian Autumnal Convention* (Worcester, 1853).

42. *Woe to Drunkards* (1673); John A. Krout, *The Origins of Prohibition* (New York, 1923), pp. 51, 140, 263, 265, 295.

friends of the cause in Massachusetts pressed for a similar law. One enthusiastic supporter from Portland wrote Higginson that seven eighths of poverty, squalor, and suffering were caused by intemperance. The amount of money the citizens of Portland spent for intoxicating drinks, he calculated, was enough "to pay for paving in a substantial way, TWENTY MILES of our streets." [43]

After a law similar to the Maine law was passed in Massachusetts in July 1852, Higginson became a chief propagandist for its enforcement. Martin Stowell was his most important Worcester ally. Stowell earlier had written a temperance tract which attacked the Secret Order of the Sons of Temperance for the immorality of its secrecy and the possession of slaves by some Louisiana members. Like the Maine temperance supporter, Higginson also argued that if the law was faithfully enforced it would suppress the chief source of crime and pauperism. He told a meeting of the Massachusetts Temperance Committee that he believed in the manifest destiny of this law to spread ultimately with the spread of the Anglo-Saxon race. For Higginson, the new law was to be interpreted as a "total abstinence pledge of the whole state." [44]

His efforts to spread the "manifest destiny" of temperance brought him to membership in the committee planning a World Temperance Convention. The meeting convened in New York in May 1853, but temperance was not discussed. For when Higginson moved that Miss Susan B. Anthony be placed on the committee on arrangements, all thoughts about the evils of alcohol disappeared. Miss Anthony, the leading political organizer for woman's rights and a strong advocate of temperance, had already become a symbol of staunch feminism. The prospect of admitting her and her bloomer-costumed cohorts goaded one Connecticut divine to charge that Higginson did not understand the distinction between reform and revolution. Bedlam ensued. Higginson tried speaking again but was shouted down. When the ladies in bloomers (Lucy Stone, Abby Foster, and Susan B. Anthony) endeavored to

43. Newburyport *Advertiser*, Feb. 14, 15, 1848; Newburyport *Union*, Nov. 11, 1850; William Hadley to TWH, Mar. 10, 1852, in *Liberator*, April 9, 1852.

44. Martin Stowell, *An Exposition of the Secret Order of the Sons of Temperance* (West Brookfield, 1848), p. 24; Alice F. Tyler, *Freedom's Ferment* (Minneapolis, 1944), p. 337; "State Temperance Committee Meeting, March 9, 1852," *Liberator*, March 18, 1852.

be heard, the Chair ruled against further consideration of Higginson's motion. Abby Foster was howled at with even more feeling than Higginson.[45]

Finally it seemed obvious that the discussion of temperance might never occur unless the woman's rights question was settled. It appeared certain that this question—even women's right to be on a temperance committee—was not going to be quickly resolved. Insisting that no World Temperance Convention could possibly succeed when half the world was excluded, Higginson demanded that his name be stricken from the committee. Others joined him. A band of about fifty agreed to bolt the meeting and reconvene at a Broadway site to arrange for a *"Whole* World's Temperance Convention." The seceders included Garrison and Phillips, along with Susan B. Anthony, Lucy Stone, Abby Foster, Lucretia Mott, and Elizabeth Cady Stanton. A call for the Whole World's Temperance Convention to meet in New York in early September 1853 was signed by an impressive list of advocates of woman's rights, Free Soil politics, and Garrisonian abolitionism: Horace Greeley, Joshua Giddings, Theodore Parker, and William Henry Channing, as well as Garrison and Phillips. Higginson's name headed the list.[46]

When the meeting convened at Metropolitan Hall, the largest and most ornate auditorium in the country, Higginson was unanimously chosen chairman. He argued that the meeting was no woman's rights convention but rather a temperance convention in which women would not be wronged. After briefly outlining women's contribution to the temperance cause, he pointed to the success of the Massachusetts law, and asked the convention to "aid those fallen ones, . . . the poor wretch who lingers by night in some polluted corner." [47]

But all did not go smoothly. A reformist convention in New York seldom did, especially when Abolitionists and wearers of the bloomer costume were concerned. They were subjected to public ridicule. Hecklers found the balcony of the new Metropoli-

45. Ibid., May 27, 1853; TWH to L. Higginson, May 16, 1853, Higginson MSS.
46. *Liberator*, May 27, Sept. 16, 1853.
47. *Whole World's Temperance Convention, Sept. 12, 13, 1853* (New York, 1853).

tan Hall very convenient. More disconcerting, however, were the acoustical difficulties caused by the hall's size and the noise from workmen completing its construction. A disparity of views from the platform was evident. The Reverend Antoinette Brown, a female Baptist minister, insisted that the degradation of women was inexorably linked to rum-selling and charged that liquor unleashed the innate sin in the soul of man. Horace Greeley, who shouted "Drunkenness is a crime!" argued that it must be punished by law, since the state must be "a guardian of the weak, a protector of the assailed, an admonisher of the beguiled and tempted." Garrison opposed any proscriptive legislation, for he said that men who needed laws to govern them were not fit to be trusted. Another reformer, a Belgian named Victor Hanot, argued that if men were given free land to cultivate they would neither steal nor drink. William Henry Channing charged that the real reasons for drunkenness were that people lacked healthful stimulants, what was needed were libaries, museums, and parks. But in the end most of the convention endorsed increased proscriptive legislation, though a minority of ninety wanted solely "argument, exhortation, and song." All agreed to adjourn by standing and reciting the "Total Abstinence Pledge." [48]

Higginson was satisfied with having "held the reins of three thousand people for two days." W. H. Channing, observing his nephew's efforts, judged him extremely well fitted for public life, and predicted that the eminent position won on the temperance platform would prove Higginson's introduction to a constantly increasing influence. [49]

On the woman's rights platform Higginson would exert a growing influence. He had been among those eighty-nine signatories in 1850 calling for the first national woman's rights convention; along with his name and Mary's appeared those of Emerson, Alcott, Garrison, Mrs. Stanton, and Gerrit Smith. Since antislavery advocates were numerous at this 1850 meeting, it resolved to "bear in our heart of hearts the memory of the trampled womanhood of

48. *Liberator*, Sept. 16, 1853.
49. TWH to Mary [Curzon], Sept. 4, 1853, Higginson MSS; Octavius B. Frothingham, *Memoir of William Henry Channing* (Boston, 1886), p. 8.

the plantation, and omit no effort to raise it to a share in the rights we claim ourselves." Although Higginson had not attended this historic meeting, Worcester had been well represented with Martin Stowell, and Drs. Oramel Martin and Seth Rogers.[50]

Higginson spoke at a woman's rights meeting in 1853; in keeping with a school report he had written in Newburyport, citing that women teachers were paid less than men for the same amount of work, he enumerated the various ways in which women were treated as inferior citizens. He mocked the idea that chivalry moved men to offer chairs to women but gave them few rights. Once one grants that women, like men, have an individual body to be protected, an individual soul to be saved, then, he claimed, the cause of women becomes clear, because the body needs civil rights and the "soul needs . . . something more than visiting, and gardening, and novel-reading, and a crochet needle, and the occasional manufacture of sponge cake." Women must be given a voice in government, for as rational and moral beings given motives for learning, women could know as much or as little as men. But he insisted that domestic tasks, because of her temperament, must remain a woman's work. His article, "Woman and Her Wishes," first printed in June 1853 in *Una*, the new woman's rights periodical, was soon reprinted by the national committee as one of its first woman's rights tracts.[51]

Along with Lucy Stone, Phillips, and Parker, Higginson addressed the Massachusetts Constitutional Convention's committee on voting qualifications in June 1853. He argued that the exodus to California had made women the majority in Massachusetts and that the general silence of this majority should be construed similarly to the silence of the black majority in South Carolina: in neither case was silence synonymous with consent. But when it became apparent that the Massachusetts Constitutional Convention

50. *Liberator*, Oct. 4, 1850; *Proceedings of First National Woman's Rights Convention, Oct. 23, 24, 1850* (Worcester, 1850).

51. J. J. Babson to TWH, Feb. 10, 1851, Higginson MSS; TWH, *Annual Report of the School Committee of the Town of Newburyport* (Newburyport, 1851); *Proceedings of the National Woman's Rights Convention, Oct. 5–7, 1853* (Cleveland, 1854); TWH, "Woman and Her Wishes," *Woman Rights Tract No. 4* (Newburyport, n.d.).

would not give women increased rights, Higginson lectured to the 1853 woman's rights meeting that their advocates used abstract arguments. The public was not yet listening, because facts were not stressed.[52]

Higginson's growing reputation caused Lucy Stone, at a subsequent woman's rights convention, to read aloud his letter challenging woman's rights opponents to explain how it could be unwomanly for women to have increased educational opportunities when it was not considered unwomanly to allow them some education; or how it could be said a woman had a voice in government through her brothers or husband when the worst laws were confessedly those relating to female property? The hecklers answered by laughing, stamping, groaning, beating on teakettles, and hissing. The press responded no less raucously. James Gordon Bennett, editor of the New York daily with the highest circulation, the *Herald* (known as the "Satanic Herald" to reformers), suggested that entertainment was available for anyone willing to attend this convention of "unsexed women." The New York *Express* billed the meeting as "The Bloomer Women, Abolitionists, and Bowery B'hoys in General Convention." The attitude of the Reverend Henry Ward Beecher did not help the cause. In response to Higginson's plea for support, Beecher wrote: "Don't ask me to be solemn about the woman question. I can't do it. . . . I should plead peace principles—dislike of quarrels—everything—anything." [53]

For Higginson, who earnestly wished the improvement of women's status, there was more than an ideological issue. When he suggested that Lucy Stone was worth hearing "not so much for the subject . . . but for the speaker," he revealed a major reason for his interest in woman's rights—his continued fondness for picturesqueness and a certain stylistic quaintness. With a touch of paternalism, he judged Miss Stone to be simple, quiet, and modest, "one of the noblest & gentlest persons whom I know, with her

52. "Remarks of Reverend Thomas Wentworth Higginson," *Constitutional Convention on Qualification of Voters, June 1853* (Boston, 1853); TWH to Lucy Stone, Sept. 15, 1853, in Elizabeth Stanton, Susan B. Anthony, and M. J. Gage, eds., *History of Woman Suffrage, 1* (New York, 1881), 131.

53. Ibid.; *Liberator*, Sept. 16, 1853; Henry Ward Beecher to TWH, May 28, 1853, Higginson-Barney MSS.

homely face & her little Bloomerized-Quakerish person—& her delicious voice; I think the very sweetest voice I have ever heard in public speaking." [54]

To him it was this kind, quiet, and modest woman, weak in voice and in body but still expressive, who best symbolized the cause of underpriviledged women. At a future convention he would assert that there was no place where a man could redeem his manhood better than on the woman's rights platform. The phrase "redeem his manhood," was not mere platform rhetoric for Higginson. Nor was the beard he grew mere fashion. On his thirtieth birthday, in 1853, he conceded that former objects of reverence had become less so with his advancing years, but "this is compensated by an increased enjoyment of those younger than myself, who look to me." Both the younger and the weaker were sought as a "source of pleasure." To his journal he confided an attachment for children and wrote of those feelings that were hidden by his controlled public countenance. "There is really no sentimental school-girl whose demand for being loved is greater or more comprehensive than mine—it makes me uncomfortable for five minutes in the room with a strange child without winning it to love me." [55] Two years before, six-year-old Margaret Channing, a daughter of the unstable marriage between Ellen and Ellery Channing, had stayed five months with the Higginsons. At first he had found her to be a "gay, bright, and noble child" who was not demonstrative. But they soon became fond of each other; they took walks before breakfast and he read stories to her at night. Initially he predicted that Mary, who had not yet had her rheumatism attack, would also enjoy having the child with them, but he soon understood that he was wrong. In a few months Mary had grown tired of "Greta" and was pleased when she returned to her parents.[56]

Mary's poor health and undisguised repugnance for children,

54. TWH to L. Higginson, Jan. 30, 1853, Higginson MSS.

55. Stanton el al., *Woman Suffrage*, 1, 634; TWH to L. Higginson, Nov. 26, 1853, Higginson MSS; TWH journal, 1853.

56. TWH to L. Higginson, Sept. 13, 25, Dec. 19, 1851, Feb. 15, 1852, TWH to [R. W. Emerson], Feb. 23, 1852, Higginson MSS. See also Frederick T. McGill, Jr., *Channing of Concord: A Life of William Ellery Channing II* (New Brunswick, 1967), pp. 136, 137, 143–47, 153.

and her husband's solicitousness, kept the Higginsons childless. Later in life he wrote in his diary that he had been "childless *not of necessity*," thus suggesting that Mary could have borne children. References in his fiction to a closely drawn archetype of her as an "unmarried" invalid, further suggest that the Higginsons very seldom had sexual intercourse.[57]

Mary's physical condition (she had to be carried up and down stairs) might put her in a dependent role but her personality, in part induced by illness, was hardly docile. After she had caught a cold from Higginson, he noted, "Poor child, she always has some ingenious added dislikes beside her regular ones." William Channing Gannett, an acquaintance, would later write: "Mrs. Higginson is very queer, a great invalid from rheumatism, a perfect mistress of the art of abuse, in which she indulges frequently with peculiar zest & enthusiasm, she has a very dry & cutting wit and is very amusing." Gannett thought that Higginson was very tender toward her. With what was meant to be affectionate solicitude, Higginson related to a woman friend: "I throw things down for her to pick up & show her off generally, like some wonderful quadruped, wholly gratis." [58] Mary demanded his attention but seems to have shown none of that reverence which he admittedly craved.

Reform activities in 1853 had given Higginson a feeling of his own strength, but by the end of the year he was despondent:

> All I ask of fate is—Give me one occasion worth bursting the door for—an opportunity to get beyond this boy's play. . . .

57. TWH diary, Dec. 23, 1866. A discussion of the characters in *Malbone* can be found in Chapter 18.

A highly respected source of sex advice, first published in 1870, approved by Andrew D. White, Horace Bushnell, and Noah Porter, suggests continence as the only recourse for a moral man with an invalid wife. The use of contraceptives was deemed immoral, and uncompleted intercourse caused "premature loss of virility and serious injury to the nervous system." George H. Napheys, *The Transmission of Life: Counsels on the Nature of the Masculine Function* (Philadelphia, 1884), pp. 191–92. Steven Marcus notes the nineteenth-century view that the desire for sexual gratification was largely a male desire and could be overcome by a strong-willed man. *The Other Victorians* (New York, 1966), pp. 23, 21. See also Norman E. Himes, *Medical History of Contraception* (New York, 1963), pp. 201, 209–85.

58. TWH to L. Higginson, May 15, July 17, 1853, Higginson MSS; William Channing Gannett diary, Aug. 8, 1860, Gannett MSS, University of Rochester.

Till then my life, frittered away in little cares and efforts for the *sick*, sad and sinful is not worth chronicling. . . . I never remember to have rested my cares on any earthly being—all with whom I have ever associated have rested theirs on me.[59]

The new year would provide Higginson with one important occasion for door bursting.

59. Quoted in M. T. Higginson, *Higginson*, p. 124.

10

Reform or Revolution

Higginson wrote to his mother in February 1854 that he was gradually waking up to the Kansas-Nebraska Bill and expected to preach about it. After he spoke, the *Liberator* found it fitting to reprint his sermon, which discussed agitation, Stephen Douglas' presidential ambitions, and the impact of the bill's passage. It was ironic, noted Higginson, that "this nation forgives no one for the agitation of slavery, except the Slaveholders themselves. Fortunately they always do it." Unlike other critics he denied that Douglas was motivated by political ambition. Everybody should recall, said Higginson, that presidential candidates have never been chosen from politically prominent figures: "they must either be military heroes or persons of whom men ask, 'Who is he?'" Not only were Whigs culpable because they had begun the process of compromising on slavery, but Douglas and the Democrats were partly correct to assert that the Kansas–Nebraska Bill was based on the precedent of previous compromises. The Douglas bill would pass, Higginson predicted, "and it will be a good thing that it does for it will finally teach men who compromised in 1850 that you cannot compromise one day and then on the next assert freedom. . . . This is not a new Compromise to save the Union, it is the repeal of the old one, which was made to save it before. . . . If this nation attaches no more importance to its compromises than it does to its principles, what have we left to trust to?" The only certain way to halt this continual backsliding was to end the strange infatuation with compromise. "Never, never, never will there be peace in this nation, until Slavery be destroyed." For the present he prescribed a homoeopathic treatment: to meet agitation with more agitation until a healthy state was attained.[1]

1. TWH to L. Higginson, Feb. 3, 1854, Higginson MSS; *Liberator*, Feb. 17, 1854.

While men in and out of Congress argued about the relevance of the principle and precedent of the Compromise of 1850 for evaluating the Kansas-Nebraska Bill, three southerners were traveling through Massachusetts searching for three fugitive slaves. Colonel Charles T. Suttle of Alexandria, Virginia, soon learned that his "property" was being employed in a Boston tailor shop. Suttle gave a description to the United States Marshal and the Massachusetts District Attorney of a six-foot, well-built, thirty-year-old Negro, who had a large scar on his cheek, and a hand distorted by a projecting bone from an improperly healed break.[2]

Near midnight, Wednesday, May 24, Deputy Marshal Asa O. Butman discovered the Negro outside a Boston jewelry shop. The deputy quickly summoned help from among the men in Peter Bent Brigham's saloon. Anthony Burns was seized and spirited to the Court House—the first fugitive arrested in Boston since Thomas Sims.[3]

Higginson received a note by private messenger from Samuel May, Jr., telling of Burns' capture and suggesting that Worcester men be recruited for a public meeting at Faneuil Hall on Friday evening. May, urged that the country back the city, and if necessary lead it. He hoped that the ill-health of Higginson's wife would not prevent his hastening to Boston.[4]

May's plea was heeded. Higginson left home on Friday morning, May 26; before boarding a train he met with Martin Stowell, the leader of the Syracuse fugitive slave rescue in 1851, urging him to bring some Worcester men to Boston in the early evening. Arriving in Boston before noon, Higginson went directly to a secret meeting of the Vigilance Committee. Wrath, despair, and anger were evident among the sixty men assembled, but no plan of action. When a lookout announced that Colonel Suttle was going to pass along the street with his bodyguard of Harvard southerners, it was proposed that the committee adjourn to point the finger of scorn at the enemy. Most men moved outside, but Higginson and others interested in a different kind of activity stayed behind. An executive

2. Dana journal, May 25, 1854, Dana MSS; Charles F. Stevens, *Anthony Burns* (Boston, 1856); Samuel Shapiro, "The Rendition of Anthony Burns," *Journal of Negro History, 44* (1959), 35.

3. *Spy*, May 26, 1854; *Liberator*, June 2, 1854.

4. Samuel J. May, Jr. to TWH, May 25, 1854, Higginson-Burns MSS.

committee was formed, composed of Higginson, Parker, Phillips, Howe, Captain Austin Bearse, and William Kemp. At Higginson's suggestion Martin Stowell's name was added. These men debated whether to attempt to free Burns forcibly that evening. Howe wanted a later rescue effort in New York. Most of the group were unwilling, now or later, to join a forcible rescue. Finally there was agreement to hold further discussion in a Faneuil Hall anteroom just prior to the great meeting. Late in the afternoon, Higginson wrote to his anxious wife: "Dearest, I don't think anything will be done tonight, but tomorrow if at all. The prospects seem rather brighter than before, & *there are better leaders than I.*" Posting the letter, he proceeded to the railroad station to meet the six o'clock train from Worcester. He carried his large black umbrella on his arm, since it appeared that it might rain before the evening was over.[5]

The Worcester train with Stowell on board arrived on time, but only fifty men were with him. Upon learning about the situation in Boston, Stowell suggested that an effort to free Burns should begin while the Faneuil Hall meeting was in session and attention not on the Court House. Higginson, finding a compatriot eager for action, enthusiastically accepted this plan and became the project's leader. With many policemen at the meeting and the Court House guard not due to be reinforced until 10:30 P.M., Stowell and Higginson went into action. Stowell hurried away to recruit more men. Higginson, using the pseudonym Higgins, made an important purchase at Gardener & Thayer, "Importers & Dealers in Foreign & Domestic Hardware & Cutlery." Receiving a 5 per cent discount for cash, he bought a dozen handaxes at one dollar each. He deposited them at the law office of Henry Bowditch, across the street from the Court House, and proceeded to the Vigilance Committee meeting. What he saw there both pleased and disturbed him. Huge crowds were pouring through the Faneuil Hall anteroom into the auditorium, the small room proving completely inadequate as a meeting place for the executive committee. Amidst the noise and excitement, Hig-

5. *Yesterdays,* pp. 147, 148, 159; Samuel G. Howe to Theodore Parker, May 1854, in *Letters and Journals of Samuel Gridley Howe,* ed. Laura Richards, *2* (Boston, 1900), 268–69; "Burns Narrative," MS, Higginson-Burns MSS; TWH to M. Higginson, May 26, 1854, Higginson MSS.

ginson and Stowell were able to get a hasty approval of the rescue plan from Howe and Parker—an approval which the latter in fact misunderstood. Phillips, already pushing toward the speaker's platform, could not be seen or reached; Captain Bearse, on the other hand opposed the expedition. Only Kemp among the executive committee, clearly consented. Lewis Hayden, the leader of the Shadrach rescue, promised to provide ten Negroes to lead the assault along with the men that Kemp, Stowell, and Higginson could muster. With this as a nucleus, further support was anticipated by alerting the crowd at the meeting.[6]

Much was expected from those in Faneuil Hall, but the small attacking band also had reason to believe in its own effectiveness. Not only were Stowell and Hayden experienced at such rescue work, but John C. Cluer, a noted activist, was part of the band. Cluer, described by a friend as an earnest, sarcastic Scotsman, had been a Chartist and had come to America in 1845. He had become involved in the ten-hour labor movement, then in temperance, and finally served as an agent for the Massachusetts Anti-Slavery Society. Only recently he had been released from a New York jail after having been arrested for bigamy. During the Sims affair Cluer and Kemp had risen at three in the morning to hiss while the fugitive was marched to the wharf for extradition. Like Higginson, Cluer had tired of speeches, hisses, and umbrella waving, and was ready for action. At Cluer's side was the Boston machinist Ira Steward, in ten years to be the organizer of the Grand Eight-Hour League of Massachusetts and a leader of the Machinists' Union.[7]

While Higginson strolled around the Court House waiting for Stowell and the other leaders to appear at the head of columns of Faneuil Hall sympathizers, Parker and Phillips were firing antislavery rhetoric from the Faneuil Hall platform. The Boston minister began by addressing the overflow crowd as "Fellow-subjects

6. "Burns Narrative"; Receipt, May 26, 1854, Higginson MSS; *Spy*, Jan. 12, 1855; TWH to S. J. May, Jr., Oct. 11, 1855, Higginson-Burns MSS. Hayden owned a clothing and variety store in west Boston and was in close contact with the black community. *Liberator*, Dec. 21, 1855.

7. N. Ware, *Worker*, pp. 134–40; *Commonwealth*, June 3, 1854; Vincent Y. Bowditch, *Life and Correspondence of Henry Ingersoll Bowditch*, 1 (Boston, 1902), 218; Selig Perlman, *A History of Trade Unionism in the United States* (New York, 1922), p. 146.

of Virginia," to which it responded with cries of "No" and "Never." "Yes," insisted Parker. "We are the *vassals* of Virginia. It reaches its arm over the graves of our mothers, and it kidnaps men in the city of the Puritans, over the graves of Samuel Adams and John Hancock. . . . Webster was right. There is no North. . . . The South goes clear up to the Canada line." More cries of "No" and more provocation by Parker brought the crowd close to hysteria. Shouts of "Let's free the slave now" grew louder. The audience now seemed ready to attack the Court House. Instead of climaxing his speech with a call to arms, however, Parker argued that the frenzied crowd was not yet unanimous in its desire to free Burns forcibly. It took the commanding voice of Wendell Phillips to bring order to the scene Parker had created. Phillips linked the Douglas bill to the Burns capture by shouting: "Nebraska I call knocking a man down, and this is spitting in his face after he is down . . . but tomorrow morning . . . the children of Adams and Hancock may prove that they are not bastards." Neither Parker nor Phillips advocated immediate action. But when the man who had been designated by Higginson to alert the crowd shouted that hordes of "Negroes were already storming the Court House and attempting a rescue!" Phillips saw his audience rush to the exits. Down the steps, out of Faneuil Hall raced hundreds of excited men.[8]

Directly outside the Court House, the sounds of the approaching crowd became the signal for attack. Hayden and Stowell clutched their pistols. The dozen new axes were in the hands of men ready to swing them into action. The assault began even when it became evident that the first breathless figures from Faneuil Hall were merely spectators rather than sympathetic members of the Vigilance Committee. Stowell reported to Higginson that his men held a wooden beam and were preparing to ram the southwest door which led to the second-floor courtroom where Burns was held. Higginson excitedly put down his umbrella and along with ten others seized the fourteen-foot beam. Two men pounded on the door with their axes. Darkness was added to the noise and confusion when one Negro confederate shinnied up a lamppost and extin-

8. *Commonwealth*, May 27, 1854; TWH to S. J. May, Jr., Oct. 11, 1855, Higginson-Burns MSS.

guished the light. Other men were throwing bricks at the Court House windows as the police began arriving to confront a crowd of five hundred. The battering-ram did its work. The door swung open momentarily and Higginson and a black companion stormed in. They were immediately pummeled with clubs and gashed by cutlasses wielded by the Court House guards, and appeared trapped inside. The others hesitated. "You cowards, will you desert us now?" bellowed the beleaguered minister. A shot from outside answered him, and one of the guards near him fell bleeding, fatally wounded by a bullet in the stomach. Now Higginson and his accomplice could flee from the Court House.[9]

Outside, the police sprang to action. They seized the man who had extinguished the streetlight, another with an ax in his hand, and still another who was clutching a brick. Cluer was arrested while attempting to stir the crowd to a mass attack on the building by shouting: "the Court House belongs to the citizens of Boston." Stowell was also arrested, but Lewis Hayden and Higginson slipped away. At 10 P.M., a half hour after the attack, Higginson wrote to his wife: "There has been an attempt at rescue, & failed. I am not hurt, except a scratch on the face which will probably prevent me from doing anything more about it, lest I be recognized. But I shall not come home till Monday morn." [10]

"I knew his ardor and courage," Dana recorded in his journal, "but I hardly expected a married man, a clergyman, and a man of education to lead the mob." [11] Few others had expected it either.

When informed that the guard, James Batchelder, had been killed during the raid, Higginson reconsidered his plan to remain in Boston until Monday. The United States Marshal increased the guard at the Court House by summoning two companies of federal troops. From President Pierce came a telegram to the Marshal: "Your conduct is approved. The Law must be executed." With a man murdered, arrests increased. By Saturday afternoon, Higginson was back in the relative safety of Worcester. That evening, he ap-

9. "Burns Narrative", Drew memo, April 4, 1877, MS, Thomas Drew to TWH, April 16, 1888, Higginson-Burns MSS; *Liberator*, June 2, 1854; *Commonwealth*, June 3, 1854; Stevens, *Burns*, pp. 42, 43.

10. *Commonwealth*, June 7, 1855; TWH to M. Higginson, May 26, 1854, Higginson-Burns MSS.

11. Dana journal, May 27, 1854, Dana MSS.

peared at an enthusiastic meeting of about a thousand men, his gashed chin bandaged. Through crowds of cheering townsmen, Higginson was escorted to the platform to plead for funds for the family and for the legal defense of the jailed Martin Stowell. Joining him in this appeal were Stephen Foster, Dr. Oramel Martin (a key figure in the Free Church), and Thomas Drew, editor of the Worcester *Spy* and once with Elihu Burritt co-publisher of a pacifist newspaper. In the afternoon, a special train had carried about a thousand Worcester men to Boston where they marched in protest around the heavily guarded Court House. On Sunday morning Theodore Parker spoke to a large audience at the Melodeon. For the dead Batchelder, Parker's epitaph read: "He was a volunteer in this service. He liked the business of enslaving a man, and has gone to render an account to God for his gratuitous work." [12]

Both Mary and Higginson's mother appeared as unconcerned as Parker about the moral issue connected with killing a defender of slavery. They worried more about whether an attempt would be made to arrest Higginson, and whether his "ferocious friends" in Worcester would forcibly try to prevent it. His brother Stephen suggested that a change of costume might be the means of averting trouble. Higginson tried to calm them by promising not to resist his imminent arrest. And as for being jailed:

> How little this seems compared with what men have to bear in France & Russia & nay in Virginia. I think that months & years in jail would be well spent as a protest against slavery. . . The men now arrested are obscure men; *their* sufferings will be of comparatively little service; but I have a name, a profession, & the personal position which make my bonds a lesson & a stimulus to the whole country. What better things could I do for liberty? What so good? [13]

12. Watson Freeman to President Pierce, May 27, 1854, President Pierce to Watson Freeman, May 27, 1854, in Stevens, *Burns*, p. 273; TWH to M. Higginson, May 26, 1854, Higginson-Burns MSS; *Spy*, May 29, 30, 1854; TWH to L. Higginson, May 29, 31, 1854, Higginson-Burns MSS; Theodore Parker, *The Lesson of the Day, May 28, 1854* (Boston, 1854).

13. William I. Bowditch to TWH, May 30, 1854, L. Higginson to TWH, June 1, 1854, Stephen Higginson to TWH, June 4, 1854, Higginson-Burns MSS.

One of those obscure men, Martin Stowell, wrote him from a Boston jail cell, more concerned about his trial than his symbolic role. Stowell knew he had been unjustly accused of wielding an ax (having in fact used a pistol) and insisted that he was imprisoned "for no other offence than loving your neighbor as yourself, and doing as you would be done by." Higginson declined Stowell's invitation to visit the jail. It is doubtful that he could have served the prisoner as well as Thomas Drew. This former pacifist, when visiting Stowell, smuggled out of the jail the pistol he had loaned the prisoner by placing it between the covers of a hollowed-out Bible.[14]

While the legal skills of Richard Henry Dana, Jr., and Charles Ellis (the latter had calmed the crowd after Higginson's speech during the Sims affair) were employed on Burns' behalf, official preparations were made for the fugitive's return. The Adjutant General of the Army had been ordered to Boston to direct operations, troops were dispatched from Rhode Island and New Hampshire, and soldiers as far away as New York City were kept under arms. Two corps of Marines, a detachment of National Lancers, a company of army artillery, joined state and local forces to provide a 2,000-man escort for Anthony Burns. The marchers included the staff for the six-pound cannon that had been summoned from Charlestown to point at the hostile crowd. The procession's route was lined by 50,000 people, many hissing and groaning. And on a few occasions, when the police line weakened, the Lancers rode into the crowd to keep it back.[15]

Higginson, who understood that Burns was lost when the Court House attack had failed, was not in Boston to view this martial epitaph to his efforts. But Howe, who was there, still wished Burns either to try to escape or then and there to strike "a knife into his own heart," rather than allow himself to be returned to slavery. At 3:20 P.M. the steamer *John Taylor* took Burns through the harbor and delivered him to the revenue cutter *Morris*.[16] A Boston merchant reported: "People in State Street were more moved . . .

---

14. Martin Stowell to TWH, June 1, 7, 1854, Thomas Drew to TWH, April 16, 1888, M. Stowell to T. Drew, June 4, 1854, Higginson-Burns MSS.

15. Shapiro, "Burns," 44, 45; *Liberator*, June 9, 1854.

16. S. G. Howe to Laura Richards, June 18, 1854, in Richards, *Howe*, 2, 270–71; *Commonwealth*, June 3, 1854.

than I ever saw them before about anything." In Worcester, the church bells sounded with funeral solemnity, many stores closed, their windows draped in black crepe. Said Parker: "Daniel Webster lies buried in Marshfield, but his dead hand put the chain on Anthony Burns. Last winter it was proposed to build him a monument. He needs it not. . . . Daniel Webster had his monument last Friday." [17]

Two days after the extradition, Higginson appeared in the Free Church pulpit for the first time since the abortive rescue attempt. The cut on his chin had healed, but a scar remained where the blade of the cutlass had struck. His words were as dramatic as his appearance.[18] He chose a text, equal to his own wrath, Jeremiah XV, 12: "Shall iron break the northern iron and the steel?" A fire, like that for the judging Lord, was kindled under Higginson's anger. Conceding that a spark of old New England heroism and enthusiasm still glimmered, he questioned whether freedom still lived. But at least, said he, freedom did not die without a struggle, and thousands had witnessed its burial. "Words are nothing—we have been surfeited with words for twenty years. I am thankful that this time there was action also. . . . Our souls and bodies are both God's and resistance to tyrants is obedience to Him . . . else we miss our proper manly life on earth." He explained the need for manly action:

> If men array brute force against Freedom—pistols, clubs, drilled soldiers, and stone walls—then the body also has a part to do in resistance, . . . and calm irresistible force, in a good cause, becomes sublime. For myself, . . . I can only make life worth living for, by becoming a revolutionist.
>
> The strokes on the door of the Court House that night . . . went echoing from town to town, from Boston to New Orleans, like the first drum beat of the Revolution—and each reverberating throb was a blow upon the door of every Slave-prison of this guilty Republic.

17. Stephen Higginson to TWH, June 4, 1854, Higginson-Burns MSS; *Spy*, June 4, 1854; Theodore Parker, *The Crime Against Humanity*, June 4, 1854 (Boston, 1854).

18. TWH, *Massachusetts in Mourning* (Boston, 1854).

Claiming that even if only 200 guards had been summoned instead of 2,000 the attack would have been worth a dozen lives, Higginson played upon Massachusetts chauvinism and the popularity of Know Nothing anti-Irish sentiment: "Lower, Massachusetts, lower, kneel still lower! . . . Down in the dust Citizen Soldiery! before the Irish Marines."

With Independence Day a month away, Higginson intoned: "I have lost the dream that ours is a land of peace and order. I have looked through our 'Fourth of July' and seen its hollowness; and I advise you to . . . revoke . . . the appropriation for its celebration . . . and only toll the bells in all the churches, and hang the streets in black from end to end."

Though so recently on the platform of the Garrisonian non-resistors and so recently a Free Soiler, he now said:

> The way to promote Free Soil is to have your own soil free.
> . . . Leave legal quibbles to lawyers, and parties to politicians,
> and plant yourselves on the simple truth that God never made
> a Slave, and that man shall neither make one nor take one
> here! . . . No longer conceal Fugitives and help them on,
> but show them and defend them. Let the Underground Rail-
> road stop here! . . . *Hear O Richmond! and give ear O Caro-*
> *line! henceforth Worcester is Canada to the Slave!*

Praising physical force again, he mixed his attack on slavery with an attack on materialism: "Life is something more than dress and show; . . . there is some nobler aim in existence than a good bargain, and a fast horse, and an oyster supper."

Needed was braveness without ignorance, the moral courage of the Puritans without their superstition, "that we may show the world that a community may be educated in brain without being cowardly in body; and that a people without a standing army may yet rise as one man, when Freedom needs defenders."

He ended with this invocation: "May God help us to redeem this oppressed and bleeding state, and to bring this people back to the simple love of Liberty, without which it must die amidst its luxuries, like the sad nations of the older worlds."

Disregarding his mother's fear that the publication of this "Massachusetts in Mourning" sermon would make him more conspicuous, he allowed it to be printed. At home, "nice tunes & plenty of laughter" filled the time before his inevitable arrest; he proposed that a daguerreotype be made of Mary and titled "Mrs. H. the Martyr's Wife." [19]

Six days after his sermon, Higginson telegraphed his mother: "Arrested for riot only." He was relieved that a murder charge was not part of the expected indictment. Just a few days previously he had admitted he was not feeling very well after the troubles in Boston. The sensation of being rather tired out, and sick from overwork, followed his intense activity. Taken to Boston by a policeman who pleased Higginson by his urbanity and politeness, the arrested minister was met at the railroad station by lawyer Dana. Dana has his head bandaged from the beating received during the Burns procession, when a blackjack-carrying hoodlum had knocked him unconscious. [20]

Higginson was accused of having assembled "with 500 or more persons . . . to disturb the peace, . . . riotously beset and attack the Court House, . . . break the glass in the windows, . . . force in and break open one of the doors of said Court House, . . . fire and discharge sundry fire-arms, . . . and . . . utter loud outcries and hurrahs." [21]

The eminent William I. Bowditch, and Higginson's father-in-law posted a $3,000 bail bond for his release. Mary, waiting for word of her husband's fate, received a telegram: "All right, return today." It was at first expected that his trial would begin in July, but the legal dockets in Boston courts were so filled with pending cases resulting from violations of the temperance law that it was delayed until April 1855. [22]

During that long interval Higginson spent much time defending the assault upon the Court House. He carefully compiled the reactions of some of the clerical brethren with whom he had had most

19. L. Higginson to TWH, June 9, 1854, TWH to L. Higginson, June 10, 1854, Higginson-Burns MSS.

20. TWH to L. Higginson, June 10, 1854, TWH to Mary [Curzon], June 7, 1854, Higginson MSS; *Commonwealth*, June 13, 1854.

21. *Spy*, June 13, 1854.

22. Ibid., June 3, July 17, 1854; *Commonwealth*, June 15, 1854; TWH to M. Higginson, June 10, 1854, Higginson-Burns MSS.

rapport. Without directly mentioning Higginson, Clarke, in a sermon, called for a peaceful war against the fugitive slave law and denounced violence or bloodshed. Samuel Johnson attacked slavery, insisting that the old party lines must be dropped, but added: "God forbid I should counsel armed resistance. . . . Bayonets are but ill proselytizers for . . . freedom." John Weiss in a sermon titled "Legal Anarchy" justified disobedience to the law if one experienced an overpowering sense of individual duty, but also insisted that no man had a right to kill another. Only Parker talked differently. Said he: "Edward Greeley Loring, . . . Fugitive Slave Bill Commissioner of the United States, . . . I charge you with the death of that man who was killed. . . . He was your fellow servant in kidnapping." [23]

Criticism by Garrisonian Abolitionists for having been injudicious hurt Higginson most, for he believed he deserved better from them. Higginson argued that he was criticized only because he had failed to rescue Burns. Too many refused to understand (and it still has not been recognized) that his effort was not an impetuous accident but the result of deliberate calculation, with careful selection of experienced confederates. "If no attempt had been made," Higginson noted, "we should have had the ineffable disgrace of seeing Burns marched down State Street under a corporal's guard only, amidst a crowd of irresolute semi-abolitionists, hooting, groaning, and never striking a blow." Perhaps it was just as well that the attempt had failed, for the shame of seeing this man returned to slavery appeared to have made a deep impression on public opinion and promised a de facto nullification of the fugitive slave law.[24] The Burns effort, Higginson declared, was the greatest step in antislavery that Massachusetts had ever taken; and he was ready to do his share over again. He summarized what had often troubled him about reformers, particularly Abolitionist reformers:

23. James F. Clarke, *Christian Politics*, June 4, 1854 (Boston, 1854); Samuel Johnson, *The Crisis of Freedom*, June 11, 1854 (Boston, 1854); John Weiss, *Legal Anarchy*, June 4, 1854 (Boston, 1854); Parker, *Lesson of the Day*.

24. S. J. May, Jr. to TWH, May 30, 1854, Higginson-Burns MSS; TWH to S. J. May, Jr. [June 1854], Misc. MSS, American Antiquarian Society; TWH to Garrison, June 28, 1854, Whitney-Benjamin MSS; TWH to Mary Curzon, June 7, 1854, Higginson MS; TWH to Garrison, Aug. 21, 1855, in *Liberator*, Aug. 24, 1855.

What paralyzes us in a slave case . . . is the timidity of the majority, the irresolution of the rest, and the want of organization of all. We have not yet learned to trust each other and ourselves; and each thinks the other plans ill-advised and injudicious. But men must risk something; not only risk danger, but even failure and disapprobation of critics. . . . A few more such defeats as that before the Court House, and we shall have a victory.[25]

Because of the Burns affair Henry Thoreau could not remain in solitude—there was no serenity even near secluded ponds and the beauty of nature. Speaking at an antislavery convention in July he said: "The remembrance of my country spoils my walk. My thoughts are murder to the State, and involuntarily go plotting against her." Higginson was more specific. To a meeting in August commemorating West Indian slave emancipation, he declared: "I hate the Fugitive Slave Law not because it is unconstitutional . . . but because it is *infernal*." He still saw some hope in political action, but now he stressed that nothing was clearer than that political action must tend to the building up of a northern union, a northern democracy. Urging his audience to take part in politics, he said: "I can a little while longer—I do not know how long . . . [and even I cannot promise to take] a very hearty part." He warned against expecting much from antislavery politicians like Senator Charles Sumner, for though "reforms can be carried by votes—by political action, I tell you the conflict with Slavery is not a reform[,] it is Revolution." [26]

Henry Bowditch sent Higginson assurances that a Boston secret society had just been organized and had pledged "to use all proper means for rendering difficult or impossible the coming or remaining of the Manhunter among us." Blackjacks had been purchased, and at one meeting a member played at being the slave catcher and the others overwhelmed and manacled him.[27] But in Worcester, in October 1854, the real test came.

25. Ibid.

26. "Slavery in Massachusetts," *Walden and Other Writings*, ed. Brooks Atkinson (New York, 1937), pp. 677–79; *Liberator*, Aug. 11, 1854.

27. William I. Bowditch to TWH, Aug. 10, 1854, Higginson-Burns MSS; V. Y. Bowditch, *H. I. Bowditch*, 1, 96.

Deputy Marshal Asa O. Butman, the man who had arrested Anthony Burns, arrived in town to search for another fugitive slave. Worcester radicals had been increasingly forced back to the realization that they could do little that was immediately tangible for abolition. From condemning slavery where it existed, to trying to prevent its spread into the territories, to endeavoring to prevent the spread of its power into Massachusetts, men like Higginson had been finally forced to say: "I am not responsible for the evils of the whole world, but I am responsible for what happens beside my own doorstep." [28] Butman's presence in Worcester portended a test of Higginson's declaration that Worcester was Canada to the slave.

Recognizing Butman on the morning after his arrival, the Worcester Vigilance Committee quickly printed and distributed handbills to Negroes, warning of his presence. The mayor prohibited his policemen from aiding the marshal. On Sunday, October 29, about sixty men kept an all-night vigil outside American House, Butman's hotel. Over and over again they chanted, "Bring out the kidnaper." Getting no response, they stoned the building. Some of the men on watch occasionally rang the doorbell and demanded to speak to Butman. The deputy marshal finally emerged, but with a gun in his hand. He warned that he would not be intimidated. At 3 A.M., a warrant was issued for Butman's arrest for carrying a concealed weapon. He spent the rest of the night in the city jail.[29]

On Monday morning Worcester's Court House overflowed with people eager to witness the trial of the deputy marshal. The aroused spectators punctuated the proceedings with taunts. When the case was temporarily adjourned, a group of Negroes reached the room in which Butman was being held and began beating him; but soon City Marshal Lovell Baker rescued him and arrested the man who had landed the hardest blows.[30]

By now the crowds outside the Court House were growing more excited—some called for lynching, others for tarring and feathering the slave catcher. When the Negro who had been arrested and jailed for striking Butman forced a window open and jumped ten

28. TWH, *Address to the Voters, 1850.*
29. *Spy,* Nov. 31, 1854. (The same details were carried in the conservative Worcester *Transcript,* Nov. 30, 1854.)
30. Ibid.

feet to safety, the crowd strained to go into action. At this point
Judge George F. Hoar appeared on the Court House steps appealing for law and order. Above the noise he argued that even in
Charleston, "low and degraded" as the citizens were, such harm as
the Worcester crowd threatened, would not occur. But the citizenry remained agitated.[31]

With the situation so incendiary, and with the mayor's continued
reluctance to supply Butman with police protection, the only
course appeared to be to remove the prisoner from Worcester before the crowd stormed the Court House. Hoar soon emerged from
the building, holding Butman's arm, and the crowd on the Court
House steps momentarily gave way. But as soon as the two men
reached the sidewalk it started to close in. At this juncture Higginson, Stowell, and Foster, along with Joseph Howland and Thomas
Drew, offered their protection for Anthony Burns' captor. Higginson, ready to display leadership and courage, took Butman's other
arm, and with Hoar moved the prisoner through the hooting
crowd. Soon, noted one observer, Higginson had to beat back
would-be assailants "with the same strong hand that burst the door
of Anthony Burns." Some policemen joined the guard as the crowd,
now numbering about six hundred, appeared ready to try to tear
Butman limb from limb. For most of the route to the railroad station it was kept at bay, but at intervals eggs and tobacco juice
splattered upon the head and face of the deputy marshal. Howland,
ideologically a nonresistor, kept shouting to the crowd: "Don't hurt
him, mean as he is! Don't kill him, mean though he be!" Thomas
Drew, though also concerned about keeping the crowd away,
would occasionally give a vigorous kick to Butman before returning to the role of bodyguard. At one point a man described as a
powerful Negro succeeded in "planting a tremendous blow behind
Butman's left ear, which made him stagger like a drunken man."
Another struggle for possession of the prisoner ensued. Foster implored the crowd: "Boys don't kill him;—don't strike him—but
abuse him as much as you can." Having many times been the target
of an anti-Abolitionist mob, he later noted: "Scenes of excitement
and peril are not new to me, but in all my past experiences I have
seen nothing like this. . . . I have often been myself the object of

31. Ibid.

popular rage, . . . but never did I feel half the anxiety for my own life which I felt for his, or made half the effort to save it." [32]

By the time the shouting mob reached the railroad station, its size had increased to a thousand. Now it called for the chance to ride Butman out of town on a rail. Allegedly for his own protection, the prisoner, while waiting the arrival of the train to Boston, was separated from the crowd by being locked in the depot privy. It was learned, however, that the train was not due into Worcester for some time. The privy door was opened, exposing Butman to more verbal and physical abuse. Finally he was pulled into a carriage with Higginson alongside him, and was sent to Boston. Later, Higginson assured Theodore Parker that he would have enjoyed Higginson's task—preaching a brief sermon to Butman after his rescue from the Worcester mob. With reason, he insisted that his efforts had saved the deputy marshal's life, "unless he has died of fright since, I never saw a man so near it." Parker praised Higginson's noble conduct and concluded that the whole affair was admirably done. Stephen Foster, who until now had had little contact with Higginson because of basic political and economic differences, noted: "He is unquestionably a man of great courage, but of his judgment I cannot speak with confidence. I hope for a more intimate acquaintance with him soon." [33]

Higginson preferred to recall the Abolitionists' efforts to protect Butman, rather than to defend the mob, as did the Worcester *Spy* which said:

> Our citizens bespattered with eggs, mud and tobacco quids, punched with umbrellas, kicked *a postiore*, rolled into the gutter and pummelled Asa O. Butman, the notorious kidnapper.
>
> The attack upon him was a natural expression of popular disgust towards the base, beastly, and brutal vocation; it was an honorable vindication of the high-tone sentiment of our community, against slave-holders and their dirty dog. . . . We rejoice that the public pulse beats so strong and full of the in-

32. *Spy*, Nov. 23, 30, 1854; *Yesterdays*, p. 163; S. Foster to A. K. Foster, Oct. 31, 1854, Foster MSS.

33. TWH to T. Parker, Oct. 31, 1854, Higginson-Burns MSS; T. Parker to TWH, Nov. 4, 1854, Higginson-Huntington MSS; S. Foster to A. K. Foster, Oct. 31, 1854, Foster MSS.

stinct of disgust towards a man so lost to the feelings of humanity or religion.[34]

The *Spy* was also gratified that the "brave" and "valiant" Abolitionists saved him from further harm. It proudly noted that though some of Butman's assailants could be recognized, City Marshal Lovell Baker thought it would be fruitless to undertake to prosecute in Worcester. But within a week six arrests were made. Howland, Foster, and Adin Thayer were accused of inciting riot by their actions in front of the American House. Three Negroes, Alexander Hamenway, Solomon Dutton, and John Angier, Jr., were charged with physically assaulting Butman. Foster, who found the results even more glorious than he had dared to anticipate, attracted most attention when he refused bail on "non-resistant principles" —Higginson noting that this was the sixth time Foster had been imprisoned for righteousness' sake. And for righteousness' sake Foster also refused to defend himself in court, claiming that he had already severed relations with the government. He subsequently demanded that his wife Abby be recognized as his counsel, in violation of a Massachusetts law which prohibited women from practicing before the bar. In any case, Higginson was sure none of the Butman rioters would be convicted. The *Spy*, upon completion of the trial, happily reported that the jury "only found bills for simple assault against the three coloured lads." [35]

Foster remained unbowed. The treatment of Butman proved, he said, that Higginson was right: Worcester henceforth would be Canada to the slave. But after witnessing the cruelty of the Worcester mob, Higginson preferred not to comment. And the *Spy*, committed to the new Republican party, now stated: "We welcome the presence among us, of fugitives from Southern slavery, and we wish to have them remain among us. . . . We do not think the atmosphere of our city is favorable for the health of kidnappers." But the newspaper did not wish to be viewed as aggressively defiant to the government; slave hunters would have to come to Worcester entirely on their initiative and not at the *Spy*'s invitation.[36]

In spite of Higginson's active defense of law and order in the

34. *Spy*, Nov. 31, 1854.

35. Ibid.; TWH to M. Higginson, Nov. 9, 1854, Higginson MSS; *Spy*, Jan. 24, 1855.

36. S. Foster to A. K. Foster, Oct. 31, 1854, Foster MSS; *Spy*, Jan. 29, 1855.

Butman riot, he still had to stand trial for violating the law in the Burns affair. Law, unlike Higginson, appeared uninterested in the consistency of heroic leadership. With his own trial imminent, he remarked that Foster had acquitted himself excellently.[37] Could those who had attacked the Boston Court House do as well?

From many sources Higginson received advice about how he should act. Before his arraignment, Francis Jackson, the wealthy Garrisonian Abolitionist, had offered to reserve space for him on a steamer either to Halifax or New Brunswick. But Higginson found this plan absurd. William Burt, hired to be his lawyer, suggested that before the trial Higginson should shave his beard, acquire a heavy sunburn, crop his hair short, and wear clothes directly contrasting to the dark coat and hat that he had worn during the attack on the Court House. This also seemed less than manly to the accused. More akin to Higginson's spirit was the advice of George William Curtis, the editor of *Putnam's Monthly*. Curtis thought Higginson should jauntily insist on the greatest pomp for the trial and perhaps memorize the dying speech suggested by the ballad of Captain Kidd, which could be delivered against a background of constables with cocked hats, including one with "a fearful golden knobbed stick." Lucy Stone, in a similar vein, asked, "Do you know that it would be best for the 'cause' if they should hang you?" A sympathetic Unitarian minister was more serious when he advised, "Suffer like a noble true martyr and the result will be good." [38]

Once it became evident that riot rather than murder was the charge, the pressure, of course, was lessened, but questions still remained. Should Higginson plead guilty? How much of a public issue could be made of the injustice of the fugitive slave law? Phillips suggested that "the opportunity of preaching to that jury is one of the things you fought for, perhaps the most important object." But it was clear to him, and to Higginson also, that it would be wrong to admit guilt. The only area open to dispute in Phillips' mind was how much and what should be confessed.[39]

When Theodore Parker learned that he too "would have the

37. TWH to Parker, Feb. 12, 1855, Higginson-Burns MSS.

38. S. J. May, Jr. to TWH, June 19, 1854, William Burt to TWH, June 26, 1854, George W. Curtis to TWH, Sept. 22, 1854, Lucy Stone to TWH, July 15, 1854, Rev. J. H. Fowler to TWH, June 30, 1854, Higginson-Burns MSS.

39. Wendell Phillips to TWH, June 14, 1854, Higginson-Burns MSS; TWH to Robert Carter, June 13, 1854, Carter MSS.

honor of being indicted" for rousing the crowd at Faneuil Hall, it became apparent that there would be much preaching in court. After hearing the good news of Higginson's arrest, Parker assured him that "the breach must widen till there is a division & perhaps a civil war." Senator Charles Sumner, in turn, told Parker he was glad he had been indicted, for the sake of the cause and Parker's own fame. After suggesting to the Boston minister that he argue the constitutionality of the fugitive slave law, Sumner agreed to be satisfied if Parker would do something historical, for the time would belong to history.[40]

Parker warmed to the task and suggested that Higginson not close his own defense but instead choose lawyer John P. Hale, who not only would be a fitting antislavery symbol but also as counsel would not be under oath to speak the truth—"a quite important distinction in *this* matter." Hale, as a politically committed antislavery leader, however, no longer represented Higginson's position. Besides, he reputedly was not strong on criminal law or the use of evidence. Higginson chose lawyers John A. Andrew, William Burt, and Henry Durant.[41]

Instead of serving as a vehicle for an attack on the fugitive slave law, Higginson desired a good defense. To Parker, who was preparing an elaborate critique of the fugitive slave law, Higginson wrote: "If I can't have the satisfaction of pleading guilty, I wish to have the satisfaction of being acquitted." [42] An acquittal was more important than verbal protest. That had ended when he lifted the battering-ram to the Court House door.

No trial took place. The first grand jury refused to indict. A second one brought indictments but, in Federal District Court, Judge George T. Curtis, with Judge Peleg Sprague concurring, quashed the indictments of all the defendants on the grounds that the government's case was based on the violation of the fugitive slave law of 1793 whose provisions pertained only to offenders resisting a federal officer serving some court order. In the case at hand

40. T. Parker to TWH, Feb. 1, 1855, Higginson-Burns MSS; C. Sumner to T. Parker, quoted in Commager, *Parker*, p. 243.

41. Parker to TWH, Jan. 17, 1855, TWH to Parker, Feb. 22, 1855, Higginson-Burns MSS.

42. Ibid.; S. Higginson to TWH, June 4, 1854, TWH to Parker, Feb. 12, 1855, Higginson-Burns MSS.

the resistance or obstruction of some legal process had not been charged. Curtis suggested that the use of the fugitive slave law of 1850 would have constituted a proper indictment.[43] Instead of heeding Curtis' advice about a new indictment, District Attorney Benjamin Hallett publicly declared that his brief had been a good and sufficient one, and then sought to avoid giving the Abolitionists further publicity by dropping the whole matter. Parker, not to be thwarted, issued his statement to the press: he cited Jeffrey and John Peter Zenger, among others, in an argument of 221 printed pages. A month later Anthony Burns' freedom was purchased for $1,300. Receiving a scholarship to Oberlin College, he became a Baptist minister. The former slave rejected the offer of $100 a week to tour the North made by showman Phineas T. Barnum.[44]

A few years after the Burns affair, Higginson received a package from one of his Negro companions in the Court House attack. An enclosed note declared that Higginson, more than anyone else, deserved to have this hand ax as a souvenir. His antislavery militancy made him a favorite on all kinds of reform platforms. One women's rights advocate warned her young daughter that some men might be as "splendid as Mr. Higginson, but . . . might not be equally worthy of the *homage* you rendered him." At abolitionist conventions he became a hero. At a meeting commemorating the mobbing of the English Abolitionist George Thompson, Higginson was introduced as a "man who had proved himself bold and fearless in opposition to the Slave Power." [45] Even more significant was praise from the veteran Abolitionist Parker Pillsbury, who had attacked "Free Soil Phariseeism" and now decided that Higginson "had grown admirably since . . . I once encountered him in Worcester defending politicians and denouncing us as impracticables. . . . He sees as I do about the prospects for the future." But what Hig-

43. U. S. v. Stowell, Case No. 16,409, *The Federal Cases: Circuit and District Courts of the United States*, Book 27, 1350 55.

44. Commager, *Parker*, p. 245; Theodore Parker, *Trial of Theodore Parker for the 'Misdemeanor' of a Speech in Fanueil Hall Against Kidnapping, April 3, 1855* (New York, 1864); Worcester *Transcript*, April 13, 1855; S. J. May, Jr. to Richard D. Webb, April 17, 1855, May, Jr. MSS.

45. Robert Morris to TWH, Mar. 19, 1856, Higginson-Burns MSS; Mary C. Wright to Ellen W. Garrison, Sept. 1, 1855, Garrison Family MSS; *Liberator*, Nov. 2, 1855.

ginson saw was more akin to the vision of W. H. Channing. After the Burns incident, Higginson's uncle advised him "the next thing to do is a guerilla war . . . at every chance." [46]

46. Louis Filler, "Parker Pillsbury: American Anti-Slavery Apostle," *New England Quarterly*, *19* (1946), 315; Parker Pillsbury to S. J. May, Jr., Nov. 22, 1855, May, Jr. MSS; William Henry Channing to TWH, July 4, 1854, Higginson-Burns MSS.

11

From the Azores to Kansas

William Lloyd Garrison sought funds in May 1855 for "putting the admirable bust of our noble Phillips in marble, hoping it will ultimately, in the revolution of public sentiment, find an abiding place in Faneuil Hall." The features and fame of Phillips deserved to be handed down to posterity, said Garrison. More than twenty years had elapsed since the first issue of the *Liberator* in which Garrison had vowed never to equivocate about the sin of slavery. Public apathy, he then charged, was enough to make every statue leap from its pedestal. And although Garrison in 1854 had publicly exhibited a copy of the Constitution, labeled it an agreement with hell and set it afire, to have a statue sculpted symbolized best the changed state of Garrisonianism. Its followers could reminisce about an iconoclastic past or dream of success in posterity, but they were growing fewer in number as they lost touch with the present. The momentous events of the fifties were reshaping and stimulating other antislavery action. To some men the recent emergence of the Republican party promised imminent political success. To others, the beginning of a revolutionary physical struggle, which had progressed from resistance to the fugitive slave law to the fight over Kansas, was shunting the Garrisonian verbal banners of non-resistance out of the vanguard.[1]

Higginson credited the *Liberator*'s editor with an essential part of his antislavery education, rightly believing that too many antislavery men, who either bypassed or broke with Garrison, had not acknowledged his pioneer influence upon divers antislavery organizations.[2] One may argue that Garrison was less important in the fifties than earlier, but partly because of his past efforts more

1. Garrison to James Buffum, May 17, 1855, Garrison Family MSS; Thomas, *Liberator*, pp. 387, 389.
2. TWH to Garrison, Sept. 5, 1855, in *Liberator*, Sept. 7, 1855.

men could no longer remain silent about slavery. For Higginson he still represented a valid kind of antislavery agitation, but not the only kind. Garrison's methods, by the mid-fifties, were not sufficiently militant for the Worcester minister.

On one point both men did agree: Abolitionists must not ignore the northern Negro's status while criticizing slavery in the south. Higginson as a member of the Worcester School Committee until 1854 (he lost his position by supporting the election of a Catholic school committeeman) had helped end the segregated "African school," and persuaded the small Worcester black population to send its children to integrated schools. A year later both Higginson and Garrison were praised by the Boston Committee for Equal School Rights for their part in bringing integration of the city's schools, which promised some clues to the capabilities of the Negro race. While Higginson stressed the sin of slavery regardless of the consequences of its abolition, he also wondered about racial inferiority and racial differences. Although the environmental effect of slavery on Negroes interested many antislavery men, inherent racial differences were more deeply believed.[3] The momentous question—What was the Negro race like?—needed an answer.

Higginson suggested that Garrison read his article in *Putnam's Monthly* because it presented quite a new view of the character and capabilities of a native African race. In this "African Proverbial Philosophy," Higginson imagined touring a West African river. In a romantic setting he described the natives as "a people active, keen, commercial, ingenious, affectionate, moral, with a remarkable language, and the most remarkable collection of proverbs ever dis-

3. TWH and James Rice, *Report of the School Committee of the City of Worcester* (Worcester, 1855); M. T. Higginson, *Higginson*, p. 123; Litwack, *North of Slavery: The Negro in the Free States, 1790–1860* (Chicago, 1961), pp. 149–50; *Proceedings of the Presentation Meeting for Equal School Rights in Boston* (Boston, 1856); *Liberator*, Aug. 17, 1855. The best discussions of antebellum racial views are: William R. Stanton, *The Leopard's Spots: Scientific Attitudes Toward Race in America, 1815–1859* (Chicago, 1960), James M. McPherson, "A Brief for Equality: The Abolitionist Reply to the Racist Myth, 1860–1865," *The Antislavery Vanguard: New Essays on the Abolitionists*, ed. Martin Duberman (Princeton, 1965), pp. 155–77, William H. Pease and Jane H. Pease, "Antislavery Ambivalence: Immediatism, Expediency, Race," *American Quarterly*, 27 (1965), 682–95.

covered among a people possessing no other literature." The best part of these proverbs was their similarity to northern epigrams. West Africans possessed "two qualities which we claim as especially American—mechanical ingenuity and commercial enterprise," wrote Higginson.[4] Perhaps the emancipated southern slave could come to resemble the white northerner.

Higginson would soon have a firsthand opportunity (in the African article he had relied upon an account by a fellow minister) to experience the values and ways of a foreign culture. Mary's ill health and his "nerves," strained by involvement in the Burns affair, led him to plan a long vacation made economically possible by supplementary income from a two-week Midwestern lecture tour. The Reverend David Wasson, who had been dismissed from a Congregational church for anti-Calvinist pronouncements, agreed to run the Free Church. The Higginsons, on October 29, 1855, sailed for the Azores and the Portuguese island of Fayal.[5]

After three weeks at sea, the white cliffs and stony black beach of Fayal provided a graphic introduction to the volcano of Pico dominating the horizon. The Fayalese port city of Horta displayed its high walls, Moorish towers, and whitewashed houses, made even more vivid by a Spanish ship in the harbor flying "her gorgeous ensign of gold and blood." Higginson, mixing the excitement of an explorer with a tourist's enthusiasm, reported: "Not a sound . . . is not new, not a square inch of surface . . . is like anything we ever saw before. . . . At Singapore . . . we should feel no farther from home. It has been a day of absolute intoxication." At the dock he was fascinated by "picturesque little half naked children, handsome Italian-looking young men with tasselled caps, women with baskets on their heads, & sick, forlorn . . . tattered beggars! All divided to let us pass & every cap was off."[6]

But by the second day, he wrote: "I see that the picturesque consists in a proper weighing of nudity and dirt. . . . I am thankful

4. TWH to Garrison, Sept. 26, 1854, Whitney-Benjamin MSS, "African Proverbial Philosophy," *Putnam's Monthly Magazine*, 4 (1854), 364.

5. TWH to Mary Curzon, July 23, Sept. 23, 1855, "Lecture Itinerary," Jan. 1855, MS, Higginson MSS; "David Wasson," Eliot, *Heralds*, p. 374.

6. TWH, "Fayal and the Portuguese," *Atlantic Monthly*, 6 (1860), 527; TWH journal, Nov. 9, 1855; TWH to David Wasson [Nov. 1855], Higginson MSS.

to see these things, but all too grateful that I was born in New England." In this tropical land of lemons and oranges, of a brightly dressed peasantry moving alongside "little donkeys clicking the rough pavements," [7] Higginson's senses would be stimulated and some previously unstated thoughts would now find expression. Fayal would serve as a prelude for later warm and equally strange days in the South.

Having left in America the sight of discreetly clothed and tightly corseted ladies, he particularly noticed the movement of the bare-legged Fayalese women carrying baskets on their heads. With apparent comparison to Mary, they represented to him "the female figure in its natural vigor and symmetry. . . . Every muscle is fresh & living . . . [in contrast to America's] diseased and tottering women." He was also impressed that despite the low standard of living, good manners were exhibited by the cap-doffing populace. Learning to speak Portuguese made him feel popular with the people.[8]

Higginson followed the path of the orange picker through the countryside, and with his characteristic audacity he climbed trees to peer into the gardens of high-walled estates, or walked into the thatched huts of the peasants. Collectively, he found them an attractive people, but quickly added, "I never for a moment prefer them to earnest and resolute Yankees." When he looked again at the character of the people he still granted their charm and their singular natural grace, but questioned "their want of all truth & honesty when there is any temptation, & the total destitution of all the heroic qualities. . . . The want of all respect for labor is detestable; no man of property will work, even in commercial business . . . the carpenter . . . has a boy carry his tools. I do not think I could tolerate these things for a year." [9]

Carnival week was no better for the vacationing minister. The Higginsons still hoped for something as picturesque as their first impressions. His evaluation of the festival was unambiguous: "Carnival is humbug. A few people have stood at their windows &

7. TWH to (?), Nov. 10, 1855, Higginson MSS; "Fayal," p. 527.
8. TWH journal, Dec. 6, 31, 1855; TWH to David Wasson, Feb. 2, 1856, Higginson MSS.
9. Ibid.

pelted passers with *beans*. . . . Little boys sit on the pavement
. . . & fill their syringes with water from puddles & display un-
couth figures cut in paper, to pin to people's backs." He facetiously
suggested that the law passed the previous year prohibiting all-out
attacks against strangers might account for the carnival's lack of
authenticity. But two days after this comment, he was hit by a
rotten orange thrown by one of those naturally vigorous Fayalese
women; with aplomb he tipped his hat and bid her thank you. With
some satisfaction he noted that later in the day he received only a
light pelting with beans and flour.[10]

The Higginsons mostly relied upon the company of the American consul in Fayal, the Bostonian Charles W. Dabney, "a man of
noble carriage, & gay and courtly manners . . . with a gracious
sweet smile like Mr. Emerson's." They enjoyed a formal dress ball
together as Mary, with the aid of a sulphur bath treatment, was
sufficiently mobile to take her husband's arm in a waltz. At parties,
charades and "Brattleboro Blind Man's Buff" brought both entertainment and memories of New England. And even a party given
by some wealthy Fayalese Frenchmen ended happily with a Virginia Reel. Higginson was growing less interested in looking at
Fayal than in making it look like America.[11]

Despite his growing cynicism about the picturesque qualities of
the customs and people of the Azores, there was one local event
that moved Higginson. That event was Holy Week. For three
days the cathedral was darkened except for the flickering candles
carried by a chanting procession of communicants. The frequent
masses and sermons during these days were accompanied by sudden views of the crucifixion: the faithful were moved to tears and
clapping their cheeks in token anguish. On Hallelujah Saturday
came the climactic end of mourning. With their foreheads leaning
upon the altar steps, the priests, in gorgeous robes, voiced their
monotonous chant, while the congregation waited expectantly for
the words *Gloria in Excelsis*. At their sound every door was suddenly thrown open, every window uncovered, and the church

10. Ibid.; TWH to David Wasson, Feb. 7, 1856, Higginson MSS.
11. TWH to L. Higginson, Nov. 13, 1855, Feb. 18, April 12, 1856, TWH to
Margaret Channing, Dec. 23, 1855, Higginson MSS.

filled with sunlight. The organ sounded and the ancient bells pealed as fresh spring flowers tossed from the gallery further accented the transcendent joy and wonder of rebirth.[12]

Such an experience strengthened Higginson's belief in the unity of life and death, of the aesthetic and the religious. It enhanced the meaning of religion based on "natural" feeling rather than on the rationalism of biblical exegesis. But he rejected what he conceived as the theological and institutional restrictions of Catholicism. Working at this time upon a discourse later to be called "The Return of the Faith, and the Decline of the Churches," he described the essay to Garrison as

> based upon the conviction that the present is the most momentous era in religious history of the world, inasmuch as all other epochs, even those of Jesus and Luther, have simply substituted one mythology for another, while the great ideas of the present age are promoting the rapid decay of all mythology, and the establishment of simple Natural Religion, of confidence in the Absolute Law of God.[13]

Even this concern for the state of religion was difficult to sustain. He found it hard to write sermons in Fayal, being "unable to take aim in the absence of birds." Clearly, Higginson was no St. Francis. Although trying to follow the events at home by reading the weekly editions of the *Liberator* and the *Tribune*, Fayal's lack of "moral electricity" made him feel too disconnected from American news. He did copy into his journal the frequently received reports of the Crimean War. By spring of 1856, Kansas events so interested him that any news was anxiously awaited. Certain that peace there was only temporary, he hoped that in Kansas "on which battleground of freedom I have dreamed myself, many times," a crusading minister was needed. Higginson announced plans to return to Boston by the first of June.[14]

There was one excursion that had to be undertaken before de-

12. TWH to Free Church of Worcester, Feb. 18, 1856, TWH to L. Higginson, Mar. 20, 1856, Higginson MSS.

13. "Fayal," pp. 541–43; TWH to Garrison, Mar. 19, 1856, in *Liberator*, May 6, 1856.

14. TWH journal, Feb. 18, 1856; "Quarry," Jan. 1856, Higginson MSS.

parting: the climbing of the steep Pico volcano. With a Fayalese guide, José, he ascended the 7,000-foot cone. Their path was literally into the clouds and onto great slabs of petrified lava. To crawl through narrow caves and leap over yawning crevices gave the journey a touch of that daring which so pleased Higginson. But perhaps what was most intense was the impact of José. Higginson bluntly described the guide as selfish and an uncommon liar. Later he would similarly complain about the beggars of Fayal, who assumed the haughty air of an exiled Stewart. The Spaniards were correct to charge that Portuguese were "mean even in their begging." Once the tourist has given them coins, Higginson noted, "you go home with a feeling that a distinguished honor has been done you." An attitude of *noblesse oblige* was satisfactory to Higginson only when those beneath him were no less generous in acknowledging their debt. The climbing of Pico and the encounter with José confirmed his feeling that he "had squeezed the orange of the Azores a little dry" and was ready to depart.[15]

After a rough ocean voyage, Cape Ann came into sight on June 7. Two days before, Higginson had written a friend: "Trust me, this is a great historic period, & the future will leave no true man unhonored." Now the harbor pilot meeting the ship came aboard with a newspaper which reported the clubbing of Senator Charles Sumner by Preston Brooks and the blockading of the Missouri River against free-state immigrants. Such momentous news, mixed with the sounds of English and the sight of bonnets and lighted shops, marked the Higginsons' arrival. Safely landed, he could say that New England was the home of "people so well dressed, so intelligent, & so sick—so unlike the robust baseness of Fayal & Pico." The Fayal peasantry later would be transformed in his writing to "little dusky creatures" who were as "harmless as birds."[16]

After visiting Louis Agassiz in Cambridge to present the naturalist with flora and mineralogical specimens from the Azores, he returned to Worcester after nine months abroad. The *Spy* heralded his arrival by predicting that "in the stirring events of the times Mr. H. will find ample scope for the exercise of his fine talents and

15. TWH journal, April 7, 1856; "Fayal," p. 544; *Yesterdays*, p. 196.
16. TWH to Moncure Conway, June 5, 1856, Conway MSS; TWH to L. Higginson, June 8, 1856, Higginson MSS; "Fayal," p. 544.

undaunted courage." At this time the paper was campaigning for the nomination of John C. Frémont as the Republican party's first presidential candidate. It had already labeled the Democrats the "border ruffian ticket." [17]

The Worcester Free Church arranged a special meeting to welcome the returning minister. Before festivities ended it was transformed into a recruiting rally to raise men and money for Kansas. The guest of honor was the leading recruiter. He observed afterward: "I find there is a great deal for me to supply, in the way of *prompt* action, as there always is." Yet any action for Kansas was a turnabout for Higginson. He had asked his congregation in June 1854: "Where is the good of emigrating to Nebraska, if Nebraska is to be only a transplanted Massachusetts, and the original Massachusetts has been tried and found wanting?" [18] Massachusetts, however, by January 1856, had responded militantly to territorial developments. What had been begun by Worcester's Eli Thayer in April 1854 as a business venture had become, to many minds, an armed crusade against the extension of slavery. Early in 1856, aided by interest in the outbreak of skirmishes along the Wakarusa River near Lawrence, Kansas, fund-raising in the North achieved its greatest success. The Reverend Henry Ward Beecher, in support of sending guns to free-state settlers for fighting slavery's defenders, wrote in the New York *Tribune* that "you might just as well . . . read the Bible to Buffaloes as to those fellows who follow Atchison and Stringfellow." But on May 21 "Beecher's Bibles" failed to prevent the sacking of Lawrence by southern "Border Ruffians," nor did they figure significantly three nights later in the massacre on Pottawatomie Creek by John Brown and his men.[19]

All this excitement was perfect fare for the action-hungry Higginson. As he later recalled: "It seemed necessary to arm any party of colonists more openly and thoroughly than had been the policy

17. TWH to L. Higginson, June 8, 1856, Higginson MSS; *Spy*, June 3, 10, 1856.
18. Ibid., June 3, 1856; TWH to M. Higginson, June 10, 1856, Higginson MSS; *Massachusetts in Mourning.*
19. Samuel A. Johnson, *The Battle Cry of Freedom: The New England Emigrant Aid Company in the Kansas Crusade* (Lawrence, 1954), p. 114; Eli Thayer, *The Kansas Crusade* (New York, 1889), pp. 130–33; Beecher quoted in W. H. Isely, "Sharps Rifles Episode in Kansas History," *American Historical Review, 12* (1907), 548; James C. Malin, *John Brown and the Legend of Fifty-Six* (Philadelphia, 1942), p. 566.

of the Emigrant Aid Society" run by Eli Thayer. Thayer, on the other hand, never sympathetic to Abolitionist crusaders, was convinced that men like Higginson were militant for fear that peace in Kansas would "quiet the Northern conscience with an apparent triumph." Not warfare in the name of political and moral anti-slavery, but peace for "business anti-slavery" was Thayer's desire.[20]

Forty-seven armed men led by Dr. Calvin Cutter (including Charles Tidd who would later be with Brown at Harpers Ferry) marched along Main Street with the Worcester Cornet Band in mid-June to receive the official good wishes at City Hall. They then countermarched to the railroad station—the band remaining behind to await its next parade. Within three days a newspaper announcement revealed that Higginson and Dr. Seth Rogers, a Worcester hydropath, were recruiting a second contingent of immigrants to Kansas. An advertisement in the *Spy* invited any Massachusetts town to send men and money to the new recruiting committee, "Reverend Thomas Wentworth Higginson, Secretary." [21] A local merchant advertised an appeal to men "who want their lives protected at a cheap rate and with perfect security . . . to get Allen's New Breech Loading Rifles, firing *eighteen* times to the minute: warranted to kill three or four of the Missourians or the [Indian] Natives, if in range at one shot." Another firm, stressing marksmanship less, offered blasting powder for the emigrant's purchase. Notwithstanding the promised accuracy of the Allen Breech Loader, Higginson, at this time, also became one of the fifteen vice-presidents at a town meeting planned to ratify Frémont's nomination. But unlike Garrison, who deviated from his customary antipolitical stand by expressing enthusiasm for Frémont, Higginson was more interested in using blasting powder than electing a Republican. Invited to speak at a Frémont rally, he replied: "I am willing to speak on Kansas, but prefer not to speak at a Republican meeting because . . . it would be hard for me not to say things which the politicians prefer to leave unsaid." [22]

The Massachusetts Kansas Aid Committee was formed at the

20. *Yesterdays*, p. 197; Thayer, *Kansas*, p. 100; Horace Andrews, Jr., "Kansas Crusade: Eli Thayer and the New England Emigrant Aid Company," *New England Quarterly*, 25 (1962), 498.

21. Worcester *Transcript*, June 18, 1856; *Spy*, June 18, 21, 1856.

22. Ibid., June 23, 1856; *Transcript*, June 25, 1856; Thomas, *Liberator*, pp. 338–89; TWH to Thaddeus Hyatt, Oct. 26, 1856, Hyatt MSS.

end of June as a militant arm of the Emigrant Aid Society, and chose as chairman George Stearns, a wealthy lead-pipe manufacturer. Stearns became a chief contributor to its rifle fund along with the Syracuse philanthropist Gerrit Smith. Within a year the committee would spend over $12,000 for arms. Pleased with progress, Higginson considered it "amazing how sluggish people have been in acting for Kansas . . . in this time of imminent need. . . . Nothing would have been done if I had not gone to work on it on the first night I came . . . for the busy give no time and the leisured no energy." [23] He soon had the opportunity to measure the energy expended in the territories.

Dr. Cutter's Worcester group had been instructed to take the land route into Kansas via Iowa, but instead went into St. Louis, took passage on a Missouri River steamboat, and was summarily disarmed by a band of Missourians. Higginson, on summer vacation from the pulpit, was dispatched by the Massachusetts Kansas Aid Committee to investigate.[24]

His Kansas education began before he reached Ohio. During dinner aboard a Lake Erie steamer he was struck by the significance of two black children being treated pleasantly by a white northern patron. Higginson began to wonder why this condition was unusual, why northerners were so often, instead, Negrophobes. His conclusion was revealing: "I'm persuaded that the great reason why there is less superficial colorphobia at the South, is because the inferiority is so unquestionable that there is no more jealousy of personal contact than in the case of dogs & horses." [25]

He anticipated little time for such reflection once he neared Kansas. To his wife, whom he addressed as "dear child" just at the time his courage came closer to being tested, he solicitously wrote, "bear it patiently darling, it's for Kansas." Higginson expected even more from Calvin Cutter and his men. "I almost hoped to hear that some of their lives had been sacrificed, for it seemed as if nothing but that would arouse the Eastern States to act," he later wrote. If none of their lives had thus far been sacrificed, the instructions he was bringing to the Cutter party could recify that:

23. Johnson, *Kansas*, p. 314; TWH to L. Higginson, July 24, 1856, Higginson MSS.
24. TWH to M. Higginson, June 29, 1856, Higginson MSS.
25. TWH to (?), June 29, 1856, Higginson MSS.

"if they met a party of Missourians not larger than five to one, to fight to the last rather than surrender." Higginson soon learned that Cutter and his men had surrendered their arms without firing a shot. He tried to assure those who had qualms about New England heroism that Cutter's Worcester party had indeed been outnumbered ten to one. Similarly, the sack of Lawrence in May, Higginson reported, had been accomplished only because the free-state men had been outnumbered ten to one.[26] What was obviously needed was more armed men.

Back in Worcester by the middle of July, he felt strong with hope. Officially appointed New England agent for the Kansas-bound parties, he wrote, "I am particularly popular in private just now for what I am doing in Kansas, & it is rather pathetic to have them thank me for doing what they ought to have taken hold of themselves, but have not." And in a jubilant unsigned article in *Putnam's Monthly*, linking Kansas militancy to sexuality, he assumed the role of a woman who had been prevented by men from joining a Mt. Katahdin climbing expedition, claiming that "there is more real peril to bodily health in a week of ball-rooms than in a month of bivouacs." [27]

At West Indian Emancipation Day, in 1856, held as usual in a grove at Abington, Massachusetts, Higginson spoke about the significance of Kansas. To those who opposed war he talked of the glory intrinsic in the white man fighting with arms to end slavery. In such a war the northern white man's present selfishness and money-grabbing would be replaced by "disinterestedness and self-devotion . . . as the more favored and privileged race finds . . . at last its highest privilege to aid the weakest, the most ignorant!" In Kansas was the first real promise of revolution, a revolution so imminent that "future historians will wonder that there was one man in the Union who could think that the crisis could be avoided." Those who talked peace and had faith in compromise were like the man in the time of the flood who said " 'Go along with your old ark; it isn't going to be much of a shower.' "

26. TWH to M. Higginson, June 29, July 1, 1856, Higginson MSS; TWH to Editor, New York *Tribune*, July 10, 1856; *Spy*, July 8, 1856; Boston *Journal*, July 8, 1856.

27. TWH to L. Higginson, July 16, 1856, Higginson MSS; *Putnam's Monthly Magazine*, 7 (1856), 256.

Higginson concluded: "I am not sure of this Union. I think LIBERTY is going to be saved." In private he admitted: "The mass of the people do not see this." [28]

As New England agent for the Massachusetts Kansas Aid Committee he shopped for supplies like a man anticipating a flood. Initially, Higginson purchased 20 Sharps rifles in Boston. Between July 17 and August 25, he had on hand $2,646.25 as contributions to the state committee. In August and September he purchased 71 Sharps rifles, 27 United States muskets, 10 United States rifles, 92 revolvers, 161 knives, 20 kegs of powder, 29 boxes of cartridges, 5,900 caps for revolvers, and a 2½-pound cannon. And there was more to come. Frank Sanborn, the Concord schoolmaster, noted that Harvard people contributed about $700 during a Cambridge meeting at which Emerson spoke for the cause. Higginson had aims different from those of Martin Stowell, who exulted in the newly settled 640 acres of Plymouth, Kansas, the town twelve miles south of the Kansas–Nebraska border, and seventy miles north of Topeka. Stowell described the lovely town and rich land, and desired to "make money & secure one of the finest homes in the world." He was comforted that the land route made the hazardous Missouri River route unnecessary. [29]

The Reverend John T. Sargent, who in the 1840's had lost his pulpit for allowing Theodore Parker to speak from it, temporarily filled the Free Chuch post while Higginson returned to the territories. Whether Higginson received a salary for serving as New England agent is unknown, but it is evident that the state committee paid his expenses. [30]

He arrived in Chicago by September 3, a crucial time in the Kansas fight. Assaults against proslavery settlements at Franklin, Fort Saunders, and Fort Titus, and the free-state town of Osawatomie had occurred in August. Acting Governor Daniel Woodson, a proslavery man, had issued a proclamation declaring Kansas in a state of open insurrection and rebellion. John W. Geary, ap-

28. *Liberator*, Aug. 8, 1856; TWH to Wm. P. Clarke, Aug. 17, 1856, copy in Villard MSS.

29. Receipt, Aug. 2, 1856, Higginson-Kansas MSS; Kansas Notebook, July 17–Aug. 25, Higginson MSS; Frank Sanborn to TWH, Sept. 19, 1856, M. Stowell to Elizabeth Stowell, Aug. 15, 1856, Higginson-Kansas MSS.

30. Kansas Notebook, Higginson MSS.

pointed governor by President Pierce to succeed Woodson, arrived in Kansas on September 7 and immediately ordered all armed forces to disband. Five days later Higginson, using the signature "Worcester," wrote the first of his "Letters from Kansas" which appeared in the New York *Tribune*, Chicago *Tribune*, and St. Louis *Democrat*. From the Missouri River town of Nebraska City he told of having spoken daily with men who had sacrificed all their property and were ready to add their lives for a revolution as fierce as any seen in Europe. But while waiting to travel into Kansas with a party of immigrants he privately conceded: "My spirit of adventure is a little checked, . . . things look discouragingly safe, and the men are beginning to fear marching in without a decent excuse for firing anything at anybody." Nebraska City was depressingly oblivious of the antislavery crusade; the main occupation of the inhabitants seem to be, according to Higginson, sitting on doorsteps, eating watermelons and waiting for the price of real estate to rise. From his "vile little tavern" in this forlorn little town he called on "Eastern Capitalists" to invest in transforming the whole blighted area into an industrious North. One way this could be done, he suggested, was by constructing a railroad from Burlington, Iowa, to the Missouri River to carry the northern immigrant.[31]

More immediate promise came from the sight of northern men on horseback who were "bearded and booted and spurred and red-shirted, sword and pistol by their side—only their sword is a bowie knife—wild manly looking riders." James Lane, the militant Kansas politician, noted for mixing self-advertisement with free-state efforts, appointed Higginson brigadier general because of his past courage and ability, and invited him to join the Kansas fight. From Nebraska City, Higginson along with Sam Tappan, a reporter for the New York *Times* and the Boston *Journal*, joined a train of twenty or thirty wagons for the six-day prairie trek to Topeka. With a surge of pride he incredulously wrote his mother: "Imagine me also patrolling as one of the guard for an hour every night, in high boots amid the dewy grass, rifle in hand & revolver

31. TWH to L. Higginson, Sept. 3, 12, 1856, Higginson MSS; Malin, *Brown*, p. 607; Johnson, *Kansas*, pp. 202, 207; "Worcester," Sept. 12, 1856, New York *Tribune*, Sept. 27, 1856.

in belt." He added plaintively, "But nobody ever came." He shot a superb hawk, however, whose wings he promised to bring back East as a trophy.[32]

En route to Topeka he enjoyed seeing men constantly armed, and Indian bands roaming the countryside. In the new village of Plymouth he met his compatriot in the Burns attack, Martin Stowell, with whom he left money and supplies as he later did with Calvin Cutter. But Geary's earnest efforts to abolish all armed bands discouraged him because the Governor was offering peace for the price of obedience to the fraudulently elected proslavery legislature. Recalling European revolutions, Higginson said: "As Hungary, having successfully resisted her natural enemy, Austria, yielded at length to the added strength of Russia; so the Kossuths of Kansas, just as they had cleared her borders of Missourians are subdued by the troops of the United States." [33]

In Topeka, Higginson directly felt Geary's power. He was awakened before dawn by news that his lodgings were surrounded by a cordon of dragoons waiting for sunrise and the order from Colonel J. T. L. Preston to search the house for leaders of Kansas immigrants. Higginson neglected acknowledging that the raid's purpose was to test the rumor that a large armed force known as "Lane's Army of the North" was marching into Kansas. Though the dragoons learned that Higginson and his companions constituted no such force, they were taken for a "half-compulsory" interview at Lecompton with Governor Geary. This confrontation further convinced Higginson that the Governor was a "little Napoleon," with "neither the mental ability to understand the condition of Kansas nor the moral power to carry out any systematic plan for its benefit." [34]

Comparing Lecompton to Lawrence, he stressed the proslavery town's paucity of schoolhouses and churches, and its streets lined with barrooms. The Virginia Saloon "is true Virginia—bacon, corn bread, and dirty negro boys and girls to wait on table.

32. TWH to Mary Curzon, Sept. 16, 1856, Higginson MSS; James Lane to TWH, Sept. 18, 1856, Higginson-Kansas MSS; TWH to L. Higginson, Sept. 18, 1856, Higginson MSS.

33. Kansas Notebook, Sept. 21–23, 1856, TWH to L. Higginson, Sept. 24, 1856, Higginson MSS; "Worcester," Sept. 25, 1856, *Tribune*, Oct. 8, 1856.

34. "Worcester," Sept. 28, 1856, *Tribune*, Oct. 10, 1856.

Southern provincialism strikes one's ear at every moment, and the town is garrisoned by . . . militia, reinforced yesterday by twenty-five precious youths from Georgia in a high state of whiskey." While visiting the free-state men imprisoned by Geary for using arms, Higginson noticed the cannon pointed at the building; he recalled June 1854, when another cannon had been pointed at Boston spectators during the imprisonment of Anthony Burns.[35]

For antislavery men like Higginson who had grown disillusioned with politics and words, Kansas represented the hope for militant activism. From the free-state town of Lawrence he wrote:

> Ever since the rendition of Anthony Burns . . . I have been looking for *men*. I have found them in Kansas. The virtue of courage (for though these two words originally meant the same thing, they have become separated now) has not died out of the Anglo-American race, as some have hastily supposed. It needs only circumstances to bring it out. A single day in Kansas makes the American Revolution more intelligible than all Sparks and Hildreth can do. . . . In Kansas, nobody talks of courage, for everyone is expected to exhibit it.[36]

He desired the courage and manliness shown in Lawrence when two hundred men battled bravely though outnumbered, and where "Old Captain Brown" had moved among the defenders telling them to fire low. This same man, Higginson had heard, also defended Osawatomic, which was abandoned only when twenty-seven men could not repulse two hundred Missouri invaders. Courage was not lacking: "A hundred dollars worth of ammunition would have prevented . . . the destruction of $60,000 worth of property." Here was a judgment with a moral that was surely directed to eastern capitalists. No less pointed was his enumeration of Lawrence's assets: its location on the water, its adjacent forests, its luscious melons, squashes, and pumpkins, and its abundance of coal and stone. "Give us freedom, and a few years will make Kansas the garden of America." [37]

35. "Worcester," Sept. 30, 1856, *Tribune*, Oct. 9, 1856.
36. "Worcester," Oct. 4, 1856, *Tribune*, Oct. 17, 1856.
37. Ibid.

It was surely not commercial speculation that attracted Higginson to Kansas. He preached on Sunday, September 8, from a Lawrence pulpit. His text was from Nehemiah: "Be not ye afraid of them: remember the Lord, which is great and terrible, and fight for your brethren, your sons, and your daughters, your wives, and your homes." It was the same passage used by the Reverend John Martin on the Sunday after he had fought at Bunker Hill. Lydia Maria Child, hearing about the sermon, commented: "What a convenient book that Old Testament is, whenever there is any fighting to be done." She judged it inconsistent for people to be greatly shocked by Higginson's course. If Massachusetts men did not come forward, "why, then indeed, the spirit of the Puritans and of '76 has died out. . . . This battle with the slave power is merely the great battle of Armageddon." [38]

But even Higginson conceded that free-state men occasionally stooped to horse-stealing. When he mentioned Osawatomie Brown, however, he left unmentioned the Pottawatomie massacre. Later in life, while judging it the most extreme act of John Brown's Kansas career, he claimed that in 1856 he had heard of no one who did not approve of the act and recognize its beneficial effects —it had given an immediate check to the armed agression of the Missourians. Regarding free-state morality he concluded: "I can see that this state of things brings out some bad qualities, but far more good ones." Despite his public statements about the heroism of Kansas settlers, he once again privately admitted that most of them were unarmed, and the idea of asserting their rights and meeting the consequences did not seem to have occurred to them. He thought settlers should feel and act as though every moment was an emergency. To his diary he disclosed non-military reasons for militancy: "I enjoy danger. Enjoy sitting in a hotel & hearing men talking about me etc. . . . while I know that I have incurred the penalty of death for treason under U. S. laws & for arming fugitives to Kansas." [39]

38. Kansas Notebook, Higginson MSS; Lydia M. Child to Lucy Osgood, Oct. 28, 1856, in *Letters of Lydia Maria Child*, ed. W. Sewall (Boston, 1882), p. 84.

39. *Yesterdays*, pp. 207–08; TWH to O. G. Villard, Sept. 8, 1910, Villard MSS; "Worcester," Oct. 4, 1856, *Tribune*, Oct. 17, 1856; Kansas Notebook, Higginson MSS.

Heading north, Higginson stopped at the proslavery town of Leavenworth. Here there were fifty saloons for a population of two thousand, but its location on the Missouri River moved him to predict that with New England enterprise it would be destined to greatness. The only enterprise he found was practiced by proslavery men to procure election votes. Strangers were encouraged to partake in a Kansas election "as if it were something to drink." He denied that making capital for Frémont was the motivation behind antislavery agitators[40]—certainly it was not his motive.

The longer he stayed in Kansas the more critical of the South he became. Describing a "representative of chivalry," Higginson wrote about "a slender puny race, with good manners and bloated faces." On a Missouri River steamer en route to St. Louis he reflected: "It is sad to think that among these sixty men on board there are not half a dozen who belong to the same nation with myself. For what constitutes a common nationality except common ideas, principles, habits, purposes? And in all these I find myself more alone than I should be among the English, French, or Russians." Northern security, Higginson concluded, would not come from relying upon southern honor nor by demanding upon Frémont's election but by supplying guns to Free Soil settlers. "Kansas may be crushed," he granted, "but not without a final struggle more fearful than that of Hungary; a struggle which will convulse a continent before it is ended, and separate forever those two nations of North and South which neither Union nor Constitution has yet welded together." [41]

Though Greeley's New York *Tribune* printed this prophecy of bloodshed over the usual "Worcester" signature, it now dissented from its militant columnist. As the November election neared, the paper supported Frémont, not continued warfare. Unlike Higginson, the *Tribune* sought revolution at the ballot box. Meanwhile, once back East, Higginson tried to thwart Governor Geary's peace efforts. But he rejected one plea for money to organize an independent antislavery guerilla band. A Kansas fighter, in return for future support, promised that "as long as there is a Ruffian in Kansas, my plan is not to show quarters, and

40. *Tribune*, Oct. 6, 1856, Oct. 21, 1856.
41. *Tribune*, Oct. 6, 9, 20, 21, 22, 23, 1856.

consequently take no prisoners, but give them their own play.
. . . Where we find them in squads, Butcher them clean by the
horde." [42]

Higginson and the militant members of the Massachusetts Kansas
Aid Committee wanted more extensive warfare. Having armed
settlers and aided such noted Kansas fighters as Jim Lane, they now
planned to enlist the support of state legislatures. Higginson addressed the Vermont legislature and met with that state's governor,
Ryland Fletcher. He pleaded for an appropriation to resist "federal
interference" in Kansas, and advocated a bill providing for a volunteer state militia to combat further "encroachment" by the United
States government.[43] The Kansas territorial government must not
be allowed to remain proslavery and bring Kansas into the union
as a slave state.

Richard Hinton and other antislavery men in Kansas kept Higginson informed about developments. Hinton, who in June had
entered Kansas with Worcester men, graphically described the
sacking of Plymouth, the Kansas town established under Martin
Stowell's leadership. Stowell, the town's judge and military chief,
was forced to flee temporarily, but noted that a rear guard still
remained: "I left Brown there in as comfortable circumstances as I
could." [44]

Buchanan's victory over Frémont stung Abolitionists more than
had been expected. While insisting that the election had decided
nothing, reporter Sam Tappan, for example, evinced some serious
doubts: "I hope we shall never have peace in this country until the
damn thing called slavery is exterminated from the land." And
James G. Birney, the pioneer candidate for the Liberty party, con-
curred. Said he in an epitaph for peaceful political abolitionism:
"I regret that a civil war should rage but if slavery cannot be
exterminated without one—& I don't see how it can be—I say let
it come." [45]

42. *Tribune*, Oct. 23, 1856; Dunn to TWH, Nov. 23, 1856, Hutchinson MSS.
43. TWH to L. Higginson, Oct. 26, 1856, Higginson MSS; TWH to Thaddeus
Hyatt, Oct. 16, 1856, Hyatt MSS; TWH to W. Hutchinson, Oct. 29, 1856, Hutchinson MSS.
44. Richard Hinton to TWH, Nov. 6, 1856, Hinton MSS; M. Stowell to TWH,
Oct. 27, 1856, Higginson-Kansas MSS.
45. Samuel Tappan to TWH, Jan. 6, 1857, James G. Birney to TWH, Oct. 27,
1856, Higginson-Kansas MSS.

Frank Sanborn, who had recently returned from Kansas, worried along with Higginson about the election's negative effects on abolition, should "timid cowards prevail and Senator Wilson . . . be followed." For Wilson and the Republicans, encouraged by their substantial vote in 1856, believed that the new party would eventually settle the slavery issue. "I am convinced," said Sanborn, "we need something different—submission for the next four years seems to me out of the question." Higginson showed his agreement by shipping a box of revolvers to Kansas to help arm a newly organized artillery company. Militancy was approved by Gerrit Smith, to whom Higginson revealed his desire to recruit state "minute men." This group would not be confined to fighting Missourians, he assured Smith, but also would be released against *any* federal opposition. Looking to the future, Higginson judged it "essential to involve *every* state in the war that is to be." [46]

Such zeal, however, had become difficult to transform into cash. Martin Conway, formerly a Free Soil member of the Kansas legislature and now in Vermont seeking a $20,000 state contribution, reported the spreading discouragement: "It seems to me that the election of Buchanan has played the devil with the public heart of those low-lived politicians. Their backbones have become entirely relaxed." [47]

Even Martin Stowell was discouraged. He wrote from Kansas that he felt "gloomy" when thinking of the sad state of his private affairs and the little real estate he had left. This especially hurt, he noted, when recalling that most people cared so little about Kansas. He plaintively asked. "What is duty O—what is duty?" Higginson, under pressure from Calvin Cutter's public statements about the Kansas Committee's loose handling of funds, felt forced to ask Stowell to consider duty more concretely: he pleaded for an account of the expenditure of $2,000 that had been sent from Worcester. Stowell's reply expressed grief, annoyance, and a poignant picture of the bookkeeping difficulties in Kansas: "I have copied my account since yesterday on a box as best I could, half-frozen and half-burned while doing so. It pains me to have *you beg*

46. F. Sanborn to TWH, Nov. 6, 1856, Higginson-Kansas MSS; Ralph V. Harlow, *Gerrit Smith* (New York, 1939), p. 357; TWH to H. B. Hurd, Nov. 12, 1856, Higginson-Kansas MSS.

47. Martin Conway to TWH, Nov. 12, 1856, Higginson MSS.

me to report." He then tried to explain a $100 loss: a personal check he accepted for cash was returned uncashed by the bank because of a closed account. Identifying the man who had written and presented the bad check, Stowell sad: "You have doubtless heard of the hero of Osawatomie, the scourge of the Ruffians and terror of their accomplices; of his having his house destroyed and all effects stolen." He concluded that one "cannot think of asking Brown to pay," adding, somewhat slyly: "If you know him and his noble sacrifices you will heartily approve of my course." Higginson thereupon accepted Stowell's bookkeeping.[48]

Although indeed aware of Brown's reputation, Higginson also looked elsewhere. While striving to procure funds in November from nothern legislatures, he was also planning a Massachusetts Disunion Convention. As he told Gerrit Smith: "Garrison and Phillips and others see that the time is come . . . to consider the idea of Disunion between Free and Slave States, *as a practical problem which the times are pressing on us.*" For thirteen years Garrisonians had advocated peaceful disunion, but now, Higginson happily reported, "they will gladly cooperate on a common platform with all who believe that the time is coming for resisting the U.S. government in Kansas, and sustaining such resistance everywhere else." Here, after having abandoned Free Soil coalitionists, was the possible fruition of Higginson's dream to unite radical Abolitionists of both the violent and nonviolent variety. Smith, prominent in both political and armed abolitionism, sympathized with Higginson's disunion desires but refused to support a Disunion Convention. "I prefer to have the South take the lead in the matter," he stated.[49]

Despite Smith's negative response, Higginson prepared for an early January 1857 convention in Worcester. While so engrossed in fomenting revolution, the thirty-three-year-old Higginson wrote: "I feel ever so much younger now than I did when I was eighteen or twenty, & I doubt if I shall ever feel any older." Since

48. M. Stowell to TWH, Nov. 12, 17, 1856, Calvin Cutter to TWH, Nov. 7, 22, 1856, TWH to Cutter, Nov. 14, 1856, Redpath to TWH, Feb. 5, 1857, Higginson MSS.

49. TWH to Smith, Nov. 22, 1856, in Harlow, *Smith,* p. 357; Smith to TWH, Nov. 27, 1856, Higginson-Kansas MSS.

it was apparent that his immobilized wife was an incurable invalid (by now she had to have meals brought to her room), it is likely that his public activity away from home was stimulated. He would later reveal his feelings about the satisfactions of carrying a gun in Kansas:

> I finally discharged my revolver and put it away in my trunk. . . . There occurred the most curious reaction from the feeling with which I had first loaded it. . . . It fully came home to me that all the tonic life was ended, and thenceforward, if any danger impended, the proper thing would be to look meekly about for a policeman, it seemed as if all the vigor had suddenly gone out of me, and a despicable effeminacy had set in.

But the aggressiveness required to seek state aid for Kansas and to plan for the Disunion Convention temporarily relieved anxiety about despicable effeminacy. These efforts clearly did not require him to search meekly for a policeman. Yet while he could be intensely earnest about his commitment to the antislavery cause, he simultaneously would blithely report that he was trimming a Christmas tree while "in the intervals, I dissolve the Union & write letters to Kansas." [50]

Two weeks before the assembling of the Worcester Disunion Convention, Higginson addressed a Faneuil Hall meeting gathered to commemorate the twenty-fifth anniversary of the Massachusetts Anti-Slavery Society. Introduced as "The Reverend General Higginson," his words lived up to the billing. Assuring his audience that he had not journeyed to Kansas to see underground railroads, he said:

> I wanted to see something above ground. . . . I was tired of reading of Leonidas, I wanted to *see* him. I was tired of reading of Lafayette, I meant to *see* him. I saw in Kansas the history of the past, clothed in living flesh before me. I saw in Charles Robinson the Puritan soldier—the Hampden of Cromwell's army; so modest, so absolutely noble. . . . And if I

50. TWH to Ellen W. Garrison, Dec. 27, 1856, Garrison Family MSS; TWH to L. Higginson, Nov. 30, Dec. 19, 1856, Higginson MSS; *Yesterdays*, p. 214.

wanted a genuine warrior of the Revolution where could I find him better than in the old Vermonter, Captain John Brown, the defender of Osawatomie. . . . Old Captain Brown, the Ethan Allen, the Israel Putnam of today, who has prayers every morning, and then sallies forth, with seven stalwart sons, wherever duty or danger calls, who swallows a Missourian whole, and says grace after the meat.[51]

Higginson no longer talked of voting. "Disunion. . . . As God is in heaven, our destiny and duty are to be found there. It is our only hope." If Garrisonian nonresistors momentarily thought they had enlisted the reverend general, Higginson quickly killed any such hope by declaring that "fire still exists, and the laws of nature are guaranty for a revival of terror." Headway could be made against the South only if the coming year were crammed with insurrections.[52]

Higginson's insurrectionary activities would be confined, at least during the first few months of 1857, to delivering militant speeches. In Boston, on January 9, he saw John Brown for what appears to be the first time (Brown claimed to have met him previously in Kansas), but Higginson only noted that Kansas was then quiet and that Brown was raising money to repulse an expected spring invasion by Missourians.[53]

51. Jan. 2, 1857, *Liberator*, Jan. 16, 1857.
52. Ibid.
53. *Yesterdays*, p. 216; TWH to L. Higginson, Jan. 9, 1857, Higginson MSS.

12

Planning for Harpers Ferry

Higginson's name headed the list of eighty-nine men who signed the call for a Massachusetts Disunion Convention. This petition noted a rapid increase in sectional hostility, the hopeless attempt to unite two opposing systems of society in one government, and the discouraging prospect of four more years of proslavery government under the newly elected Buchanan. Using the *Liberator*'s technique, the Worcester *Daily Bay State* printed the eighty-nine names surrounded by a black mourning border, suggesting that South Carolinians also should have been offered the opportunity to sign this treasonous document. It categorized the signers as a "band of mischievous fanatics, designing demagogues, and weak minded spiritualists." Boston papers joined the *Bay State* in ridiculing the leaders: the *Evening Ledger* captioned an editorial, "The Lunatics Let Loose." [1]

At Worcester's City Hall, on January 15, Higginson called the meeting to order. Francis Bird was elected the convention's president, Garrison one of its vice-presidents, and Wendell Phillips and Higginson business committee members. Bird, once a Free Soiler and recently the key Republican politician behind Sumner's successful legislative campaign for re-election, delivered the opening address—an attack on the Republican party. "If the wires of Republican abolitionist dynamite had been directed to the citadel of slavery, it would have been blown to atoms; but the operators conducted the charges into the territories, and it was lost." Massachusetts Senator Henry Wilson, who had traveled from Free Soil party to Know Nothing party to Republican party, received the brunt of Bird's criticism. Most disturbing, said the speaker, was Wilson's suggestion that slavery's continuance must be decided by each

1. *Proceedings of the State Disunion Convention* (Boston, 1857), p. 3; Worcester *Bay State*, Dec. 31, 1856; *Ledger* quoted in *Liberator*, Feb. 13, 1857.

southern state. Even more foolish to Bird was that Senator John P. Hale of New Hampshire, a leader of political antislavery men, sugested appealing to the conscience of slaveholders. Something more was necessary than waiting for the South's compliance or the Republican party's triumph.[2]

After Bird, Higginson read extracts from letters sent by public figures unable or unwilling to attend the convention. Congressman Amasa Walker of Massachusetts sympathized with discussing disunion but took no stand on the issue itself; Senator Wilson opposed the meeting. Congressman Joshua Giddings of Ohio was against making military preparations in the North to counter southern preparations. He cited important Republican congressional victories and argued: "Ours is the cause of truth and justice, which needs no arms, no violence, no shedding of blood."[3]

Charles Francis Adams questioned the value of disunion:

> Conceding . . . that slaveholding is sin, . . . I do not understand it as part of the Christian theory, that we are to have no society with it on that account. If such be the doctrine as to sinners, where are we to stop at home, and who of us will have a right to claim exemption from excommunication? . . . There are high-minded honorable, conscientious men and women scattered thick all over the slave states. . . . Shall we help this excellent class by deserting them?[4]

Theodore Parker had militant reasons for opposing the immediate dissolution of the Union: "The North must do well by those four millions of slaves and those four millions of 'poor whites'; we must bring the mixed multitude even out of the inner house of bondage, peaceably if we can, forcibly if we must." He concluded: "I used to think this terrible question of slavery in America would be settled without bloodshed; I believe it no longer."[5]

Higginson presented the business committee's resolutions: they stressed the impossibility for any government on earth to reconcile

2. *Disunion Convention*, pp. 6–11; TWH to Theodore Parker, Jan. 9, 185[7], Higginson-Huntington MSS.
3. *Disunion Convention*, p. 11
4. Ibid., p. 9.
5. Ibid., p. 5.

the North and South in the Union. Necessary, therefore, was "the expulsion of the Slave States from the confederation in which they have been an element of discord, danger, and disgrace." Politics was equated with acquiescence in slavery, disunion with opposition to it. The resolutions predicted, however, "It is not probable that the ultimate severance of the Union will be an act of deliberation or discussion—but that a long period of deliberation or discussion must proceed it; and this we must begin." Again it was said: "peace or war is a *secondary consideration*." [6] The business committee had avoided bowing to Garrison's pacifism.

Daniel Mann, a farmer from Sterling, Massachusetts, delivered the day's most chauvinistic words. The South, said Mann, "is a sink of every ignoble vice and loathsome pollution. . . . We the most industrious and enterprising people of the world, who despise idleness and incapacity as a crime, are squandering our money to support and encourage a horde of loafers and swindlers." Higginson's address sought to provide the solution. As a former advocate of political antislavery, he recalled how the Republicans had warned that Frémont's election was freedom's last hope, and how they predicted that whichever party won the election would control the country for the next thirty years. Subsequent Democratic victories, added Higginson, would continue to depend upon courting the South and acceding to more proslavery villainy. A militant alternative thus was imperative: "Give me a convention of ten who have drawn the sword for right, and *thrown away the scabbard* and I will revolutionize the world. . . . You say we are 'weak'. . . . Give us five years, and let us see. . . . All we ask is, open the doors of your powder magazines, and let us try!" [7]

He recalled the attempted Anthony Burns rescue which brought the country to the verge of civil war. "Give us . . . another chance to come face to face with the United States Government . . . and see if we have not learned something by the failure. . . . No sir! disunion is not a desire, merely; it is a *destiny*. It is in vain to talk of difficulties in *effecting* the process. The laws of human nature are taking care of these difficulties very rapidly." He recalled the presence of those laws even in Iowa, once considered a weak spot

6. Ibid., p. 18.
7. Ibid., pp. 15, 19.

among the free states. When in Iowa, "I laid my hand upon the earth; and everywhere the soil grew hotter and hotter with the suppressed volcano." Both militant action and inevitable laws would bring the antagonistic sections into collision. "In God's name let it come quickly." [8]

While opposition newspapers (and subsequent historians) would dismiss the Disunion Convention as simply another platform for Garrisonian doctrine, the open clash between Garrison and Higginson contradicts this. Garrison followed Higginson with a plea for immediate disunion "for the sake of true religion." Force, he argued, had failed, thus "every fugitive who comes to Boston is counselled to make his way to Canada." Just at this point, Higginson interrupted Garrison by asserting: "When a fugitive comes to Worcester, we always advise him to stay." The audience applauded but Garrison replied: "It remains to be seen whether Worcester will be able to protect the slave, when seized by the United States Government." Here was a basic doctrinal and functional confrontation between Higginson and Garrison. For Higginson, who had explored and rejected political antislavery, armed force by Abolitionists had to be employed whenever necessary. Wendell Phillips had wished to be by Higginson's side during the Burns attack, but now remained closer to Garrison by saying: "What I want to do . . . is . . . to familiarize the public ear to the word Disunion . . . and when that is done, leave events to stereotype it into practice." [9] Higginson was most militant by demanding that men use more than abolitionist rhetoric to bring disunion.

Although the convention resolved that another disunion convention would meet during the current year to join representatives of all the free states, agreement for further action was indefinitely delayed. A petition containing six thousand names for a national convention in July subsequently was drawn, but the economic re-

8. Ibid., p. 19.

9. Ibid., pp. 21–23. The important clash at the Worcester Disunion Convention between Garrison and Higginson over the use of violence has been ignored in even the most reliable discussions of abolitionism, eg. Bartlett, *Phillips*, p. 204; Thomas, *Liberator*, pp. 391–92; Walter Merrill, *Against Wind and Tide, a Biography of William Lloyd Garrison* (Cambridge, 1963), p. 271; Louis Filler, *The Crusade Against Slavery* (New York, 1960), pp. 258–59; John Demos, "The Antislavery Movement and the Problem of Violent Means," *New England Quarterly*, 37 (1964), 501–26.

cession of 1857 would force the cancellation of the meeting. At the Worcester Disunion Convention were heard the most explicit statements concerning the differences among various kinds of radical antislavery men. The convention's meaning was perhaps best summarized in the last song rendered by the Hutchinson family singers: "Right and Wrong, or the Good Time Coming." [10] How the Right would come was in doubt, but all agreed that it was inevitable.

While some men at the convention wanted to be recorded for disunion largely because they were "sick of the Southern gas on the subject," Higginson felt committed to it. With emotion he wrote his mother: "I am sorry, dearest mother, you differ from me about it, but I never was more sure of being right. . . . Five years hence it will be generally admitted that we did right." But even in this letter about an unequivocal commitment, he spoke of a peaceful and dignified policy and omitted the need for physical force. Having reached the point of rejecting both Garrisonianism and political antislavery, he momentarily withdrew from embracing violent means. Stung by a letter from George William Curtis who said, "I suppose an arrogant and vindictive self-conceit to be philosophically an integral part and necessity of every radical reformer," Higginson replied: "Under an apparent rashness I have a great deal of caution, & being naturally very good tempered, I am seldom charged with personal severity." He defended the convention's criticism of the Republican party and its Massachusetts leaders, Henry Wilson and Nathaniel Banks. Granting that Wilson "has real anti-slavery feeling," Higginson declared: "he is a politician in grain, & is *weak* among stronger persons." As for Banks, he "knows as much of Anti-Slavery as those busts in the Atheneum." [11]

Curtis' criticism of Higginson was mild compared to the treatment the press gave the convention. The Worcester *Bay State* labeled those attending, "a set of weak-minded men and strong-minded women—making on a fair average, a numerous set of men-

10. *Disunion Convention*, p. 23; *Call for a Northern Disunion Convention, July 8, 1857* (Boston, 1857).

11. S. J. May, Jr. to TWH, Dec. 14, 1856, TWH to L. Higginson, Dec. 14, 1856, George W. Curtis to TWH, Jan. 22, Feb. 5, 1857, TWH to Curtis, Jan. 25, 1857, Higginson MSS.

tal eunuchs." Of the convention's organizer, the paper said: "there is Fayal Higginson, with the wound in his head yet gaping, apparently wholly unconscious that when the brains were out the man would die." And the Boston Daily *Bee* reported:

> The nine tailors of Tooley Street, who proclaimed themselves "The People of England" were a modest body compared with a score or two of crack-brained Abolitionists who have resolved upon the dissolution of the Union. . . . Is there anyone in New England so given up to delusion as to suppose that Tom Higginson or Amasa Walker could by any possibility, be considered dangerous animals! . . . Surely, the Union is safe against such men as these! [12]

But other newspaper editors worried. The Paterson *Democrat,* for example, prophesied that "unless the violent and inflammatory appeals . . . on the subject of slavery are stopped, the day is not far distant when the public mind will be ripe for an overt act of treason." The Boston *Atlas* feared the way in which southern Democratic papers reported the convention, "the responsibility for which they falsely ascribe to the Republican party." [13]

The Boston *Courier* bluntly dealt with possible results of disunion—the migration of Negro slaves to Massachusetts. "We would be obliged to re-enslave them to protect ourselves," for "the natural intelligence of the race cannot be improved," and unless serving a master, Negroes would practice "utter cannibalism and licentious barbarism." Higginson, on the other hand, simply predicted that for every slave that now escaped to the North, ten would do so once the Union was dissolved, thus disagreeing with Parker that remaining in the Union was necessary to end slavery. Disunion, Higginson was certain, at least would make slavery impossible in the border states.[14]

While the meeting received relatively extensive press coverage, it received no support from any but distinctly abolitionist journals. The Worcester *Spy,* so often friendly to Higginson's words and deeds, now noted: "The Disunion Convention has been held, and

12. Quoted in *Liberator,* Feb. 13, 1857.
13. Ibid.
14. Ibid.; TWH to L. Higginson, Jan. 27, 1857, Higginson MSS.

yet the Union is not dissolved, but will probably survive long after the agitators of that movement have passed from the stage of life." [15] There were two men, however, imbibing the radical spirit of the convention who would transform its words into action. The lesser known one was an editor of a small Italian language newspaper, *The European*. This was "Colonel" Hugh Forbes, a former soldier under Garibaldi, a Siennese silk merchant, a fencing instructor, and a translator for the New York *Tribune*. Higginson had notified Forbes about the convention in late 1856, assuring him that *The European* had many Worcester readers. Forbes' reply foretold his later behavior. His main interest was not the value of disunion but rather the commercial one: "*The European* makes an impression where other papers cannot go." Forbes blatantly suggested that it be resolved at the convention that every reading room in the country subscribe to *The European*. This resolution never emerged from committee, though the colonel was appointed a committee member. [16]

Possibly, at the convention, Forbes first grasped the monetary opportunities of association with abolitionist revolutionary schemes. Also present, in search of funds, was John Brown. While there is no evidence that Forbes was introduced to Brown until March 1858, the Worcester meeting was probably the first time he saw him. [17] The path which was to wind from Worcester's City Hall to the engine house at Harpers Ferry was yet indistinct, but the course charted by Higginson in January 1857 would help lead to that insurrectionary effort.

While Higginson planned a national disunion convention, Frank Sanborn endeavored to agitate matters in Kansas, where, because of Geary's peace efforts, the situation continued to look bad. Sanborn reported Brown's appearance at the Boston State House hearing on Massachusetts' aid to Kansas. Initially, Sanborn had cautiously said he liked the man from what he had seen. Now he asked Higginson, "Can anything be done for the good old man in Worcester County among your friends?" Higginson approved

15. *Spy*, Jan. 17, 1857.

16. Hugh Forbes to TWH, Jan. 5, 1857, Higginson MSS; Oswald G. Villard, *John Brown* (Boston, 1911), p. 285.

17. Malin, *Brown*, p. 301; Villard, *Brown*, p. 285.

Brown's plan to raise $30,000 for Kansas from private sources; state
legislatures were reluctant about appropriating money and shyer
about supplying recruits from the state militia to oppose federal
troops in Kansas. While even the Republican Worcester *Spy* suggested that Boston officials present Brown with a testimonial showing their esteem before he went West, Higginson understood that
the "Ethan Allen of Kansas" wanted something more immediately
negotiable than an inscribed plaque. Confident in his ability to raise
money, Brown was already looking past Kansas warfare when in
February 1857 he ordered a thousand pikes, useful weapons for
men unaccustomed to handling firearms—as were southern slaves.[18]

Higginson received his first letter from Brown on April 1, 1857.
It asked him to gather Worcester funds raised on Brown's behalf to
make them easily more accessible. "My heart grows sad," he told
Higginson, "in the fear of a failure of the enterprise." Others were
more explicitly confident. Daniel Foster, chaplain of the Massachusetts General Court, told Higginson, "I expect to serve in Capt.
John Brown's company in the next Kansas war, which I hope is inevitable and near at hand." And the chance for action was a reason
for Higginson's announcement on April 10 that he planned to resign from the Free Church pastorate. To be able to lecture, preach,
and write without being weakened from overwork as had recently
happened to Theodore Parker, was another cause for his decision.
Because of "the present condition of the country, . . . which is
likely to exist for several years, there will be an increasing demand
on me from outside," he explained.[19] Eventually David Wasson
would be his replacement, but a church trustee feared that Wasson
would never fill the house as Higginson had. "There is something
in your son's appearance," he told Higginson's mother, "that calls
out the Masses." [20] Little Mrs. Higginson, now seventy years old,
must have wondered where her tall and handsome son would lead
them once he called them out.

18. Sanborn to TWH, Jan. 5, Feb. 19, 1857, Higginson-Brown MSS; *Spy*, Jan.
8, 1857; Villard, *Brown*, pp. 283, 284.

19. Brown to TWH, April 1, 1857, Higginson-Brown MSS; David Foster to
TWH, April 2, 1857, Higginson-Kansas MSS; TWH to L. Higginson, April 11,
1857, Higginson MSS.

20. Oramel Martin to L. Higginson, April 22, 1857, Higginson MSS.

Now receiving from $25 to $50 for public lectures, Higginson had turned from the pulpit for the last time. The desire to speak to men "in one form or another," which he had articulated during his Divinity School days, had remained undissipated; he had become more keenly aware of the diverse ways one spoke to men. Words had become linked to physical action as a means of communicating. Even the plethora of words that he began to publish in the new *Atlantic Monthly* frequently advocated physical action. An article appeared in March 1858 in which Higginson complained: "One of the most potent causes of the ill-concealed alienation between the clergy and the community, is the supposed deficiency, on the part of the former, of a vigorous, manly life." [21]

Accepting an invitation from Samuel May, Jr., to speak at the annual meeting in New York of the American Anti-Slavery Society in May 1857, he again referred to force.[22] He told the convention that theoretical discussion about the nature of the Constitution was meaningless. "The question of slavery," said Higginson, "is a stern and practical one. Give us the power, and we can make a new Constitution, or we can re-interpret the old one. How is that power to be obtained? By politics? Never. By revolution, and that alone." Once again he heralded Worcester's ability to become Canada for the fugitive slave. Remembering a recent letter from Boston which said that a fleeing slave was being sent to Worcester because it "should afford . . . as much safety as this accursed Union can give," Higginson told the convention about the result: "We looked at the man, and saw the measure of him. Such sinews I never saw. That man could take a barrel of flour in his arms, lift it easily, and hold it out at arm's length. We looked at him and said to him, 'Those arms are a better argument for staying, than your legs are for going, so stay where you are.' He stayed." Higginson pointedly added that his Worcester townsmen had informed federal authorities that the fugitive was there, yet no slave catcher appeared. This was proof that a willingness to take

21. Bode, *Lyceum*, p. 138; "Saints and Their Bodies," *Atlantic Monthly*, 1 (1858), 581.

22. S. J. May, Jr. to TWH, Mar. 3, Mar. 27, 1857, Higginson MSS; TWH, *The New Revolution* (Boston, 1857); *National Antislavery Standard*, June 20, 1857.

physical action was manliness, and manliness triumphed. Boston, he sarcastically suggested, also should strive to become Canada to the slave and be "as free as if . . . ruled by a Queen."

Not scheduled to speak at the annual meeting of the Massachusetts Anti-Slavery Society in January 1858, Higginson rose from the audience to reiterate his disagreement with Garrisonian nonresistance. "The moral position of this society," he conceded, "is the highest and noblest possible, but their practical position does not take hold of the mind of the community." [23]

While Higginson had been talking revolution, John Brown, with his own plans, had been tapping rich reservoirs of wealth. He understood that the enforced calm in Kansas had left interested northerners in a quandary about where to invest money for antislavery action. His prediction of a Missouri invasion, and his willingness to resist it forcibly, moved men like George Stearns and Samuel Howe, therefore, to give Brown financial aid. Benefiting from a successful subscription to support his wife and five children, and an additional $13,000 in arms and property, Brown was promised $12,000 more if he needed it. By the middle of May 1857, Brown forthrightly informed Stearns that he needed $1,000 at once to pay for a farm which he had purchased from Gerrit Smith. When Sanborn questioned this request, Brown suggested that the money be promptly raised, and told Sanborn to become "conscious that I am performing that service which is equally the duty of millions, who need not forego a single hearty dinner by the efforts they are called on to make." Brown well understood the importance of playing on the guilt felt by those who had limited their antislavery actions to verbal and monetary contributions.[24] The details of his relationship with the Abolitionists continued to be revealing.

Despite the tightening of the national money market during the

23. *Liberator*, Feb. 5, 1858.
24. Testimonial of 1857 by A. A. Lawrence, Dec. 1884, newspaper clipping, Higginson MSS; Brown to G. Stearns, May 13, 1857, Brown to Sanborn, May 15, 1857, Higginson-Brown MSS. For a discussion of Brown's relationship with the Abolitionists and how he has been treated by historians and some present-day civil rights advocates, see Tilden G. Edelstein, "John Brown and his Friends," *The Abolitionists: Immediatism and the Question of Means*, ed. Hugh Hawkins (Boston, 1964), pp. 71–79.

August financial panic, Brown received more funds. "May God reward you all a thousandfold," he wrote Sanborn. Then characteristically not wasting an opportunity, he requested additional funds in case trouble came up. He informed Sanborn that Colonel Hugh Forbes had established a military training school at Tabor, Iowa. Realizing that Stearns in the midst of the financial panic was worried about new monetary commitments, Brown asked Sanborn to "Please say to him, that *provided* I do not get into *such a speculation* as shall swallow up all the property I have been furnished with, I intend to keep it *all safe,* so that he may be remunerated in the end." The property to which Brown referred was the goods of the Massachusetts Kansas Aid Committee, covertly put into Brown's hands, with dubious justification, by Stearns. Included were 200 Sharps rifles, 200 revolvers, 4,000 ball cartridges, and 31,000 percussion caps.[25]

Sanborn relayed to Higginson Brown's plea for more money and his readiness for future service, adding "how true he is amid all his trials." The $3,000 held by the Worcester County Kansas Committee, Sanborn suggested, should be donated to Brown rather than kept idle. But Higginson replied with some skepticism about Brown's past accomplishments and suggested caution in showing him such overwhelming favor. Sanborn was unsympathetic to the warning. He correctly reminded Higginson that Smith had favored Brown soon after they first met, as did other prominent committee members. Besides, lectured Sanborn, Brown "is as ready for a revolution as any other man. . . . I believe he is the best Disunion champion you can find, and with his hundred men, when he is put where he can use them and drill them (he has an expert drill officer with him) will do more to split the Union than a list of 5,000 names for your convention—good as that is." He would make possible, Sanborn concluded, "a movement which has all the elements of fitness and success—a good plan, a tried leader and a radical purpose." To Sanborn, the purpose at this juncture specifically meant upsetting Governor Geary's pacification of Kansas.[26]

25. N. H[awkins] to Sanborn, Aug. 27, 1857, Higginson-Brown MSS; Villard, *Brown,* p. 247; J. Brown to G. L. Stearns, April 28, 1857, Brown MSS, Library of Congress.
26. Sanborn to TWH, Sept. 11, 28, 1857, Higginson-Kansas MSS.

Brown, however, sought bigger game. By the end of 1857 he looked to action in the South and was organizing his raiders. Only later did some of his eastern benefactors learn of these preparations. Artfully playing off his key supporters against each other in order to give each the feeling of being his closest confederate, Brown wrote Parker that "none of them understand my views as well as you do." He tried to persuade Higginson that concealing his whereabouts was "for good reasons . . . not for any anxiety about my personal safety. I now want to get for the *perfecting* of BY FAR the most *important* undertaking of my whole life, from $500 to $800 within the next Sixty days." Endeavoring to make Higginson feel a share in conspiratorial excitement, Brown asked that he "consider this communication *strictly confidential:* unless it may be such as you are *sure* will *feel,* & *act* and *keep very still.*" What he specifically wanted he expressed quite candidly: "Can you be induced to operate at Worcester, & elsewhere during that time to raise from *Anti*-slavery *men* & *women* (or any other parties) some part of that amount?" [27]

But Higginson, wanting something more specific than Brown's assurances, shrewdly baited him with his own letter: "I am always ready to invest in treason, but at present have none to invest. . . . But I'll raise *something* if only $5 & send it on. I *may* be able to persuade a Committee who have a trifing balance left." [28] The committee in question was the Worcester County Kansas Committee with its balance of $3,000.

Sanborn again sought to assure Higginson about Brown, though "he speaks of *a* plan but does not say what it is. Still, I have confidence enough in him to trust him with the moderate sum he asks for—if I had it—without knowing his plan." Sanborn reported without comment the charge that Brown was of little service in Kansas, but strongly denied the allegation of his insanity. It was rumored, he noted, that Brown had been talking of overthrowing slavery "in a large part of the country." Sanborn volunteered, "I should not wonder if his plan contemplated an uprising of slaves—though he had not said as much to me." Apparently fearing, and

27. Villard, *Brown*, p. 675; Brown to Parker, Feb. 2, 1958, Parker MSS; N. Hawkins to TWH, Feb. 3, 1858, Higginson-Brown MSS.
28. TWH to Hawkins, Feb. 8, 1858, Higginson-Brown MSS.

wrongly so, that Higginson might be shocked by this last prophecy, he reminded him: "The Union is evidently on its last legs and Buchanan is laboring to tear it in pieces. Treason will not be treason much longer, but patriotism." [29]

Brown also tried to fire Higginson's imagination by acknowledging the Worcester man's interest in treason. A "Rail Road business on a *somewhat* extended scale," he wrote, "is the *identical* object for which I am trying to get means. I have been connected with that business as *commonly conducted* from my boyhood; and never let an opportunity slip. . . . I now have a measure on *foot* that I feel sure would awaken in you something more than a common interest if you could understand it." Higginson, Brown hoped, would join Stearns, Sanborn, Smith, and himself at a meeting in Peterboro, New York, to discuss further plans, and promised that he would "never regret having been one of the council." Not knowing his man, he solicitously added, "I would most gladly pay your expenses had I the means to spare." [30] Brown was striving mightily for Higginson's support and the concomitant release of the Worcester County Kansas Committee funds.

But he would have to be less condescending before he could win Higginson, who delayed a full commitment pending knowledge of specific details from Brown. Stearns, having invested much already, also waited. Sanborn, however, remained enthusiastic and journeyed to Peterboro, where on Washington's Birthday, with Smith and Edward Morton (a tutor in the Smith family whom Higginson had recommended), he heard Brown unfold his plans. As they sat together in an upper room of the Smith mansion, Brown jolted them by reading his authoritarian "Provisional Constitution and Ordinances for the People of the United States." By means of a small conspiratorial band and an armed slave insurrection, his government was expected to be born. Sanborn, it appears, well understood that Brown intended to launch his plans with an invasion of Virginia. Smith and Sanborn, walking and talking together at sunset, agreed they could not "give him up to die alone." [31]

29. Sanborn to TWH, Feb. 11, 1858, Higginson Brown MSS.

30. Brown to TWH, Feb. 12, 1858, Sanborn to TWH, Feb. 19, 1858, Higginson-Brown MSS.

31. Harlow, *Smith*, p. 402; TWH to Smith, May 29, 1855, Smith MSS, Syracuse University; Frank Sanborn, *Recollections of Seventy Years*, 1 (Boston, 1909), 147.

Two days after the Peterboro meeting, Higginson submitted his formal resignation to the Free Church. By the 6th of March, along with Parker, Howe, Sanborn, and Stearns—five of those who became known as the Secret Six—he met with Brown at the American House in Boston. Sanborn, after the Peterboro meeting, had briefed Higginson and Parker, but now Brown's presence, his personal intensity and power, gave a new dimension to the plan. Each man agreed to pay a $100 assessment as a shareholder in the enterprise. Further fund-raising was begun in earnest.[32]

Upon receiving Higginson's $100 in late April, Sanborn asked for more money and reported that Brown had just left Canada for the West "to move his furniture and bring in his hands. . . . If not embarrassed by want of means [he] expects to turn his flock loose about the 15th of May." But for a time, Virginia pastures would remain untrod. It was not lack of funds that delayed "the shepherd" but rather the monetary desires of enterprising Colonel Hugh Forbes, who suddenly opposed the "present speculation" and threatened a full disclosure if he was not appointed to replace Brown. Sanborn now regretted that the colonel had ever been included in the "wool business." Parker and Stearns, after learning that Forbes had approached Senator Henry Wilson, wished to defer Brown's plans for another year, and Sanborn tended to agree. Gerrit Smith went farther: he saw his chance to be free of the whole affair. He told Sanborn: "I never was convinced of the wisdom of his scheme. But as things stand it seems to me madness to attempt to execute it." Along with Brown, Howe and Higginson opposed delay. At this point Higginson wished he had the funds to "buy out the other stockholders & tell the veteran to go on." [33]

Higginson denied knowing Forbes, whom Sanborn now designated as "either a madman or a villain." Perhaps during the excitement of the Worcester Disunion Convention, Higginson indeed had forgotten their correspondence and his meeting with the editor of *The European*. Agreeing with Brown that Smith was timid,

32. *Spy*, Feb. 24, 1858; Brown to TWH, Mar. 4, 1858, Stearns to TWH, Mar. 18, 1858, Sanborn to TWH, Mar. 21, April 1, 20, 1858, Higginson-Brown MSS.
33. Sanborn to TWH, April 20, 1858, Smith to Sanborn, May 7, 1858, TWH to Sanborn, May 18, 1858, Higginson-Brown MSS.

Higginson wrote Brown's son, Jason: "I utterly protest against any postponement. *If* the thing is postponed it is postponed forever—for H. [ugh] F. [orbes] can do as much harm next year as this." That Stearns and Smith, "leading stockholders," could enforce their wishes through financial pressures hardly placated Higginson. With reason, he believed that when these men delayed it really meant they feared any action.[34] During the debate between the cautious stockholders and the more aggressive managers, Higginson delivered a bold address to the American Anti-Slavery Society. Without mentioning Harpers Ferry or Brown, he explained why he thought Brown's plans suited disunion and abolition.

> We white Anglo-Saxons are too apt to assume the whole work is ours. . . . I see it otherwise now. Never in history was there an oppressed people who were set free by others, and it will not begin here and now. I have wondered in times past, when I have been so weak-minded as to submit my chin to the razor of a colored brother, as his sharp steel grazed my skin, at the patience of the negro shaving the white man for many years, yet kept the razor outside of the throat . . . but I was foolish to make this a test of courage.
>
> Behind all these years of shrinking and these long years of cheerful submission . . . there may lie a dagger and a power to use it when the time comes. . . . We speak of the American Slave as if he was never to do anything for his own emancipation. We forget the heroes of Santo Domingo, in fact great negro heroism has already been shown and thus charges of timidity are wrong.[35]

Unequivocally now, Higginson said about slavery: "It is destined, as it began in blood, so to end." Hopeful about coming insurrection, he directed a question to his audience for the first time: "Is there a man here who would fight to put down a slave insurrection?" And when someone shouted, "Yes," Higginson coolly told him

34. S. G. Howe to TWH, May 7-8, 1858, TWH to Jason Brown, May 7, 1858, Higginson-Brown MSS.

35. May 12, 1858, *Liberator*, May 28, 1858.

to go to it with the certainty that such resistance would extinguish his life.[36]

Zeal for insurrection moved him to try to convince Theodore Parker that Forbes, "a blundering blockhead," could be outwitted by immediate action. For Higginson the time had come to strike. "Any betrayal afterward," he told Parker, "will only increase the *panic* which is one element in our speculation." Further dependence on Stearns and Smith for additional supplies was unnecessary. For the plan, argued Higginson, had been to make the outbreak look like a spontaneous local flurry with no resources *at all*. Besides, even if men, arms and ammunition were sparse, "fame & fear will exaggerate them." On the same day he wrote this letter, Higginson assured Brown, "I, for one, am willing to leave the whole matter to you." [37]

Parker disappointed Higginson. "You are a better soldier than I," soothed the Boston minister, "but I think I'm right in the matter." Brown, on the other hand, was a different kind of soldier from Higginson. He wanted to be well outfitted—an unattainable goal without further financial support from Stearns and Smith. Promise of receiving an additional two or three thousand dollars, if the project was postponed until the winter or spring, sufficed to cool Brown's ardor for taking the field immediately. Higginson sulked and grew skeptical about the courage of his fellow conspirators. He disregarded Sanborn's invitation to a Boston meeting in June with Brown and the Secret Six, though he was in town at the time. Knowing that the meeting would oppose immediate action, he preferred casting his vote by boycotting it.[38]

But he was noticeably mollified when Brown personally reported to him, and argued that Forbes' knowledge, if made public, would hurt their plan by revealing its magnitude and thereby initiate counterrevolutionary preparations. Higginson, however, suggested that "the increased terror produced would perhaps counterbalance this." Brown, not one to alienate a desired ally, then altered his position by saying that if he had the means he

36. Ibid.
37. TWH to T. Parker, May 18, 1858, TWH to John Brown, May 18, 1858, Higginson-Brown MSS.
38. Parker to TWH, May 10, 20, 1858, Sanborn to TWH May 31, 1858, Higginson-Brown MSS.

would begin immediately, and that the other conspirators over-rated the obstacles and basically were not men of action. Stearns and Parker, Brown charged, did not have an overabundance of courage. Higginson now happily concluded that Brown agreed entirely with him. The shrewd campaigner's simultaneous agreement with two opposing views about delaying action, Higginson explained this way: "The sly old veteran . . . had not said this to them, & had appeared to acquiesce far more than he really did; it was essential that they should not think him reckless, & as they held the purse he was powerless without them, having spent nearly everything received thus far. . . . But he wished me not to tell them what he had said to me." [39]

Only when Brown appeared to appreciate Higginson's militancy, gave him his confidence, and agreed entirely, did he show enthusiasm. When others became more important to Brown, when Brown showed an independence, or during periods when he rarely heard from Brown directly, Higginson became correspondingly skeptical and uninterested in the Harpers Ferry plan. Unlike so many northern admirers who had met Brown, Higginson was not hypnotized by his "flashing eyes," his "penetrating genius," or by his other so-called trancendental qualities. For Higginson, he indeed was the "sly old veteran."

Higginson willingly kept Brown's secret from the Secret Six, especially after learning that Forbes' threatened disclosure had moved most of the committee (to avoid direct responsibility) to want to know as little as possible about insurrectionary plans, and to leave Brown to his own discretion. As Sanborn succinctly explained: "The business of the Kansas Committee was put in such shape that its responsibility for the arms in Brown's possession should no longer fetter his friends in aiding his main design." But Higginson and Sanborn kept abreast of the fascinating design. It has not been recognized how well informed they were about Brown's insurrectionary plans. His other northern supporters knew he needed money and that he planned insurrection. Brown kept

39. TWH memo, MS, Higginson-Brown MSS; Villard, *Brown*, p. 340. Villard found the word "sly" illegible though it is perfectly readable, and Higginson frequently was consulted during the writing of the book: see Edelstein, "Brown," p. 75.

them interested by asking them to name the earliest date possible. He noted: "Little business can be accomplished until we get our Mill in operation. I am *most* anxious about that." Brown's recruit, the reckless and genial John E. Cook, once employed as both a schoolteacher and lock-tender, was already settled at Harpers Ferry to reconnoiter the area in advance of the shepherd and his flock. He would have time enough to marry a Harpers Ferry girl before Brown finally arrived.[40]

Higginson, while pleased that Brown still anticipated action, apologized to him in late October about being able to raise so little money for the enterprise. Distinguishing himself once again from other conspirators, he wrote, "I trust that your enterprise may not be deferred longer than next spring that I may yet be able to render it some service besides good wishes." A month later Higginson published an article in the *Atlantic* called "Physical Courage":

> Life is sweet, but it would not be sweet enough without the occasional relish of peril and the luxury of daring deeds. Perhaps every man sometimes feels this longing . . . when he would fain leave politics and personalities, even endearments and successes behind, and would exchange the best year of his life for one hour at Balaklava with the 'Six Hundred.'[41]

Further evidence of Higginson's awareness and approval of Brown's plan is contained in a vital exchange of letters during late November 1858 with Lysander Spooner, a Boston lawyer who had become known for his well-circulated pamphlet "The Unconstitutionality of Slavery," published in 1845. His argument was based on a natural-law interpretation of the Constitution, although it mistakenly had gained its renown for being a strictly legal argument. Wendell Phillips, as a Garrisonian, attacked Spooner by citing previous court decisions that upheld slavery's constitutionality. Spooner, on the other hand, assailed the Garrisonian belief in inevitable disunion, arguing that the South would not voluntarily

40. Sanborn, *Recollections*, *1*, 466; Brown to Sanborn et al., Sept. 10, 1858, Higginson-Brown MSS; Villard, *Brown*, p. 408.
41. TWH to Brown, Oct. 29, 1858, Higginson-Brown MSS; *Atlantic Monthly*, *1* (1858), 729.

secede from the Union. Now, some ten years later, Spooner asked Higginson's opinion about distributing throughout the country his new broadside: "A Plan for the Abolition of Slavery." [42]

This plan, to be achieved "*by force if need be*," called for the "non-slaveholders of this country in their private capacity as individuals—without asking the permission . . . of the government —to go to the rescue of the Slaves from the hands of their oppressors." Southern non-slaveholders should receive special appeals to raise money and military equipment to achieve this end. Said Spooner: "The tea must be thrown overboard, the Bastille must be torn down, the first gun must be fired, by private persons, before a new government can be organized, or the old one be forced (for nothing but danger to itself will force it) to adopt the measures which the insurgents have in view." [43]

He had only one reservation regarding force: "We are unwilling to take the responsibility of advising any insurrection, or any taking of life, until we of the North go down to take part in it, in such numbers as to insure a certain and easy victory." [44]

Touched by these sentiments, Higginson in turn confided to Spooner:

> The increase of interest in the subject of Slave Insurrection is one of the most important signs of the times. It is my firm conviction that, within a few years, that phase of the subject will urge itself on general attention, and the root of the matter be thus reached. I think that this will be done by the action of the slaves themselves, in certain localities, with the aid of *secret* co-operation from the whites.
>
> This is greatly to be desired. The great obstacle to the anti-slavery action has always been the apparent feebleness & timidity of the slaves themselves. Had there been an insurrection every year since the American Revolution, I believe that Slavery would have been abolished ere this. . . . The Northern people . . . would have been forced back on the funda-

42. John A. Alexander, "The Ideas of Lysander Spooner," *New England Quarterly*, 23 (1950), 204, 207; Lysander Spooner to TWH, Nov. 28, 1858, Spooner MSS.
43. Ibid.
44. Ibid.

mental question of liberty; instead of the partial & superficial aspects of the matter, upon which our politicians have dwelt. A single insurrection, with decent temporary success, would do more than anything else to explode our present political platforms.[45]

But still Higginson opposed Spooner's plan. His explanation gives a good glimpse of his revolutionary mind. "I think in Revolutions the *practical end* always comes first & the theory afterwards. . . . For one man who would consent to the *proposition* of a slave insurrection, there are ten who would applaud it, when it actually came to the point. People's hearts go faster than their heads." He argued that the fugitive slave cases and the Kansas troubles had in some degree prepared the public mind for an insurrection. "In place therefore of . . . propounding insurrection as a *plan*, my wish would be to secure it as a *fact*. The concrete will arouse more sympathy than the abstract." [46]

Only with great restraint did Higginson not say more than this: "Were I free to do it, I would give you assurance that what I say means something, & that other influences than those of which you speak are even working to the same end. I am not now at liberty to be more explicit." [47]

If Brown could evade capture, "I think we may look for great results from this spark of fire," predicted Sanborn. Although apprehensive about being arrested before launching his Virginia attack, Brown understood that some risk was necessary to keep money flowing to him, and so he ventured upon an occasional foray followed by a personal appearance at the sources of wealth. At times he would be paraded before rich admirers to show their own heroism by association. Howe arranged such an appointment for him with the wealthy industrialist John Murray Forbes and sent a letter of introduction: "If you would like to hear an honest, keen and veteran backwoodsman disclose some plans for delivering our land from the curse of slavery, the bearer will do so. . . . He is of the Puritan militant order. . . . He has a martyr's spirit. He will ask nothing of you but the pledge that you keep to yourself

45. TWH to Spooner, Nov. 30, 1858, Spooner MSS.
46. Ibid.
47 Ibid.

what he may say." Brown, of course, also asked for money. The cotton manufacturer eventually contributed to his visitor's wool business.[48]

At other times Brown sought less conventional ways to raise funds; much to Howe's chagrin, he sought to defend his success at stealing horses. And in towns where outright gifts were scarcer, Brown would request, for example, someone to sell "a little cannon & carriage as an old relic; or for the sake of helping me a little: I am certainly quite needy; and have moreover a family to look after." [49]

For twenty-five cents admission in Cleveland and for voluntary cash contributions in Peterboro, New York, Brown appeared in person. At the Cleveland lecture the journalist Artemus Ward described him as quick as a cat and a man of iron, who "could lick a full yard of wild cats before breakfast without taking off his coat." Few people came to see for themselves. At Peterboro, however, Gerrit Smith wept upon hearing Brown and contributed another $400.[50]

In March 1859, Sanborn reported that Brown "is ready *with some new men* to set his *mill* in operation, and seems to be coming east for that purpose." Higginson was asked to raise money in Worcester "in admiration for B's late achievements." Brown's Missouri raid in December 1858, during which eleven slaves were freed and a slaveholder killed, were the achievements to which Sanborn was referring. Higginson sent $20.[51]

Brown again came to Boston for funds in late April. But Higginson refused to solicit money in Worcester: "I have drawn so largely on others, within the last years, for similar purposes, that I find it hard to obtain more now, when many of our best men are involved in business difficulties." Besides, he explained, "it is hard for me to solicit money for another *retreat*, when I think retreat

48. Sanborn to TWH, Jan. 19, 1859, Higginson-Brown MSS; Sanborn to S. Johnson, March 8, 1859, Johnson MSS; S. G. Howe to John M. Forbes, Feb. 5, 1859, in Sarah Forbes Hughes, *Letters and Recollections of John Murray Forbes,* 1 (Boston, 1899), 178; Villard, *Brown,* p. 390.

49. Ibid., p. 391; Brown to Jesse Brown, Mar. 3, 1859, Higginson-Brown MSS.

50. Sanborn to TWH, Mar. 14, 1859, Higginson-Brown MSS; Villard, *Brown* p. 394.

51. Sanborn to TWH, Mar. 4, Apr. 19, 1859, Higginson-Brown MSS; Villard, *Brown,* p. 394.

is not needed." He promised to send something, however, once Brown was truly launched, and assured him: "I have perfect confidence in you. All you do will be well done. And I long to see you with adequate funds in your hands, set free from timid advisers, & able to act in your own way." Adding, "Did I follow only my own inclinations, without thinking of other ties, I should join you in person if I could not in purse. But for the present I am restrained." [52]

Mary's poor health, of course, was the most obvious restraining influence. It also appears that Higginson now seriously doubted that Brown ever would begin another Balaklava. Should Brown act, Higginson, in any case, did not relish risking his life to be merely one of the "Six Hundred."

Despite fund-raising difficulties, Brown obtained a pledge for $2,000 during a visit to Boston in May. He also received a small amount by speaking in Concord about his Missouri invasion to an audience that included Alcott, Emerson, and Thoreau. Impressed with his surprising sense, courage, and religious earnestness, they all contributed. When Brown returned to Boston, a final meeting was arranged at Howe's home. "He is a character, I assure you," Howe remarked afterward. Higginson had been invited to see Brown before he left, but he was not in Worcester when the invitation arrived.[53]

Sanborn reported in June that Brown had taken $800 with him with assurances that Stearns would see that the remainder of the $2,000 was forwarded. Sanborn noted that Brown meant to be on the ground as soon as he could, to begin perhaps by the fourth of July.[54]

Telling Higginson that this might be the last chance to help, Sanborn suggested that, because of the shortage of available Boston Negroes, Higginson should go to Canada with Harriet Tubman to recruit fugitive slaves for Brown's forces. Sanborn himself felt unable to do so because of teaching commitments at Concord. He recommended Higginson because he already had some ac-

52. TWH to Brown, May 1, 1859, Higginson-Brown MSS.
53. Sanborn to TWH, May 9, 1859, Higginson-Brown MSS; Howe to J. M. Forbes, May 9, 1859, in Hughes, *Forbes, 1,* 179; Sanborn to TWH, May 30, 1859, Higginson-Brown MSS.
54. Sanborn to TWH, June 4, 1859, Higginson-Brown MSS.

quaintance with Canadian sympathizers and would know where to go. In spite of a visit from the female "Moses," Harriet Tubman, Higginson declined.[55] This was not the sort of secondary work to whet his enthusiasm. He would not run a recruiting errand for Brown, especially when he was asked to substitute for young Sanborn and had not even been asked directly by the captain. Higginson well remembered that since their May 1858 meeting he had rarely heard from Brown.

Still, Higginson kept well informed about him. Sanborn visited Worcester in late June and Higginson visited Sanborn in Concord in late July. Sanborn's letters suggest that Brown continued to be discussed between them. In late August he told Higginson that more money was urgently needed. Again Higginson provided nothing even when Sanborn implored: "you must raise $50 if possible, you see the emergency and how others have met it." The arrival of another fourth of July with slavery still flourishing increased Higginson's skepticism. Only when George Stearns personally requested more funds did he respond with $20 of the $50 asked of him.[56]

John Brown wrote his children on October 1, urging them to "save this letter to remember your Father by." On the 6th, Sanborn noted that a nephew of Abolitionist Francis Jackson, Francis Merriam, an eager youth of twenty-two who was en route to Brown, had agreed to contribute $600 in gold plus his own service and would stop at Worcester to see Higginson. Merriam, in September 1858, had told Wendell Phillips of a desire to supply money for "stealing slaves down South," and to participate in such action. Confessing doubts about how much he would dare do, he asked Phillips: "Could poison or a deadly weapon be passed to a prisoner caught in the South for stealing slaves?"[57]

Although it may have been literally true that nobody explicitly mentioned Harpers Ferry, as was later claimed, both Higginson

55. Ibid.; TWH to L. Higginson, June 17, 1859, Higginson MSS; *Yesterdays*, p. 222.

56. TWH to L. Higginson, June 17, July 22, 1859, Higginson MSS; Sanborn to TWH, Aug. 24, 1859, Sept. 4, 1859, G. Stearns to TWH, Sept. 14, 1859, Higginson-Brown MSS; L. Hayden to Mrs. G. L. Stearns, April 5, 1878, copy in Villard MSS.

57. Copy in Higginson-Brown MSS; Sanborn to TWH, Oct. 6, 1859, ibid.; Merriam to Phillips, Sept. 22, 1858, Villard MSS.

and Sanborn knew enough to send Merriam to Kennedy's farm on the Maryland border. "Perhaps you will have something to say to him or some message for the shepherd," suggested Sanborn. But instead of relaying a final message, Higginson was stunned. He found the one-eyed, frail Merriam to be either mentally unbalanced or severely retarded—a discovery that made him wonder if the whole expedition would be a fiasco. Sanborn's reply strongly castigated Higginson for his lack of faith in Brown, informing him that the "business operation" was to commence on the next Saturday, October 15: "Have we seen so little fruit from the agent's labors that we should distrust his Fabian valor? Who saved Kansas in '56 and invaded Missouri in '58?" [58]

As for using the unbalanced Merriam in this arduous venture, Sanborn's jubilance at having secured both money and a recruit suddenly made explicit a new aspect of the Harpers Ferry effort and the relationship of Brown and his northern supporters. Of this man sent to Brown on the eve of the raid, the Concord schoolteacher said:

> 'Tis a virtue posted in numbskulls, to give money freely. . . . I consider him about as fit to be in this enterprise as the devil is to keep a powder house; but everything has its use & must be put to it if possible. Out of the mouths of babes and sucklings come dollars by the hundred, and what is wisdom compared to that? I do not expect much of anybody . . . but when a plum drops in your mouth shall you not eat it because it is not a peach or a pumpkin? [59]

58. Villard, *Brown*, p. 421; TWH to Hinton, Mar. 15, 1890, Hinton MSS; Sanborn to TWH, Oct. 6, 1859, Higginson MSS; TWH to (?), October 16, 1859, Misc. MSS, American Antiquarian Society.

59. Sanborn to TWH, Oct. 13, 1859, Higginson-Brown MSS. There is no mention of this letter in Villard's *Brown*, but it has been copied in the Villard MSS.

13

"Swart-Minded Higginson"

Writing forty years after the Harpers Ferry raid, Higginson attempted to recollect that October morning in Worcester when he heard a neighbor declare: "Old Osawatomie Brown has got himself into a tight place at last!" Higginson recalled having hurriedly read a newspaper account and how his first feeling about Brown had been one of remorse because the men who had given him money and arms were not at his side. In his own case, however, he said that the justification was clear.[1] Forty years allowed his memory to distort more than just his feelings at the first news of Harpers Ferry.

Not remorse but ecstasy describes his initial reaction. The raid, he wrote at the time, was the most formidable slave insurrection that had ever occurred, and it was evident through the confused and exaggerated accounts that there were leaders of great capacity behind it. He was sure that they could long withstand an attack from "all the force likely to be brought against them, & can at least retreat to the mountains & establish a Maroon colony there, like those in Jamaica & Guiana. Meantime the effect will be to frighten & weaken the slave power everywhere, & discourage the slave trade." Assuming that Brown had roused an army of southern slaves to join the battle, Higginson again noted that nothing had so strengthened slavery as the timid submission of the slaves thus far. Far different was the reaction of his old Amesbury neighbor and ally in Free Soil politics, John Greenleaf Whittier, who said, "I have just been looking at one of the *pikes* sent here by a friend in Baltimore. It is not a Christian weapon; it looks too much like murder." [2]

1. *Yesterdays*, p. 223.
2. TWH to L. Higginson, Oct. 17, 1859, Higginson MSS; Whittier to Lydia M. Child, Oct. 21 [1859], quoted in TWH, *Whittier*, pp. 78–79.

Higginson, in subsequent months, would have reason to regret that four of the Secret Six had not been among those besieged in the engine house. For in retrospect the actions of Sanborn, Smith, Stearns, and Howe before and after the raid appeared far less heroic than the stand of Leonidas at Thermopylae. One can wonder whether Higginson, forty years after the event, wanted also to include Francis Merriam among those attacked by Colonel Robert E. Lee and the marines. For neither was Merriam at Brown's side at the surrender; he had fled north to Canada via Concord, to visit Sanborn. But the Concord schoolteacher refused to see him, allegedly out of regard for Merriam's safety. He dispatched Thoreau instead, who introduced himself as a Mr. Lockwood and put Merriam on the next train north. Merriam, Sanborn now concluded, was "wholly crazy." [3]

By no means was Higginson alone in revising his memories of the raid. The changing reactions of the Republican Worcester *Spy* well illustrated the politically committed antislavery mind. At first it said:

> This old man, whose experiences in Kansas made him a mono-maniac on such matters as slavery and border ruffiianism, has gone so far in this madness, and become so wild with it, as to invade Virginia at the head of an army of seventeen white men, all as crazy as himself. . . . The madness is so evident in all he has done at Harpers Ferry as to leave no room for doubt.[4]

Attacked by the Democratic press, the paper a week later characterized the Harpers Ferry affair as "one of the rashest and maddest enterprises ever," but perhaps remembering that it had once agreed that Brown be given a plaque for his Kansas heroism, plaintively added that he had never lacked prudence or shrewdness in the territories. Subsequently aided by Brown's own denial from prison that he had ever contemplated slave insurrection or bloodshed, and by the actual heroism he displayed when confronted with a Virginia death sentence, the *Spy* began depicting him as a

3. Sanborn, *Recollections, 1,* 204; Sanborn interview by Katherine Mayo, Jan. 19, 1909, Villard MSS.
4. *Spy*, Oct. 20, 1859.

zealous hero devoted to a noble cause. It would finally conclude that Brown had acted from conviction.[5]

Others who had been closer to Brown also changed their tune after Harpers Ferry from a militant revolutionary air to one that sounded *lento pianissimo*. Three days after Brown was captured, Frank Sanborn forewent his chance to lead his Concord students in their annual chestnut-hunt. From Portland, Maine, en route to Canada, he wrote Higginson: "According to advice of good friends and my own deliberate judgement I am to try change of air for my old complaint . . . whether my absence will be long or short will depend on circumstances. . . . Burn this." [6]

Although Higginson chose not to burn Sanborn's letter, and would continue to ignore such requests, Gerrit Smith was busy burning all the Brown correspondence he possessed; moreover, he dispatched his son-in-law to do the same in Boston and at the Ohio home of John Brown, Jr. His personal secretary, Edward Morton, and his ally in conspiracy, Frederick Douglass, both sailed for England. Smith too was plagued by an "old complaint," which manifested itself in acute insomnia. His physician indicated that it was not "trouble of the Brain" but constipation caused the disability. The patient was confined for a month, however, at the New York State Asylum for the Insane at Utica. In later years, when Sanborn planned to disclose Smith's generous financial aid to Brown, Smith's daughter noted that similar symptoms once again plagued her father.[7]

Once Brown's trial began, George Stearns and Samuel Howe left for Canada, remaining there until Brown was hanged. But Howe was not silent. He issued a statement denying the rumor that linked his name with Harpers Ferry and John Brown. Said Howe: "That event was unforeseen and unexpected by me; nor does all my previous knowledge of John Brown enable me to reconcile it with his characteristic prudence and his reluctance to shed blood, or excite servile insurrection. It is still to me a mystery, and a marvel." Theodore Parker was the only conspirator who was out

5. Ibid., Nov. 5, Dec. 2, 1859.
6. Sanborn to TWH, Oct. 21, 1859, Higginson-Brown MSS.
7. *Spy*, Nov. 11, 1859; Harlow, *Smith*, p. 411.

of the country for health reasons not connected with the Harpers Ferry epidemic. In Italy, living out the last month of a terminal illness, he was still certain that "without the shedding of blood there is no remission of sins." To the nonresistant Abolitionist Francis Jackson, Merriam's uncle, he wrote: "Of course I was not astonished to hear that an attempt had been made to free the slaves in a certain part of Virginia, . . . such 'insurrections' will continue as long as Slavery lasts. . . . All the great charters of humanity have been writ in blood. . . . It is plain now that our pilgrimage must lead through a Red Sea, wherein many a Pharoah will go under and perish." [8]

Parker's statement gave him the distinction of being the only member of the Secret Six who was consistent (certainly more consistent than Brown) before and after Harpers Ferry. When Stephen Vincent Benet later put the John Brown story into verse, he reflected the judgment of historians by writing, "only the tough swart-minded Higginson kept a grim decency, would not deny." [9] This was true to the degree that Higginson was the only member of the Secret Six who remained in the country throughout Brown's trial, his execution, and during the congressional investigation into the Harpers Ferry affair; he was also the only member of the conspirators who did not burn letters and who truly wished to testify at Brown's trial. It has not been recognized that he denied in another way. Never again would Higginson admit what he had so jubilantly hailed upon first reading of the attack, when its success seemed possible. He would never again admit that John Brown's actions, and his own words and deeds until Brown's utter defeat, were clearly directed toward "the most formidable slave insurrection."

Not only had the raid failed to end slavery but it failed to accomplish what Higginson wanted so badly: "the end of the apparent feebleness & timidity of the slaves." He had hoped that with one blow a slave insurrection would destroy the northern view that all

8. Villard, *Brown*, p. 530; Harold Schwartz, *Samuel Gridley Howe* (Cambridge, 1956), pp. 238–40; Howe to TWH, Feb. 16, 1860, Higginson-Brown MSS; *Tribune*, Nov. 16, 1859; Theodore Parker to Francis Jackson, Nov. 24, 1859, in John Weiss, *Life and Correspondence of Theodore Parker*, 2 (New York, 1864), 172.
9. Stephen Vincent Benet, *John Brown's Body* (New York, 1941), pp. 58–59.

slaves were as submissive as Uncle Tom. Two facts made defeat devastatingly complete: Brown had utterly failed as a military strategist, and the first man killed was a Negro who was fleeing from him. Two years later Higginson made a veiled attempt to explain the absence of a slave uprising by noting that in the Denmark Vesey insurrection not even sympathetic white men were able to gain the slaves' confidence. In this context Oliver Wendell Holmes' lines assume a special irony:

> All through the conflict, up and down
> Marched Uncle Tom and Old John Brown.

Contrary to his own words and deeds prior to Harpers Ferry, Higginson claimed forty years later that in 1859 he knew Brown's "postponement had somewhat disturbed the delicate balance of the zealot's mind, and had made him . . . defy the whole power of the United States government, and that within easy reach of Washington. . . . Anything like slave insurrection, in the ordinary sense of the word, was remote from his thoughts." [10]

After Higginson had learned of Brown's absurd military conduct and the ease with which his force's had been overcome, he appeared less than compassionate about the prisoner's fate. "Of course I *think* enough about Brown," he rather touchily asserted. "I don't feel sure that his acquittal or rescue would do half as much good as being executed; so strong is the personal sympathy with him. We have done what we could for him by sending counsel & in other ways that must be nameless." [11] But once Brown's trial had begun and once the Secret Six had begun developing "old complaints," Higginson's sympathy turned increasingly toward Brown as did his antipathy toward his former fellow conspirators. In jail, Brown acted and talked like a manly hero; in contrast, his northern supporters seemed more like cowardly politicians.

Higginson was unsympathetic to Smith's illness and Howe's denial of complicity, especially since it had been agreed before the

10. "Denmark Vesey," *Atlantic Monthly*, 5 (1861), 737; "The World's Homage," Oliver Wendell Holmes, *Complete Poetical Works* (Boston, 1895), p. 272; *Yesterdays*, pp. 223, 225.

11. TWH to L. Higginson, Oct. 27, 1859, Higginson MSS; Circular "to aid in the defense of Captain Brown . . . ," Villard MSS.

raid not to deny. Sanborn argued that Brown and his men were not suffering from concealment of their support. Reminding Higginson of the unmanly confession of Brown's man John Cook, he asked whether he would want to put himself in a similar position.[12] Higginson hotly answered by posing his own questions: "Sanborn, is there no such thing as *honor* among confederates? . . . Can your clear moral sense be so sophisticated . . . [as] to justify holding one's tongue in face of this lying—and lying under the meanest of circumstances—to save ourselves from all share in even the reprobation of society when the nobler man whom we have provoked on into danger is the scapegoat of that reprobation—& the gallows too?" Sanborn replied that he had destroyed all letters that might be used against anyone. Anticipating this, Higginson retained a copy[13] and continued to plague him. The Concord schoolteacher was being forced to pay for the top conspiratorial position he had held during Harpers Ferry preparations.

For a time there was one voice that denied nothing. It belonged to James Redpath, a friend of Brown in Kansas. Three days after Brown's imprisonment, Redpath began a series of articles in the Boston *Atlas & Daily Bee*, variously titled "Reminiscences of the Insurrection" and "Notes on the Insurrection." The author claimed to be qualified for the task because Brown's men had been his intimate acquaintances, and because one of the raiders had called him "the rashest and most reckless man he knew." Redpath boasted of having traveled to Haiti with Francis Merriam in order to examine the benefits of slave insurrection.[14]

For John Brown, of course, he saved his most important words, and expressed them just before the trial:

> Living he acted bravely, dying, he will teach us courage. A Samson in his life; he will be a Samson in his death. Let cowards ridicule and denounce him; let snake-like journalists hiss at his holy failure—for one, I do not hesitate to say that I love him, admire him, and defend him. GOD BLESS HIM! [15]

12. Sanborn to TWH, Nov. 17, 1859, Higginson-Brown MSS.
13. TWH to Sanborn, Nov. [17], 1859, Sanborn to TWH, Nov. 19, 1859, Higginson-Brown MSS.
14. Boston *Atlas & Daily Bee*, Oct. 21, 24, 29, 1859.
15. Ibid., Oct. 24, 1859.

Redpath said that Brown believed slavery would be abolished only by servile insurrection. He concluded that there was "no greater compliment" to Brown than being hanged by the state of Virginia.[16] With both points John Brown strongly disagreed. His subsequent denial of having even contemplated slave insurrection or bloodshed reflected his doubt that hanging was an honor.

By the fourth day of the trial Brown became markedly interested in saving his life. Tired of being the instrument of militant-speaking nonparticipants, his request for legal help included the admonition: "Do not send an ultra Abolitionist." The dispatch of George Hoyt, a twenty-one-year-old Abolitionist lawyer from Athol, Massachusetts, to provide Brown's legal defense hardly proved that his supporters were anxious to prevent his execution. Hoyt, a "beardless boy," was obviously in Charles Town to help plan Brown's escape. But the prisoner knew how heavily guarded Charles Town was and did not relish the risk of once again sustaining the kind of physical beating he had received when captured at Harpers Ferry. Hoyt's report about a jail break was unequivocal: "The country all around is guarded by armed patrols & a large body of troops are constantly under arms. If you hear anything about such an attempt, for Heaven's sake do not *fail to restrain the enterprise.*" Brown said he opposed a rescue attempt for fear of betraying his kind jailer.[17]

After reading the prisoner's moving speech to the court and the cowardly words of the Secret Six, Higginson showed signs of reversing his view that Brown was better dead than alive. He took a trip to the Adirondacks and the Brown family homestead at North Elba, New York, and was struck by the family's simplicity and disinterestedness. Impressed by their high morale in the face of what he now admitted was the "utter downfall" of years of planning, Higginson assured these "calm, cheerful, strong" people that the Harpers Ferry raid and Brown's trial had done more than Sumner or Kansas to reawaken antislavery agitation throughout the country. Perhaps he also was trying to reassure himself. But to give

16. Ibid., Oct. 28. 1859.
17. Brown to Thomas Russell, Oct. 27, 1859, in Villard, *Brown*, p. 493; W. Phillips to TWH, Oct. 26, 1859, George Hoyt to John Le Barnes, Nov. 30, 1859, Higginson-Brown MSS; TWH to L. Higginson, Nov. 5, 1859, Higginson MSS.

consolation to Mrs. Brown, of whose thirteen children only four had survived, and whose husband faced certain execution, was not the reason for his trip. He was on a mission to bring her to Boston and then send her to the Charles Town jail to convince her husband that an escape was desirable. At the very least, her appearance at the side of the condemned man would evoke public sympathy.[18]

Mrs. Brown was greeted in Boston by the antislavery people with gifts, kisses, and counsel. Her husband, however, beginning to grow in his role as condemned man, greeted with dismay the news of her impending visit to his cell. Boston lawyer George Sennott, in Charles Town to defend four of the six Harpers Ferry survivors, telegraphed Higginson collect: "Mr. Brown says for gods sake dont let Mrs. Brown come. Send her word by telegraph wherever she is." [19]

At this news, Higginson demanded an explanation from Charles Town while simultaneously informing the Philadelphia Abolitionist J. Miller McKim, who had already reached Baltimore with Mrs. Brown, that "it can hardly be a matter of *sentiment* on his part. . . . It may be that something has occurred; or it may be that he fears her being called as a witness." Nevertheless Brown's wishes should be regarded, Higginson told McKim, at least temporarily. Brown insisted that he was a better judge in this matter than anyone else. But Mrs. Brown was eventually brought to Charles Town.[20]

Even at the point of death, John Brown had to resist being used by his offstage northern supporters. Against his repeated statements opposing an escape attempt, plans were made to free him. The prospect of procuring a militant abolitionist martyr was not as promising now to some of his northern supporters as thwarting Virginia justice. When the fugitive slaves Thomas Sims and Anthony Burns had not tried to escape their southern captors, it had been a great disappointment. Perhaps the downfall of the Harpers Ferry plan could be mitigated.

18. *Spy*, Nov. 3, 1859; TWH to L. Higginson, Nov. 5, 1859, Higginson MSS; TWH to [J. Miller McKim], Nov. 3, 1859, McKim MSS.

19. TWH to L. Higginson, Nov. 5, 1859, Higginson MSS; George Sennott to TWH, Nov. 5, 1859, Higginson-Brown MSS.

20. TWH to J. M. McKim, Nov. 5, 1859, McKim MSS; Alfred M. Barbour memo, Dec. 1, 1859, Brown MSS, Library of Congress.

Lysander Spooner, a bold advocate of armed insurrection in the South, now proposed securing a hostage for Brown's life. He received encouragement, in mid-November, for a plan to kidnap (in Richmond) Virginia's governor, Henry A. Wise. John Le Barnes, a lawyer employed at the Boston Waterworks Company and the man who had hired George Hoyt to help execute Brown's escape, judged that the Spooner plan had the merit of audacity. Higginson agreed that it would terrify the South as much as Harpers Ferry. More important, if it succeeded, Massachusetts, not Virginia, would be the final victor.[21]

After enlisting mercenaries and finding a boat reputed to be faster than any gunboat in the Richmond area, a major obstacle arose: $10,000 to $15,000 would be necessary to cover costs. To raise that amount quickly proved especially difficult when so many affluent northerners, including Abolitionists, thought Brown better dead than alive. Le Barnes finally told Higginson what he undoubtedly already knew very well: "*Success* would be *brilliant* defeat fatally inglorious."[22] Despite defiant public statements by the Abolitionists about the victory at Harpers Ferry, their morale could not bear the humiliation of another such rout.

A new plan was soon conceived: an overland assault on the Charles Town prison by volunteers. Again Brown's wishes were not relevant. The fugitive slave Shadrach had been forcibly carried from a Boston courtroom to freedom without asking his consent; why could not Brown be an instrument to exhibit Abolitionist heroism? The Boston sculptor Edwin Brackett, permitted to stand outside Brown's cell to model the condemned man's head, had an imagination not restricted, like Hoyt's, by the exactitude of legal training. Asked to report on the feasibility of a direct attack on the jail, Brackett answered that it could be done.[23]

A group of German refugees, who had fled the revolution of 1848 and settled in New York, agreed to lead an overland attack after a rendezvous with a band rumored to be headed by John Brown, Jr. The plan required reaching Charles Town secretly on foot, freeing the prisoner, and seizing the horses of the cavalry

21. John Le Barnes to TWH, Nov. 15, 1859, Higginson-Brown MSS.
22. Ibid., Nov. 22, 1859, Higginson-Brown MSS.
23. Ibid., Nov. 14, 27, 1859, Higginson-Brown MSS.

companies for the escape. Even the enthusiastic Le Barnes told Higginson: "They are confident strange as it may seem to us—of success." Their price was $100 each plus compensation for their families in event of capture or death. "The men are ready. They ask for *funds*. It is for you in Boston to say 'go' or 'stay,'" reported Le Barnes. Sanborn, fittingly, sent him the answer: "Object abandoned." He wrote Higginson: "So I suppose we must give up all hope of saving our old friend." [24]

Those closest to Brown had become so eager to save his life that a week before the execution date they even agreed to have Hoyt present to Governor Wise an affidavit of John Brown's insanity. No longer were they claiming that Virginia, not Brown, was insane. The various plans to save him, however, worried James Redpath, who had candidly declared that Brown's aim was slave insurrection and he welcomed Brown's execution by Virginia. Rapidly completing *The Public Life of John Brown*, he told Higginson that he would withhold publication "until Old B. is in heaven." Having worked so frantically to complete his manuscript, he nervously asked: "I have not the faintest hope of his escape from martyrdom: have you?" [25]

Four days before Brown's execution, Higginson admitted to Lysander Spooner that the only way the honor of the free states could have been redeemed was by the rescue of John Brown and his comrades. Despite Brown's heroic comportment even up to death, Higginson believed that Virginia had defeated them. Indicating that it was not only in Virginia where honor had been lost, he acidly advised Spooner: "There is no need to burn this." [26]

Of course the final words pronounced about Brown were not those delivered at the execution by Colonel J. T. L. Preston, who declared: "So perish all such enemies of Virginia! All such enemies of the Union! All such foes of the human race!" James Redpath had different judgments to will to posterity. His book appeared soon after the execution. Not only were its sentiments different from Preston's but also from those Redpath had previously writ-

24. Ibid., Nov. 27, 1859, Sanborn to TWH, Nov. 28, 1859, Higginson-Brown MSS.

25. James Redpath to TWH, Nov. 13, 1859, Higginson-Brown MSS.

26. TWH to L. Spooner, Nov. 28, 1859, Spooner MSS.

ten about Brown the revolutionary. As if to help "old B." to heaven,
he prudently refrained from relating Brown in Kansas to Brown at
Harpers Ferry. This, he shrewdly told Higginson, "degrades him
from the position of a Puritan 'warring of the Lord' to a guerrilla
chief of vindictive character." Redpath also left slave insurrection
unmentioned. Brown's plans had simply been to liberate slaves, to
free them in Virginia, and to keep them there—not revolution but
justice. As for the satchel of conspiratorial letters which had been
seized at the Kennedy farm after the raid (letters whose discovery
terrified Brown's northern accomplices) it contained unimportant
notes. And to show the heroic qualities of Mrs. Brown and the survivors at North Elba, Higginson allowed Redpath to include in the
book his own essay, "Visit to the John Brown Household." This
newly acquired prudence won Redpath an endorsement from both
Brown's widow and his son Salmon and netted Mrs. Brown a large
percentage of the profits. In a short time the book would be selling
"wondrously." [27]

Toward Brown's surviving sons Higginson felt empathy, compassion, and a touch of envy. "Were he my father," he wrote
Brown, Jr., "*I know I* should feel all pangs of sorrow merged in
gratitude for his being the means of a great good. *He has failed in
his original effort only to succeed in a greater result.*" [28]

On the night after the execution, Higginson participated in a
John Brown memorial meeting in Worcester. Although stressing
the good that Brown's deeds had accomplished, he reminded his
audience, which included at least nine ministers, that "Virginia acts;
Massachusetts talks. If ever a man despised words when deeds were
needed that man was John Brown." Eulogies were not enough:
"John Brown is now beyond our reach; but the oppressed for
whom he died still live." Higginson had not specifically said how
Brown's memory could be used to stimulate future deeds. Much
had been asked of Brown and his family by northern supporters,
but there was one sacrifice the Brown family refused to make. It
denied Higginson's request that John Brown's body be moved to

27. Villard, *Brown*, p. 557; James Redpath, *The Public Life of John Brown*
(Boston, 1861), pp. 233, 270; Redpath to TWH, Nov. 13, 1859, Sanborn to TWH,
Jan. 16, 1860, Higginson-Brown MSS.

28. Nov. 10, 1859, Dec. 2, 1859, Higginson-Huntington MSS.

a grave at Cambridge's Mt. Auburn Cemetery. Whether John Brown used his northern supporters more than they used him indeed is questionable.[29]

The question of courage was less difficult to determine. Once John Mason of Virginia was appointed chairman of a Senate committee to investigate the events surrounding the Harpers Ferry affair, the fears which had plagued Brown's northern supporters when he had first been captured returned. Frank Sanborn uneasily waited to be called as a witness. Determined to refuse to testify in Washington, he threatened a public exposure of Senator Henry Wilson's knowledge of Brown's plans should the Senator fail to help Sanborn. Wilson cooperated, however, for he neither wished to implicate himself nor the Republican party. Warning that Higginson, Sanborn, Howe, Stearns, and Amos Lawrence would be summoned by the Mason Committee, he urged them to refuse to testify.[30] Sanborn agreed with Wilson. He reminded Higginson that Richard Realf, who in 1858 had been elected Secretary of State under Brown's "Provisional Constitution," already had named the Worcester man at one session of the hearing. Trying to convince Higginson to avoid testifying, Sanborn argued: "there are a thousand better ways of spending a year in warfare against Slavery than by lying in a Washington prison." He added his usual closing sentence: "I hope you burn all my letters about these things." [31]

Once back in Canada to escape the congressional summons, Sanborn was even more articulate. Further schemes like Harpers Ferry, he predicted, were possible. "Such is my prophecy of the future, and I mean to reserve myself for that. . . . Some of us are so fond of charging bayonets that for fault of any enemy we rush upon our friends." But after this thrust at Higginson, he pleaded that "in case you are summoned . . . do not tell what you know to the enemies of the cause, I implore you." [32]

29. *Spy*, Dec. 2, 1859; Ruth B. Thompson to TWH, Dec. 27, 1859, Higginson-Brown MSS; see C. Vann Woodward, "John Brown's Private War," *America in Crisis*, ed. Daniel Aaron (New York, 1952), p. 112.

30. *Report of the Select Committee of the Senate appointed to inquire into the late invasion and seizure of public property at Harper's Ferry*, Rep. Com. No. 278, 36th Cong., 1st Sess. (Washington, 1860).

31. Henry Wilson to TWH, Dec. 24, 1859, Sanborn to TWH, Dec. 20, 25, 1859, Jan. 2, 1860, Higginson-Brown MSS.

32. Sanborn to TWH, Jan. 29, 1860, Higginson-Brown MSS.

Higginson disagreed, but he was not summoned to Washington even though Richard Realf had indeed told the investigating committee on January 21, 1860, "that a clergyman, whose name is Thomas Wentworth Higginson, who . . . resides at Worcester, Massachusetts, was an intimate friend of John Brown, and . . . was one of those who supplied him with funds to enable him to prosecute his movements in behalf of freedom in Kansas, and had given him a general promise to assist him in whatever enterprises he might undertake." It remains unclear why Higginson was not subsequently summoned to Washington as were Martin Conway of the National Kansas Committee, Samuel Howe, George Stearns, Charles Robinson, Frank Sanborn, James Redpath, and Thaddeus Hyatt. No evidence was introduced to question the veracity of Realf's statement.[33] Furthermore, Virginia's Governor Henry Wise had received a note in October which was signed by a "Friend of Order":

> There are two persons in Massachusetts, and I think only two, who if summoned as witnesses, can explain the whole of Brown's plot. Their names are Francis B. Sanborn of Concord, and T. W. Higginson, of Worcester, Mass. No time should be lost, as they may abscond, but I do not think they will, as they think you would not think it best to send for them.[34]

Higginson believed that he was not called simply because congressmen, when "white men are concerned . . . will yield before the slightest resistance. The reason why Phillips & I have not been

33. *Senate Harper's Ferry Report*, p. 112 and *passim*.

34. Oct. 1859, Brown MSS. Sanborn, in 1909, accused Higginson of having written the letter in a disguised handwriting, but it was vigorously denied. Higginson branded the charge an "almost incredible libel." After examining the letter he believed that the author was Rev. Samuel J. May. Attempting to resolve the dispute, Worthington Ford, President of the Massachusetts Historical Society, compared the anonymous letter with May's handwriting and decided that Higginson was the writer.

Higginson surely was capable of writing such a letter in 1859 and there is a resemblance in handwriting. But I do not think that the phraseology is Higginson's, especially the last sentence, and I believe that Higginson would have accepted authorship in 1909 if the letter were his—his reminiscences tended to stress his past acts of bravado. See *Yesterdays* p. 25; TWH to Villard, Oct. 23, Nov. 18, 1909, Villard MSS; TWH diary, Nov. 10, 11, 1909; TWH to Worthington Ford, Nov. 30, 1909, Ford to TWH, Jan. 11, 1910, Higginson MSS.

summoned is that it is well understood that we are not going to
Canada." If one fled the country, the Mason Committee could
charge guilt without risking armed defiance in some northern city.
But Higginson was unwilling merely to test the Mason Committee.
More aggressive action was necessary—action that would elevate
Higginson and his followers to the heroic role, "and redeem the
honor of the Free States." [35]

Public sympathy for the Brown survivors manifested in cash
contributions soon allowed something bolder. Rescue plans to free
Brown had all been hampered by a shortage of cash. Higginson,
by late December, recalled his earlier observations about the
Browns: "money seemed to be flowing for them in all directions"
and they were in any case "not so totally destitute as many
think." [36]

Apparently with the Browns' permission, funds contributed to
them were diverted to try one last rescue. Freeing Aaron Stevens
and Albert Hazlett, the two imprisoned members of Brown's band
thus far not executed, might yet prove as audacious as Harpers
Ferry. Higginson's justification for not being more active for
Brown prior to his imprisonment apparently was not as certain as
he alleged in that recollection forty years after.

To lead a guerrilla force at night through the mountainous
countryside of western Virginia and then descend upon the Charles
Town jail to liberate the prisoners would certainly serve Higginson's purposes. With ample funds and sufficient daring the expedition had great promise. He began recruiting, in early January,
some of the former Kansas marauders and the Harpers Ferry men
who had escaped capture. Charles Tidd, the only Brown man free
and still in the country, was the first to consent to join Higginson.
But Tidd was unwilling to return to Virginia. A week later Richard Hinton, once active in Kansas, agreed that Stevens and Hazlett
must be saved, and enlisted in the cause. Catching the conspiratorial spirit, he suggested that all letters be written "either in some
cypher or with iodine." He embarked for the West to persuade

35. TWH to Sanborn, Mar. 3, 1860, Nov. 13, Dec. 25, 1859, Higginson-Brown
MSS.
36. Anne Brown to TWH, Jan. 17, 1860, Higginson-Brown MSS; TWH to
L. Higginson, Nov. 22, 1859, Higginson MSS.

James Montgomery, the chief free-state guerrilla leader, to join the action.[37]

John Le Barnes assured his German forty-eighters that this time their price would be met. S. J. Willis, a Kansan who had helped in the escape of a free-state man from a prison in St. Joseph, Missouri, notified Higginson that he was on call. "Where duty's path is plain," said he, "I hope to God I may never falter." In Brown's footsteps, Willis sought to smooth his path to duty: "Now it is necessary for me to speak of some things that I regret to say are important and must be considered—first I am entirely without funds and in debt." Willis also received assurance that this should not keep him from joining the action. Enthusiasm and money seemed available. Hinton, in fact, was too enthusiastic. Higginson learned that he freely told anyone interested that he was on a secret mission.[38]

Higginson, by the end of January, arranged a Midwestern lecture tour to coincide with a trip to Harrisburg, Pennsylvania. Under the apt pseudonym, "Reverend Theodore Brown," he directed preparations but was pessimistic because he recognized that campfires would be necessary for the cold weather. He left for Harrisburg after sending eight revolvers to Le Barnes for his German forty-eighters and instructions to alert them. En route to the Harrisburg rendezvous Higginson characteristically addressed his wife in the manner he used when on a daring venture. This time he called her "you dear little ignoramus." He wrote: "As I grow older, darling, I think I feel more & more that I have no right to risk myself without strong reasons. I hope for some dinner which is all my physical man needs." [39]

But a dinner no longer seemed enough to satisfy his appetite for action when he learned that Montgomery and his men were on their way to Harrisburg. Instead of stifling the project or perhaps

37. TWH to Stevens, Mar. 12, 1860, copy in Higginson-Brown MSS; Charles P. Tidd to TWH, Dec. 8, 1859, R. Hinton to TWH, Dec. 13, 27, 1859, Higginson-Brown MSS.

38. Le Barnes to TWH, Jan. 19, 1860, S. J. Willis to TWH, Jan. 19, Feb. 27, 1860, Mrs. S. C. Pomeroy to TWH, Jan. 23, 1860, Higginson-Brown MSS.

39. TWH memo, Feb. 10, 1860, Higginson-Brown MSS; Villard, Brown, p. 575; Le Barnes to TWH, Feb. 4, 1860, copy in Villard MSS; TWH to M. Higginson [Feb. 16], 1860, Higginson MSS.

allowing Montgomery to proceed without his direction, he again assumed the role of the enthusiastic leader: "Montgomery is strong in hope. . . . He is a man to inspire infinite hope." Not only did he strike Higginson as "the most charming person I ever saw," he also had brought seven experienced Kansas men. Montgomery planned to reconnoiter the route to Charles Town. Warming to the task, Higginson instructed Le Barnes to choose his forty-eighters from those who had been troops of the line. If Montgomery reported favorably, Higginson would lead the raiding party into Charles Town. Montgomery and Silas Soule, another participant in the St. Joseph jail rescue, embarked for Charles Town on February 21. Higginson continued his Midwestern lecture tour; he asked his wife to give him credit for wisdom in not canceling it to go with them. While Montgomery and Soule were away, his pessimism about a successful rescue returned.[40]

En route to Charles Town, Montgomery, a Kentuckian by birth, deepened his southern accent. Soule, playing the part of an inebriated Irishman, succeeded in being put in the same Charles Town jail that held Hazlett; he learned that Hazlett was as undesirous to test a wild escape plan as Brown had been. Montgomery, in addition, reported to Higginson that the entire countryside was alerted for any rescue attempt. The last two Harpers Ferry men would go to the gallows. The cost of the Harrisburg venture had been nearly $2,000.[41]

Higginson, on March 1, inscribed in his notebook a line from Dickens' *A Tale of Two Cities:* "Recalled to Life." Relieved at not having to embark on a foredoomed rescue effort, he wrote his own words of consolation to Aaron Stevens: "Death is only a step in life, & there is no more reason why we should fear to go from one world into another than from one room into another." A full year after Harpers Ferry, Higginson would judge that the attempt to free Stevens and Hazlett had done one important thing: it had allowed him to regain his self-respect.[42]

40. TWH to Le Barnes, Feb. 17, 1860, Higginson-Brown MSS; TWH to M. Higginson, Feb. 9, 17, 1860, Higginson MSS.

41. TWH to Le Barnes, Feb. 25, 1860, Higginson-Brown MSS; TWH to Hinton, Mar. 24, 1860, Hinton MSS.

42. "Field Book," Higginson MSS; TWH to G. Stearns, Mar. 12, 1860, Higginson-Brown MSS; TWH journal, Oct. 1860.

14

On the Brink of War

The effects of Harpers Ferry still were being felt through New England in the spring of 1860 when Higginson joined a bodyguard of Massachusetts men gathering in Concord to protect Frank Sanborn from seizure by federal officials. Sanborn recently had narrowly avoided arrest for refusing to heed a summons of the Mason Committee. A hurriedly mustered *posse comitatus* had saved him, but a ruling by the Massachusetts Supreme Judicial Court was anxiously awaited. Would conservative Chief Justice Lemuel Shaw again decide against antislavery advocates as he had done in the Burns case, and would the United States again try to arrest Sanborn? To meet the possible crisis, Higginson rushed to defend the man he had so sharply criticized for deviousness in the Brown affair.[1]

His militancy was thwarted again. Shaw denied the legality of federal jurisdiction and the government made no further attempt to arrest Sanborn. And while James Redpath, expecting to be seized by federal authorities, promised to fire at the first intruder, no such attempt occurred. Only Thaddeus Hyatt, of New York, was arrested and imprisoned in Washington. The days of militant abolitionism were waning. Politically active men who talked of an "irrepressible conflict" were becoming, at times unwittingly, the real vanguard of abolition. Martin Stowell, important in the Jerry rescue, the Burns attempt, and in staking a New England claim in Kansas, reflected the change. Now settled in New Jersey, he anticipated the approaching conflict but confined efforts to his interest in temperance agitation.[2]

1. Sanborn, *Recollections*, *1*, 209–18; William Handy to TWH, April 4, 1860, Hinton MSS.

2. TWH to M. Higginson, April 4, 1860, Hinton MSS; Redpath to TWH, April 20, 1860, Stowell to TWH, April 15, 1860, Higginson-Kansas MSS; Villard, *Brown*, pp. 582, 583.

Higginson began again to write for literary magazines. Neither able nor wishing to change his activities as completely as Stowell, he remained in touch with abolitionism. Because it was "a good subject & can be useful & somewhat lucrative," he started writing a history of slave insurrections. The first piece had been written while Brown was in prison, and it did not mention the word insurrection. But now, six months after the raid, with the South nearing secession, he was eager to predict the inevitability of revolt. Implicitly defending Brown's violent aims in an article about the Maroons of Surinam, he generalized about the actions of the Negro slave by suggesting that during an insurrection a slave would of course commit some outrages: "If it is the normal tendency of bondage to produce saints like Uncle Tom, let us offer ourselves at auction immediately." [3]

The May news of the momentous split between northern and southern Democrats at the National Democratic Convention in Charleston pleased him. He judged that it helped Seward's chances for nomination and for election, and proved that disunion was inevitable. But he moved no closer to the exciting nomination battle that transpired in Chicago at the Republican Convention. As had repeatedly happened in the past, Higginson's periods of most intense militancy were followed by isolating himself from society. It was a withdrawal mistaken for self-containment.[4]

In his field book he recorded impressions that were reminiscent of those days along the Merrimack when nature, not man, surrounded him. As he had done in the past, he turned to Thoreau for justification: "I have at last, after a good many years of tolerably hard work, resolved to say with Thoreau, that 'I do not wish to practice self-denial, unless it is quite necessary.'" He felt moved by some internal force to that "old happiness in nature. . . . A thousand delicate tendrils seem to be tremulously thrusting forth within me, to bind me to the blissful world once more." This time, he discovered, by writing about nature, some connection between contemplation and action, between receiving sense experiences and expressing them in print. "There are out-door moments so rich," he

3. TWH to L. Higginson, April 18, 1860, Higginson MSS; "Maroons of Surinam," *Atlantic Monthly,* 5 (1860), 553.
4. TWH to L. Higginson, May 11, 1860, Higginson MSS.

explained, "it seems as if a single walk would furnish an essay. But I do not wish my essays to be milk, but cream. They must skim the wealth of many days & nights, besides 36 silent years behind." [5]

Briefly interrupting his absorption in nature to write an article for the *Atlantic* in memory of Theodore Parker, who had recently died at age fifty, Higginson sought to explain his own winding course. Parker, he suggested, had died from overwork. Although he was not moved by "any petty egotism, . . . Parker stood ready to take all the parts. . . . One sometimes wished that he had studied less and dreamed more." Benefiting from this lesson, Higginson hoped to direct his energy away from cities and men, but in the fall of 1860 he was attracted once more to the continuing crises. [6] For the next two years he was torn between the sounds of abolitionist activity and the silence of nature. Along with more resolute writers and intellectuals of the 1850s, Higginson was unable to find peace in solitude. His dilemma was greater than Parker's, Thoreau's, or Emerson's because he was justifiably less certain of his intellectual and artistic abilities.

Supporting political action for the first time since 1854, Higginson, in September, spoke to the Worcester Convention of radical political Abolitionists, organized by Stephen Foster, about whether a radical Abolitionist party was needed to oppose the Republicans. Gerrit Smith thought so, and Wendell Phillips, after evaluating the Republicans and their limited free soil antislavery plank, concluded that Lincoln was worse than Senator Mason of Virginia and should be labeled "*Abraham Lincoln—The Slavehound of Illinois.*" Higginson told the convention that its antislavery interpretation of the Constitution was meaningless. He proclaimed the excellence of Lincoln and declared his support of the Republican ticket. Foster was moved to say: "I love my friend Higginson, but if there is anything I loathe it is his opinions." [7]

By supporting the Republican party Higginson was sanctioning a platform which not only condemned John Brown's raid but was

5. "Field Book," Aug. 1860, Higginson MSS.

6. "Field Book," May 20, 1860, Higginson MSS; "Theodore Parker," *Atlantic Monthly*, 5 (1860), 451, 453; James R. Lowell to TWH, June 28, Sept. 22, 1860, Higginson MSS.

7. *Liberator*, Sept. 28, 1860; TWH, "Anti-Slavery Days," *Outlook*, 60 (1898), 51.

less firmly antislavery than the 1856 plank he had rejected. Now he foresaw the growing strength of the party's radical wing and looked to the beneficial pressure of events upon future political developments. Encouraging were the results of the recent Massachusetts Republican Convention in Worcester where Sumner and Bird succeeded in overwhelmingly defeating Governor Nathaniel Banks' bid to nominate his own successor. The selection of John A. Andrew by a two-to-one majority constituted an endorsement of a radical candidate who had praised Brown and subscribed money both for the raid and for legal counsel. And Sumner's frequent campaign speeches on Andrew's behalf had become more unequivocally antislavery than ever. He asked Massachusetts to choose between the tradition of the Mayflower and that of the first slave ship. The subsequent election of both Andrew and Lincoln also appeared to vindicate, at last, the effectiveness of long years of Abolitionist agitation. Higginson, like Garrison, had come to believe that Republican opposition to the extension of slavery foreshadowed a more radical policy.[8]

Unlike most Americans, including Garrisonian disunionists, he acknowledged the imminence and desirability of "a state of temporary war." Assuming, as did the disunion Abolitionists, that slavery would crumble once secession brought the loss of federal protection, Higginson also understood that if secession spread, the North would have to fight to hold certain strategic areas below the Mason-Dixon line: he argued in February 1861 that Maryland, Washington, and the Mississippi River must be kept. Not expecting merely a temporary war at this point, he admitted with no misgivings: "it is hard to predict the end." [9]

War was preferable to compromise. Involvement in the Burns affair, the Worcester Disunion Convention, and the Harpers Ferry raid had strengthened Higginson's conviction that disunion and peace were incompatible. While some disunion Abolitionists wavered regarding the need for violence, he was strongly for it. During the secession crisis of 1860–61 his desire for war increased. The

8. TWH to James T. Fields, Sept. 18, 1860, Higginson MSS; Donald, *Sumner*, p. 365; Thomas, *Liberator*, pp. 399–404.

9. TWH to L. Higginson, Nov. 23, 1860, Feb. 8, 1861, Higginson MSS; James M. McPherson, *The Struggle for Equality* (Princeton, 1964), pp. 37–43.

advocacy of peaceful disunion no longer remained the monopoly of radical Abolitionists: adopted by southern firebrands and embraced on the other hand by some northern moderates, it ceased to be associated with the abolition of slavery.[10] At Harpers Ferry, force had been sanctioned to end slavery. It was not the failure of force but the failure of southern slaves to join Brown to fight for their own freedom that had most impressed Higginson. To various kinds of antislavery men, Harpers Ferry indicated that the northern whites would have to emancipate the slave. After the raid, the lingering hope that the slave would free himself had largely disappeared, though talk continued that the South would be destroyed by slave insurrection.

Higginson, by January 1861, witnessed what he believed were the last manifestations of public opposition to abolition. There was a new sting in the words of radicals like Wendell Phillips, for they no longer could be ignored as the ravings of an eccentric minority. Since December, Phillips had become a marked man, a target for rowdies, Democrats, and Negrophobes. Conspicuous were "well-dressed young men"—prominent Boston lawyers, merchants, and brokers—who wanted concessions made to the South. When Phillips spoke in Theodore Parker's old pulpit in the Melodeon, Higginson headed a band of sixty armed sympathizers protecting the speaker. Surrounded by a hooting and threatening mob, Phillips had to be escorted home and his house guarded. Four days later, at the annual January meeting of the Massachusetts Anti-Slavery Society at Tremont Temple, Higginson served as commander-in-chief of the civilian guard and in the possibly more hazardous role of platform speaker.[11]

During the meeting, Phillips and Emerson were subjected to cat-calls and tossed pillows. For a full hour Phillips was inaudible because of the noise of the hostile crowd; and Emerson, no more successful, was provoked to shout: "Let me say to those young for-

10. TWH to Fields, Sept. 18, 1860, Higginson MSS; Kenneth Stampp, *And the War Came* (Baton Rouge, 1950), pp. 248, 260; David Potter, "Horace Greeley and Peaceable Secession," *Journal of Southern History*, 7 (1941), 145–49; Donald, *Sumner*, pp. 365–71.

11. TWH to L. Higginson, Jan. 21, Feb. 22, 1861, Higginson MSS; *Liberator*, Dec. 1, 1860, Jan. 25, 1861; TWH to Sumner, Jan. 27, 1861, Sumner MSS; McPherson, *Equality*, pp. 42–44.

eigners, to those young strangers, that I was born on the spot where the post-office now stands, that all my education has been in her town's schools, here in her college, and all the best of my life spent here. . . . I think the same record cannot be shown by the young people who have endeavored to interrupt this meeting." [12]

This hardly quieted the crowd, and Emerson finally had to withdraw without completing his address. Higginson was still determined to speak. The volume of his voice, the brevity of his address, and the hecklers' eventual weariness allowed his words to be heard. Higginson reminded the crowd that he had not spoken from the Society's platform for almost three years; he had been fighting for the slave in ways different from those advocated by the nonresistant, nonpolitical Massachusetts Anti-Slavery Society. But he now felt compelled to speak for a cause more fundamental than abolition. "The slave today," he declared, "must take care of himself, for the moment, while we are defending the right of white men in Massachusetts to be heard in Boston." [13]

Higginson continued to guard Phillips through February and March. Not only did he exercise at the new Worcester gymnasium but in the *Atlantic* he urged physical fitness for everybody so that men of "solid strength" would be produced. And he proudly reported to his mother on the progress of a military school, composed of thirty gentlemen learning military drill. "I am one, as I always wanted to learn it." [14]

Troubled by the hesitation of the *Atlantic*'s editor about publishing "war matter," he urged Fields to print at least his article on the Denmark Vesey slave insurrection of 1822: "these times are particularly seasonable for that." The Vesey article stressed that southerners did not understand that all slaves desired freedom and that the most humanely treated Negro was the first to kill his master. Fields held back, however, and the article did not appear until June 1861. Instead, the April *Atlantic* contained a Higginson essay with the title taken from Tennyson's *In Memoriam*: "Can trouble dwell with April days?" But before many of the magazine's

12. *Liberator*, Feb. 1, 1861.
13. Ibid.
14. TWH to Sumner, Jan. 26, 1861, Sumner MSS; TWH to L. Higginson, Feb. 22, Mar. 22, April 5, 13, 1861, Higginson MSS; "Gymnastics," *Atlantic Monthly*, 7 (1861), 301.

readers were able to examine the article, the April days of 1861 were shattered by the cannons of Civil War. "I think the world is growing better all the time," was Higginson's response to the war's first sounds.[15]

Spring air and martial music were an invigorating mixture. Emerson, so accustomed to a sweet New England April, now remarked: "sometimes gunpowder smells good." In Worcester, on the evening of April 16, a mass meeting was held at which the city's leading men spoke, Higginson among them. "Tonight we have more than enthusiasm," he told the cheering crowd, "we have unanimity." He urged all men to prepare to serve. The next day the Worcester Light Infantry was dispatched to Washington and quartered in the Senate chamber. Each man had been presented with a Bible by the city of Worcester.[16] The strange enthusiasm that Webster had deplored appeared to have triumphed.

Jubilant about the apparent obliteration of factionalism, Higginson noted: "Never before since I lived here (or anywhere else) has there been absolute unanimity on a single subject, great or small." Not only were Worcester's leading Democrats heralding the war, but even Wendell Phillips soon declared: "I rejoice . . . that now, for the first time in my Anti-slavery life, I stand under the stars and stripes, and welcome the tread of Massachusetts men marshalled for war." [17]

Higginson remained jubilant even after such characteristic public statements about northern war aims as that of the Worcester *Spy*: "It is not the slavery question in any form that is now an issue between the administration and the secession conspirators." The war, however, in Higginson's view would at least fulfill the predictions made in 1857 at the Worcester Disunion Convention, and he now prophesied: "We shall fight a little while—the harder the shorter

15. TWH to James Fields, April 9, 1861, Higginson MSS; "Denmark Vesey," *Atlantic Monthly*, 7 (1861), 742–43; TWH, "April Days," *Atlantic Monthly*, 7 (1861), 385–94; TWH to L. Higginson, April 17, 1861, Misc. MSS, Houghton Library.

16. Quoted in William M. Salter, "Emerson's View of Society and Reform," *International Journal of Ethics*, *13* (1903), 416; *Spy*, April 17, 1861; Ellery B. Crane, ed., *History of Worcester County*, *1* (New York, 1924), 517.

17. TWH to L. Higginson, April 17, 1861, Higginson MSS; Phillips quoted in John G. Palfrey, "Boston Soldiery in War and Peace," *Memorial History of Boston*, ed. Justin Winsor (Boston, 1880–81), *4*, 318.

—& then have a treaty of separation forever." Emancipation, he suggested, would be the South's penalty for being defeated. He did not acknowledge that Lincoln sought to save the Union. Yet he believed there could be no reunion with slavery. "Even should we end the war with a compromise," he predicted, slavery's prestige would be much weakened. Through union or disunion, slavery would die.[18]

In a public lecture Higginson cautioned against criticizing Lincoln, and privately sought to raise a company of men headed by John Brown, Jr., to be deployed at the Pennsylvania border. "I want to at least get the *name* of John Brown rumored on the border & then the whole party may come back & go to bed—they will frighten Virginia into fits all the same." The plan, so in keeping with the antebellum daring of militant Abolitionists, reflected Higginson's estimation about the war. A week after the first call to arms he summarized the military situation: "I have no anxiety about Washington nor do I expect a long war. In money, arms, drill, & means of manufacture and transportation, the Free States have immensely the advantage, & no inferiority in any other way." [19]

When Governor Andrew approved Higginson's John Brown, Jr., project but had no available contingent fund to finance it, Samuel Howe introduced Higginson to some State Street bankers who pledged close to $2,000. Traveling to Harrisburg, he was pledged another $1,000 by Governor Andrew Curtin. But such irregular proceedings with their prospect of antagonizing the border states were feared by the federal government; it was having sufficient difficulties with more orthodox organizational problems and shunned association with John Brown's name. The Worcester *Spy* did obligingly report that a reliable source in Ohio had learned that young John Brown had an army in the field "to explore Virginia, and perhaps make a visit to the place where his father was hung." The army was said to be composed of 400 Negroes with another 500 soon expected. Higginson knew it was an army of rumor and

18. *Spy*, April 16, 1861; TWH to L. Higginson, April 17, May 30, 1861, Higginson MSS.

19. Newspaper clipping, April 1861, TWH to L. Higginson, April 23, 1861, Higginson MSS.

not of men. "The Harper's Ferry men," he privately conceded, "were so far crushed by that affair that they shrunk from making themselves *outlaws* again, with a terrible shrinking." [20]

Nature proved insufficiently soothing to Higginson's frustrated militancy. "All this beauty seems tame & unexciting," he mourned, "I find myself longing for the tonic of war." But he did not seek to obtain that tonic. It was not the government's refusal to emancipate slaves that restrained him, for he disagreed with Lydia Maria Child who said of the administration: "When it treats the colored people with justice and humanity, I will mount its flag in my great elm tree . . . but until then I would as soon as wear the rattlesnake upon my bosom as the eagle." Nor was it fear that a plan to colonize southern Negroes in Haiti would reach fruition. For Higginson, like Garrison, praised the Republican party's radical wing and had faith in its bringing abolition and being able "to conquer the prejudice against color." Through his articles in the *Atlantic* he sought support for the radical cause. When his Denmark Vesey article was printed uncut, he endeavored to go farther. The only way, he told Fields, to sustain the magazine's circulation during "these absorbing excitements is to make the excitement feed it, by having articles of current interest." [21] Higginson's most audacious ones were published successively in July and August of 1861.

He appeared undiscouraged by evidence of southern military strength. In a long war, "the ultimate military emancipation of slaves is inevitable," he explained to Fields. But the printed article refrained from talking of a long war: "Tethered to their homes by the fear of insurrection . . . it is almost a moral impossibility that a slave-holding army should be strong." The real questions were happily emerging:

> Either slavery is essential to a community, or it must be fatal to it, there is no middle ground; and the Secessionists have taken one horn of the dilemma with so delightful a frankness as to leave us no possible escape from taking the other. Never

20. *Yesterdays*, p. 246; M. T. Higginson, *Higginson*, p. 205; *Spy*, May 21, 1861; TWH to Sydney H. Gay, May 5, 1861, Gay MSS.

21. Sewall, *Child*, p. 150; TWH, "Haitian Emigration," *Liberator*, July 19, 1861; "Field Book," April 30, 1861, TWH to J. T. Fields, May 27, 1861, Higginson MSS.

in modern days, had there been a conflict in which the contending principles were so clearly antagonistic.[22]

The Negro slave also would be important in the final decision. Conceding that slave insurrection was certainly terrible, war itself was terrible and "if the truth were told, it would be that the Anglo-Saxon habitually despises the Negro because he is *not* an insurgent. . . . Our race does not take naturally to nonresistance, and has far more sympathy with Nat Turner than with Uncle Tom." Regardless of "our desires, the rising of the slaves in case of continued war, is a mere destiny." Northern victory would come when its generals shut their mouths and opened their batteries.[23]

Higginson's article, "Nat Turner's Insurrection," was no less pointed. The full terror of insurrection—"nothing that had a white skin was spared"—was softened only by the greater horror of its suppression by white southerners. The heroism of Turner with his selfless desire for "retribution" was emphasized; so too was the assertion that the leader never drank and his men committed not one "indecent outrage against a woman." [24] Nat Turner, in Higginson's view, was an Uncle Tom on horseback—morally pure but militantly fierce.

Higginson enviously watched the marching men of Worcester clad in colorful Zouave uniforms with red skullcaps and bouquets on their bayonets. He listened as they sang "The John Brown War Song," a plaintive Methodist tune, and said, "I never heard anything more impressive, & it seemed a wonderful piece of popular justice to make his name the war song." Such sounds and sights animated his optimism; even the northern defeat at Bull Run seemed a victory because of the subsequent congressional Confiscation Act emancipating all slaves used in rebellion, and because of the instructions of Secretary of War Simon Cameron to General Benjamin Butler approving the utilization of Confederate-owned slaves who were within Butler's lines. The reverse at Bull Run, said

22. TWH to J. T. Fields, June 2, 1861, Higginson MSS; TWH, "Ordeal by Battle," *Atlantic Monthly*, 8 (1861), 90.

23. Ibid., pp. 89, 94.

24. TWH, "Nat Turner's Insurrection," *Atlantic Monthly*, 8 (1861), 176, 179, 185, 187.

Higginson, caused "the greatest step in advance taken by our government since its formation. . . . Now for the first time it is a government of emancipation." Countering the criticism of Wendell Phillips, he even defended Charles Devens, his old nemesis in the Sims fugitive slave incident, who had become an active field officer and was now returning to the front as a colonel of a regiment. "This is a new era & we must forgive the past," said Higginson.[25]

Where was Higginson in this new era? Where was the man who had decried words and extolled actions? Others like Dr. Calvin Cutter of Kansas days and Dr. Oramel Martin of the Worcester Free Church had gone to war. Unlike Phillips, who was critical of Lincoln's caution, Higginson expected that "a policy of emancipation will be reached by stages so as to unite public sentiment." But he spent his days walking in the woods and paddling his wherry through isolated waters. A diary entry in mid-August, written with the dogmatism that always indicated uncertainty, revealed his inner conflict: "I have thoroughly made up my mind that my present duty lies at home—that this war, for which I long and for which I have been training for years is just as absolutely unobtainable for me as a share in the wars of Napoleon." Although once again wanting to feel like Napoleon, as he had during the Sims and Burns incidents, he vowed, because of Mary's dependency, to swallow down all rebellious desires, hoping that good would yet come from enforced abstinence. More than ever before, by surrounding himself with nature he would seek to forget both his past and the present. But they were not calm days. Spending hours watching insects and birds, he recorded in his field book: "I burn with insatiable desire to penetrate their consciousness." [26] Being a commander without a military command moved him to direct his *Atlantic* articles toward nature's regiments of flora and fauna.[27]

At first he judged that nature was no substitute for vigorous ac-

25. TWH to L. Higginson, Aug. 4, 13, 1861, Higginson MSS.
26. *Spy*, Aug. 3, 1861; TWH to L. Higginson, Aug. 23, 1861, TWH diary, Aug. 15, 1861, "Field Book," Aug. 1861, Higginson MSS.
27. "My Outdoor Studies," *Atlantic Monthly*, 8 (1861), 302–09; "Snow," *Atlantic Monthly*, 9 (1862), 188–201; "Life of Birds," *Atlantic Monthly*, 10 (1862), 368–76; "Procession of the Flowers," *Atlantic Monthly*, 10 (1862), 649–57.

tion. Yet he did state: "We cannot transform the world except very slowly. . . . Nature . . . does her work almost as imperceptibly as we." His descriptions of scenes outside Worcester suggested what they meant for his frustrated militancy. By means of a strange voyeurism his imagination could even transform the trees into submissive maidens:

> The trees denude themselves each year, like the goddesses before Paris, that we may see such unadorned loveliness in the fairest. Only the unconquerable delicacy of the beech still keeps its soft vestments about it, . . . however, . . . the beech has good reason for her prudishness, and possesses little beauty of figure; while the elms, maples, chestnuts, walnuts, and even oaks, have not exhausted all their store of charms for us, until we have seen them disrobed.[28]

When news reached Worcester on October 25 of the crushing defeat at Balls Bluff of Devens' 15th Massachusetts Regiment, Higginson could no longer repress the desire to act. Upon learning that half the regiment had sustained casualties and that the wounded, heroic Charles Devens during the retreat across the Potomac had narrowly missed drowning, he hurriedly prepared to enter the war. Governor Andrew, by November 1, authorized him to begin raising a Massachusetts regiment. According to the Governor's instructions it would become part of a brigade commanded by Rufus Saxton, who was then serving in Admiral Samuel Dupont's naval expedition just landed at Port Royal, South Carolina. So conscious of making history, he felt he now could find his special role in the war: "No prominent anti-slavery man has yet taken a marked share in the war, & as I am satisfied that there are a great many who would like to go *if I do*, I have made up my mind to take part in the affair, hoping to aid in settling it the quicker." [29]

Requesting James Freeman Clarke to serve as chaplain of his new regiment he wrote: "I think that the army is becoming a power so

28. "Field Book," Sept. (?), 20, 1861, Higginson MSS; "April Days," p. 391.
29. *Spy,* Oct. 26, 1861; TWH to L. Higginson, Nov. 1, 11, 1861, Higginson MSS.

formidable that [it] is essential to the safety of the nation, that a high tone of character *should* prevail in it." The army's power and character appeared almost as important as antislavery in moving him to war, and the meaning of these issues to him was subsequently clarified. "If Democrats & Irishmen do most of the fighting," said Higginson, "they will have—& deservedly—most influence on the policy of the war. The only way for anti-slavery men to share in the control is to share in the sacrifices. . . . All I ask now, is an opportunity to fight, . . . carrying with me such men as I can raise." Apart from advocating emancipation, he was cautious about war policy. Even after the news of the successful expedition to Port Royal, South Carolina, Higginson disapproved "a general & indiscriminate arming of slaves." [30]

As for responsibilities to his invalid wife, he now decided that "a man has no right to make his home duty paramount to another." Besides, "if men feel that they must go to war," stated this supporter of woman's rights, "women must not try to prevent them, but quietly submit & hope for the best." [31]

Nature, his battleground since Sumter, was now submerged by war, but a crushing blow followed two weeks after the decision to enlist. One of the sudden terminations of recruiting left him sorrowfully reporting that his regimental prospects were in entire chaos. The shattering of his military plans reversed his aims again:

> Years I have wasted in efforts to do people good—preaching, lecturing, conventioning, organizing, politics, newspaper-writing, private philanthropies etc.—in all of which I have succeeded as the average, perhaps better—but never with the hearty zest a man feels when he knows he is leading his true life. Now I have wrenched myself away from all these things, feeling that I have served my time at them and got my Experience—and I have come back to the one thing which I have always enjoyed, a quiet life with literature and nature. It has cost me all these years to *dare* to do this.[32]

30. TWH to J. F. Clarke, Nov. 5, 1861, TWH to L. Higginson, Nov. 1, 1861, Higginson MSS.
31. Ibid.
32. "Field Book," Nov. 16, 21, 1861, Higginson MSS.

Continuing to avoid politics, he drifted deeper into solitude, feeling the mirage of nature surrounding him again, noting that "the world has of late become to me sort of a fairy palace . . . far surpassing the tales of Arabian enchantment." During these weeks, Higginson would wander home from the countryside with his pockets filled with flowers, lichens, chrysalids, baby turtles, and scraps of written paper with notes for nature essays. The Worcester Natural History Society was a more welcome place than the recruiting platform; at the end of February 1862 he spoke to the society on the twenty-five species of Orchidaceae found in Worcester County.[33]

In an *Atlantic* article, "Letter to a Young Contributor," written in January while his chances for joining the war seemed nil, he stressed how unimportant war was in the context of life. And it has not been recognized that perhaps it was this theme, this talk of "the trivialities of war," that "war or peace, fame or forgetfulness can bring no real injury to one who has formed the fixed purpose to live nobly day by day," which moved secluded Emily Dickinson to write her first letter to Higginson. Knowing his reputation as a militant Abolitionist, she understood that he too was engaged in renunciation. His talk of resuming the important affairs of life "when the fire is extinguished" had more meaning to her than his literary advice. She also turned to him because she genuinely admired his essays and sympathized with his unorthodox commitment to Protestantism. "Letter to a Young Contributor" served to inaugurate a relationship, developing after the war, which would be of primary importance to Miss Dickinson and of haunting importance to Higginson. From the outset there was much incongruity. She had miscalculated the depth of his renunciations, for as Higginson later explained, "Letter to a Young Contributor" merely reflected that he had been "temporarily disappointed" about going to war. By the time she read the article in the April *Atlantic* and sent him four of her poems asking him to tell her if they "breathed," and what was "true," he was no longer in isolated loneliness, nor looking upon war as trivial. On the day her first letter arrived, he was in the Worcester gymnasium introducing a

33. "Field Book," Oct., Dec., 1861, Higginson MSS; *Spy*, Feb. 25, 1862.

Miss M. A. Drake, who, with a troupe of energetic girls, put on a wooden dumbbell exhibition. Higginson publicly endorsed the competency of the instruction and the excellence of the method of exercise for women.[34] Neither exercise nor war was of much interest to Emily Dickinson.

Whenever Higginson discussed the war he usually minimized its difficulties. He confidently stated that "either they or we will emancipate the slaves in some form & so remove prospectively the only real obstacle to peace & prosperity, & then the bequest of debt & hate will be surmounted in a generation or two." Thus the natural course of events, not his participation, was made paramount. On the other hand, when his chances of entering increased again, he criticized government policy, charging, for example, that General David Hunter was the sole high-ranking antislavery officer in the regular army. Reversing himself about Lincoln's commitment to abolition, he argued that only with Union military defeats would an emancipatory policy emerge. Higginson's interest was gradually heightened after speaking with returning Worcester soldiers about the war's progress, and he wrote another insurrection article.[35]

Stonewall Jackson's sweep through the Shenandoah Valley in the spring of 1862, the routing of Union forces at Winchester, and the subsequent retreat of Banks' army across the Potomac all reverberated in Worcester. Secretary of War Stanton telegraphed northern governors to send troops to defend Washington, and Governor Andrew replied that it would be difficult to raise Massachusetts men before the federal government gave northern Negroes the opportunity to enlist in the Union army. Higginson, for the first time since the early days of the war, made a public plea for volunteers, observing a month later that a new regiment was growing very slowly: "People feel that it is near the end of the war & don't like the prospect of garrison or police duty somewhere for

34. "Letter to a Young Contributor," *Atlantic Monthly*, 9 (1862), 409, 411; E. Dickinson to TWH, April 15, 1862, in Thomas H. Johnson, *The Letters of Emily Dickinson*, 2 (Cambridge, 1958), 403; TWH to Brander Matthews, Jan. 6, 1892, Matthews MSS; *Spy*, Apr. 17, 1862.

35. TWH to L. Higginson, Feb. 6, 21, 1862, TWH to Fields, Mar. 26, April 17, 1862, Higginson MSS.

three years." To his diary he tersely summarized his own state as "my powerlessness to stir, because of Mary, while yet I am not clear whether it is conscience or weakness." [36] The presidential call for a draft and the inauguration of the shorter, nine-month enlistment term helped focus his long personal crisis.

In early August he asked Worcester's mayor Emory Aldrich, not to exempt him from the draft because he was a clergyman, for he no longer had a pulpit. He then announced: "Settled with Mary that if drafted I shall go." But it became evident that Worcester's quota would be filled without a draft; he would have to volunteer to serve nine months. "I ought to go for that time without a draft," he wrote in his diary. "I have not mentioned it to Mary, & may not have the strength to carry it through, but it seems to me that if I do not, I shall forfeit my self-respect & be a broken man for the remainder of my days. I have sacrificed the public duty to this domestic one as long as I can bear." [37]

On the next day he spoke to his wife: she would room and board at Lincoln House in Worcester with Margaret Channing and a part-time maid. Six days later he wrote to his mother that he had obtained official authority to enlist a company for nine months and serve as captain. "Recruits were raised slowly here," he incorrectly asserted, "& I decided that I never could hold up my head again in Worcester or even elsewhere if I didn't vindicate my past words by actions, though tardy." [38]

An announcement, four times the size of all others, signed by Higginson, soon appeared in the Worcester *Spy*. It read like a sermon that he had been preaching to himself:

> Nine months is not much to offer to save the very existence of the institutions that reared you.
>
> What will you say to your children's children when they say to you, 'a great contest was waged between Law and Disorder, Freedom and Slavery, *and you were not there'?*
>
> Criticism is idle without action. . . .

36. John Andrew to Edwin Stanton, May 19, 1862, in *Spy*, May 26, 1862; TWH to L. Higginson, June 20, 1862, "Field Book," July 23, 1862, Higginson MSS.
37. "Field Book," Aug. 9, 1862, Higginson MSS.
38. TWH to L. Higginson, Aug. 15, 22, 1862, Higginson MSS.

Have not sixteen months of war given time enough for deliberation?

If you are going, go now. It is designed that this company shall be filled, organized, and *in camp* while the doubters are making up their minds.[39]

A recruitment meeting in City Hall on the succeeding night ended with the chairs being pushed aside and the new enlistees being drilled by Higginson. The threat of being drafted and an increased enlistment bounty helped fill the company, by the end of August, to a full 110 men. To the beat of drums the new captain marched his men through Worcester streets and passed his own house—"much to Mary's edification." Higginson enjoyed drilling his men two hours every afternoon while awaiting assignment to barracks. "I don't think I ever did anything better than I have done all this, so far," he said with pride in the present and some doubt about the future.[40] A Negro visitor to Worcester observed that the captain was "entering with his whole soul into his work." Unlike the man in his semi-autobiographical short story, "The Monarch of Dreams," Higginson succeeded in leaving the reverie of nature for the reveille of war.[41]

39. *Spy*, Aug. 16, 1862.

40. Ibid., Aug. 18, 30, 1862; TWH to L. Higginson, Sept. 7, 1862, Higginson MSS.

41. Forten journal, Nov. 27, 1862, in *The Journal of Charlotte Forten*, ed. Ray A. Billington (New York, 1953), p. 137; TWH, "The Monarch of Dreams," *Higginson Writings*, 5, 233–36; Edward Bellamy to TWH, Dec. 20, 1886, Higginson-Barney MSS.

15

Crusading in Enemy Territory

Higginson and his company, by mid-September 1862, were settled in their barracks just outside Worcester at Camp John E.
Wool, as part of the 51st Massachusetts Regiment. Reveille
sounded at 5 A.M., marching filled the day, taps were blown at
9:30 P.M. No guns were issued for two months; comradeship and
military discipline were more evident than war. He enjoyed
watching his men attend evening prayers or relax with tea and
baked apples while a quartet sang. The recruits entertained themselves in the barracks, some taking the parts of ladies for a waltz
or polka, with two fiddlers providing the music. Such scenes
seemed especially wholesome to Higginson because "without the
excitement of love or wine . . . they dance like Maenads or Bac-
chanals . . . and show such a passionate delight that one would
say dancing must be reminiscent of the felicity of Adam before
Eve appeared." Happily all this levity, he noted, was without
swearing or vulgarity. On other nights, even those men who
found their relaxation with the help of alcohol provided a certain
satisfaction when they stumbled back to camp singing: "Old Hig-
gie is so strict, so strict." [1]

Looking "like a piece of caste-iron happiness," he proudly
marched his men through town in perfect step behind him. Sometimes they partook of the amenities offered by civilian hosts, gathering in an apple grove decorated with an American flag, to eat
doughnuts, cheese, and apples and then to serenade the appreciative
townsmen. With a visit to Mary every other day, Antietam was
indeed distant. He cheerfully predicted that when his men got
their first furlough it would seem like a holiday from school. [2]

1. TWH to L. Higginson, Sept. 15, Oct. 4, 13, 26, Nov. 3, 1862, Higginson MSS.
2. Frank Le Baron to Samuel Johnson, Oct. 18, 1862, Johnson MSS; TWH to
L. Higginson, Oct. 4, 1862, Higginson MSS.

There were obstacles at Camp Wool which interfered with the comforting sensation of feeling like "the father of a family." Those few officers who had had war experience tended to view contemptuously their untried and eager colleagues, and since these veterans lacked "intelligence and refinement," Higginson was doubly upset. Among his superiors only Colonel Augustus B. Sprague, who used "a silken glove and a hand of iron," made being a subordinate comfortable. Higginson denied aspiring to become colonel of a regiment, because an experienced leader was needed. Seeking recognition of a different sort, he asked New York *Tribune* managing editor, Sydney Gay: "would you like to have me write for the *Tribune* . . . & at what price?"[3]

Before Gay replied, Higginson, on November 14, was surprised to receive a letter from Brigadier General Rufus Saxton, Military Governor of the Southern Department with headquarters in Beaufort, South Carolina. Saxton offered him the colonelcy of the 1st South Carolina Volunteers. A few days later, a letter arrived from the Reverend James H. Fowler which emphasized that the new regiment was being recruited from freed slaves. Fowler, having recommended Higginson to Saxton, was certain that the success or failure of the regiment would be most important in the solution of the Negro question. He had last written before Higginson's trial in the Burns affair, then advising him to prepare to suffer martyrdom.[4]

After a day's sincere hesitation because of the government's tenuous commitment to the Negro, Higginson enthusiastically informed Fields: "In a few days I expect to go to Beaufort S C to take command of a black regiment, which I would rather do than anything else in the world, if the enterprise can be carried through in good faith." Seventy-two hours later, Higginson was almost totally committed; to assure space on the next Beaufort steamer he even requested a mattress for sleeping on deck. He headed South armed with a letter of introduction from Colonel Sprague to General Saxton attesting to his skill as a field officer and devotion to

3. TWH to L. Higginson, Sept. 26, Oct. 26, Nov. 9, 1862, Higginson MSS; TWH to Gay, Nov. 4, 1862, Gay MSS.

4. Rufus Saxton to TWH, Nov. 5, 1862, J. H. Fowler to TWH, Nov. 10, 1862, TWH to L. Higginson, Nov. 16, 1862, Higginson MSS.

the "cause of the oppressed by long & persistent effort with a good knowledge of human nature & an ability to govern." [5]

The New York *Times*, an advocate of arming Negroes, heralded Higginson's appointment by announcing that "the hour and the man" had arrived. "The negroes," the paper reported, "need men to lead them . . . not fops and imbeciles, nor yet speculators, who unable 'from want of capacity' to earn three hundred dollars a year at an honest calling, have decided to commit a worse sin upon the country by officering a colored regiment." The prominent industrialist, John Forbes, who knew Higginson and who also was a strong advocate of enlisting ex-slaves (partly because he was concerned about the loss of northern factory laborers to the army), believed that the government could have found "some old army officer of more experience than Wentworth Higginson!" For surely, he argued, there must be men of "equal bravery and just about as little discretion!" [6]

Any remaining doubts about accepting the command vanished upon Higginson's arrival on November 24 when he first saw the picturesque plantations, magnolia avenues, and live oak groves. General Saxton's welcome and the "simple New England good sense and earnestness" of this "abolitionist of the West Point school" much complimented him. [7] With his English whiskers and mustache, Saxton was a reassuring kind of man.

As military governor, Rufus Saxton, according to Higginson, had to contend with a horde of teachers and preachers, a "mixture of desirable and undesirable zealots" who had come from the North to educate young and old freedmen in letters and morality. Even more contentious were the power-seeking military men and the northern civilians who ran the rich Sea Island cotton plantations. One of the most influential plantation managers expected that the attempt to raise a Negro regiment would fail "from the imbecile character" of black recruits. Others, both civilian and

5. TWH to J. T. Fields, Nov. 17, 1862, Misc. MSS, New York Public Library; TWH to Seth Rogers, Nov. 24, 1862, Misc. MSS, American Antiquarian Society; A. R. Sprague to R. Saxton, Nov. 19, 1862, Higginson MSS.

6. Quoted in *Spy*, Dec. 5, 1862; J. M. Forbes to Charles Sumner, Jan. 17, 1863, Sumner MSS; George W. Smith, "Broadsides for Freedom: Civil War Propaganda in New England," *New England Quarterly*, 21 (1948), 303.

7. TWH to Sarah [Bowditch], Nov. [27,] 1862, Higginson MSS; TWH journal, Nov. 27, 1862.

military, expressed repugnance for the Negro far surpassing this.[8]

But to Higginson the future seemed adventurous and exotic. "As I sit in my tent in the cool moonlit evening," he reported from Camp Saxton, "the level sands, the glistening tents, the flickering fires, the graceful palmetto cook-houses, the wild carousals—make it all seem some far off Oriental realm." The subjects of this realm seemed to vary "only in their degree of unintelligibility & their shades of inkiness. . . . I have hardly seen even a mulatto, almost all are as black as printer's ink." Outside, under plumes of waving moss, he saw the fire reflecting "gorgeously from their red [trousered] legs & . . . from their shining cheeks and white teeth & rolling eyes."[9] He watched their "unequalled comic display," concluding after his first few weeks at Port Royal that if you "give these people their tongues, their feet, & their leisure . . . they are happy." At first Higginson judged their dialect immature and childlike. "I think it is partly from my notorious love of children," he reflected, "that I like these people so well." They appeared simple, docile, observing, shrewd, and imaginative; they had none of the "upstart conceit one sometimes sees among the free negroes of the North."[10]

The discovery that some of his men were not truthful, honest, or chaste he preferred first to blame on slavery and later not to mention. He pictured himself as the leader of innocent and childlike individuals, "simple & lovable," who said "the brightest things" from behind their masks of "hopeless impenetrable stupidity" and who proved that northern minstrels were "no caricature."[11] His romantic faith in intuitive perception, in judging right and wrong with a single glance, was now attributed to the perceptive abilities of his black soldiers. His personal need to feel his own power of leadership, of course, helped perpetuate the image of the Negro's docility in his mind.

8. Higginson Notebook, MS, Higginson MSS; Elizabeth Ware Pearson, *Letters from Port Royal* (Boston, 1906), p. 102. A superb account of the "Port Royal Experiment" is Willie Lee Rose's *Rehearsal for Reconstruction* (New York, 1964).

9. TWH to Sarah Bowditch, Nov. 17, 1862, Higginson MSS; TWH to James Rogers, Nov. 24, 1862, Misc. MSS, American Antiquarian Society.

10. TWH to L. Higginson, Nov. 28, 1862, TWH to M. Higginson, Dec. 10, 1862, Higginson MSS; TWH journal, Dec. 6, 20, 1862.

11. Ibid., Nov. 27, Dec. 3, 1862.

The Negroes responded well to his drill commands: Their "imitativeness and musical ear" convinced Higginson that there were few white troops able to surpass his men in marching and drilling. Sergeant William Brunson of Company A, one of the few Negroes who was not illiterate, requested the "Armies Regulation Book" even "if it cost[s] me one Months wages." Working earnestly with the men on hand and with the ever-increasing number recruited to bring the regiment to its full complement, Higginson joyfully wrote his mother, "If I don't come home jet black you must be very grateful." He asked for the *Life of Toussaint L'Ouverture* and another book titled *Colored Patriots of the Revolution.* He already had a copy of *Les Miserables* in hand.[12]

During the first two months at Port Royal, General Saxton was his most earnest ally, so earnest that Higginson feared the reluctant government would be irked by this champion of the Negro. Saxton visited the Sea Island plantations trying to persuade Negroes to enlist in the regiment, suggesting that they could trust the new colonel who had stood loyally by Anthony Burns to the point, according to Saxton, of actual imprisonment. The General promised to elevate Higginson to head a brigade.[13]

No ally, however, was the acting commanding general of the area, John M. Brannan. He seemed more like a hussar on horseback than a man devoted to the delicate task of proving the Negro soldier's worth. General David Hunter, absent until mid-January, would prove, in his own way, an even more formidable senior officer. So eager to raise a black regiment, he practiced ruthless recruiting tactics and exerted great pressure on subordinates to conscript Negroes.[14]

Some of Higginson's junior officers had been trained in Hunter's unauthorized Negro regiment, but most had had as little military training as himself. He found them reliable, but not cultivated. His

12. TWH to John Andrew, Jan. 19, 1863, Civil War Scrapbooks, TWH to Fields, [Nov. 1862], TWH to L. Higginson, Nov. 27, 1862, Higginson MSS; Brunson to TWH, Feb. 20, 1863, Negro Papers, Library of Congress.

13. Forten journal, Nov. 27, 1862, in Billington, *Forten,* pp. 137, 138; TWH journal, Nov. 27, 1862.

14. Ibid.; William H. Pease, "Three Years Among the Freedmen: William Gannett and the Port Royal Experiment," *Journal of Negro History,* 42 (1957), 113; Rose, *Reconstruction,* p. 179.

most experienced staff officer was Captain Charles Trowbridge, who had been a stonemason in Brooklyn before the war and subsequently had led the first Negro company on a bountiful foraging expedition in October 1862. The brawny captain's ability to discipline his men and follow Higginson's orders seemed more important than his lack of respect for the personal sensitivities of his troops. He mimicked their dialect and behaved "like a good natured overseer, who will resent every tyranny but his own." Captain L. W. Metcalf, formerly a Maine confectionary salesman, led the company that responded best to drill, discipline, and sanitary regulations.[15]

Of all the officers, Dr. Seth Rogers, regimental surgeon, was Higginson's closest companion. Having been a Worcester neighbor and fellow reformer, Rogers was recommended for the post by Higginson.[16] Together they were the bulwark of abolitionist leadership in the regiment.

While "de Cunnul," as Higginson heard his men call him, drilled the troops he began recognizing some individual differences. Usually saying that they shared a common docility which made them easy to train, he found some who were forlorn and were unwilling to become soldiers, men for whom it was "too late to be anything but a 'nigger.'" The word nigger, he learned with surprise, was almost commonly used by his recruits as by prejudiced white men. After visiting the local plantations he decided, incorrectly, that the southern planters who had fled had left behind "the blacker & duller fieldhands." Actually those left behind were the most rebellious and independent. These plantation Negroes reminded him of Fayal, leading to the discouraging conclusion that "a peasantry is a peasantry I suppose, black or white, slave or free." The Negro women also disappointed him with their toothless smiles and their way of encouraging the men to "strike through the sand into a subsoil of sensuality." He concluded: "most of the black women are utterly repulsive in aspect & attire."[17]

He was proud of his troops especially when they performed

15. TWH journal, Nov. 27, 1862, May 17, 1863; TWH to James Rogers, Nov. 24, 1862, Misc. MSS, American Antiquarian Society.

16. TWH to L. Higginson, Dec. 10, 1862, Higginson MSS.

17. TWH to M. Higginson, Dec. 21, 1862, Higginson MSS; TWH journal, Dec. 3, 8, 11, 16, 1862.

smartly at his command for the frequent official visitors. Most white officers were either skeptical about using Negro troops or were strong Negrophobes, but to Higginson they all seemed courteous, at least to his face, and no one had yet made him feel inferior as a drillmaster.[18]

The uniqueness and importance of his role continued to fascinate and please him. The monotonous chants sung by his men to the accompaniment of their own handclapping and drumming of feet drew Higginson toward the campfires. "When I am tired and jaded in the evening," he wrote, "nothing refreshes me more immediately than to go and hear the men singing in the company streets." [19]

As he listened to the chants he attempted to record the obscure words of these "spirituals." Here was a come-outer earnestness that thoroughly convinced him of the southern slaves' religious intensity. "There is no parallel instance," he later asserted, "of an oppressed race thus sustained by the religious sentiment alone." Only infrequently did he recognize the rebellious defiance against the white man that was disguised in these songs. They were as "simple and indigenous" as the Scottish ballads that had fascinated Sir Walter Scott. In keeping with the prevailing view that the Negro had no cultural heritage, Higginson failed to recognize any African influence in the spirituals. He characterized them as picturesque, quaint, elementary, mystical, sweet and touching, and, of course, religious. That this religious sentiment was, sometimes influenced by the white man is suggested by one of the Negroes' "most thrilling & impassioned prayers":

> Let me so lib dat when I die I shall *hab manners*, dat I shall know what to say when I see my Heabenly Lord.[20]

18. TWH to Sarah [Bowditch], Nov. 27, 1862, Higginson MSS; TWH journal, Dec. 16, 1862.

19. TWH journal, Dec. 3, 10, 11, 1862.

20. Ibid., Dec. 14, 1862; TWH, "Negro Spirituals," *Atlantic Monthly, 19* (1867), 691, 685. Melville J. Herskovits; *The Myth of the Negro Past* (New York, 1941), completely accepts the survival of the African heritage in America; more cautious and convincing is Rose, *Reconstruction*, pp. 96–100, 422–23. Also see Miles Mark Fisher, *Negro Slave Songs in the United States* (Ithaca, 1953).

As he lay in his tent after taps he could hear the "wild curlews hover & wail all night, invisibly around us in the air, like vexed ghosts of departed slave-lords of the soil." It was strange to be in a land where figs and oranges were ripening during the Christmas season and where ceremonies were planned to celebrate not Christmas or New Year but the Emancipation Proclamation. Plans for the celebration did faintly remind him of the first of August in New England when West Indian Emancipation Day was remembered by abolitionist societies. There was a difference though, despite Lincoln's words, "These men will have to fight to get the promise fulfilled." [21]

Ten oxen had been roasted on New Year's eve for the next day's celebration. In a large grove of live oaks outside Camp Saxton, a crowd of civilian and military men and women heard the Reverend Mr. Fowler deliver the opening prayer of the "Freedom Jubilee." Dr. William Brisbane, a South Carolinian who had freed his slaves before the war, read the Emancipation Proclamation to the assembly; Higginson was presented with a stand of colors for the regiment by the Reverend Mansfield French, a leader of the first band of northern teachers who had come to Port Royal in March 1862. As Higginson was about to acknowledge receipt of the regimental flags, a group of Negroes with seeming spontaneity began singing "My Country 'Tis of Thee." "It seemed the choked voice of a race at last unloosed," wrote Higginson. He accepted the standards, reported another, with tears in his eyes and seemed inspired upon presenting the American flag to his color-sergeant, Prince Rivers. He admonished Rivers to act as if his life were chained to it, and to die to defend the flag that would make him free. Rivers, "as superb as a panther," responded by telling his comrades that if he were shot, the flag must first be saved. Corporal Robert Sutton, the Colonel's favorite, made the point better than any white Abolitionist. Sutton vowed that no black soldier would be satisfied until all his brothers and sisters were free. "Boys we will take Christ for our Captain who never lost a battle." [22]

21. TWH to L. Higginson, Dec. 22, 1862, Higginson MSS.
22. Jan. 1, 1863, "A Surgeon's War Letters," *Proceedings of the Massachusetts Historical Society*, 43 (1910), 340 (hereafter cited as Rogers). Forten journal,

It was indeed a day of promise. A week later Higginson would wonder about the reality of the promise.

> I cannot believe it, but sometimes I feel very anxious about the ultimate fate of these poor people. After Hungary, one sees that the right may not triumph, & revolution may go backward, & the habit of inhumanity in regard to them seems so deeply impressed upon our people, that it is hard to believe in anything better. I dare not yet hope that the promise of the President's proclamation will be kept.[23]

Higginson had good reason for anxiety. Lincoln had continued to delay a declaration bringing Negroes into the Union ranks. Even in the Emancipation Proclamation the President had conceded the use of Negroes for garrison duty only. He did not seem interested in proving the Negro's lack of timidity. He had no desire, as one newspaper noted, "to carry out this war for the purpose of elucidating a theory." [24] The decision to extend the Negro's role in the war, and presumably his role in his own future, would chiefly depend upon military and political pressures. Union losses during 1862 in the Pennsylvania campaign, at Second Bull Run, at Antietam, and at Fredericksburg were hastening the need to tap the potential of black manpower. The increasing reluctance of northern men to enlist made the problem critical. Finally, radical Republicans were exerting more pressure on the President to commit the country to the Negro cause. By the end of March 1863, Lincoln, who had talked of compensated emancipation and colonization four months previously, would believe that the Negro population was the "great *available* and yet *unavailed* of force for restoring the Union." The President sounded like an echo of the exaggerated assertions of militant Abolitionists when he said: "The bare

Jan. 1, 1863, in Billington, *Forten*, p. 154; H. Ware, Jan. 1, 1863, in Pearson, *Port Royal*, pp. 129–31; Edward L. Pierce, "The Freedmen at Port Royal," *Atlantic Monthly*, *12* (1863), 298; *The Free South*, Jan. 10, 1863, Civil War Scrapbooks, Higginson MSS.

23. TWH journal, Jan. 8, 1863.

24. Dudley Taylor Cornish, *The Sable Arm: Negro Troops in the Union Army, 1861–1865* (New York, 1956), p. 96; New York *Times*, Jan. 9, 1863.

sight of 50,000 armed and drilled black soldiers upon the banks of the Mississippi would end the rebellion at once." [25]

But such statements would not be made until March. In January, only the 1st South Carolina Volunteers had full War Department authorization, for the President, as a friend of Higginson noted, was "backing slowly into God's faith with his face always turned to Kentucky." Generals Benjamin Butler in Louisiana and James Lane in Kansas had no more sanction for their enlistment of Negroes than the fact that they had not received a government reprimand. General David Hunter, however, had been officially censured. He was informed in May 1862 that no commander was authorized to recruit Negroes, and his actions were declared void. It was Higginson who became the leader of the first slave regiment legally mustered into the army, a group which therefore "deserves to be called the first American Negro regiment," says a recent historian.[26]

General Hunter returned to command the Department of the South in late January. He had missed by three days the sight of Higginson parading his regiment through the streets of Beaufort with "every polished musket having a black face beside it, and every face steadily front." Jeering, taunts, and the striking of a black soldier by a white one had occurred during the march, but Higginson had minimized these as a "few trivial exceptions." He avoided describing these incidents, though the regimental surgeon, Dr. Rogers, reported that it had been necessary to help the accosted Negro: "We wheeled our horses upon the rabble, and Major Strong, with drawn sword persuaded the offender, with the point of that instrument a little nearer to the fellow's back than seemed wholesome. . . . The effect was magical, no more audible sneers." [27] Higginson simply stated that nothing but a parade was so stirring as real war. Even Rogers agreed that in all, the parade left him feeling that he had "never [in his] life, felt so proud, so

25. *The War of the Rebellion: A Compilation of Official Records of the Union and Confederate Armies*, *3* (Washington, 1880–1901), 103 (hereafter cited as *O. R.*).

26. Samuel Johnson to George Stearns, Dec. 29, 1862, Johnson MSS; Cornish, *Sable Arm*, p. 92.

27. TWH journal, Jan. 19, 1863; Rogers, Jan. 17, 1863, p. 345.

strong, so large." It helped abate his despair of a few days before over thoughts of keeping the men from scurvy for lack of proper food, treating the sick without medicines, and amputating without knives.[28]

General Hunter first viewed Higginson's regiment during battalion drill and told the troops that he desired to recruit 50,000 more Negroes. A plan was quickly initiated to send the regiment up the St. Mary's River on the Florida–Georgia border for cotton, lumber, and especially Negro recruits. Higginson was more concerned than Hunter that "success or failure may make or mar the prospects of colored troops." [29]

Higginson was troubled that the Negroes at Camp Saxton seemed so different from the fiercely independent slave portrayed in his *Atlantic* insurrection articles. The romantically conceived Negro of Denmark Vesey or Nat Turner fame, who combined virtue with heroism, did not coincide with Higginson's "docile" troops, and the insurrectionary Negro portrayed had refused to follow the most sympathetic white man into battle. He thought this was probably why John Brown had failed to put those thousand pikes into the hands of Virginia slaves. Doubt still existed in Higginson's mind whether an Uncle Tom would fight or a Denmark Vesey would follow a white leader.

Saxton remained confident that Higginson's men were unsurpassed in discipline and morale. The New Englander in charge of the Sea Island plantations, however, was skeptical: "Any other race of men under the sun would fight for their own freedom, but I doubt whether there is the requisite amount of pluck in them . . . even when we are ready to lead them." [30] Higginson maintained that their courage already had been successfully tested during two skirmishes fought prior to his arrival at Port Royal, yet he remained dubious about their toughness. Dr. Rogers expressed the prevalent feeling when he recorded in his diary: "It remains to see how they will fight." [31]

28. TWH journal, Jan. 19, 1863; Rogers, Jan. 18, 19, 1863, p. 346.

29. TWH journal, Jan. 19, 1863.

30. Saxton to Stanton, Jan. 26, 1863, newspaper clipping, Higginson MSS; Edward S. Philbrick, Jan. 2, 1863, in Pearson, *Port Royal*, p. 136.

31. TWH to M. Higginson, Dec. 20, 1862, TWH to John Andrew, Jan. 19, 1863, Higginson MSS; Rogers, Jan. 23, 1863, p. 348.

Only two days after Hunter's return, Higginson, commanding three boats and 462 officers and men, steamed down the Beaufort River. He led the expedition from the *Ben de Ford*, a ship armed with a six-pound cannon and carrying most of the men. The *John Adams*, a double-ended East Boston ferry, was expected to provide most of the firepower with its thirty-pound and two-pound Parrot guns plus an eight-inch howitzer. The third ship, the *Planter*, had already achieved fame in May 1862 when a Charleston Negro, Robert Smalls, had skillfully run this Confederate ship through the Charleston harbor fortifications and delivered himself and the boat to the Union blockading fleet outside. The Higginson expedition was further armed with numerous copies of the Emancipation Proclamation to enlist skeptical slaves into the Union ranks.[32]

The ships were to rendezvous at St. Simons Island, which lay abandoned though under virtual control of the Union navy. Because the *Planter* was delayed with mechanical difficulties, the men of the *John Adams* and *Ben de Ford* were sent on a foraging expedition onto St. Simons. There they uncovered a substantial amount of railroad iron that had been concealed in the abandoned rebel forts. When the *Planter* did arrive two days later, the three ships sailed south to the Union post at Fort Clinch in Fernandina, Florida. On the same evening of January 26, Higginson crowded 200 men onto the *John Adams*. The objective was to travel fifteen miles up the St. Mary's River, disembark at Township Landing and surprise a rebel cavalry company known to be encamped nearby. A quick victory and some experience under fire were expected.[33]

The *John Adams* moved slowly and silently up the river. With Higginson leading and Corporal Robert Sutton serving as guide, 175 men landed just past midnight. They quietly marched through the pine woods for two miles while those remaining on the *Adams* awaited news of the successful encirclement of the cavalry. Suddenly, those aboard the ship heard the crack of musketry in the woods. Dr. Rogers prepared to receive the wounded.[34]

In the woods it was Higginson, not the Confederate cavalry,

32. Rogers, Feb. 1, 1863, p. 355; O. R., *14*, 195; TWH, "Up the St. Mary's," *Atlantic Monthly*, *15* (1865), 423; Benjamin Quarles, *The Negro in the Civil War* (Boston, 1953), pp. 71–73.

33. O. R., *14*, 197; "Up the St. Mary's," p. 425.

34. Rogers, Jan. 26, 1863, p. 349.

who was surprised. About 35 of the cavalry men had spotted his advanced guard and had swung into action. Almost instantly Private William Parson of Company G was hit in the chest and fell dead at the side of his white colonel. A rapid response by three black soldiers narrowly prevented another shot at Higginson. And when the rest of the men opened fire, the heavily outnumbered Confederate force fled. Its lieutenant had been killed and two soldiers wounded.[35]

Higginson immediately abandoned the plan to attack the rebel camp. His men, he decided, had proven their ability to fight under the duress of surprise attack at night, and the expedition's main task of getting supplies and black recruits was paramount. Seven wounded men—one near death—were carried back to Dr. Rogers. Higginson with some of his officers and men spent the remainder of the night in an abandoned plantation house. One of the sentinels remained on duty without reporting the buckshot lodged in his shoulder from the skirmish of "One Hundred Pines." Only the sounds of musketry from Higginson's overanxious sentries broke the night's silence.[36]

He reported the encounter as an undisputed triumph. Dr. Rogers, however, candidly recorded that the "object of our raid was to surprise and capture a company of rebel cavalry pickets, but as usual in this war, the enemy seemed to know the secret plan, and we only succeeded in making them skedaddle after a few rounds." In the morning, Higginson partially succeeded in preventing the looting of the plantation house except for the confiscation, with his permission, of a piano later presented to some schoolchildren. But the house, because of its use to the enemy, was set afire just before the *Adams* sailed down the river.[37]

The next stop was the already heavily shelled town of St. Mary's, a short distance from Fort Clinch, where some abandoned lumber was taken on board. Higginson initially opposed burning the seemingly deserted town until the *Adams*, about to depart, was fired upon from the shore. He then commanded his men to fire the town.

35. "Up the St. Mary's," pp. 425–27; *Floridian and Journal*, Feb. 14, 1863, Civil War Scrapbooks, Higginson MSS; Forten journal, Feb. 7, 1863, in Billington, *Forten*, p. 183.

36. Rogers, Jan. 27, 1863, p. 349; "Up the St. Mary's," p. 428.

37. Rogers, Jan. 26, 1863, p. 349.

Even Dr. Rogers, who had wanted every house burned to the ground and three old ladies there imprisoned, was satisfied with the "immense fire." Higginson, who wished to observe the amenities of warfare, confided to his journal: "Oh how beautiful they blaze." [38]

After returning to Fernandina, he dispatched the *Planter* and the *Ben de Ford* for brick and lumber. Meanwhile the *Adams* began a 40-mile trip up the St. Mary's to recruit slaves from the Alberti plantation. Corporal Sutton, formerly a slave on that plantation, carefully guided the ship through the narrow river. Finally, just before sunrise, she reached Woodstock, and Higginson sent two companies ashore. They met no opposition. At daylight, Higginson landed with Dr. Rogers and most of the remaining men. Rogers carried the copies of the Emancipation Proclamation. [39]

A few forlorn southern soldiers had already been captured by Higginson's men before he came ashore, but no slaves were found on the Alberti plantation. Only a slave-jail remained, with three stocks and "a machine" designed to manacle a prisoner into a position where he could not stand, lie, or sit. The keys and shackles were soon taken aboard along with rice, sheep, and corn. Colonel Higginson, relishing the ceremonial symbolism, decorously introduced Robert Sutton to Mrs. Alberti, his ex-owner. [40]

The most dangerous part of the trip lay ahead. Confederate units usually saved their fire for foragers returning with their treasure. True to this pattern, southern pickets from the bordering Florida and Georgia bluffs opened fire on the *Adams*. In her course downstream the ship became the target for all the enemy could muster. One of the first barrages of bullets killed the *Adams'* captain. Higginson ordered his men below decks and they were forced to content themselves by firing their rifles futilely through the portholes. The gauntlet run, the *John Adams* finally steamed into Fernandina. [41]

Joining the flagship *Ben de Ford* and the *Planter* once again, the three boats sailed for Beaufort. Back on his flagship, Higginson jubilantly wrote his mother, "I will merely say that we have made

38. TWH journal, Feb. 4, 1863.
39. *O. R., 14*, 197; "Up the St. Mary's," pp. 431–32.
40. *O. R., 14*, 197; "Up the St. Mary's," p. 433; TWH journal, Feb. 4, 1863.
41. *O. R., 14*, 198; TWH journal, Feb. 4, 1863.

one of the most daring expeditions of the war, . . . fought a cavalry company in open field & defeated it overwhelmingly. . . . The men have behaved splendidly & I have enjoyed it inexpressibly. When the whole is known, it will establish past question the reputation of the regiment." [42]

In Beaufort by sunrise, Higginson hurried to the quarters of General Saxton, had him awakened, happily presented the keys from the Alberti slave prison, and related the story of the St. Mary's expedition. Saxton approved the official report which Higginson had drafted en route to Beaufort. Well aware that he was reporting more than just another foraging raid and that northern newspapers would quote his account of the venture, Higginson wrote for the men who were wondering about the wisdom of recruiting ex-slaves into the Union army:

> These men have been repeatedly under fire . . . and have in every instance come off not only with unblemished honor but with undisputed triumph. . . . Nobody knows anything about these men who has not seen them in battle. I find that I myself knew nothing. There is a fiery energy about them beyond anything of which I have read, unless it be the French Zouaves. It requires the strictest discipline to hold them in hand. [43]

The Negroes' childlike nature was not mentioned here, nor that they probably had saved his life.

Higginson denied that the river expedition had been a gesture of mere bravado. Like an overly zealous auctioneer he listed among the collected treasure: 250 bars of much-needed railroad iron valued at $5,000; yellow pine ties "said to be worth $700"; and 40,000 bricks, "valued at about $10,000 in view of the present high freights." He defined the meaning of his expedition for the future:

> No officer in this regiment now doubts the key to the successful prosecution of the war lies in the unlimited employment of black troops. . . . They have peculiarities of temperament, of position and motive, which belong to them alone.

42. TWH to L. Higginson, Feb. 1, 1863, Higginson MSS.
43. Quoted in Saxton to Stanton, Feb. 2, 1863, in *O. R.*, 14, 194.

Instead of leaving their homes and families to fight they are fighting for their homes and families. . . . It would have been madness to attempt with the bravest white troops what I have accomplished with the black ones.[44]

A New York *Times* editorial criticized Higginson for thinking it necessary "to convince the public that the negroes will fight." [45]

General Saxton, as enthusiastic as Higginson about the accomplishments of black troops, reported to Secretary of War Stanton that the St. Mary's expedition had been a complete success. Like Higginson he suggested the establishment of posts on the mainland which could be used to recruit more ex-slaves for the army.[46] Unrecorded, however, is the reaction of General Hunter and other officers in the Department of the South to the fact that Higginson had brought back no new recruits and relatively little lumber. These, after all, had been the expedition's main purpose. Railroad iron from abandoned St. Simon's Island was available anytime.

It pleased Higginson that even while the expedition was in progress, James Montgomery, the charming and zealous Kansan, was commissioned to raise a second Negro regiment. The fame of the 1st South Carolina Volunteers made it a spectacle for both the prejudiced and the curious. The great number of unsympathetic observers moved Higginson to deride the "military flunkies" and conclude that "never was a great army, probably with so many accidental great men; my respect for them diminishes every day. . . . There is much that is petty and unsatisfactory. . . . I enjoy the method & the system of the army, but its very nature puts so much power into such poor hands, from McClellan downward." [47] At least Montgomery was an experienced and true friend of abolition. Dr. Rogers was more specific than Higginson: "I am sick of talking to men whose limited capacity renders it necessary for me to explain that humanity lies somewhat deeper than the integument of the human body." Neither Higginson nor Rogers agreed with Beaufort's Union newspaper, *The Free South*, that a "reck-

44. Ibid.
45. *Times*, Feb. 10, 1863.
46. Saxton to Stanton, Jan. 26, 1863, Civil War Scrapbooks, Higginson MSS; *O. R.*, *14*, 198.
47. TWH journal, Feb. 20, 24, 1863

less and prostituted" South had been replaced by "a spotless virgin" from the North.[48]

Rogers believed that only more success in battle could overcome the feeling against Negroes. After a discussion with General Hunter about the prejudice at Port Royal manifested by the 24th Massachusetts Regiment, Higginson knew a major Negro victory was necessary. The place for such a victory was Florida. "I am satisfied," he said, "that these people, having once tasted freedom could sustain themselves there indefinitely." [49]

For men like Saxton and Higginson there was more to war than military triumphs by black soldiers. With words that could have been Higginson's, Saxton urged the white officers of the 1st South Carolina Volunteers that "in addition to training our men to fight for their liberties—it's our duty to try to elevate them in the moral scale. I have learned with sorrow that the habit of profane swearing is becoming prevalent." Other breaches of morality appeared among the Negro soldiers as some slipped out of camp to attend a dance at a nearby plantation; one soldier was fatally shot by a sentry when he failed to halt. The very scandalous reports from the local ladies prevented Charlotte Forten, whom Higginson called "The Daughter of the Regiment," from joining his next expedition to serve as schoolteacher.[50]

Three armed ships filled with approximately a thousand men, consisting mostly of Higginson's regiment plus two still incomplete companies of Montgomery's, steamed out to sea and headed south near dawn on March 8. Higginson, aboard the *Boston*, was instructed to proceed with the *John Adams* and the *Burnside* to join a few naval gunboats from the Florida blockading fleet and to commence an invasion of Jacksonville, the city which had been twice taken and abandoned by Union forces.[51]

Orders from Saxton instructed Higginson to

48. Rogers, Feb. 6, 1863, p. 368; *The Free South*, Jan. 10, 1863, Civil War Scrapbooks, Higginson MSS.

49. TWH journal, Feb. 6, 1863; TWH to L. Higginson, Feb. 20, 1863, Higginson MSS.

50. Saxton to officers of 1st S.C. Vols., Feb. 28, 1863, Misc. MSS, Houghton Library; Rogers, Mar. 3, 1863, p. 369; Forten to J. G. Whittier, June 13, 1863, Whittier MSS.

51. Cornish, *Sable Arm*, p. 138.

carry the proclamation of freedom to the enslaved; to call all loyal men into the service of the United States; to occupy as much of the State of Florida as possible; . . . and to neglect no means consistent with the usages of civilized warfare to weaken, harass, and annoy those who are in rebellion against the Government of the United States.[52]

At the outset Saxton told Stanton that the expedition had departed with insufficient ammunition because of a shortage in the Department of the South. But he still hoped that besides recruiting able-bodied Negroes, it would aid the forthcoming Charleston assault by forcing General Beauregard to divert some troops to Jacksonville. As if to assuage his own doubt as well as Stanton's, Saxton exaggeratedly reported that Higginson's regiment had killed or wounded sixty enemy soldiers during its recent St. Mary's skirmish.[53]

Once Higginson's forces were joined by the naval gunboats *Norwich* and *Uncas*, the five ships, at 2 A.M., March 10, began their ascent of the St. Johns River toward Jacksonville, about thirty miles away. Several times during the night a ship ran onto one of the many sandbars in the channel. The *Norwich*, heaviest in fire power, was grounded a few miles below Jacksonville; only the next tide could free her, and she was unable to join the initial invasion.[54]

It had been planned to enter Jacksonville at daybreak, but now the landing would have to be made under the bright noon sun. Children, seemingly oblivious to war, were the first people sighted as the small task force neared Jacksonville. The ships' gunners were at their stations waiting for the sound of enemy fire before opening the cannonading. But the city seemed as much apart from the war as the children.[55]

The *Uncas* steamed to the big upper pier, the others docked at a wharf downstream. Small howitzers were quickly mounted on both wharves as Colonels Higginson and Montgomery led the men

52. Saxton to Stanton, Mar. 6, 1863, in *O. R.*, *14*, 423.
53. Ibid.
54. Rogers, Mar. 12, 1863, p. 372.
55. TWH journal, Mar. 8, 1863; Report of Col. John D. Rust, April 2, 1863, in *O. R.*, *14*, 232–33; TWH, "Up the St. John's," *Atlantic Monthly*, *16* (1865), 311–25.

into Jacksonville. Confederate General Joseph Finegan, commanding the District of Florida, explained four days later that the city
was occupied with such speed and secrecy that it had been taken
before his forces were aware of it.[56]

The first day went swiftly as the invaders hurriedly prepared
entrenchments. It was known that a Confederate camp was near,
though the number of men was undetermined. With defenses incomplete, Higginson and his men spent a very anxious night at the
only mainland Union post in the Department of the South. On the
second day he ordered houses burned on the outer edge of town to
give his artillery a clear field and to shorten the line of defense for
the small force. Trees were felled to make barricades, and advance
pickets were deployed beyond the barricades.[57]

Now that Jacksonville was theirs, the force of a thousand men
hardly seemed sufficient to hold the town and also embark upon
needed forays into the interior. This was readily apparent on the
second day when the advance pickets encountered a formidable
Confederate reconnaissance party in a skirmish that spilled the first
Union blood. An enemy cavalry charge by 200 men forced Higginson to withdraw his pickets behind the barricades. Until Florida
Negroes could be recruited to augment the occupying forces, he
would have to depend upon the big guns of the *Norwich* and
Uncas to restrain the enemy. The naval gunboat *Paul Jones* had
been ordered by Admiral Dupont to sail beyond Jacksonville and
"assume a bold front in the St. Johns, or we shall be forced to abandon the river." But it never sailed past the town. The *Paul Jones*
had arrived there on the 12th and her commander judged the Union forces insufficient to hold Jacksonville without its assistance.[58]

Higginson's anxiety about the enemy was still less than Confederate General Finegan's whose estimate grossly exaggerated the in-
vading force at 4,000 Negroes and a company of white soldiers.
What was even more horrendous was contemplation of the Yankee's aims. "Negroes," Finegan feared, "may escape in large num-

56. Mar. 14, 1863, *O. R.*, *14*, 272; Rogers, Mar. 12, 1863, p. 372.

57. TWH journal, Mar. 13, 1863; TWH to L. Higginson, Mar. 19, 1863, Higginson MSS.

58. March 20, 1863, *Official Records of the Union and Confederate Navies in
the War of the Rebellion*, *13* (Washington, 1894–1932), 742 (hereafter cited as
O. R. N.).

bers to the enemy. . . . The entire negro population of East Florida lies within easy communication of the [St. Johns] river. . . . A few weeks will suffice to corrupt the entire slave population of East Florida." Finegan issued orders for all troops within four or five days of Jacksonville to prepare to defend the countryside against a marauding enemy. A proclamation was drafted to alert the people of the district and state the news that "our unscrupulous enemy has landed a large force of negro troops." From Charleston he requested siege guns with which to blast the "Abolition troops" from Jacksonville.[59]

Higginson was not expecting to be bombarded. On the third day of occupation, which had been marked by the welcome arrival of the *Paul Jones*, he felt sufficiently secure to write his mother: "We have taken the prettiest town I have seen, without a gun. . . . My abode is a sort of palace: one of the finest I ever saw, even with a billiard room." From his captured mansion, Higginson directed the occupation forces and contended with about 500 citizens remaining from a peacetime population of 5,000. The intricacies of judging who in Jacksonville was loyal to the Union were evident. To be confronted with Unionist slaveholders was especially strange for an Abolitionist officer. Higginson decided to consider all residents semiloyal and to give food rations where needed. But he refrained from administering the oath of loyalty as freely as commanders less committed to antislavery might have done and was unsympathetic to those who pleaded for protection from the "niggers." He answered: "These are United States troops and they will not dishonor the flag." His own men, many originally from Florida, disliked the residents but refrained from going beyond confiscating an occasional pig or chicken. This caused them some hardship, for food was scarce.[60]

During the first week of occupation, military action was confined to skirmishes at the barricades, reconnoitering, and raids up the river. A small force under Montgomery returned from its first raid heavily laden with poultry, pigs, ducks, and geese. The main work of the occupation, however, continued to be the building of

59. *O. R.*, *14*, 229.
60. TWH to L. Higginson, Mar. 12, 1863, Higginson MSS; Rogers, Mar. 12, 13, 14, 1863, p. 372.

fortifications. By the fourth day, advance pickets were deployed and recalled at sunset; all military personnel were forbidden outdoors at night. In the darkness, gunfire from the Union sentinels could be heard. Higginson sought encouragement by reading frequently from the author who had meant much to him in his youth —Jean Paul Richter. It was an appropriate time to recall how a man, as in Richter's *Titan*, had eliminated unhappiness and doubt through sheer heroism.[61]

At Port Royal, Rufus Saxton was confident. He had dispatched the 8th Maine Regiment to Jacksonville to reinforce Higginson's garrison. Reminding Secretary Stanton that the expedition's object was "to occupy Jacksonville and make it the base of operations for the entire state of Florida," Saxton assured him that many prisoners had already been taken, and the black troops had never flinched. But more guns and ammunition were necessary to conquer all of Florida. Saxton did not know that his first reinforcements were caught in rough weather and would arrive in Jacksonville from four to eight days late. And he did not know that the manpower shortage was seriously hampering Higginson's operations.[62]

Higginson, meanwhile, was gratified when the *Adams*, foraging upriver, returned with thirty new Negroes, eighteen horses, and eleven head of cattle. The *Burnside* was then dispatched to try foraging. His force "might even become self-supporting at this rate," Higginson noted with irony. The Confederate commander, also pressed for supplies, especially long-range guns, reported the raiding with neither restraint nor accuracy: "They are robbing and plundering everything on the east bank of the St. Johns River."[63]

Since the foragers had confiscated bridles and saddles with the horses, Higginson now appeared on horseback. For $125 he purchased the animal from its new owner, the federal government.

61. TWH journal, Mar. 12, 1863; TWH to L. Higginson, Mar. 16, 1863, Higginson MSS.

62. Saxton to Stanton, Mar. 14, 1863, in *O. R.*, *14*, 226; TWH to L. Higginson, Mar. 22, 1863, Higginson MSS.

63. TWH journal, Mar. 16, 1863; Joseph Finegan to Thomas Jordan, Mar. 20, 1863, in *O. R.*, *14*, 838.

Mounted on "Rinaldo," he proceeded to lead two companies on the first large-scale reconnaissance venture of the expedition. About forty enemy cavalry men were encountered—shots were exchanged but soon the southerners withdrew. On the next day the Confederates sent word that women and children should be evacuated from Jacksonville within twenty-four hours because it was going to be shelled. About 150 people left the city on the following day, and in the evening the shelling began.[64]

This seemed the low point for Higginson's forces. Fatigue from continuous duty and ill-health, especially dysentery, were depleting the small garrison. For ten days a comparatively inexperienced and undermanned force, with no relief, had held Jacksonville. Only the effectiveness of the naval gunboats and exaggerated estimates of Union strength had discouraged a sustained Confederate attack. But now shelling during the night promised a more aggressive enemy. The southern force had recently been augmented with men, some small artillery, and a 32-pound rifle gun. The 32-pounder, on board a platform car, was moved in at night to shell the town. Instead of leading an offensive operation into enemy territory, Higginson and his troops were entrenched in a besieged city. On the second evening of shelling, however, the Union position changed. The 6th Connecticut Regiment landed at midnight to provide the first reinforcements. Two days later, 200 men of the 8th Maine arrived, followed by the rest of the regiment under Colonel John D. Rust. Treasury Agent, Judge Lyman Stickney, always eager to control Florida, arrived with the troops.[65]

Higginson welcomed the reinforcements which swelled the occupation forces to about 3,000 but also noted, "Now I have to show, not only that blacks can fight, but that they and white soldiers can act in harmony together." Men like General Hunter, confident in the fighting abilities of Negro troops, had similar doubts. Hunter, as late as March 7, had informed General Henry Halleck that "the colored troops . . . cannot consistently with

64. TWH journal, March 19, 20, 1863; Duncan to Dupont in *O. R. N.*, *12*, 745; A. H. McCormick, Mar. 17, 1863, in *O. R.*, *14*, 839; Rogers, Mar. 18, 1863, p. 373.
65. Ibid.; Finegan to Jordan, Mar. 20, 1863, in *O. R.*, *14*, 838; TWH to L. Higginson, Mar. 12, 1863, Higginson MSS.

the interests of the service (in the present state of feeling) be advantageously employed to act in concert with our other forces." [66] Higginson's and Montgomery's failure to find sufficient Florida slaves to supplement their Negro troops had necessitated either the sending of white reinforcements or the immediate abandonment of Jacksonville. Again military necessity had become the determinant in establishing a more radical race policy.

There is no evidence that any significant clash occurred between the white and black troops, though Dr. Rogers anxiously conceded that the "prejudice of the white soldiers is very strong." He feared a subsequent collision because the Negroes occupying Jacksonville had endured sufficient hardships to make them impatient with taunting. Higginson was determined to prevent such a catastrophe by exercising military discipline. By dividing the duties of the whites and Negroes, he hoped to use his own troops for taking new posts in Florida while the white troops did the garrison duty. "The colors are better apart, for military services," he declared. Although they were not separated in Jacksonville, the conclusion of a Confederate prisoner probably summarizes the climate of integration: "There is much bad feeling among the whites against the negroes." [67] But it never exceeded bad feeling, as it had in Beaufort. The pressing danger of the enemy blunted overt antagonism.

The Confederate railroad gun came within an audacious mile and a half of Jacksonville to lob its shells. The Union gunboats returned the fire, but the major effect was on the nerves of men who lay wounded in the Union hospital. The enemy's ability to move into shelling range proved the need for an expedition to dislodge and possibly overwhelm the smaller forces. Higginson, therefore, led ten companies (four black and six white) four miles outside of town, marking the first time during the Civil War that so many whites and Negroes were together in combat. With their advance, the southern cavalry and its railroad gun pulled back. Acting under orders from his superior officer, Colonel Rust, Higginson then ordered his men to return. Only as they withdrew did

66. TWH journal Mar. 20, 1863; Hunter to Halleck, Mar. 7, 1864, in O. R., *3,* 425.

67. Rogers, Mar. 22, 1863, p. 378; TWH to L. Higginson Mar. 22, 1863, Higginson MSS; Henry Bryan to Thomas Jordan, Mar. 26, 1863, in O. R., *14,* 845.

the Confederate railroad gun advance; it succeeded in killing two men and wounding two others of the Maine regiment. With the destruction of some railroad tracks and the posting of advance pickets, however, the Confederates were no longer able to come so close to Jacksonville.[68]

At the time the white troops arrived, only seventy Negroes had been added to the ranks. The vision of hundreds of slaves flocking to Jacksonville had not materialized, and even so zealous a recruiter as James Montgomery had not significantly increased their numbers. But a penetration deeper into Florida's interior promised additional recruits. To achieve this, Montgomery with 120 black troops boarded the gunboat *Paul Jones* for a 75-mile trip up the river to Palatka. Higginson planned to follow with a raid at Magnolia, 35 miles from Jacksonville. Depending upon the intensity of enemy opposition, posts were to be established at Palatka and Magnolia.[69]

Montgomery reached Palatka safely, although when a landing was attempted, his men came under heavy fire from a Confederate cavalry company. The *Paul Jones* answered with its own cannonade, but the vigorous Confederate defense convinced Montgomery to abandon the plan for taking Palatka. The enemy cavalry captain, having halted a superior force, allowed his joy to influence his official report. He informed Finegan that from 600 to 700 Negroes "under the command of the notorious Montgomery" had been repulsed, with some twenty or thirty colored troops dead or wounded. Later, the *Paul Jones* expedition had some success when it stopped a few miles down river at Orange Mills and gathered bales of cotton, rifles, horses, and fourteen freedmen. Further foraging might eventually compensate for the repulse at Palatka.[70]

But before Montgomery could continue, he received orders to return immediately to Jacksonville. Upon his arrival, he learned that General Hunter had commanded all Union forces to return to Beaufort. The command had been received at Jacksonville on the day that General Beauregard, unknown to Union forces, had

68. Rogers, Mar. 22, 1863, p. 378.
69. Rogers, Mar. 23, 1863, p. 378.
70. *The Free South*, April 4, 1863, Civil War Scrapbooks, Higginson MSS; J. J. Dickinson to Finegan, Mar. 27, 1863, in *O. R.*, *14*, 238–39.

notified his distraught commander in the East Florida district that he could spare him only 300 Enfield rifles and 300 rounds. Meanwhile, General Hunter rejected a plea from Saxton to allow the continued occupation of Jacksonville. Troops and gunboats were badly needed for the big Union attack on Charleston.[71]

Higginson called the evacuation order a great blow. And as embarkation preparations were being made, Rogers aptly expressed the feeling of those men so interested in proving a theory, when he wrote in his diary: "This is one of the sad days of my life. The evacuation of Jacksonville is the burial of so many hopes I had cherished for the oppressed, that I feel like one in attendance at the funeral of a host of his friends." [72]

The proceedings accompanying the evacuation did not sweeten his feelings, or Higginson's—the departing forces burned most of the city, including the Catholic and Episcopal churches. The fires appear to have been begun by the 8th Maine, though Colonel Rust insisted in his official report that the deed had not been confined to any one regiment. Both Higginson and Rogers denied this. Rogers, looking out at the burning scene asserted that "it is established beyond all controversy that black troops, with worthy commanders, are more controllable than white troops. Whether this would be with a less conscientious Colonel, I cannot say." [73]

Also disturbing Higginson was an act for which he had complete responsibility. Fifty Jacksonville citizens had been granted permission to travel back to Beaufort with the Union troops. As the six ships detailed for the evacuation were being loaded, it became obvious that not all the civilian furniture could remain on board. Higginson's task was to order some of these personal items returned to the wharf. Upon seeing their property removed, the evacuees vigorously assailed him as a heartless tyrant. This personal attack, he believed, was the height of ungratefulness: their lives were being saved if not their featherbeds. Ignoring the horse

71. TWH journal, Mar. 28, 1863; Rogers, April 2, 1863, p. 384; Beauregard to Finegan, Mar. 27, 1863, in *O. R.*, *14*, 846; Forten journal, Mar. 26, 1863, in Billington, *Forten*, p. 175.

72. TWH to L. Higginson, Mar. 30, 1863, Higginson MSS; Rogers, Mar. 29, 1863, p. 384.

73. Duncan to Dupont, Mar. 29, 1863, in *O. R. N.*, *12*, 794; Report of Col. John D. Rust, Mar. 29, 1863, in *O. R.*, *14*, 233; Rogers, Mar. 30, 1863, p. 384.

and small sailboat being transported to Beaufort for his own use, Higginson pondered anew the problem of treating the southerners' loyalty to the Union. He now found sympathy for the view expressed by his men, who distrusted all southerners. After all, he said, the southern Negro represents "the only real Union population of the South." [74] During Reconstruction he would remember this attitude.

With the Union departure from Jacksonville the threat to Florida slavery disappeared. A similar but more aggressive expedition of 20,000 men would return to the city a year later, only to be decimated at the battle of Olustee. For Higginson and his men there had been neither great victory nor overwhelming defeat. Upon hearing the news of Jacksonville's abandonment, General Beauregard surmised that "the object of the expedition was to make me divide my forces." President Lincoln, making his only comment directly concerning Higginson's war activities, wrote General Hunter:

> I am glad to see the accounts of your colored force at Jacksonville. I see the enemy are driving them fiercely, as it is to be expected. It is important to the enemy that such a force shall not take shape and grow and thrive in the South, and in precisely the same proportion it is important to us that it shall. Hence the utmost caution and vigilance is necessary on our part. The enemy will make extra efforts to destroy them, and we should do the same to preserve them and increase them.[75]

When Lincoln wrote this letter he had not yet learned that Jacksonville had been evacuated; and by the time Hunter received it the troops had arrived in Beaufort. Only the spirit of the President's words remained important. The abandonment of the city failed to sustain Rogers' fear—the burial of Negro hopes. Not only had Lincoln committed the government to enlist slaves by the spring of 1863 but he also authorized the recruitment of northern Negroes. In Massachusetts, April and May would be marked

74. TWH journal, April 1, 1863.
75. Cornish, *Sable Arm*, pp. 27–69; Beauregard to James Seddon, Mar. 30, 1863, in *O. R., 14,* 850; Lincoln to Hunter, April 1, 1863, in *O. R., 14,* 435–36.

by the organization (led by George Stearns and Frederick Douglass) of the Negro 54th Regiment under Robert Gould Shaw, and the 55th Regiment under Norwood Hallowell. By the end of 1863, twenty black regiments would be formed in the Mississippi Valley alone. By the time Higginson had brought his men back to Beaufort he thus no longer carried the heavy responsibility of leading the only official Negro regiment. His had been the first to be mustered and to take part in any fighting, but the future action of other Negro regiments would eclipse the limited action of the 1st South Carolina Volunteers. Higginson, with reason, believed that the Jacksonville occupation had helped shape government policy.[76]

The utilization of Negro troops provided a meaning to the war that transcended the initial secession issue. It is doubtful, however, whether even many of the radicals within the Republican party were aware, at this juncture, of how far radicalism might lead. One European journalist, writing for the New York *Tribune*, was sure that he knew the effect. Wrote Karl Marx: "A single negro regiment would have a remarkable effect. . . . A war of this kind must be conducted on revolutionary lines while the Yankees have thus far been trying to conduct it constitutionally." [77] From 1864 through 1877 the revolutionary aspects of the Civil War would continue to emerge.

76. Cornish, *Sable Arm*, pp. 234–40.
77. Marx to Engels, Aug. 7, 1862, in Karl Marx and Frederick Engels, *The Civil War in the United States* (New York, 1961), p. 253.

16

Concluding a "Military Picnic"

After returning from Jacksonville, Higginson and his men were assigned to advance picket duty seven miles from Beaufort on Port Royal Island. The bulk of Hunter's forces were attacking Charleston while the 1st South Carolina Volunteers protected a seven-mile shore line along the Coosaw River. Higginson's own duties chiefly consisted of galloping through miles of lanes with sprays of immense roses to check on his men. He was quartered at the Milnes plantation in a comfortable four-room house with a fireplace and a piazza. But he complained that even the southern woods lacked "those pure, clean, innocent odors which so abound in the New England forest. There was something luscious, voluptuous, almost oppressively fragrant" about South Carolina. The climate reminded him of the nature and temperament of southern women: they had "passion, & fire, without fineness or depth." [1] Adding to the alien feelings was the reverberating reminder of war from the great guns booming at intervals from Charleston. Also, his troops could hear the taunts of nearby rebel pickets from the South Carolina mainland; Higginson ordered silence from his men to avoid exchange of obscenities. [2]

The leisure of picket duty enabled him to reflect further upon his relationship with the troops with whom he had now spent six months. To his journal he confided: "I am conscious of but little affection for individuals among them, if a man dies in [a] hospital or is shot down beside me, I feel it scarcely more than if a tree had fallen." But "over their *collective* joy & sorrow I have smiles and tears." He likened this feeling to the love of animals for their young: a willingness to die for their collective progeny, but a lack

1. TWH journal, April 6, 7, June 27, 1863.
2. TWH to L. Higginson, April 8, 1863, Higginson MSS; Rogers, April 7, 1863, p. 387.

of concern about the individual. At times, some men showed a "sublime eloquence," but "more commonly they are just children." [3]

The appeal of immediate danger which had seemed absent was revived a few days after the inauguration of this "military picnic," when the small Union gunboat *George Washington,* making its nightly patrol around Port Royal Island, lingered in the channel near sunrise. A shot from Confederate light artillery struck the boat's boiler room. At 5:30 A.M. Higginson's pickets were confronted by the sight of the blazing gunboat, its crew scrambling off. The colonel was hurriedly summoned, and arrived to find the enemy preparing what seemed to be an invasion of Port Royal Island. Soon after the first sounds of rebel artillery, four regiments of Union troops were dispatched to Beaufort from the Charleston expedition. The excitement had inflated the assault on the *Washington* to the belief that Beaufort had been attacked and burned. Union artillery fire quickly halted the removal of additional cannon from the stricken ship. On the following night, a boatload of southern soldiers, emboldened by their success, sought to capture a squad of Higginson's pickets, but the alert men drove them back into the darkness.[4] Subsequently, except for an infrequent exchange of artillery fire or a small foray, the war again receded.

Higginson made one trip at night to the wreck of the *Washington,* marooned in the Coosaw channel, to ascertain the number of guns still remaining aboard. He did not delegate this hazardous task to a man of lesser rank, he explained, because he had to treat himself to a little adventure. Once aboard the gunboat he learned that only elaborate equipment and great effort, under enemy fire, could possibly free the heavy cannon.[5]

On another night, primarily for personal excitement, he embarked on a "swimming reconnaissance" across the Coosaw channel, close to enemy pickets. The story of this daring exploit would be the first account of his war experiences to be published. He told how when he had swum back to his own lines and emerged naked

3. TWH journal, June 27, May 27, 1863.
4. Ibid., April 12, 1863; Rogers, April 15, 1864, p. 388.
5. TWH journal, April 16, 1863.

from the water, revealing himself as "a man and brother," the startled Negro sentry had snapped into present-arms.[6]

While there was little war action on picket, many amenities of Port Royal life were available to Higginson: dinner and tea on the piazza, a "charming life among cherokee roses & peach blossoms," or a gallop through the woods on Rinaldo. His headquarters at the Milnes plantation was frequently visited by the women schoolteachers from nearby plantations. He enjoyed reading the ballads of Robert Browning to an admiring Charlotte Forten or dining with the attractive Shakespearean actress Mrs. Jean Lander, who served as an army nurse. In the sailboat he had brought from Jacksonville he could cross to some little island that was even farther from war. Occasionally there was a dress parade and some drilling, but usually there was ample time to pick "rosebuds or see if any more of the small magnolias had opened their cloying flowers. . . . Lazy evening, piazza, fireside, chess." Life was indeed "pleasant and tropic." [7]

His men, he believed, also enjoyed their military picnic. Those who set up evergreen awnings in front of their tents "looked like lizards beneath their shelter." In the evenings he observed them cleaning their guns, mending clothing, or silently moving their lips while engrossed in the book that was their favorite reading primer because of its large type, short words, familiar subject, and fascinating pictures—McClellan's *Bayonet Exercises.* "Think of the great dethroned idol," noted Higginson, "banished from all other temples, still reigning in the primary school of the blameless Ethiopian." The colonel remained fascinated, also, by their "negro English" as they transformed the sentinel countersign "Carthage" to "cartridge," "Concord" to "corncob." Unknown to him, some men were spending their evenings with a bottle of liquor surreptitiously purchased in camp.[8]

The addition of white troops to his Negro pickets appeared to

6. Ibid., May 19, 1863; TWH, "A Night in the Water," *Atlantic Monthly, 14* (1864), 393 398.

7. TWH journal, April 17, 19, 22, 27, 1863; TWH to L. Higginson, April 10, 22, 1863, Higginson MSS.

8. TWH journal April 19, 26, June 27, 1863; Oct. 20, 1863, in Pearson, *Port Royal,* p. 225.

be working without friction. "This is creditable all around. At the same time it always makes me feel anxious, for if a quarrel should arise, ever slight, the whole lumbering hostility would awaken instantly & might be the destruction of all of us." But the only significant quarrel did not occur among Higginson's men. Since Montgomery's black regiment was still not at full complement, General Hunter renewed the policy that had proved so disastrous in 1862—impressing the area's freedmen. When Montgomery returned from Jacksonville this order was carried out in earnest; he scoured the local plantations for likely draftees. Exercising his usual vigor, Montgomery swelled his ranks from about 250 men to 600. To find reluctant recruits he raided Negro churches and searched through the local marshes. In one instance a fifteen-year-old Negro boy was caught and in another, a seventeen-year-old was wounded in the head. Higginson only later learned of Montgomery's methods, for at this time he observed "these are queer creatures, these freedmen, they are so used to having their destinies determined for them that they acquiesce at once when drafted." [9]

For Higginson the discipline of his men became less a matter of keeping them alert on picket duty than of seeing that they did not become like some of the white soldiers, "the undisciplined, unbuttoned mob we call an army." His tasks were becoming too routinized: boring paperwork, he was certain, would have been handled by a clerk in a white regiment, and he realized that he and his regiment no longer represented the antislavery vanguard. In May 1863 he reflected:

> For many months the fate of the whole movement for colored soldiers rested on the behavior of this one regiment. Mutiny, an extensive desertion, an act of severe discipline, a Bull Run panic, a simple defeat, might have blasted the whole movement for arming the blacks—through it the prospects of the war & of the race.[10]

There was a growing number of officers with few scruples about destroying and capturing enemy property and more willing to risk

9. TWH journal, April 19, 1863; Rupert S. Holland, ed., *Letters and Diary of Laura Towne* (Cambridge, 1912), pp. 107–08; TWH to M. Higginson, April 16, 1863, Higginson MSS; Cornish, *Sable Arm*, p. 38.
10. TWH journal, May 10, 16, 1863.

the lives of Negro troops. One of the most audacious and least successful of these leaders was Francis Merriam, the unbalanced young man who had been sent to John Brown. Merriam caught Hunter's fancy and convinced him of a plan for a wild foray on the mainland with a few picked men from Higginson's regiment. Saxton and Higginson predicted disaster and they proved to be correct. The raid resulted in a complete rout. Merriam shot one of his men and demanded that three others (including Corporal Robert Sutton) be court-martialed for an alleged act of mutiny. Only the concerted support of Higginson and his officers saved Sutton from conviction. Higginson believed that Mrs. Saxton was right when she called Merriam "a lunatic." [11]

James Montgomery had greater success. He was sent on a foraging raid into Georgia on May 25, nine days after the Merriam fiasco. Even with the draft, Montgomery's regiment remained below its full complement, but a week in enemy territory rectified this. He returned to Port Royal with 800 new recruits. Higginson, who had come to dislike Montgomery for his ambition and lack of regard for system and order, had to concede that the raid was a brilliant success, but added, "I don't believe in burning private homes, as he does." [12]

The aggressive, if distasteful, acts of Merriam and Montgomery, formerly his allies in abolition militancy, were probably factors that stimulated Higginson to make his own move. He convinced Hunter to permit a raid on the mainland. With a band of sixty men, Higginson embarked for the point where the Coosaw ferry had formerly connected Port Royal with the mainland. Five hours later they returned, having been easily repulsed by the Confederate pickets. Lieutenant Frank M. Gaston, one of the regiment's finest officers, was accidentally killed by one of his own men.[13]

General Hunter preferred Merriam's and Montgomery's aggressiveness to Higginson's seemingly fastidious interest in drill and discipline. Merriam he promoted to captain in the newly formed 3rd South Carolina Volunteers; Montgomery was en-

11. TWH to M. Higginson, May 16, 1863, TWH to L. Higginson, June 5, 1863, Higginson MSS.

12. TWH journal, May 5, 1863; TWH to L. Higginson, June 5, 1863, Higginson MSS.

13. TWH journal, May 28, 29, 1863

couraged to forage and was promised promotion to brigadier general. As commander of the first Negro regiment, Higginson felt pushed aside. But isolation, of course, was impossible. "I have experienced more annoyance & discourtesy from Montgomery," Higginson wrote in his journal, "than from any pro-slavery functionary in the Department. . . . If he only was noble & generous in thought as he is daring & successful in action. . . . He thinks me strait-laced & red-tapish—I think him fitter to command a hundred men than a thousand." [14]

The dramatic news that Montgomery had ordered the plundering and burning of Darien, Georgia, by his Negro troops appalled many northerners and allowed Higginson to elevate his differences with the Kansan from personality to principle. "Montgomery's raids are dashing," he admitted, "but his brigand practices I detest & condemn—they will injure these [black] people & make a reaction at the North. I never allowed such things are according to strictly military principles & it is perfectly easy to restrain the negroes; they are capable of heroic abstinence." Higginson declared that he would permit only civilized warfare in his regiment. Privately he concluded, however, that Montgomery was not an evil man, "but a mixture of fanaticism, vanity, and genius." [15]

Besides criticizing the brigandage of Montgomery, Higginson denied that colored troops *as such* were responsible for burning and pillaging. He observed: "I do not see why we should be savages, when J. E. B. Stuart in Pennsylvania was *not*." Soon Governor John Andrew joined the growing controversy by opposing the elevation of Montgomery to brigade commander of Negro troops. But he also opposed the promotion of Higginson, the senior colonel. Andrew reminded Stanton that Higginson has never seen much service, and had never been in the field until he went to South Carolina. The Governor feared that Higginson's letters to Senator Sumner and the *Tribune* might bring his promotion.[16]

14. Ibid., June 16, July 7, 1863; TWH to M. Higginson, June 10, 1863, Higginson MSS.

15. TWH journal, June 16, July 7, 1863; TWH to L. Higginson, June 19, 1863, Higginson MSS; Cornish, *Sable Arm*, pp. 148–49; Rose, *Reconstruction*, pp. 252–54.

16. TWH to Sumner, June 20, 1863, Sumner MSS; TWH to Sydney Gay, June 20, 1863, Gay MSS; TWH journal, May 17, 1863; Edward L. Pierce to

Another man committed to civilized warfare was Robert Gould Shaw, the twenty-six-year-old leader of the North's first black regiment, the 54th Massachusetts. Under the command of Montgomery during the destruction of Darien, Shaw was horrified. "Bushwacker Montgomery," he observed, "allows no swearing or drinking in his regiment and is anti-tobacco . . . but . . . looks as if he would have a taste for hanging people!" Like Higginson, Shaw aspired to lead his regiment to heroic feats. Both got their opportunity in early July. Shaw and the 54th Massachusetts were ordered to take Morris Island, a strategic point in the entrance to Charleston harbor. Higginson's force was assigned an indirect role in the attack as it was expected to cut the important Charleston and Savannah Railroad by destroying a bridge at Jacksonboro, South Carolina.[17]

The 1st South Carolina Volunteers were to travel twenty miles up the South Edisto River and seize and temporarily hold the town of Wiltown Bluff to allow small boats with demolition equipment to proceed ten miles on shallow river to the railroad bridge. While 10,000 troops were readying for the Morris Island attack, Higginson led his three ships from Beaufort on July 9. Relying upon moonlight to help navigate the winding river, they approached Wiltown Bluff at 4:00 A.M. under a slight fog cover. The town was taken after a brief exchange of fire. Most of the Confederate force fled, but the Union men captured young G. Henry Barnwell whom Higginson proudly identified as being of the well-known southern family. The major surprise was the hurried arrival of excited Negroes who came running to the shore soon after the first shots were fired.[18] There was no need to read them the Emancipation Proclamation.

Sumner, June 18, 1863, Sumner MSS; Andrew to Stanton, June 29, 1863, in *O. R.*, *3*, 423.

17. Robert G. Shaw to Mrs. R. G. Shaw, June 6, 1863, Civil War Scrapbooks, Higginson MSS; E. L. Pierce to Sumner, June 18, 1863, Sumner MSS; Cornish, *Sable Arm*, p. 151; Gilmore to Saxton, July 8, 1863, Memo Book, Higginson MSS; Gilmore to Halleck, July 21, 1863, TWH to Saxton, July 11, 1863, in *O. R.*, *28*, 201–02.

18. TWH to Saxton, July 11, 1863, in *O. R.*, *28*, 201–02; Col. H. K. Aiken to Brig. Gen. Thos. Jordan, July 12, 1863, in *O. R. 28*, 196; TWH, "Up the Edisto," *Atlantic Monthly*, *20* (1867), 157–65; Lt. Thos. White to Capt. F. R. Malony, July 13, 1863, in *O. R.*, *28*, 199. ,

While pickets were deployed, Captain Trowbridge supervised the removal of wooden piles in the river, which the enemy had placed to obstruct passage to Jacksonboro. The initial effort to reach the railroad bridge soon failed as both the *Governor Milton* and *Enoch Dean* ran aground; they backed off and returned to the protective cover of the *John Adams'* guns until the next flood tide. The second ascent was smoother, and the *Dean*, with Higginson aboard, was within two miles of the bridge before it ran aground and developed engine trouble. The tug *Governor Milton* was ordered to proceed alone to its destination but it came under sudden heavy fire from a six-inch shore battery. Her engineer was killed and her engines disabled; the tug was forced to float back down river. The *Dean*, with its own engine trouble, alternately towed the *Milton* and drifted downstream. The enemy fire increased and the summer sun beat down upon the crippled boats.[19]

The sound of splintering wood seemed to alternate with artillery fire as the Confederate shells smashed the *Dean*. Two men were killed instantly. Higginson saw the head of another one of his soldiers shot off. He himself felt a sudden fierce blow near his stomach which doubled him up; he staggered to a nearby chair, feeling paralyzed on one side. Surprisingly, his uniform was not ripped. He had been barely grazed by grapeshot or an exploded shell and was taken below deck. His side was soon covered by a large purple bruise.[20]

Weakened and stunned by the blow, Higginson was not comforted by the concurrent events. The *Milton*, having survived enemy fire, became impaled on some of the remaining river piles. Without his knowledge she was inexpertly set afire and hastily abandoned—not even her guns were destroyed. Higginson slept through the remainder of the doleful journey. After an absence of thirty-six hours, the two remaining ships limped into Beaufort. Nurse Jean Lander supervised the removal of the wounded and the dead to waiting ambulances.[21]

Four men had been killed, including one Wiltown Bluff Negro.

19. TWH to Saxton, July 11, 1863, Aiken to Jordan, July 12, 1863, Capt. Geo. H. Walter to Malony, July 12, 1863, in *O. R.*, *28*, 202–3, 196, 199.
20. *Yesterdays*, p. 263; TWH to Saxton July 11, 1863, in *O. R.*, *28*, 202–03; TWH to L. Higginson, July 12, 1863, Higginson MSS.
21. Gilmore to Halleck, July 21, 1863, in *O. R.*, *28*, 201–02.

One sailor lost a leg, while Higginson and one freedman suffered less severely. The expedition returned with two hundred freedmen, six bales of cotton, and two prisoners. But trains on the Charleston and Savannah Railway were unhindered because of the failure to destroy the bridge at Jacksonboro. A week later Shaw's 54th Massachusetts Regiment was cut to pieces while attacking Fort Wagner. Shaw was killed in this assault and was buried by the enemy in a mass grave with his Negro troops. The only victory for Higginson and Shaw lay in the fact that by the end of 1863 the number of Negro regiments being recruited reached sixty, and talk of "tenacious and brilliant valor displayed by troops of this race" became more prevalent.[22]

Convalescing in a Beaufort hospital, Higginson was not bothered by pain but only by a lingering stiffness and bruise. An early recovery was expected, for the blow had not caused peritonitis—a bit of good fortune he attributed to a lifelong abstinence from hard liquor. One hospital visitor, however, was shocked to see how feeble and underweight the usually vigorous Higginson had become.[23] By mid-July he decided upon a twenty-day furlough to Worcester, hoping to speed his recuperation. He left Beaufort after nine months of duty with a people he had scarcely envisioned during his days as a militant Abolitionist. Only the whip scars on the backs of some of his men seemed to relate the Negro of abolitionist oratory and the Negro of the Sea Islands. As a disunion Abolitionist he had ignored the consequences of abolishing slavery; that slavery was evil seemed sufficient then. Now he had seen Negroes showing "a dumbness that is pathetic" and forbearing "in silence." But he had seen more than that. "They are self-supporting & industrious," he observed, "& have impressed me very favorably—far more than I dared to hope. Every morning the road is full of women & old men walking . . . with great baskets of fruits and vegetables on their heads. . . . Nor did they even seem idle at noon; & the crops look well."[24]

22. TWH to Saxton, July 11, 1863, in *O. R., 28*, 202–03; Cornish, *Sable Arm*, p. 56.

23. TWH to M. Higginson, July 12, 1863, Higginson MSS; Forten journal, July 21, 1863, in Billington, *Forten*, p. 194.

24. TWH journal, June 27, July 19, 1863; TWH to L. Higginson, June 10, July 27, 1863, Higginson MSS.

As for those who were soldiers, he was equally hopeful. Higginson assured the visiting representatives of the American Freedmen's Inquiry Commission that the experience of military life would be of great value to the Negro once peace came. What Negroes wanted most was land, which he suggested should be given to them as a bounty. Much also depended upon the kind of leadership they would have after the war, since the Negroes, he believed, depended more than the white soldiers upon their officers.[25]

Arriving in Worcester July 27, Higginson, after four days home, still felt weak and extended his furlough an extra four days. By the end of the first week in August he was better, had some photographs taken in his full-dress uniform, and prepared to return South. He looked forward to seeing his men again. What greeted him upon his arrival, however, was discouraging. The temperature was 97° in his shaded tent and malaria was raging. The obvious possession of liquor forced him to have one of his officers, Captain George Dolly, court-martialed. Dolly, who had been a Maine lumberman, was admittedly a good officer, but his coarseness and swearing plus a "tendency to drink" finally exasperated Higginson. Later, after Dr. Rogers left, he had difficulty finding a surgeon who did not imbibe.[26]

Faced with disciplinary problems, Higginson also prohibited Negro women from visiting the camp except on Sundays. He found that desertions had reached alarming proportions since his men received only $10 a month pay instead of the promised $13. One unsympathetic plantation superintendent charged that desertions could be blamed on the regiment's colonel, "whose heart is . . . [so] bursting with tenderness for the negroes' former woes, that he cannot treat them like men, but like babies." [27] After hearing his "black children" singing in the evening, Higginson wrote

25. *O. R.*, *3*, 435.

26. TWH to L. Higginson, July 31, Sept. 8, 30, 1863, Feb. 7, 1864, TWH to M. Higginson, Aug. 19, 1863, Higginson MSS; TWH journal, May 17, Aug. 22, Sept. 22, 1863.

27. Arthur Sumner to Nina Hartshorn, Dec. 19, 1863, Arthur Sumner MSS, Penn Community Center, St. Helena Island, South Carolina; Harriet Ware to Elizabeth Ware Pearson, Oct. 20, 1863, in Pearson, *Port Royal*, p. 255.

in his journal: "I feel as if they were a lot of babies in their cradles cooing themselves to sleep, the dear, blundering, dusky darlings." [28]

By early October Higginson was ill, suffering from "general debility," night sweats, and diarrhea. From eight to twelve drops of sulphuric acid was prescribed to curb the sweating. Eventually malaria was diagnosed, and he was sent to convalesce on St. Helena Island at "The Oaks" plantation where the indefatigable schoolteacher Laura Towne reigned. He admiringly described her as the "homeopathic physician of the department, chief teacher, and probably the most energetic person this side of civilization." Arsenic was the remedy she recommended. It appeared to help him though he could neither walk nor ride without fatigue.[29]

His men were assigned picket duty in November at the newly named Camp Shaw on Port Royal Island, but for a time Higginson was unable to join them. More and more his thoughts turned to life after the war: "To solve the great problem of emancipation many hands & brains will be needed, & though I feel *now* no call to connect myself with it how can I tell how I might feel by & by?" [30] His soldiers also seemed to be looking ahead as they formed a building association to buy confiscated southern plantations from the government. Higginson believed they were right in wanting to be owners, not tenants. He agreed that every colored man would be a slave until he could raise his own cotton and say *"Dis is mine!"* The view held by some northern plantation supervisors, that if the Negro got land he would waste it by planting corn and live by fishing and selling eggs and chickens, Higginson judged incorrect. "They are all sharp enough," he asserted, "to see the vastly greater profits to be made on cotton." He exulted at the idea of preempting 20-acre lots at $1.25 an acre for the freedman. The Negroes' war service now seemed commonplace—what was extraordinary was the future: "One has the feeling of course that the

28. TWH journal, Sept. 5, 12, 1863
29. TWH to L. Higginson, Oct. 24, 1863, TWH to M. Higginson, Oct. 16, 24, 1863, Higginson MSS; Forten journal, Sept. 19, Oct. 18, 1863, in Billington, *Forten*, pp. 222, 223.
30. TWH to M. Higginson, Nov. 6, 1863, TWH to L. Higginson, Nov. 18, 1863, Higginson MSS.

negroes are the true owners of the soil & so long as they are here, it seems as it should be." [31]

His illness lingered. Interest in his command was only temporarily stimulated by his men doing police duty in Beaufort to "enforce the law in the scene of their old bondage." Happily, he reported seeing one of them confront a recalcitrant Beaufort citizen by pointing to his chevrons and saying "Know what dat means . . . ? Dat means Guvment." [32] But Higginson remained concerned that his men were given more fatigue duty than white soldiers.

His time was increasingly spent as a judge in the scores of court-martials occurring in the area. Since his wound and illness, Higginson's interest in fighting had receded. Being in charge of the civilian and military procession at the Beaufort celebration of the Emancipation Proclamation on January 1, 1864, provided none of the old satisfaction. Neither the grand parade of the white friends of freedom, the colored regiments, and the plantation freedmen nor the ceremony held under the wooden arches labeled Washington, Lincoln, Adams, Toussaint L'Ouverture, Shaw, and John Brown seemed to stir him. When presented with a sword and asked to speak he sounded defensive. Granting that his regiment had not fought in any of the great battles of the war, Higginson reminded his audience that he and his men had overcome "a fortress of prejudice . . . stronger than Fort Wagner"; they had *made Port Hudson and Fort Wagner possible*" by giving "colored soldiers an opportunity." [33] While he expressed appreciation for being presented with a sword, he noted that the sword of Confederate General Johnson Hagood, which he had captured at Wiltown Bluff, was the one he had been wearing. Hagood, it was believed, had given orders to bury Colonel Robert Gould Shaw "with his niggers." Wiltown Bluff, of course, was where Higginson had been wounded. "I cannot promise," he explained, "to value your pres-

31. TWH to L. Higginson, Nov. 10, 26, 1863, Higginson MSS; TWH journal, Nov. 21, 24, 1863, Jan. 20, 1864.

32. TWH to L. Higginson, Dec. 21, 1863, Higginson MSS; TWH journal, Dec. 28, 1863.

33. TWH to L. Higginson, Dec, 21, 29, 1863, Jan. 6, 1864, Higginson MSS; *First Anniversary of the Proclamation of Freedom in South Carolina, Held at Beaufort, S. C., Jan. 1, 1864* (Beaufort, 1864), pp. 4, 5, 16, 17.

ent more than this." New Year's Day, 1864, was far different from the Freedom Jubilee of the year before.

By the end of January he made explicit what had been implicit since his wound had been compounded by lingering malaria: "As to the *war* I feel that I have done my duty entirely & have no more compunctions." He was concerned, however, about the termination of government plans to give the freedmen pre-emptive rights to plantation lands and the failure to pay his black troops the same as white soldiers. "The colored people here," he noted, "are losing every vestige of faith in Government. . . . When rules vacillate, the people bleed." [34] Consenting to have his letter to the New York *Times* printed as a broadside, he observed that Negro troops had been promised $13 a month, had been paid only $10, and now even that was being reduced to $7. "Meanwhile the land sales are beginning, and there is danger of every foot of land being sold beneath my soldiers' feet." Such injustice was augmented because white soldiers received additional pay for re-enlisting and Negroes who remained civilians were able to buy land with the higher wages of plantation laborers. Higginson was proud that two thirds of his men refused to accept any pay rather than take "wicked, wanton & suicidal" reduced pay. [35]

The continued elevation of aggressive opportunists like Milton Littlefield further irritated Higginson's sense of justice. General Gillmore was no longer so attractive as he had seemed when he replaced Hunter. From Higginson's view, Gillmore cared nothing about prevailing injustices; the former engineer seemed like a "smart, driving railroad conductor, suddenly lifted into dominion, . . . perfectly indifferent to persons, white or black." [36]

When it seemed that Higginson and his men would be sent to join a large force under Brigadier General Thomas Seymour for the recapture of Jacksonville, he plainly was unenthusiastic. Florida's climate, Higginson feared, would make him an "invalid for life." With smallpox currently devastating the ranks, he had no desire to crowd into a transport for a return to Jacksonville. Nei-

34. TWH to M. Higginson, Jan. 28, 1864, TWH to L. Higginson, Dec. 21, 1863, Higginson MSS.

35. TWH to W. P. Fessenden, Feb. 13, 1864, Misc. MSS, New York Historical Society; TWH to Sydney Gay, Feb. 13, 1863, Gay MSS; *Times*, Jan. 22, 1864.

36. TWH journal, Jan. 25, 29, April 17, 1864.

ther did he relish being a subordinate to Seymour. At the last minute, a reprieve came when news reached Beaufort that Union forces had been routed at Olustee. Higginson was at a Beaufort ball when General Saxton burst in with word of the disaster and of the arrival of 240 wounded men. Saxton ordered the party terminated.[37]

Higginson and his men were returned instead to picket duty on Port Royal Island. As his chronic diarrhea and debility continued, he feared that his health would worsen when the weather became warm and that he might become permanently disabled. The imminence of relinquishing his command enabled him to view his soldiers differently: "In every way I see the gradual change in them, sometimes with a sigh as parents watch their children growing up and miss the droll speeches and the confiding ignorance of children. Sometimes it comes over me with a pang that they are growing more like white men, less naive and less grotesque." But he added: "Still I think there is enough of it to last." [38]

In the middle of one March night Higginson found that he could not sleep. Moved by an "irresistible desire" to write, he sat by candlelight and wrote until the sound of reveille. He started an introduction to a book: "I desire to record as simply as I may, the momentous military experiment, whose ultimate results were the re-organization of two races on the continent." Here was the first draft of *Army Life in a Black Regiment*, a book which would not be written for five years. But that strong desire to write for publication was the first such feeling since he had come to the South. Five days later he wrote his wife that he would support both of them from literature, and that, despite his preference for living in Massachusetts, he would accept her wish to leave Worcester and live in Newport, Rhode Island.[39]

"It gives an autumnal tinge to this beautiful opening spring to think that I shall, in a few weeks, leave it perhaps forever," he wrote in his journal on April 17, 1864. "Still my mind naturally

37. TWH to L. Higginson, Feb. 9, 1864, TWH to M. Higginson, Feb. 13, 1864, Higginson MSS; TWH journal, Feb. 18, 1864.

38. TWH to L. Higginson, Mar. 2, April 20, 1864, Higginson MSS; TWH journal, Feb. 11, 1864.

39. Notebook, Mar. 29, 1864, TWH to M. Higginson, April 4, 1864, Higginson MSS.

turns to home associations & all other beauty has a vague and alien look; I cannot bring it near to me." Ten days later he procured a medical certificate attesting to his ill health. But officially his resignation was attributed to "disability resulting from wound." He left Beaufort on May 14 and arrived in Newport by the end of the week. Before the war he had judged "good citizenship a sin and bad citizenship a duty"; now his first article to appear in the *Atlantic* said that "personal liberty in the civilian must be waived for the preservation of the nation." He labeled "capital" Edward Everett Hale's story about Phillip Nolan, *The Man Without a Country*.[40] Like the long exiled Nolan, Higginson was now ready to say: "This is my own, my native land."

40. TWH to James Rogers, April 27, 1864, Misc. MSS, American Antiquarian Society, Worcester, Mass.; Adjutant General, *Massachusetts Soldiers, Sailors, and Marines in the Civil War*, 7 (Norwood, Mass., 1933), 300; TWH, "Regular and Volunteer Officers," *Atlantic Monthly*, *14* (1864), 349; TWH to M. Higginson, Dec. 5, 1863, Higginson MSS.

17

The Reconstruction of Colonel Higginson

Hoping to relieve Mary's invalidism in a more moderate climate than Worcester's, the Higginsons settled in Newport. Great elms shaded the boardinghouse of Mrs. Hannah Dame where they lived, and eighteenth-century houses surrounded it. The couple's life was much different from that of other Newport citizens. Those with wealth built lavishly along the shore, inhabiting their large homes only during the cool and fashionable summer. During winter these structures stood mausoleum-like in their quietness. Little interchange took place between the residents of the old and new sections of town; Higginson preferred calling his section "Oldport," to differentiate it from the Newport of ostentation. But an arbored residential area provided an attractive place through which the wealthy rode in coach and four. Mrs. August Belmont, for example, could be identified in a passing carriage by the beauty of her horses and by two postillions in bright liveries, short jackets, tight breeches, and smart jockey caps.[1] Newport, though not yet referred to as the Babylon of America was still a fitting location from which the Colonel could learn about Reconstruction and about the Gilded Age.

Unlike some Union soldiers, Higginson came home without any war spoils. His most valuable trophy was the $75 silver sword which had been presented to him at the 1864 Freedom Jubilee. The inscription on the handle read: "Tiffany and Co., N.Y." [2]

In the war he had sought a religious and moral meaning—not an economic one; the glories of war, he had hoped, would drown the growing northern materialism in a purifying stream of heroism

1. TWH to L. Higginson, Apr. 20, 1864, Higginson MSS; Maude Howe Elliot, *This Was My Newport* (Cambridge, 1944), pp. 83, 133; TWH, "Letter from Newport," New York *Independent*, Aug. 30, 1866.
2. TWH to Sarah Bowditch, Mar. 6, 1864, Higginson MSS.

and Christian righteousness. The South, stained by the evil of slavery, would have to be physically beaten by a North which itself needed redemption for long having acquiesced to a sinful union with slavery. A militant crusade to free the slave and prove the capabilities of the Negro was necessary not only for the progress of mankind but also for the reassertion of a religious ideal—the humanity and unity of all men. Once in the army, however, many of Higginson's hopes had been assaulted by jealousy, prejudice, and pain. When peace came, he granted that the North had passed "through a Red Sea which no one would have dared to contemplate." But he added: "we have attained the Promised Land by the sublimest revenge which history has placed on record." [3]

In retrospect, other compensations besides revenge made the war's costly sacrifice worthwhile. As the editor of a two-volume biographical memorial to Harvard men killed in the war[4] (Higginson also wrote twelve of the ninety-five essays), he said that the war showed that college-educated American gentlemen, many of whom descended from colonial and revolutionary ancestors, were moved by conscience and patriotism. Any previous misapprehensions were now dispelled regarding "some supposed torpor or alienation prevailing among cultivated Americans." Their sacrifice proved the soundness of our collegiate education. And in epitaph to the pre-war anti-institutionalism held by many New England intellectuals, Higginson concluded: "I do not see how any one can read these memoirs without being left with fresh confidence in our institutions, in the American people, and indeed in human nature itself."

Tall, lean, and strikingly erect, with hair still black despite his war experience and forty-two years of life, Higginson shaved off his army beard (but clung to his army title) and prepared for peacetime living. Soon after coming North, he wrote Emerson of his intention to be "an artist . . . lured by the joy of expression itself." Emerson responded: "We are all deeply in debt to you, & I more than most . . . [for you] were a soldier of Character, as well as eminent abilities." [5]

3. TWH, "Fair Play the Best Policy," *Atlantic Monthly*, 15 (1865), 623.
4. TWH, *Harvard Memorial Biographies*, 1 (Cambridge, 1866), iv–v.
5. Elliot, *Newport*, p. 82; TWH to L. Higginson, May 18, 1864, Higginson

Through essays, literary criticism, fiction, and history, Higginson would endeavor to be a self-supporting writer. Much to his dissatisfaction, limited success made it financially necessary to engage in public lecturing. Seldom during his Newport days did Higginson's annual income exceed $3,000.[6]

With the war's end, Frederick Douglass well expressed the dilemma of many Abolitionists: "What should I do . . . ? Outside of the question of slavery my thought had not been much directed and I could hardly hope to make myself useful in any other cause than that to which I had given the best twenty-five years of my life." Higginson, on the other hand, after re-examining his army diary, felt that the life recorded "seems to belong to someone twin-born with me, but who led a wholly different life from me." [7] He lacked Douglass' loss of purpose for his antebellum activity had been diversified: liberal religion, woman's rights, and literature. He soon understood that the Negro question had not been finally answered by war. And once again he became a public spokesman for reform.

Higginson most frequently expressed his views about reconstruction of the South in the *Atlantic* and in the radical *Independent*. The best way to prepare freedmen for their new citizenship, he suggested, was not by the gradualism of apprenticeship but by immediate justice and freedom. The North must remove all southern obstructions to ownership of land for the Negro and grant him full social and political rights. He urged making permanent Sherman's Special Field Order Number 15, which had given freedmen temporary possession of land in the Sea Island region. Then the freedmen "can dispense even with our love." If such fair play was practiced, soon the northern Negro would receive better treatment too. For segregation in Philadelphia streetcars, in New York schools, and in Boston theaters "must inevitably pass away with the institution which they merely reflect." Even now, he observed, neither conviction nor prejudice caused northern dis-

---

MSS; TWH to Emerson, July 6, 1864, Emerson to TWH, July 18, 1864, Higginson-Huntington MSS.

6. TWH to Anna and S. Louisa Higginson, Sept. 22, 1866, Higginson-Huntington MSS diary, Dec. 11, 1868.

7. Frederick Douglass, *Life and Times of Frederick Douglass* (Hartford, 1881), p. 454; TWH to S. L. Higginson, Dec. 30, 1864, Higginson MSS.

crimination; rather it existed because of "an impression in each citizen's mind that there is some other citizen who is not prepared for the change." Objections to ending segregation were "merely traditional." [8]

Higginson, however, was not waiting for southern racial justice before pressing for equal treatment of the northern Negro. Appointed to Newport's School Board in 1865 he was soon fighting the city's policy of school segregation. The issue was opened by a Newport Negro who wished to transfer his son from one of the two black schools to a white school. Despite public protest, Higginson persuaded the School Board to vote for desegregation. Subsequently, the Rhode Island legislature desegregated all the state public schools. Newport's Negro schools were closed by 1867 from lack of enrollment. But Higginson was defeated for re-election to the School Board,[9] and his greatest attention remained focused on the South.

He was especially critical of former antislavery allies who opposed Negro enfranchisement. When Parker Pillsbury equated Negro enfranchisement and radical reconstruction with "gingerbread and Whiskey" and argued that Negro illiteracy should block the right to vote, Higginson demurred. He suggested that Pillsbury "abandon soap and sanctity" and instead understand that Reconstruction could succeed only "with the ballots of the unwashed." Higginson was no less critical of Garrison's opposition to immediate Negro enfranchisement: he canceled his *Liberator* subscription in January 1865. "I do not feel bound to sustain it as a matter of duty while in its present attitude," he informed its editor.[10]

From 1864 through 1866 Higginson moved away from Garrison's primary concern for educating the freedmen before enfranchisement and toward Phillips' desire to give them the vote and land. He stood with Phillips when Garrison sought to dissolve the American Anti-Slavery Society in January 1865; and Higginson again supported him when an open clash occurred in May 1865. Garrison, failing to carry a vote for dissolving the Society, felt

8. "Fair Play the Best Policy," pp. 624–26, 630.

9. Irving Bartlett, *From Slave to Citizen* (Providence, 1954), pp. 53, 54, 56; M. T. Higginson, *Higginson*, pp. 253–54; Thomas, *Liberator*, p. 443.

10. TWH, "Freedom *vs.* Pillsbury," New York *Tribune*, Nov. 24, 1864; TWH to Garrison, Jan. 2, 1865, Antislavery Letters, Boston Public Library.

compelled to resign as its president. Higginson then joined Phillips and the *Anti-Slavery Standard* to battle for radical Reconstruction.[11]

Realism, not idealism, was Higginson's major argument for immediate Negro enfranchisement:

> It might be very pleasant to have . . . [Southern States] consist entirely of college graduates, or of gentlemen in white kid-gloves or of albinos with pink eyes. But as all these classes seem likely to be small in those regions, for some years to come, it will be necessary to go beyond those precious and privileged classes and take the best we can get.[12]

He questioned the moral squeamishness of those skeptical of the freedman's fitness to vote. Since it had been long certain that the Irish vote was Democratic, why "should there be Republicans who shrink from enfranchising negroes, though equally sure that every negro will be a Republican vote?" And even allowing that "an ignorant class, newly enfranchised, will be led by demagogues, here is a case where the demagogues will be on the right side. If the demagogues manage the colored, it will be the business of the loyal North to manage the demagogues, which can be easily done." Besides, said the Colonel, "this vote will not . . . be controlled by demagogues, except in a minor degree. Ignorant men are governed by instinct, like children, and know their friends. And when in the present case, their friends are the nation's friends and their enemies are the nation's enemies, this is quite enough for them to begin with." [13]

Higginson warned that every unrepentant rebel knew that his political future depended upon the North's "lingering colorphobia" which prevented the enfranchisement of the freedman. For with southern congressional representation no longer limited by the three-fifths clause, the political results of the Civil War would be

11. McPherson, *Equality*, pp. 296–99; TWH to Garrison, Jan. 2, 1865, Anti-slavery Letters, Boston Public Library. An explanation of Garrison's position is Louis Ruchames' "William Lloyd Garrison and the Negro Franchise," *Journal of Negro History*, 50 (1965), 37–49.

12. TWH, "Use the Materials," Boston Weekly *Commonwealth*, June 24, 1865.

13. TWH, "Damning with Faint Praise," *Commonwealth*, June 24, 1865.

a "consolidated body of rebels in Congress, equally malignant, and eleven votes stronger." The Lord's retribution would be great, he predicted—and the Democrats' perhaps even greater, he implied—"if our sense of color now proves more valid than our sense of right." To pursue Reconstruction without the Negro as an active participant would be to "play anew the tragedy of Hamlet with Hamlet's part omitted." [14] Subsequent developments are an ironic reminder that Higginson had not really fathomed the betrayal of the Danish prince.

Although never much concerned with monetary issues, Higginson predicted what it would mean to admit an unrepentant and unchecked South back into the Union. If such a "sudden fanaticism of magnanimity took possession of our people . . . it would . . . [lead] to the repudiation of the public debt, and the reenslavement or pauperization of the blacks." Another Civil War was also possible if the South was not tightly controlled against counterrevolution.[15] Repudiating the public debt was sufficiently horrible for many of his readers to contemplate without the added worry about the Negro's fate.

To anyone charging that this former clergyman had forgotten the Golden Rule, Higginson denied vindictiveness. The issue was southern treason, not northern revenge: "We will yet, by proper military and civil processes, utterly exterminate from our whole country, whether North or South, every vestige of treason, all who sympathize with it, whatever their station and wherever they are." General Robert E. Lee must be held responsible for the barbaric treatment of Union prisoners in Confederate jails, while much effort was exerted to catch the assassin of one man—the President —we "have only compliments and courtesies for the assassin of thousands." [16]

The best way to exterminate treason was to employ colored

14. Ibid.; "Use the Materials." In an introduction to his translation Higginson wrote that Epictetus well expressed the "inevitable laws of retribution," *The Works of Epictetus—A Translation from the Greek based on that of Elizabeth Carter* (Boston, 1865), p. ix.

15. TWH, "The Popular Reaction," *Commonwealth*, April 29, 1865.

16. Ibid.; TWH, review of *Narrative of Practices and Sufferings of U.S. and Soldiers While Prisoners of War in the Hands of the Rebel Authorities*, by Commission of Inquiry of U.S. Sanitary Commission, *Atlantic Monthly*, 14 (1864), 777–78.

troops in a southern occupation force, argued Higginson. While northern moderates and conservatives advocated the conciliation of the South, he wrote:

> It may be said you cannot expect at once to convert the white Southerners to loyal ideas. It is a matter of considerable indifference to us whether they are immediately converted or not. We do not expect to let all the burglars to remain at large till they have experienced religion. If they still think burglariously that is their own affair for the present; but they must take care how they put their thoughts in actions.[17]

The South's defiant willingness to elect rebels to postwar offices reminded Higginson of the ignorant chamberlain at the court of Frederick II who forgot whether he was the besieged or the besieger, or whether it was himself or his brother who had been killed. The South remembered the Civil War, he conceded, but it seemed hopelessly confused about who had won. And while he had once been certain that "the last great struggle of the land is over" and that "there can be no other war, worth naming, in store for us," Higginson now advocated military training for schoolboys with no exemptions except for physical disability.[18] A distinct possibility existed, he warned, of the freedmen independently taking up arms against the unrepentant new southern governments. A strong Union garrison was necessary in the South "till all parties have learned their duties." At the same time Higginson was sounding general quarters, he confided privately that he had refused a position as agent for the New England Freedman's Aid Society because "I do not want to give any more years of my life exclusively to those [black] people now, as much as I am attached to them."[19]

Higginson had never been eulogistic about President Lincoln; at one time he had been skeptical about the real worth of the Emancipation Proclamation. His estimation of Lincoln had been

17. TWH, "Southern Doughfaces," *Commonwealth*, Aug. 19, 1865.
18. "The Logic of Must," *Independent*, Sept. 7, 1865; TWH, "New Year's Glimpses, *Commonwealth*, Jan. 7, 1865; TWH, "Our Future Militia System," *Atlantic Monthly*, *16* (1865), 372, 377.
19. TWH, "Safety Matches," *Independent*, Sept. 21, 1865; TWH to A. and S. L. Higginson, Oct. 8, 1865, Higginson MSS.

higher than Wendell Phillips' but he had not been moved to eulogy even after the assassination. The President's death, he predicted, would unite the country behind radical Reconstruction. Like other radical Republicans, he welcomed President Johnson, who near the war's end had made some strong statements about the treatment of rebels. Higginson thus pictured the new President as the best guarantee against a "mush of concession." He also cautioned that only "so long as he holds firm, the people will stand by him." [20] Although he attacked Johnson's southern amnesty program by June 1865, he had not yet attacked the President.

In a speech at Lancaster, Pennsylvania, in early September 1865, Senator Thaddeus Stevens, who understood the danger of Johnson's reconstruction policy to the freedmen and to continued Republican rule, presented a dramatic proposal. Why not, asked Stevens, confiscate the land of 70,000 of the largest former slaveholders and put it to humanitarian uses? Forty acres for every freedman, increased pensions for Union soldiers and the families of the slain, and the reimbursement of northern and southern loyalists whose property had been damaged, destroyed, or seized, would still leave more than thirty billion dollars for paying the national debt. [21] Stevens was doing more than seeking support from men who understood the economic possibilities of Reconstruction, but the unfriendly reception his speech received temporarily dampened his hopes. Greeley's shrill protest to "any warfare against Southern property" epitomized the reaction. After getting no results, Stevens was rightly discouraged about radical prospects for the coming 39th Congress. "I fear we are ruined," he wrote Sumner on October 5. Three weeks later he was even more discouraged and concluded that "the [presidential] patronage is hard to fight against." [22]

On the next day Higginson published in the *Independent* his first direct attack on the man with this patronage power. The observations of Carl Schurz, recently returned from a three-month southern tour, seem to have been his source. Like Stevens, Higginson was moved by the plight of the freedmen. Objecting to

20. TWH, "The Popular Reaction," *Commonwealth*, April 29, 1865; "Using the Materials."

21. Ralph Korngold, *Thaddeus Stevens* (New York, 1955), p. 282.

22. Ibid., pp. 283, 291.

the restoration of land "to the former lords of Southern soil, . . .
ground that the black loyalist cultivated"; to the disarming of
"black loyalists" while "white rebels are armed again under the
name of 'militia' "; to the "re-establishment of slavery under the
name of 'apprenticeship' "; to the revival of "the old assumption
that 'the people' of the South means the white population, rebel
or otherwise and that the black loyalists are something less than
'the people,' " Higginson exclaimed: "All this we of the North
have done and are doing, by and through our national executive,
Andrew Johnson." [23]

Higginson then turned from listing abuses, and succinctly
stated:

> What most men mean to-day by the 'president's plan of re-
> construction' is the pardon of every rebel for the crime of
> rebellion, and the utter refusal to pardon a single black
> loyalist for the crime of being black. . . . The truth is that
> we are causing quite as much suffering as a conqueror usually
> does. It is simply that we are forgiving our enemies and tortur-
> ing only our friends.[24]

Before passage of the Mississippi Black Codes and the conven-
ing of the crucial 39th Congress, Higginson was solidly on the
side of the radical Republicans. The legislature, not the executive,
should be dominant. Sumner, who charged that Johnson "whitewashed rebels," should be looked to for leadership.[25] But it was
Stevens, aided by Johnson's blundering and the South's recalci-
trance, who turned the tide for radical congressional power with
the formation of his Joint Committee on Reconstruction.

As the radicals in Congress exercised their power against the
President, Higginson accelerated his attack. It was a proslavery
policy that the President wanted, he charged. And a dramatic
proof of this, the kind that appealed to even those northerners
skeptical about the radical program, was that the "anti-negro
General" John Brannan remained in command in Georgia while
the pro-Negro General Rufus Saxton had been mustered out.

23. TWH, "Too Many Compliments," *Independent*, Oct. 26, 1865.
24. Ibid.
25. TWH to Charles Sumner, Feb. 18, 1866, Sumner MSS.

Brannan had agreed that Augusta schoolchildren should be prevented from placing flowers on the graves of men who had been loyal to the Union. Higginson's article, "The South Victorious in Georgia," argued that "there will neither be conscience in our army, nor loyalty in the South, nor redemption for the nation" until such attitudes were altered.[26]

As the crucial 1866 Congressional campaign drew near and the Fourteenth Amendment was submitted to the states for ratification, Higginson emphasized the personal attack on Andrew Johnson. He was reminded of the drunkard sitting all night on the sidewalk watching houses reel about him and waiting for his own front door to come around. "Far be it for me to draw an analogy between the ways of the President and those of a man given to drink. But he himself has stated . . . that he is engaged in observing a general 'swing around' of Northern and Southern radicalism; and the inference is obvious that he is waiting for the reappearance of his front door—the entrance namely, of the White House . . . in 1868." Worried about the defection of Republicans from radical ranks, Higginson claimed that it was the "abstract reverence of a President, . . . without examining who the man is," that was causing this danger.[27]

In "Two Kings Dethroned," Higginson sevely attacked the defection of Horace Greeley: he paralleled the fall of "King Cotton" with the decline of this "other imaginary monarch," the conservative editor masquerading as a radical. His "whipped spanielism" in advocating the release of Jefferson Davis from a federal jail hardly improved his credentials. Higginson was also critical of conservative Republicans like Samuel Bowles, editor of the Springfield *Republican* and friend of Emily Dickinson and her family.[28]

Of course Andrew Johnson remained his favorite target. "What has made the nation despise its President is not a political but a moral difference; not merely that he misuses his office, but

26. Rufus Saxton to TWH, Dec. 28, 1866, Higginson MSS; TWH, "The South Victorious in Georgia," *Independent*, May 24, 1866.

27. TWH, "Swing Round," *Independent*, June 21, 1866.

28. *Commonwealth*, April 8, 1865; TWH review of Samuel Bowles' *Across the Continent: A Summer Journey to the Rocky Mountains, and the Pacific States with Speaker Colfax* (Boston, 1866), in *Atlantic Monthly*, 17 (1866), 524–25.

that he degrades it." Higginson asked Sumner: "Will people ever learn that it is only a man of principle who can be a prophet?" Sumner did not reply, but one Massachusetts congressman who prophesied the impeachment of Johnson was later censured for his part in the Credit Mobilier scandal.[29] Higginson was not yet able to discern the shadow of corruption that threatened the bright hopes of Reconstruction.

Higginson joined Wendell Phillips on the American Anti-Slavery platform in support of radical Reconstruction. In May 1867 he told a New York audience that "the nation must recognize that even political power does not confer safety when it is conferred upon a race of landless men." But he refrained from explicitly criticizing the Republican party for not following Stevens' plan to have Congress grant land to the freedmen. And six months later the test of Higginson's party loyalty came with word of the likely nomination of General Ulysses S. Grant. Attending the meeting of the New England Anti-Slavery Society, Higginson heard a resolution declaring that there was "no evidence that General Grant sympathizes with the radical statesmen of the party," and that only "unreasoning and mad idolatry" would give him the presidency.[30]

Wendell Phillips, the major figure in the Society, was even more certain about Grant's views. "General Grant," said he, "was a reticent, taciturn, conservative man. No drop of his blood or fibre of his constitution was Radical." An important neophyte in the organization, Ira Steward, carried this criticism further. Steward, the leader of the recently organized National Labor Union, assailed the Republican party for favoring business interests; he argued for fostering the mutual interests of both black and white labor. Higginson, of course, preferred Sumner to Grant as the Republican nominee, but like Garrison he remained with the party.[31] When Grant's nomination became official, Phillips and Higginson once again clashed.

Phillips argued that General Grant did "not mean to waste one

29. TWH, "Lions and Tiger," *Independent*, July 4, 1867; TWH to C. Sumner, Sept. 6, 1867, Higginson MSS; Oakes Ames to Edward L. Pierce, Mar. 7, 1867, Pierce MSS.

30. *Anti-Slavery Standard*, May 18, 1867, Feb. 1, 1868.

31. Ibid.; TWH diary, Oct. 27, Nov. 1, 1868; McPherson, *Equality*, p. 423.

atom of unnecessary virtue" to secure his election. Higginson, on the other hand, while admitting that Grant might not fully comprehend the problems, was sure that he would suffice. "God will get his work done through him," predicted Higginson. Furthermore, a leader too radical would be out of joint with the times. "We can make no sudden changes in the constitution of men either at the North or South. I do not look to see in this generation, a race of Southern white men who shall do justice to the negro." No longer did Higginson argue that radical Reconstruction could end racism. Having here abandoned immediatism, he suggested that the quality of southern political leaders must be recognized and utilized. The post-war North had become too self-righteous— especially in criticizing southern treatment of the freedmen while often refusing civil rights to northern Negroes. Northern men were "willing that the negro should be a man at the South, to spite the white man, but not willing that he should be a man at the North, when it offends their prejudices." But he expressed faith that "the more enduring Northern mind" would eventually bring the end to prejudice.[32]

Higginson accepted Grant's nomination (ultimately Phillips did too) and a Republican platform which equivocated about Negro suffrage in the South and stated that in the North, where Negro suffrage had been rejected by eight states after the war, this question properly belonged to the people of these states. The party failed to advocate national Negro suffrage.[33] Subsequently, the General became President. The cooling of Higginson's radical ardor did not begin, however, with Grant's nomination. His ebbing involvement in radical politics, like all his changes of direction, had a more personal source. It first became evident in an *Atlantic* article of January 1867, simultaneous with his advocacy of Reconstruction. While he had continued during the year to speak and write for radical Reconstruction, the extent of his commitment was declining. Having supported a variety of reforms, having written

32. *Anti-Slavery Standard*, May 30, 1868. See McPherson, *Equality*, p. 420, which interprets Higginson's position differently by neglecting the reference to "no sudden changes in the constitution of men . . . ."

33. TWH, "The American Lecture System," 21 (1868), 56; C. Vann Woodward, "Equality, America's Deferred Commitment," *The American Scholar*, 27 (1958), 469.

poetry and literary criticism, and having been a clergyman and militant Abolitionist, Higginson now asked: "Why should we insist . . . on playing all the parts? The proper path of the statesman and the artist may often touch, but will rarely coincide." Amidst the sluggish efforts to ratify the Fourteenth Amendment in the North and the outright opposition to it in the South, he said: "There are a thousand rough-hewn brains which can well perform the plain work which American statesmanship now demands without calling the artist to cut blocks with his razor." An artist needed privacy, not glaring publicity, to be productive. And before Congress passed the first Reconstruction Act, he defended a self-imposed silencing of his radical voice: it was necessary to bind oneself "to the mast like Farragut, to resist dazzling temptations of paths alien." [34]

This pronouncement was soon followed by the dispatch of his first story to the *Atlantic*'s editor with a request for an opinion of it; if encouraged he would seek to write fiction. The story appeared in the April 1867 issue. Although hampered by a *deus ex machina*, "The Haunted Window" was a promising effort which evidenced the author's skill in maintaining suspense. The main character had a fertile and uncontrolled imagination which leads to his premature death. The fact that Emilia was the name given to the shadowy and mysterious heroine at a time when Higginson was corresponding with Emily Dickinson, appears to confirm his simultaneous attraction and repulsion for the Amherst poet. This "imaginative sketch" that made imagination a fatal flaw, did not stop further fictional efforts. Solaced somewhat by his very few gray hairs, he nevertheless confided to his diary that he sometimes felt that he had accomplished very little.[35] Higginson was soon fully launched upon his first novel.

He again affirmed his literary interest, by the end of 1867, in publicly lamenting the lack of "great tonics." Now that "we seem nearly at the end of those great public wrongs which require a special oral earthquake to end them . . . there seems nothing left which need be absolutely fought for; no great influence to keep us

34. TWH, "A Plea for Culture," *Atlantic Monthly*, *19* (1867), 34.

35. TWH to James T. Fields, Jan. 10, 1867, Higginson MSS; TWH, "The Haunted Window," *Atlantic Monthly*, *19* (1867), 429–37; TWH diary, Dec. 22, 1867.

from a commonplace and perhaps debasing success. . . . One must feel an impulse of pity for our successors, who seem likely to have no convictions that they can honestly be mobbed for." [36]

The way to fill this chasm was not by standing firmly for radical Reconstruction but rather by increased interest in the creation of American literature. To him, the issues of the Civil War and Reconstruction seemed resolved; writers who had left seclusion to fight by pen and sword for the Negro's emancipation and rights must now return to more purely literary pursuits.[37] Yet it was never fully possible for Higginson to "bind himself to the mast" since habits of gregariousness, humanitarianism, and the need for immediate response were always pressing him to break the bonds. He would never achieve an isolation from people nor feel entirely immune from the irritation of social ills. Croquet with Newport ladies and speeches from the public platform remained part of his life.

Both the newly organized Radical Club and the Free Religious Association attracted Higginson's interest in the spring of 1867. The Radical Club, primarily concerned with religious and aesthetic subjects, was composed of laymen and clergymen. The meetings were viewed by many as a latter-day transcendental circle. Emerson, Alcott, and Hedge represented the original Transcendentalists; Higginson, John Weiss, and Cyrus Bartol were the second-generation Transcendentalists. Whittier, Henry James, Sr., David A. Wells, Frank Sanborn, John Fiske, O. W. Holmes, Sr., and Benjamin Peirce added to an impressive list of participating members. The Reverend John T. Sargent, a former associate of Theodore Parker, provided a link, as did Higginson, Wasson, and Weiss, with an ecumenically conceived religion that Parker and his followers had desired. Mrs. Sargent served as the hostess at these gatherings in her home where papers were read and discussion encouraged. "The Immanence of God," "Religion and Art," "Pantheism," "Indian Ethics," and "The Impossible in Mathematics" were among the papers delivered. Occasionally poems were written for "Poetical Picnics." An invited guest on one occasion was Wendell Phillips,

36. TWH, "Literature as an Art," *Atlantic Monthly,* 20 (1867), 745. See TWH, "Americanism in Literature," *Atlantic Monthly,* 25 (1870), 56–63.
37. "Literature as an Art," p. 745.

who spoke of the "limitations of human nature" and argued that "democracy is not a good government, but it is the best we can get while we have only this poor, rotten human nature to work with." [38] Such talk was out of harmony with the optimism of most Radical Club members—as was Phillips' radicalism.

Two other men who attended the meetings were Francis A. Abbot and William J. Potter, major figures in forming the Free Religious Association. The F.R.A., whose organization a recent historian has called "one of the most significant events in the history of American democratic thought," [39] publicly convened in Boston on May 30, 1867. It shared many members with the Radical Club. The F.R.A., however, had public meetings and stressed religious humanism rather than a devotion to the diverse intellectual discussions of the Radical Club. Active in both organizations, Higginson, after the first F.R.A. gathering noted: "Very noble meeting. I did not believe I could ever care so much for a convention again." Here was an organization that joined Protestants, Catholics, and Jews and sought to include other religions.[40] Back in 1848, when still a young Unitarian clergyman at Newburyport, Higginson had hoped for this sort of pluralistic religious organization.

Much of Higginson's interest in abolitionism had derived from the view that the best way to make religion meaningful, and check sectarianism and anarchic individualism, was by uniting people of all beliefs in a humanitarian cause. The antislavery movement was meant to provide the cause; the Civil War was supposed to be the crusade. But when the war was over, Higginson could only say, "Perhaps the great currents of American life are outgrowing the power of one sect or any dozen." [41] With the F.R.A., a great hope was revived: again and again he spoke from its platform along with

38. TWH, "The Boston Radical Club," *Independent*, Nov. 5, 1874; *Tribune*, Oct. 30, 1871, Oct. 7, 1874; Mary E. Sargent, *Sketches and Reminiscences of the Radical Club* (Boston, 1880), pp. ix, xi, xii; Bartlett, *Phillips*, p. 369.

39. Ralph H. Gabriel, *The Course of American Democratic Thought* (New York, 1940), p. 173.

40. *Anti-Slavery Standard*, Feb. 1869; Stow Persons, *Free Religion* (New Haven, 1947), *passim*; Clarence Gohdes, *The Periodicals of American Transcendentalism* (Durham, 1931), pp. 231, 239; TWH diary, May 31, 1867, Feb. 12, 1879; *Proceedings of Free Religious Association 1868–1877* (Boston, 1868–77); TWH, "A Glance at Mohammedism," in *Proceedings . . . 1870*, pp. 90–94.

41. TWH, "Heresy Crystallizing," *Commonwealth*, April 15, 1865.

his religious allies of former days. Many of these men had been Unitarian clergymen who had revered Theodore Parker and sympathised with his Free Church movement. Participating ministers were William Henry Furness, John Weiss, and William Henry Channing; and the Hutchinson Family singers performed between speeches just as they had done at antislavery conventions.[42]

On the other hand, the social zeal of the past was missing. Interest in the religion of humanity was substituted for the airing of concrete social issues. On one occasion, Higginson helped carry a motion to table a discussion of such issues.[43] For him the religious pilgrimage had ended. The rout had been a circular one. Religious commitment had first helped him move to militant social action; now it helped him move away from such action.

At work during the early months of 1868 on his novel, Higginson noted, "this Romance is in me like the statue in the marble. . . . I have rather held back from it, but a power within steadily forces me on, the characters are forming themselves more and more . . . and it is so attractive to me that were it to be my ruin in fame and fortune I should still wish to keep on." As the manuscript took shape he revealed: "For the first time, perhaps, I have something to write which so interests me it is very hard to leave it even for necessary exercise." Recalling the past he observed: "I do not think that anything except putting on a uniform and going into camp has ever given me such a strange fascinating life, as the thought that I can actually construct a novel. It is as if I had learned to fly." Soon he even lost sight of the memory of his war experiences and in order not to interrupt the writing of his novel, postponed making a book from his military days despite its relevancy for buttressing radical Reconstruction.[44]

42. Ellen Garrison to Lucy M. Garrison, Dec. 2, 1870, Garrison Family MSS; *Proceedings . . . 1868*, p. 89

43. *Proceedings . . . 1878*, p. 14; *Proceedings . . . 1873*, p. 12.

44. TWH diary, Jan. 1, Mar. 14, 20, April 5, 1868, Sept. 25, 1868, Sept. 22, 1869.

18

"With Malice Toward None"

A notice that Higginson's first novel, *Malbone: An Olport Romance*, would appear serially in the *Atlantic* during the first six months of 1869 promised that it would differ from most American fiction by featuring cultivated people and resembling "the often praised but little read novels of Jane Austen." [1] Having indeed purchased a set of Miss Austen's novels in 1866, Higginson would seek to use the drawing room and witty conversation to set the tone of his book. The time was before the Civil War, before "the great storm of the great Rebellion broke over the land [and] its vast calamity absorbed all minor griefs." The main scene was Newport's old Hunter mansion, with its secret staircase and pilasters topped with delicate Corinthian capitals and cherub heads. The town's seventeenth-century Jewish cemetery—with barely visible Hebrew, Spanish, Portuguese, Latin, and English gravestone inscriptions—served as the site for one of the most melodramatic scenes in an exceedingly melodramatic book.[2]

The leading character, handsome Philip Malbone, was a very active man with a "perfectly sunny temperament," who was "never too busy to be interrupted, especially if the intruder were a woman or a child. . . . Almost all women loved him, because he loved all; he never had to assume an ardor, for he always felt it. His heart was multivalved; he could love a dozen at once in various modes and gradations, press a dozen hands in a day. . . . Humanity is the highest thing to investigate, he said, and the proper study of mankind is woman." Malbone also liked to watch black children strumming on the banjo, and he liked to note the ways

1. Springfield Republican, Dec. 9, 1868, quoted in Jay A. Leyda, *The Years and Hours of Emily Dickinson*, 2 (New Haven, 1960), 134.
2. TWH to A. and S. L. Higginson, Jan. 19, 1866, Higginson MSS; *Atlantic Monthly, 23* (1869), 661.

of well-dressed girls and boys at croquet parties, or to sit at the club window and hear the gossip." [3]

Part of Philip Malbone, of course, resembled the author, another part was drawn from his friend of the forties and fifties, William Hurlbut (Higginson later said Hurlbut had been the model). He remembered Hurlbut as "so handsome in his dark beauty that he seemed like a picturesque oriental." In Theodore Winthrop's *Cecil Dreeme*, Hurlbut had been portrayed as a mysterious young painter who was really a girl, and Higginson had said he was like some fascinating girl. The disloyalty with which he had returned Higginson's affections was reflected in the novel by Malbone's evolving into an unfaithful lover of the faithful and pure Hope. Malbone, like Hurlbut, is ultimately exiled.[4]

Malbone's villainess, variously described as a passionate, reckless, beautiful, inexperienced, and ignorant girl, was, as in his first short story, called Emilia. Conceptions of Emily Dickinson and Margaret Fuller appear to have been Higginson's sources. Subject to motionless trances, Emilia ultimately drowns during an abortive effort to reach her Swiss lover, Antoine, in a storm-tossed sea. But not before she destroys her half-sister Hope's true love for Philip Malbone.

Most of the men in the book are insensitive; the women possess insight and imagination. The heroine Hope is a "Saxon type. . . . Her girlhood had in it a certain dignity as of a virgin priestess or sibyl. Yet her hearty sympathies and her healthy energy made her at home in a daily life, in a democratic society." She seems closest to Higginson's unmarried sister Susan Louisa.[5] The strongest character is Aunt Jane, who solves problems and issues aphoristic wisdom. Confined to a rocking chair because of "ailments," she "has chosen to remain unmarried." Very close in age and character to Higginson's wife, she possesses a "severity tempered by wit." Aunt Jane sounds the book's theme by criticizing "that Rousseau-like temperament." In what must be construed as Higginson's re-

3. *Atlantic Monthly*, 23 (1869), 140.

4. *Yesterdays*, p. 107; M. T. Higginson, *Higginson*, p. 125; Van Wyck Brooks, *The Times of Melville and Whitman* (New York, 1947), p. 177.

5. *Atlantic Monthly*, 23 (1869), 8, 9; Higginson hoped his sisters would not be "dismayed" to find themselves in his novel: TWH to A. and S. L. Higginson, Sept. 3, 1868, Higginson MSS.

pudiation of his past faith in the primacy of feelings, she lectures:
"It is the high-strung sentimentalists who do all the mischief; who
play on their own lovely emotions, forsooth till they wear out their
fine fiddlestrings, then have nothing left but the flesh and the D."
The author later notes that "no human being when met face to
face with Aunt Jane, had ever failed to yield up to her the whole
truth she sought." [6]

Some of Higginson's views about writers, politicians, and businessmen are also presented in *Malbone*. Philip Malbone is made to
appear inaccurate and cynical when he mocks American writers
or says that nobody succeeds in politics without bribing the men
he despises. Higginson's position, on the other hand, appears in a
description of John Lambert, a self-made businessman who once
had peddled gingerbread on a railroad train. In politics, Lambert
"had no concept of honesty, for he could see no difference between a politician and any other merchandise. He always succeeded in business, for he thoroughly understood its principles;
in politics he always failed in the end, for he recognized no principles at all." [7] Virtue, Higginson believed, brings political success,
not business success. Thus politics, despite gross private economic
corruption, provides an institutional foundation for honesty.

Since the novel ended with Hope losing the Malbone she loved,
as well as her half-sister Emilia, Higginson resorted to an epilogue:
"Were this life all, its very happiness were sadness. If, as I doubt
not, there can be another sphere, then that which is unfulfilled in
this must find completion. . . . And though a thousand oracles
should pronounce this thought an idle dream, neither Hope nor
I would believe them." [8] The critics' harsh reception of the novel
made it certain that only in heaven, not in a sequel, could Hope
find happiness.

Malbone, said the *Nation*'s reviewer, "is very thin; there is an
occasional witticism that is rather small." One critic noted that
the book might have been "delightful if the speeches had not the
air of having been studied overnight for the effect." Another
wondered about the masculinity of Philip Malbone. An English

6. *Atlantic Monthly, 23* (1869), 139, 652.
7. Ibid., 397–98.
8. Ibid., 661.

critic suggested: "If this book had been published anonymously, we should have said that it was written by an American lady who had carefully studied George Sand and Nathaniel Hawthorne." [9] The *Anti-Slavery Standard* and the Newport *Journal* provided the most sympathetic comments. The *Standard* praised Higginson for having his characters lucidly preach morality; the *Journal* attested to the accurate description of Newport sites.[10]

The excessively studied quality of Higginson's literary efforts was a basic and consistent criticism. Even his friend David Wasson criticized his language as "a little fastidious, a little inclined to purism." And when some of his recent *Atlantic* essays were collected and reprinted, another critic commented that Higginson's style revealed that "He does not yet see that culture is only a means to an end, . . . that when it attracts attention to itself [it] is a solecism, like fine manners or overdressing." [11] More abrasive was the comment that "there is an air of drawing-room elegance about Mr. Higginson, a suggestion of rustling brocades and rich laces and ribbons, . . . something which suggests the dancing master and the dress maker, . . . but masculine directness, resolution, and vigor are noticeably absent. As an ambassador to a nation of females, Mr. Higginson would be admirable." The *Golden Age*, a periodical edited by the staunch New York radical Theodore Tilton, criticized Higginson's fastidious culture and suggested that he was "too much of a moralist to lose himself in literature . . . and too much of a literateur to throw himself into reform. . . . Higginson never quite loses himself in anything, never touches the high mark of his power. . . . If he would only lift Harvard College out of his experience." [12]

Appearing to understand his major literary shortcomings well before his critics spoke, Higginson confided to his diary: "I have fineness . . . but some want of copiousness & fertility which may

9. Malbone Scrapbook, *Liberal Christian* [n. d.], New York *Citizen*, July 10, 1869, *Examiner and London Review*, Oct. 9, 1869, Higginson MSS.

10. *Anti-Slavery Standard* [n. d.], Newport *Journal*, July 24, 1869, Higginson MSS.

11. David Wasson, review of *The Works of Epictetus*, translated by TWH, *Atlantic Monthly*, *16* (1865), 761; *British Quarterly Review*, January 1873.

12. Chicago Evening *Journal*, Mar. 9, 1872; *Golden Age*, Sept. 1871, Higginson MSS.

give a tinge of thinness to what I write, fine as the texture is. . . .
I wish I could write with . . . exuberant & hearty zeal." But he
had to add—"without sacrificing polish." When he later advised
young Woodrow Wilson to avoid politics because he had a literary touch,[13] much of his own life and writings served as the
basis for this advice.

Having been one of the Transcendentalists who revolted against
Unitarian rationalism, Higginson had come to conceive of the
emotions as dangerous weapons requiring careful control by reason
and will. In antebellum days he had overcome a feeling to try
to produce literature and had stifled his desire to have children.
As a militant Abolitionist he had sought ways for self-expression to
alleviate the desire to "scream in the open air" and "burst the
door." Turning to fiction only after his mother, who had opposed
it, died in 1864, Higginson could not overcome certain inhibitions.
The vigor of his antislavery speeches and Reconstruction articles
were in marked contrast to the fastidious style of his more literary
efforts.

Helen Hunt Jackson, also a literary boarder at Hannah Dame's
Newport home, vividly described the domestic difficulties under
which Higginson labored:

> On the whole I think him an astonishing success under diffi-
> culties! What would become of *you*, for instance, or me, to
> sleep where he sleeps—embrace what he embraces!—I think
> however there *was* an original touch of the truest flavor of
> manhood about him. [But now] he steps too softly—knocks
> like a baby at the door, & then opens it only a quarter of the
> way & comes in edgewise![14]

Higginson, who admitted that he wrote *Malbone* under great
disadvantages, characterized himself as a man "whose home is a
hospital & who sees the only object of his care in tears of suffering
daily." [15] Because of severe digital paralysis Mary was now forced

---

13. TWH diary, Feb. 20, 1869; TWH to Woodrow Wilson, Sept. 14, 1891,
in Katherine Brand, "Woodrow Wilson in His Own Time," *Library of Congress Quarterly Journal of Current Acquisitions*, 13 (1956), 63.
14. March 7, 1866, Leyda, *Dickinson*, 2, 111–12. I have italicized "was".
15. TWH diary, Dec 23, 1866.

to use a wand to turn pages of a book and required that her husband frequently remain at her side. Higginson, burdened by Mary's nervousness and ill-temper, confided to his diary: "I do not think any vitality & elasticity less than mine could have withstood this steady drain of so many years." He vowed to have one window of their bedroom opened slightly at night to relieve his own feelings of being suffocated. But not until three weeks later did he have the courage to discuss the matter with his wife. "Began after a talk, to open window morning & afternoon & a crack at night." On the next day he noted: "felt much better after a single night & day of open windows, showing conclusively what it was that depressed my physical [state]." A few days later he reported: "Last night window *shut*—awakened . . . short breathed— opened window a crack & slept refreshingly. I am more & more sure about this and think next winter I must have another room." Two years later, however, he talked of his blood being poisoned by the air and by the contagious influences and was anxious about the arrival of winter when the windows could not be opened. "In spite of my fine physique this life of confinement & anxiety is telling on me," he concluded.[16]

Writing undoubtedly provided some escape from his confinement, but his most vigorous relief took place in a Newport gymnasium. His good health, impaired by war duty, had returned, and he now exercised on the parallel bars and with ropes and weights. Gymnastic exercise, he felt, alleviated his feelings of depression. "In gymnasium climbed rope to top with arms only. I know no other man of fifty who is so good in gymnasium." In another entry: "afternoon—parallel bars a few times. It was astonishing how much they did for me." And again: "best gymnasium afternoon I have ever had, best condition,—forward & back somersaults in bars several times—hung by bent right arm, . . . circled bar without spring, . . . felt no fatigue & wished to keep on beyond an hour."[17] Said one Newport resident: "Col. Higginson . . . is an example to be followed by all the under developed muscle of the country. . . . No pleasure party among

16. Elliott, *Newport*, p. 83; TWH diary, Nov. 10, 1866, Sept. 25, 1868, Mar. 9, 29, 30, 31, April 3, 1871, April 18, 1873.
17. TWH diary, March 29, 1870, Sept. 15, 1871, Dec. 16, 1873, May 31, 1876.

literati is complete without the genial presence of the 'muscular Christian' par excellence." [18]

After his novel went to press, the woman's rights platform, once characterized by Higginson as the best place to redeem one's manhood, attracted him again. Mrs. Higginson told a woman friend: "My dear, I don't dare die and leave the Colonel, there are so many women waiting for him!" [19] Despite his professed commitment to literature, Higginson, after the 1868 election, wrote: "After Grant —what? Why woman's suffrage to be sure. That case stands next on the docket." Conservative Republicans and tired Abolitionists may slumber if they must, "but let those of us who had the luck to be born ultraists and men of the future stick to our function." [20] No sooner did he order the charge toward woman's suffrage when smoldering dissension and outright rebellion rose from within the ranks of the faithful.

Why not enfranchise both Negroes and women, queried Lucy Stone? Mrs. Stone, once active in the abolitionist movement, had recently returned from fruitlessly campaigning for woman's suffrage in Kansas. From there she had written: "The negroes are all against us. These men ought not to be allowed to vote before we do because they will be a dead weight to lift." Elizabeth Cady Stanton and Susan B. Anthony went further by supporting "Educated Suffrage," which would enfranchise most women and leave most freedmen without the vote. Clearly distraught by the amount of energy some prominent reformers had been expending for radical republicanism, Lucy Stone had said: "I have been for the last time on my knees to Phillips, Higginson or any of them." [21] Mrs. Stanton and Miss Anthony also were determined to stay on their feet: they marched to the Democratic camp for support. But other heavy artillery was being recommissioned for the fray. A rapprochement took place in 1868: Higginson, Phillips, Garrison,

18. Springfield *Republican*, Sept. 6, 1865, in Leyda, *Dickinson*, 2, 101.

19. Elliot, *Newport*, p. 84; Springfield *Republican*, May 31, 1869, in Leyda, *Dickinson*, 2, 138.

20. TWH, "The Next Great Question," *Independent*, Nov. 12, 1868.

21. Lucy Stone Blackwell to Susan B. Anthony, May 9, 1867, in Ida Harper, *The Life and Work of Susan B. Anthony*, 3 (Indianapolis, 1908), 274–75; E. C. Stanton to TWH, Jan. 13, 1868, Collection of Autographs of Women, Boston Public Library.

Douglass, and Tilton all supported the Fifteenth Amendment as an exclusively Negro suffrage law. And Lucy Stone, deciding that Miss Anthony and Mrs. Stanton were hurting the woman's rights cause, rejoined Higginson.[22]

The closing of ranks was temporary. Policy differences between Garrison and Phillips regarding the relative importance of woman's rights, Negro suffrage, Negro education, and loyalty to the Republican party had made the rapprochement tenuous. The inheritance of $10,000 in 1867 from the will of Abolitionist Francis Jackson aggravated the differences between the two men. Since the bequest was intended to be used for abolition, various interpretations now obviously were possible. Garrison wanted the money employed exclusively for educating the freedmen; Phillips wanted to subsidize his radical *Anti-Slavery Standard* in fighting for Negro suffrage. Higginson sought to effect a compromise but was unsuccessful. The issue went to the Massachusetts Supreme Court which decided in Garrison's favor. The internecine warfare became a bitter public spectacle, and the two pioneer Abolitionists would never be fully reconciled. Both this split and the Fifteenth Amendment clash weakened the reform movement and the drive for equality.[23]

Higginson for a time found more rapport with Garrison, since Phillips was questioning the perfection of the Republican party, becoming more interested in Ira Steward and the labor question, talking of the New York Legislature sitting in the railroad's counting rooms, and ultimately praising both Ben Butler and the Communards of France. Garrison ignored labor problems and was most interested in woman's suffrage; Higginson promised to turn to labor problems once women were enfranchised. While Phillips recently had been acknowledged to be the key agitator in the abolitionist cause, Higginson now changed his view of history and

22. Alice Stone Blackwell, *Lucy Stone. Pioneer of Woman's Rights* (Boston, 1930), p. 209; James McPherson, "Abolitionists, Woman Suffrage, and the Negro," *Mid-America*, 47 (1965), p. 43; TWH diary, Aug. 25, 1869.

23. W. L. Garrison, II, to W. L. Garrison, June 3, 30, Aug. 26, 1867, Garrison MSS; Boston Daily *Advertiser*, Feb. 1869; TWH to Charles Allen, Feb. 23, 1869, May, Jr. MSS; TWH to James F. Clarke, Feb. 25, 1869, Higginson MSS; McPherson, "Woman Suffrage," p. 47; Elinor R. Hays, *Morning Star: A Biography of Lucy Stone* (New York, 1961), pp. 211, 213.

found that "Mrs. Stowe did more than any man, except Garrison and John Brown, to secure its right solution here." [24]

Tilton also became estranged by supporting the newly formed National Woman Suffrage Association whose members had bolted from the American Equal Rights Association. Led by Miss Anthony, Mrs. Stanton, and Parker Pillsbury, and financed by George Francis Train, a wealthy eccentric who had supported peace Democrats and Clement Vallandigham in 1864, the N.W.S.A. inaugurated a woman's rights newspaper, *The Revolution*. In opposition, Higginson, Lucy Stone, Henry Blackwell, and Mary Livermore then founded the American Woman Suffrage Association and issued the weekly *Woman's Journal*. Miss Anthony's N.W.S.A., unlike the A.W.S.A., opposed the ratification of the Fifteenth Amendment because women were not also enfranchised, sought other woman's rights as well as suffrage, and strove to press Congress for action rather than state legislatures. Higginson tried to reconcile the two associations and their leaders, but Susan Anthony and Lucy Stone, still nurturing a personal feud that had begun in 1857, could not be reconciled. When the volatile Victoria Woodhull, an advocate of free love, briefly served as publicist for the N.W.S.A., Higginson defended her right to speak but denounced her as the leader of the "anti-legal marriage faction." Committed to the A.W.S.A., Higginson served for fourteen years as co-editor and frequently contributed to the *Woman's Journal*.[25]

The woman's rights meetings provided a sociability which Higginson enjoyed, and gradually Newport grew more appealing. He also became active in the Town and Country Club organized by Julia Ward Howe. Like Higginson, she loved clubs where sophisticated and intelligent men and women could gather to say urbane and witty things. Meetings were convened outdoors when the subject warranted it. Once a botanical lecture was combined

24. TWH to W. L. Garrison, Oct. 11, 1868, Anti-Slavery Letters, Boston Public Library; *Anti-Slavery Standard*, April 17, 1869; *The New Age*, June 9, 1867; TWH, *Common Sense About Women* (Boston, 1881), p. 314.

25. Henry Ward Beecher to TWH, April 11, 1870, Higginson-Barney MSS; TWH diary, April 11, 1870; TWH, "Fighting Under Cover, *Independent*, Oct. 19, 1871; Robert Riegel, "The Split of the Feminist Movement in 1869," *Mississippi Valley Historical Review*, 49 (1962), 487–92.

with a pleasant picnic, where Mrs. Howe sang her saucy song, "O So-ci-e-ty," irreverently mocking aloof Beacon Street.[26]

Higginson described one summer season as the most brilliant he had ever known as to numbers and dress and equipages. The antagonism of Oldport and Newport, for him, became less sharp. Since Mary was so crippled the Higginsons could not reciprocate with a fancy dress ball, but they hired a string quartet and presented an impressive chamber music concert. Of course this fete did not compare with the reception he attended in honor of Blaque Bey, the Turkish minister. But all understood that Higginson had more charm, sophistication, and culture than he had money. He was becoming so well accepted that even Samuel Bowles, his old nemesis at the Springfield *Republican,* suggested that he be considered for the newly vacant presidency at Harvard. When Charles W. Eliot was appointed instead, Higginson commented: "I am glad it is no worse. He is Boston-y, but I liked his articles in the *Atlantic.* . . . It is not a place for a large man." [27]

By late 1869, when Higginson moved to complete *Army Life in a Black Regiment,* work on it had become a chore because his interest in Reconstruction and the Negro had seriously waned. But *Malbone's* failure had shattered his hope of becoming a novelist and necessitated his return to nonfiction. About half of *Army Life in a Black Regiment* had appeared in the *Atlantic* as individual articles, and Higginson reprinted these unchanged.[28] He added an introduction, a conclusion, several chapters, an appendix containing a roster of officers, and his letters in behalf of equal pay for his troops. The book stands as a skillful and valuable account of the Civil War role played by Higginson and his regiment. By far his best writing, it deserves to be ranked high among nineteenth-century literature. To recall, however, that its testimony at times

26. Elliot, *Newport,* pp. 104–06; TWH to A. and S. L. Higginson, (?) 1875, TWH to A. Higginson, 1871, Higginson MSS.

27. TWH diary, Aug. 28, Oct. 10, 1868; TWH, "The Watering Place," *Independent,* Oct. 19, 1871; TWH to (?), Sept. 8, 1868, TWH to A. and S. L. Higginson, Feb. 17, 1867, Mar. 22, 1869, Higginson MSS. In June 1869 Harvard awarded Higginson an honorary M.S. degree (Harvard College Papers); this was twenty years later than it customarily was awarded.

28. *Atlantic Monthly, 14* (1864), 348–57, 521–29, 740–48; *15* (1865), 65–73, 422–36; *16,* 311–25; *19* (1867), 271–81, 685–94; *20,* 157–65.

conflicts with that of other reliable observers means that it cannot be uncritically employed as a document. Also, it has not been recognized that many of its pages were written more than five years after the actual experience, and by a man whose commitment to the Negro and the aims of radical Reconstruction had seriously lessened. In both form and content the book was significantly different from the original manuscript journal. Only two months of the eighteen-month journal appeared in print. Criticism of various officers was sharply modified; most of his doubts about the combat capability of the regiment and his admission of insensibility about the death of individual black soldiers were deleted. The joy he had experienced in conquering the enemy was omitted or tempered. The once militant colonel now wished for a world "where there is triumph without armies and where innocence is trained in scenes of peace." [29]

Quite unlike his zeal prior to 1868 for immediate equal rights for the southern Negro and his former impatience with southern bigotry, Higginson wrote in *Army Life in a Black Regiment*: "It is not in nature that jealousy of race should die out in this generation." And in an important summary chapter, "The Negro as a Soldier," he revealed how some of his own racial views were influenced by the tenacity of southern prejudice. Again stressing peculiar temperament and singular religious faith, he put greater emphasis than before on the Negro's patience. Admittedly seek-

29. *Army Life in a Black Regiment* (Boston, 1870). Higginson edited another edition of *Army Life* (Boston, 1900), making some minor language changes and adding his article from the *Atlantic* of 1878 which described his visit to the South in that year. He dedicated the new edition to General Rufus Saxton, conceding that the "ultimate civil equality" promised by the Civil War "You and I may not live to see."

Three editions of *Army Life* have been published since 1960, with introductions by Howard Mumford Jones (East Lansing, 1960), John Hope Franklin (Boston, 1962), and Howard W. Meyer (New York, 1962). Jones' introduction is most suggestive, I think, because he places Higginson and this "forgotten masterpiece" in the context of the romantic view of warm lands which was held by many important nineteenth-century writers, painters, and sculptors. Both Franklin and Meyer have relied too heavily upon Higginson's *Cheerful Yesterdays* for biographical material and especially reflect this in their discussion of Higginson during and after Reconstruction. None of the editions emphasize the disparity in context, content, and form between Higginson's manuscript journals and *Army Life*.

ing to allay popular fear about the bestial quality of the Negro race—especially its sexual aggressiveness—Higginson reasserted his belief in its affectionate, docile, and lovable qualities. White women had been far safer from verbal or physical molestation from his regiment than from a white one, he reported. While the Negro lacked a high standard of chastity, he suggested that this was the bequest of slavery, and that marriage was growing more widespread.[30]

A major theme of the book was that black soldiers had been as humane and courageous as white soldiers, but Higginson insisted that there were differences between the two races. He claimed that had he been a slave, his life "would have been one long scheme of insurrection." [31] Granting that perhaps their self-control and their failure to revolt had been wise, he judged that neither their physical nor moral temperament gave them the toughness that sustains the Anglo-Saxon.[32] *Army Life in a Black Regiment* stressed the Negroes' human qualities rather than their resemblance to white men. Affected, like much abolitionist thought, by the era's anthropological view of different racial temperaments, Higginson's book was eloquently antislavery but by no means equalitarian.

When it went to press in September 1869, he wrote in his diary: "It is amazing how indifferent I feel as to the reception of the book, compared to *Malbone* which was so close to my heart. It scarcely awakens the slightest emotion." Tilton, in the *Independent*, hailed *Army Life in a Black Regiment*, but noted that it would have been a *capital* book published during the battle for Reconstruction.[33] Howells, in the *Atlantic*, expressed the dominant view, which Higginson also shared. Said the editor:

> The lively national mind is . . . doubtless a little faded by the thought of a race with which it was really occupied a long time. . . . We should not venture to commend Colonel Higginson's book if it were a celebration of the negro in any of his familiar aspects of martyr or hero, or present 'transi-

30. *Army Life* (1870), pp. 243-65, *passim*.
31. Ibid., p. 248.
32. Ibid., p. 262.
33. TWH diary, Sept. 22, 1869; *Independent*, Nov. 4, 1869.

tional state' of bore, however we must praise it as excellent and charming literature.[34]

Reconciled to abandoning what he considered the most creative writing—fiction and poetry—Higginson relied upon his past acquaintance with New England's famous literary figures and his activity as an Abolitionist to provide material for essays and books. Soon after the publication of *Army Life in a Black Regiment*, Higginson was writing an elementary school textbook, published in 1875, called *Young Folks' History of the United States*. It pointedly did not record past wars because "the true glory of a nation lies, after all, in orderly progress." He did write about the heroism of Robert Gould Shaw and black troops. And he saw a lesson in the Missouri Compromise: "Like compromises of principle generally, it only postponed the evil day . . . by letting it [slavery] grow, it was allowed to reach such power, that it required for its abolition a great civil war, and the lives of many thousands." Declaring that the issues on which the Civil War turned are to a great extent settled, Higginson urged his readers to look instead to the spread of literature, science, and art.[35]

He continued to care about the freedmen and was always willing to defend them against people like E. L. Godkin, who in his haste to end Reconstruction, seemed to deny their humanity. Higginson now believed that he had been wrong to expect northern prejudice to end with the abolition of slavery. As the votes turned against radical Reconstruction and its critics multiplied, he refrained from predicting, as he had in 1868, that justice to the southern Negro would have to wait for the next generation. Rather, Higginson counseled the freedman to rely on that familiar forbearance, "not special legislation, but centuries of time."[36]

With leaders of Massachusetts Republicans talking in 1870 of removing anything calculated to engender strife or promote sectional animosities, as did Henry Wilson; or of reducing government expenditures and of placating the South, as did Charles Sumner, Higginson felt he was moving with the warm tide of

34. *Atlantic Monthly*, 24 (1869), 644
35. *Young Folks' History of the United States* (Boston, 1875), pp. iv, 256.
36. TWH to Editor, April 19, 1874, *Nation*, 17 (1874), 282; TWH, "An Ex-Southerner," *Independent*, June 30, 1870.

reconciliation. No longer would he have to defend the Republican party on purely expedient grounds: "If we alienate the 'carpet baggers,' the Democrats stand to pick them up." Instead he could be a good Republican by saying that "the South with all its lovely climate and luxurious vegetation, was no place for self-respecting Northern emigrants until years should have passed and the hostility inspired by war should have died away." [37]

The emigration southward of northern capital, described by Wilson and Sumner as a patriotic duty, was not similarly viewed by Higginson. If the South complained of a paucity of northern investment and of the scoundrelish behavior of the carpetbagger, he correctly urged that she remember that her own social ostracism and resentment eventually had caused the better northern immigrants to depart, leaving behind the speculators and exploiters. Both the North and the South, he suggested, had become trapped in their respective self-righteousness. [38] Higginson did not say, however, that some of these traps had been set in antebellum days and kept open during the war and Reconstruction.

Despite occasional environmental explanations about the slave's character, both Harriet Beecher Stowe and many antislavery advocates far more radical than she had attributed docility, forbearance, religiosity, childlike behavior, and a scrupulous morality (the asexuality of Uncle Tom was an essential part of his morality) to innate racial causes. Before the war, James Freeman Clarke had articulated this view by both acknowledging the environmental effect of slavery upon the Negro and suggesting that the Negro was innately different from the white man because he was more imitative, passive, and religious. Exemplifying how a reformer could simultaneously hold antislavery and racial views, Clarke had asked: "Is this an inferior race—so inferior as to be fit only for chains?" Lincoln's antislavery views in his debate with Douglas, were even more tinged with a racial inequalitarianism, as were his statements to a Negro delegation in August 1862. And most Amer-

37. Henry Wilson, "New Departure of the Republican Party," *Atlantic Monthly*, 27 (1871), 11; *Congressional Globe*, 41st Cong., 2nd Sess. (March 2, 10, 1870), pp. 1624–29, 1831–32; TWH, "The Contest of Carpetbags," *Independent*, Feb. 17, 1870; TWH, "Who Is Responsible for the Carpet-Bagger?" *Independent*, Feb. 12, 1874.

38. Ibid.

icans far exceeded Lincoln and reformers in their reliance upon racial views.[39]

During the war, men like Higginson, Saxton, and Rogers had observed slaves recently freed: they extolled their courage but also stressed an eager readiness to follow their white superiors. Rogers, an unsentimental Abolitionist and a reliable observer, illustrated the racial frame of reference when he vowed to prove that the blacks were subject to quite different diseases from those of the whites and less likely to contract fatal ones. Higginson had admitted feeling disappointment that they were growing more like white men, but he expected that they would never be identical. Having listed all the Negro racial characteristics which justified white paternalism, he repeated them in 1869 in *Army Life in a Black Regiment*. After the war one of his major arguments for enfranchising the freedman had assumed that the Negro by instinct, once again would follow enlightened northern leadership.[40]

Racial views also were voiced by the New England Freedmen's Aid Society (Higginson was a vice-president), one of the most important Reconstruction organizations working in the interest of the freedman. Its recruitment and payment of teachers to go South and teach the Negro was a project of momentous significance. Through its journal, The *Freedmen's Record*, it denied "the absolute inferiority" of any race or nation but was certain "that races, like nations and individuals, have their peculiarities." As to these peculiarities: "In the negro race we believe that the poetic and emotional qualities predominate, rather than the prosaic, mechanical, and merely intellectual powers." Further characteristics were "great

39. See James Baldwin, "Everybody's Protest Novel," *Notes of A Native Son* (Boston, 1953), pp. 3–23; J. F. Clarke, *Slavery in the United States* (Boston, 1843), p. 24; Pease and Pease, "Antislavery Ambivalence," pp. 682–85.

The best defense of abolitionist equalitarianism is McPherson, "The Racist Myth," pp. 156–77.

40. Rogers, Feb. 8, 1863, p. 359; TWH journal, Feb. 11, 1864. A provocative discussion of Negro personality and the racial attitudes of the master class is in Stanley M. Elkins, *Slavery* (Chicago, 1959), pp. 81–139, 217–22. If Elkins, as some have argued, has overdrawn his generalization about the slave's actual docility, there is little dispute about the master's *belief* in paternalism. Both the major elements of paternalism and romanticism, however, were not peculiarly southern; Higginson and other friends of the Negro shared some of these attitudes while simultaneously opposing slavery and supporting equal rights.

sensitiveness to beauty, sensibility to religious emotion, warm affection, undoubting faith." [41]

The same issue in which the *Record* warned that the black man is on trial, noted:

> In the hardier qualities, perhaps in those which constitute greatness, pre-eminent distinction, the African is inferior to the Anglo-Saxon race. Does it follow that therefore the colored peoples are doomed henceforth to be only barbers and waiters and stevedores and porters and servants that they are for the most part now? There are a good many people in America who somehow can succeed in being something more than these even though they cannot boast an Anglo-Saxon lineage. [42]

With many other advocates of radical Reconstruction Higginson shared both this desire for equal rights for the Negro and a belief in racial differences. Theodore Tilton and Moncure Conway, for example, supported equal rights, but also noted the innately "feminine" and graceful qualities of the Negro. Such characteristics were distinct impediments in a masculine-dominated world. Even Wendell Phillips, who judged Negroes and whites to be equal in ability, tended to think of Negroes as more imitative by nature. Of course, in the context of popular Negrophobia and the so-called anthropological evidence, even to advocate equal rights was enlightened. [43]

Higginson appreciated the aesthetic quality of Negro music when northern crowds were flocking to see "nigger minstrels" cavort. But seldom did he or other reformers acknowledge the possible existence and relevance of the Negro's African cultural heritage; the freedmen were rarely conceded a meaningful past prior to becoming slaves. Hence spontaneity, intuitiveness, and

41. *Freedmen's Record*, March, Aug. 1865.

42. Ibid., Sept. 1868.

43. McPherson, "The Racist Myth," pp. 164–71. McPherson's valuable argument for the Abolitionists' belief in racial equality is weakened, I think, by his use of Tilton and Conway to prove that some supporters of equal rights believed in racial equality and others in racial differences. Tilton and Conway are employed to prove both positions. Also see Bartlett, *Phillips*, p. 85.

childlike behavior served both as descriptions and explanations of Negro behavior—and as justifications for white paternalism.[44]

The task, then, of Reconstruction regarding the Negro was to elevate him to the Anglo-Saxon's level without losing too many of the alleged purities and attributes of childhood en route. A paternalism that stressed wardship, education, and increasing amounts of self-help served as the underlying relationship. If old Uncle Tom was the legacy of the past, young George Harris—Mrs. Stowe's runaway mulatto slave who could pass for a cultivated white New England gentleman—seemed to be the hoped-for future. But the goal was always less clear than the legacy. While preference for the light-skinned Negro was strong, so was opposition to miscegenation. Racial assumptions limited real hope for the growth of the childlike freedmen. Their behavior also contained much that was too exotically attractive for northern friends to be very desirous for change. And granting humanity to the Negro— as southern slavery had legally not done—was crucially different from saying that the Negro could eventually become the equal or be the superior of the white man. For once one conceded the indefinite progress of the Negro race, then the all important paternalism would be unnecessary. Equality in thought and in practice was indeed a "deferred commitment." [45]

Toward keeping the line of paternalism intact the *Freedmen's Record* commended a report from one of its southern agents who stated:

> The pure blooded Africans are superior to the mulattoes. Mixture of blood diminishes vitality and force, and shortens life. What is gained in cerebral development is lost in the tendency to scrofula and other diseases. . . . 'Miscegenation' is the last measure to be recommended for the elevation of the negro race, whether morally or physically.[46]

44. TWH, "Negro Spirituals," 685–94; W. E. B. DuBois, *The Souls of Black Folk* (New York, 1957), p. 252. The discussions of the importance of a pristine past to men of the nineteenth century in Marvin Meyers, *The Jacksonian Persuasion* (Stanford, 1957), and R. H. B. Lewis, *The American Adam* (Chicago, 1955), can be related to the widespread racial view of the Negro.

45. Woodward, "Equality: The Deferred Commitment."

46. *Freedmen's Record,* Sept. 1865.

Undoubtedly the anti-Negro northern vote and the corruption of some radical southern legislatures helped disillusion those whose humanitarian idealism or hatred for the South had attached them to radical Reconstruction. Many of the courageous Abolitionist idealists were ill-fitted for the detailed administrative problems of Reconstruction. Their revolutionary values were insufficiently radical to sustain an attack on property rights and maintain their desire to provide the freedmen with land. In this they too were part of "The Liberal Tradition in America." But it was the Sambo–Uncle Tom image, based upon the racial assumptions held by North and South, radical and conservative, that provided the main ingredient in souring men on Reconstruction. The height of Uncle Tom's morality was an impossible norm for any man, especially a freedman handicapped by poverty and illiteracy. The depth of Sambo's docility and childlike qualities—*real or imagined*—made him an orphan who might be placed under the care of either a paternal North or a paternal South.

Now that Reconstruction and the Republican party ceased to be synonymous, no longer would Higginson have to exhibit his party loyalty by being skeptical about mugwump advocacy of civil service reform or by gingerly accepting the tone which Grant, whom he came to see as honest, but narrow and obstinate, had given to the Republicans.[47] In an age of gross corruption, Higginson had never asked favors in return for his support of the party. Consequently, he attended the good government conference at New York's Fifth Avenue Hotel in May 1876. Carl Schurz had invited him and he was asked to speak. Men like Schurz, Bryant, and C. F. Adams, Jr., listened. Also listening was young Theodore Roosevelt, not yet embarked upon his own moral crusades.[48]

"I don't believe there is a man here," said Higginson, "whom it cost more to come here than it did me. I don't believe that there had been a blacker Republican than I." He went on to say that now there was an issue "more important than the results of reconstruc-

47. TWH to Moncure Conway, Nov. 8, 1874, Conway MSS; TWH, "Competitive Examinations and Their Unreliability," *Commonwealth*, Feb. 26, 1870; TWH, "Competitive Examinations," *Independent*, Dec. 28, 1871; TWH to A. and S. L. Higginson, July 23, 1872, Higginson MSS.
48. Carl Schurz to TWH, June 20, 1876, Higginson-Barney MSS; *Tribune*, May 16, 1876.

tion—for what is reconstruction worth if the Government that you have reconstructed is not an honest one?" Insisting that no one in the audience was a greater friend of Negro rights, he promised to continue to be true to Negroes, but noted that if these people at the South are the nation's wards, we owe it to them to give them an honest nation. And with unintended irony he said: "It is because we are some of us black Republicans that we need to do what we can to make the nation white." What was needed was a "President who was true to the moral integrity which lies below the principles of reconstruction, because it is the principle of the Universe." [49]

Perhaps a shorter speech which Higginson delivered two months later to a group of history teachers was more relevant—if not entirely accurate. He told them something he had never quite believed before: there are always two sides to historical questions.[50]

The distinguished men at the Fifth Avenue Hotel subsequently welcomed the Republican nomination of Rutherford B. Hayes, and many of them, including Higginson supported his campaign. But racial terrorism in August against South Carolina Negroes, especially in Hamburg, prompted some doubts. "The assertion of peace and order in the Southern states controlled by the whites," he remembered, "is precisely like the old assertions of Northern travelers that the slaves were happy and well off in slavery." After the national election in November and during the dispute over the result, Higginson recalled the bloody Hamburg riots in which the Negro trial justice, Prince Rivers, a favorite in his regiment, was overwhelmed by a white supremist mob. The "Hamburg massacre," he said, "instantly postponed for at least four years all those fine questions of civil service reform, and the rest, on which many Republicans, with Governor Hayes at their head, were sincerely desirous to employ themselves." At this point the South had failed to provide leaders who were working in harmony with their former slaves, to whom their superior intelligence and political experience would be a source of education.[51]

But when the disputed election results were finally officially de-

49. *Tribune*, May 16, 1876
50. Newspaper clipping in TWH diary, July 7, 1876.
51. TWH, "Miss Forten and the Southern Question," *Woman's Journal*, Dec.

cided in Hayes' favor in March 1877, Higginson found it "a relief to have the presidential question settled, though I have no actual anxiety it has yet worn on my nerves." When writing about Hayes' actions to end Reconstruction, he admitted: "I find it hard today to say just what I wish." [52] Only in part was his concern for the increasing graveness of Mary's ill-health the cause of this uncharacteristic inarticulateness.

Unlike Garrison, Phillips, Pillsbury, and some two thirds of the Abolitionists who criticized Hayes' policy, Higginson finally wished to be counted as one who approved heartily, cordially, and unreservedly the action of the President in withdrawing the garrisons from the State House of South Carolina and Louisiana. Rebellion, he declared, no longer existed, and sporadic outrages could not justify utilizing federal troops in South Carolina to decide the disputed election between incumbent Daniel Chamberlain, a radical Republican, and the conservative Democrat, Wade Hampton. It would be "a stretch of power so great that no State in the Union ought to tolerate it—so great that it ought to be resisted by every peaceful means." It was more important than even the immediate welfare of the colored people to maintain the right of each state in the Union to manage its own affairs in its own way, so long as peace was kept and the Constitution obeyed. It was a mistake for radical Republicans to criticize Hayes or question his motives for, "If the united Republican party succeeded, in 1876, by so slender a majority, a divided Republican party can only mean defeat in 1880." In sharp contrast to Higginson's previous support for the justice of Reconstruction, he now argued: "Of all people in the republic, the colored man of the South can least afford to benefit by an arbitrary stretch of power which may, in other hands, be used to crush him." [53] Higginson's early loss of interest in Reconstruction had turned to outright opposition.

30, 1876; TWH, "Border Ruffianism in South Carolina," *Independent*, Aug. 6, 1876; Hampton Jarrell, *Wade Hampton and the Negro* (Columbia, 1949), pp. 112–13.

52. TWH diary, Mar. 3, Apr. 4, 1877.

53. James M. McPherson, "Coercion or Conciliation? Abolitionists Debate President Hayes's Southern Policy," *New England Quarterly*, 39 (1966), 490; TWH to Editor, *Tribune*, Apr. 28, 1877; TWH, "Border Ruffianism in South Carolina"; *Woman's Journal*, July 21, 1877.

With the federal troops withdrawn from the South, with Hayes in the White House pleasurably reading the recently published biography of the late Charles Sumner, and with the South clamoring for opportunities to show its energy and its newness, Higginson planned to take his first trip below the Potomac since the Civil War. This weary man of fifty-three, trying to reconcile himself to diminishing agility in the gymnasium and lack of fulfillment as a writer, was also seeking to abate the pain he felt from the death on September 2, 1877, of his wife Mary. Pressed by mental strain and loneliness during that terrible last year of her life, Higginson had turned to collecting newspaper reports of "Crimes Against Women," which he furtively pasted between the covers of an *Edinburgh Review*. When Mary's death had seemed imminent, he sadly confided to his diary: "I resolve on a new effort to make my life fine and brave and noble. I look out into the falling snow and think—my life indeed has disappointed me in the tenderest places and I have not had what I needed most—children and freedom. But how few lives succeed!" After her death, he wrote: "With all Mary's strength she was such a child in her dependence on me & asked so often this year, 'You'll stay by me, won't you?'" An obituary in the *Woman's Journal* stressed her humor, independence, and fortitude and her ability, despite physical weakness, to be a "tower of strength," and an "invalid queen." It also revealed that "she was not especially fond of children, being, as she declared, afraid of them." [54]

Higginson's trip South was meant as a well-deserved tonic, as self-assurance that his life had really succeeded by having been involved with the Negro's cause, and with efforts to bring progress to the country. He journeyed first to Florida, where he stopped at Jacksonville, the point of his furthest penetration into the South during the war. There he was greeted by his former Worcester friend and army companion, Dr. Seth Rogers, who had brought his hydropathic practice south and established a home for invalids in what looked like an old plantation house. Higginson noted: "I was alone with my ghosts of 15 years ago . . . & got a horse, &

54. Rutherford B. Hayes to Edward L. Pierce, Nov. 1, 1878, Pierce MSS; TWH Diary, Feb. 15, Dec. 12, 1876, Sept. 30, 1877; *Woman's Journal*, Sept. 5, 1877.

went wandering around searching for my past. An individual seems so insignificant in the presence of the changes of time—he is nothing, even if his traces are mingled with fire & blood." He saw the old places where the regiment had been quartered and where there had been skirmishing with the enemy. The evidence of the new South in Jacksonville impressed him, and he was reminded of the day when he could have burned it at a word. He met some of his former Negro soldiers and attended services at a colored church— he heard the shouting he used to hear in the regiment. "I feared it was all gone," he admitted.[55]

From Jacksonville he traveled to Beaufort and the scenes of the major portion of his army life. The strangeness of returning made him feel a likeness to Rip Van Winkle. Even the freedman's village which had been named after Higginson had been blown away by the wind.[56]

What he saw in the South was assuring. The Beaufort area swelled with "Northern energy." Most encouraging was what he believed to be the improvement in the Negro's condition: Higginson found one Negro in poverty, but this man was unmarried and a habitual drinker. Race relations looked good too. There seemed to be outward peace and no conspicuous outrages, and positive signs of a less tense white–black relationship. Negroes were "still a subordinate race, doubtless, but what a difference in the degree of subordination!" In Virginia and South Carolina he observed colored people riding in first-class cars without remark. The South, he concluded, had done as well or better than New England in its treatment of the Negro. Admittedly, second-class transportation was required for Negroes in Georgia, but there was "always a decent second-class car" and they were not segregated. Danger of re-enslavement, he assured any doubtful compatriots, was as remote as the Negro's past expectation that the federal government was going to give him five acres and a mule. "There is the same sort of feeling toward the colored race as voters, that we so often hear toward Irish voters at the North; yet both are accepted as necessary evils." All future hope rested with the Negro's effec-

55. TWH diary, Feb. 21, 22, 25, 1878.
56. TWH "Some War Scenes Revisited," *Atlantic Monthly*, 42 (1878), 1; *Woman's Journal*, Mar. 2, 1878.

tively using his ballot by choosing for office the educated minority and such patriarchs as Governor Wade Hampton.[57]

Higginson returned to the South twice more within the five years that followed the end of Reconstruction. In 1879, with his new wife, Mary Thacher Higginson, who was twenty-two years his junior, he chose the South for a honeymoon. The town in which they stayed was Harpers Ferry. In the room in which the newlyweds lodged, a wooden table was scarred by bullets from the war.[58]

Colonel and Mrs. Higginson walked around the town together and visited the engine house, by the Baltimore & Ohio Railroad tracks, on which hung a sign reading "John Brown's Fort." They traveled to Charles Town, West Virginia, along the road on which Brown and his men were brought from Harpers Ferry. In Charles Town they saw the jailyard where he had been confined, the courthouse in which he was tried—they even examined the record of his trial. Finally, they saw where John Brown was hanged. The Higginsons also talked to a tall lady of "old fashioned Virginia elegance, a cousin of the Lees of Arlington, but also warmly interested in the condition of the negroes, whom she heartily and warmly praises and thinks are making great progress." [59]

The whole visit, naturally enough, left Higginson with a curious feeling. He also found curious the transformation of the non-resident Garrison into a "conscious conqueror." But time, said the Colonel, had fortunately proved President Hayes right and Garrison wrong.[60]

As Governor John D. Long's representative at the Charleston, South Carolina, anniversary celebration of the Battle of Cowpens, Higginson was the after-dinner speaker. The Colonel, now graying and slightly portly, though still handsome and erect, commended the fact that in the South with the aid of time, that great healer, the two races were learning to live together. Sympathetically he told his southern audience:

57. *Atlantic Monthly, 42,* 2, 3, 6, 7–9; *Woman's Journal,* Mar. 9, 16, 1878.
58. *Class Book, 1841,* Harvard College Papers; TWH to Anna Higginson, April 17, 1879, Higginson MSS.
59. Ibid.
60. TWH, "Two Anti-Slavery Leaders," *International Review, 9* (1880), 146.

No people ever had to face a harder problem. We of the North, believe me, are not ignorant of the difficulties, the temptations, the mutual provocations; nor can we forget the great responsibility must rest upon the more educated and enlightened race. *Noblesse oblige!*

In the words of President Lincoln at Gettysburg [sic]: With malice toward none . . .[61]

Glasses were raised by the southerners to "The New England States, The Cradle of Liberty." Higginson acknowledged the toast but offered none of his own. The reason for not doing so was probably only that the Colonel was a temperance man.

61. Charleston *News and Courier*, May 12, 1881, newspaper clipping, Higginson MSS; TWH diary, Feb. 24, 1877, Dec. 23, 1875; TWH to Sydney Gay, May 13, 1881, Gay MSS.

19

Historian, Essayist, and Literary Critic

Six months after his first wife's death, Higginson had moved from Newport to Cambridge into a small apartment on Kirkland Street, near the house in which he had been born. His new quarters faced Memorial Hall, a Victorian Gothic building honoring the Harvard men killed fighting for the Union. Soon after, he had found another residence—the old William Ware house, one block from the Yard. To this house Higginson took his thirty-three-year-old bride, the "exquisitely refined and dainty" Mary Thacher.[1]

At Newport he had known Miss Thacher, a niece of the first Mrs. Henry Wadsworth Longfellow, in a "literary way." She had published *Seashore and Prairie*, a discursive volume of essays, including one entitled "Water-Lilies in Newport," in which she described a "Professor, who having no sons or daughters, made all childhood and youth his own . . . [and] kept a watchful eye upon us."[2] The Professor, who had published "Waterlilies" in the *Atlantic* of 1858, became her husband in February 1879. They were married by the Reverend Samuel Longfellow in the home of the bride's father, lawyer Peter Thacher.

Higginson characterized his bride as shy and modest, an old-fashioned girl perfect in all household arts, who never wore a low-necked dress or had her ears pierced. News of the marriage had shocked some of his acquaintances because the new Mrs. Higginson looked younger than twenty. Higginson, now fifty-five, reported feeling unparalleled happiness with his "Pallas Athene."[3] Within a year a daughter, named Louisa after his mother, was born. And a year and a half after the seven-week-old child was stricken fatally

1. TWH to Ellen Conway, Nov. 4, 1878, Conway MSS.
2. Ibid. and Jan. 31, 1879; *Seashore and Prairie* (Boston, 1877), p. 15.
3. TWH to Ellen Garrison, Nov. 4, Dec. 6, 1878, Mar. 24, 1879, Conway MSS.

with cerebral meningitis, a second daughter was born. Of little Margaret Waldo Higginson, her father declared: "A more blissful possession no one ever owned." Marriage to Mary, whom he came to call Minnie (probably to distinguish her from his first wife), moved him to write in his diary: "no man ever had a sweeter or lovelier angel for a wife & more adapted to his needs." [4] During the coming years, which were to be the most productive of his literary career, Minnie was his collaborator in several volumes of poetry as well as a constant admirer of his writing. Less critical than the first Mrs. Higginson, she devotedly encouraged his literary career.

With a steady income from articles and reviews in the *Atlantic*, *Scribner's*, the *Nation*, the *Woman's Journal*, and the annual royalties from his *Young Folks' History of the United States*, the Higginsons were able, in December 1880, to move into a Queen Anne cottage which they had built on Buckingham Street in Cambridge. *Young Folks' History* would sell 200,000 copies and be Higginson's most popular work; its success and his continued interest in historical writing induced him to begin an adult history. *A Larger History of the United States* (to the end of Jackson's administration), published in 1885, sought to incorporate the work of Sparks, Hildreth, Parton, George Bancroft, Von Holst, and Lewis Henry Morgan—"to reduce these accumulations into compact shape, select what is most characteristic and make the result readable." [5]

The book's historical point of view reflected Bancroft's defense of Puritan society, Hildreth's allegiance to the Federalists and his criticisms of Jefferson, and Parton's disdain for Jackson. Conceding that some Federalists were narrow minded and some Jeffersonians far-sighted, Higginson concluded, however, that the less scrupulous became Jeffersonian Democrats. Jefferson's response to British maritime encroachments epitomized the prejudice of Virginia planters toward commerce. It was difficult, noted Higginson, "for those whose commerce his embargo had ruined to be patient while he rubbed his hands and assured them that they would be better

4. M. T. Higginson, *Higginson*, pp. 294, 298, TWH to Ellen Conway, Jan. 31, 1879, Mar. 27, 1880, Dec. 10, 1883, Conway MSS; TWH diary, Jan. 20, Mar. 20, 1879.

5. Ibid., Feb. 2, 1895; George W. Cooke, "T.W.H.," *Authors at Home*, J. L. and J. B. Gilder, eds. (New York, 1888), p. 157; *Larger History of the United States to the Close of President Jackson's Administration* (New York, 1886), p. vi.

off without any ships." [6] Higginson's Federalist father and grand-father would have agreed.

Andrew Jackson was narrow, ignorant, violent, and unreasonable because he practiced the spoils system in appointing public officials, which to Higginson was comparable to being opposed to the civil service reform movement of the 1880s. Jackson appeared no better than Benjamin Butler, who was seeking monetary and labor reform. "It is easier," Higginson noted, "for the demagogue than for anyone else to pose for a time as a reformer, and even be mistaken for one." [7]

Reflecting a commitment to woman's rights, the *Larger History of the United States* emphasized, even more than Charles and Mary Beard later would, the role of women in American history. It also revealed his preference for narrative history rather than either the prevailing "scientific" or philosophic history. The anecdotal and narrative style were so evident that one critic correctly said that the information at times read as if it had been gathered "at the club." [8]

Higginson was more scholarly in other historical writings and recognized the importance of research in the books of the historian highest in his esteem, Francis Parkman. He approved the vivid styles of Parkman and Bancroft, but justly criticized both historians for not understanding that the New England Puritans were devoted to truth, not liberty. And though preferring Bancroft's histories to the lack of color of the scientific school, Higginson suggested that Bancroft composed speeches for his heroes like Thucydides, but without the prerequisite of having been at the event. While Sparks in his biography of George Washington had occasionally bowdlerized, Higginson believed that he still had been more accurate than either Bancroft or Hildreth. Prescott, Ticknor, Motley, and Hildreth lacked Sparks' historical imagination for re-creating an era. [9]

Discerning about the era's young historians, Higginson favorably compared Moses Coit Tyler's *History of American Literature* with

6. Ibid., pp. 198, 358, 373.

7. Ibid., pp. 322–23, 432, 448, 451.

8. Franklin Sanborn, review of *Larger History* in *Atlantic Monthly*, 57 (1886), 559.

9. *Larger History*, p. 198; TWH, "George Bancroft," *Nation*, 52 (1891), 64–66; TWH to Brander Matthews, Mar. 7, 1896, Matthews MSS; *Yesterdays*, p. 56.

Parkman's work. A "whole department of human history," wrote Higginson in a review of Tyler's book, "is rescued from oblivion" and made a "matter of deep interest to every thinking mind." Also receptive to the antebellum history being written by young Albert Bushnell Hart, he supplied him with financial aid and historical information.[10] Higginson further praised Edward Channing's historical writing and collaborated with him in an *English History for American Readers*. Channing, his brother-in-law, was an assistant professor of history at Harvard; he wrote the first draft of the book, stressing the English events relevant to American history. Higginson revised the manuscript for popular readability. "History written as it should be, is all Swiss Family Robinson," noted Higginson. One book reviewer suggested, however, that its simple language, at times so close to nursery phraseology, indicated that, "like the earlier work of one of its authors, it is addressed to 'young folks.' " The book went through three editions.[11]

Because of his skill and grace as an essayist and because his experience with antebellum literary and reformist life provided a valuable source, both Tyler and Hart valued Higginson's historical writings. In some of his biographical studies, especially of Francis Higginson, Stephen Higginson, and Margaret Fuller, previously unused primary sources were employed. But he did not seek to be a full-time professional historian. Rather he was one of those literary patricians of the era who pronounced the magisterial verdict of history upon men and events by making moral judgments. When Higginson's appointment to the Harvard history department was being considered by President Eliot, a retired Harvard professional historian recorded that "all agreed to keep him at arm's length, but if he is to be taken any where it should be in the English Department, not Historical." [12]

10. TWH, review of *A History of American Literature* (New York, 1879), *Nation*, 28 (1879); M. C. Tyler to TWH, Jan. 18, 1879, Higginson-Barney MSS; TWH diary, May 5, 1908, TWH to A. B. Hart, Dec. 24, 1890, Mar. 25, 1891, Hart MSS.

11. *English History* (New York, 1893); TWH to Brander Matthews, Oct. 1, 1892, Matthews MSS; TWH, "History in Easy Lessons," *Atlantic Monthly*, 46 (1905), 386; review of *English History, Nation*, 57 (1893), 215.

12. Hart to TWH, Aug. 3, 1899, Tyler to TWH, Jan. 18, 1879, Higginson-Barney MSS; Tyler, *American Literature*, pp. 165, 180; Ephraim Gurney to Charles W. Eliot, Aug. 12, 1886, Eliot MSS, Harvard University.

Infrequently written poetry and very frequently published criticism of poetry helped establish Higginson's literary reputation. During his adolescence and early manhood he had published a few reform-oriented poems; after the war his poetry, while occasionally maintaining this concern, more often described domestic life. "Sixty and Six: Or a Fountain of Youth" and "The Baby Sorceress," for example, described his reaction to his young daughter Margaret.[13] The beginning of the latter poem is representative of their genre:

> Joy of the morning,
> Darling of the dawning,
> Blithe, lithe little daughter of mine!
> While with thee ranging
> Sure I'm exchanging
> Sixty of my years for six years like thine.

Occasionally more inspiring were Higginson's poems about nature. But in "Sea-Gulls at Fresh Pond" [14] he frankly acknowledged the truth about his poetry.

> I am no nearer to those joyous birds
> Than when, long since, I watched them as a child;
> Nor am I nearer to that flock more wild,
> Most shy and vague of all elusive things,
> My unattainable thoughts, unreached by words.
> I see the flight, but never touch the wings.

Higginson's most popular poems were those commemorating the Civil War. Most publicly recited was "Waiting for the Bugle," first read in 1888 before a group of Cambridge war veterans.[15] The last lines read:

> Though the sound of cheering dies down to a moan
> We shall find our lost youth when the bugle is blown.

Dedicatory poems to Whittier, Helen Hunt Jackson, and Edward Bellamy express far less disappointment and pessimism than

13. TWH, *Afternoon Landscape* (Cambridge, 1889), pp. 17, 20–21.
14. Ibid., p. 33.
15. Ibid., p. 57.

his other types of poetry.[16] Whittier is credited with opening the nation's eyes to the need for abolition, and Mrs. Jackson for "Lifting with slender hand a race's wrong." "Heirs of Time" assures Bellamy that the "tread of marching men,/The patient armies of the poor . . .

> Some day, by laws as fixed and fair
> As guide the planets in their sweep,
> The children of each outcast heir
> The harvest-fruits of time shall reap.

Higginson's poems are generally lyric in structure. Conventional meters and verse forms, four-line stanzas, alternating rhyme, and iambic pentameter are most often employed. While there is some lyric variety, he showed no interest in experimenting with unorthodox forms. In this traditionalism his poetry remained akin to antebellum poetry and to such postwar contemporaries as Edmund Clarence Stedman and Thomas Bailey Aldrich. It has been correctly suggested that Higginson was more adept as a translator than as an original poet. In *Petrarch*, for example, the weakness of his poetic fancy does not excessively mar the result.[17]

Poetry, Higginson believed, was the "highest kind of literature . . . for it culls the very best phrase of the language, instead of throwing a dozen epithets to see if one may chance to stick." He knew, however, that his own poetic efforts achieved no such height. A volume of 1893 containing the best poems from Higginson and his wife was modestly titled *Such as They Are*. But humility did not characterize his conception of himself as a critic of poetry. Recognized as a major literary critic by his contemporaries, Higginson believed that poetry could do what the novel or the essay could not: raise the mind and carry it "into sublimity by con-

16. Ibid., pp. 6, 49, 52.
17. *Fifteen Sonnets of Petrarch* (Boston, 1903); Howard W. Hintz, "Thomas Wentworth Higginson: Disciple of the Newness," Unpublished doctoral dissertation, New York University, 1937, p. 693. Although they also have not utilized the extensive unpublished manuscripts, very helpful in studying Higginson's literary career are two other accounts: Edgar L. McCormick, "The Aesthetic Criticism of Thomas Wentworth Higginson," Unpublished doctoral dissertation, University of Michigan, 1952; Sister Catherine Thomas Brennan, "Thomas Wentworth Higginson: Reformer and Man of Letters," Unpublished doctoral dissertation, Michigan State University, 1958.

forming the show of things to the desires of soul, instead of subjecting the soul to external things." [18] His responses to the poetry
of Emily Dickinson, Walt Whitman, and Sidney Lanier provide a
revealing test of his literary opinions.

By the time of Higginson's second marriage, seventeen years
had passed since his first letter from Emily Dickinson. During this
interval their relationship had changed significantly. Gone was the
spirit of intensity and mutual interest between a mentor and an
aspiring young poet. Higginson had become a popular, frequently
published man of letters, and she had accepted her status as a "private poet." Fearing for her reason at the time she first had written
to him, Emily Dickinson had looked for some poetic guidance and
especially for a person who represented the world outside her
mind. She had referred to him as her "preceptor" and "master,"
and to herself as his "scholar," "pupil" and "gnome." Any hope and
empathy that she had felt from reading in the *Atlantic* of 1862 his
"Letter to a Young Contributor" never developed into more than
the most tenuous relationship. His concern for nature, children,
women, death, and immortality was far different from her own.
And the stress in his essay on the poet's privacy and the life of renunciation had not been sustained. But she continued writing to
him, taking him at his word that even the most cultured man could
not match the easy grace of a bright woman's letters.[19]

Always most comfortable in the paternal role, Higginson had
initially viewed Emily Dickinson as childlike, ingenuous, and
simple. Her poetry both fascinated and bewildered him, for the
"strange power" of its "luminous flashes" were also filled with unconventional dissonances and startling irregularities of syntax. The
books he recommended suggest his belief that Emily Dickinson
still lacked the necessary culture to meet his requirements for a
mature poet. At the outset, Higginson thought she needed him to
take her "by the hand" to help end her isolation and begin the careful revision of her poetry. Accustomed to confront aspiring woman
writers directly and bring such relationships down to the level of

18. TWH, *Atlantic Essays* (Boston, 1871), pp. 27, 78; *Such as They Are* (Boston, 1893); TWH, *Whittier*, p. 150.

19. Emily Dickinson to TWH, Apr. 25, June 7, 1862, July 1862, Aug. 1862, Mar.
1878, Feb. 1863, in Johnson, *Dickinson Letters*, 2, 409, 412, 415, 607, 424; Johnson,
Dickinson, pp. 31, 83. See my earlier comments, pp. 250–51, 308, 313.

simple truth and every-day comradeship—as he had done with Harriet Prescott Spofford, Rose Terry, and Helen Hunt Jackson —he tried to meet Emily Dickinson. When she failed to come to Boston to see him, despite his assurance that all the ladies did, Higginson journeyed to her home in Amherst.[20]

They met on August 15, 1870, in the Dickinson parlor. Appearing in white piqué and a blue net shawl, and carrying two lilies in her hand, Emily Dickinson first apologized for her shyness and then, according to Higginson, "she talked soon and thenceforward continuously . . . sometimes stopping to ask me to talk instead to her—but readily recommencing. . . . She seemed to speak absolutely for her own relief, and wholly without watching its effect on her hearer." Her letters had led him to believe that she would look attractively sensitive, but on seeing her he thought she was prosaically "plain." Higginson found her views about poetical sensibility and the state of mankind "the very wantonness of overstatement, as if she pleased herself with putting into words what the most extravagant might possibly think without saying." Too extravagant was her assertion that she could recognize true poetry when "it makes my whole body so cold no fire can ever warm me. . . . If I feel physically as if the top of my head were taken off." Her effusiveness reminded him of the verbosity of Bronson Alcott. He failed to understand that it was possible to conceive of poetic statements as normal, and logical ones as fantastic. Higginson's beliefs in the dignity of man and democracy were sorely affronted, furthermore, when she asked: "How do most people live without any thoughts? There are so many people in the world (you must have noticed them in the street). . . . How do they get enough strength to put on their clothes in the morning?"[21]

After the horrendous lack of rapport at their first meeting, Higginson reconsidered his plan to draw closer to Emily Dickinson. "I never was with anyone who drained my nerve power so much," he admitted. "Without touching her, she drew from me. I am glad

---

20. TWH, "Emily Dickinson's Letters," *Atlantic Monthly, 58* (1891), 453; TWH to E. Dickinson, May 11, 1869, in Johnson, *Dickinson Letters, 2,* 461–62; Theodora Ward, *Capsule of the Mind: Chapters in the Life of Emily Dickinson* (Cambridge, 1961), pp. 185–86.

21. TWH to M. Higginson [Aug. 16, 1870], in Johnson, *Dickinson Letters, 2,* 473–76; TWH diary, Aug. 16, 1870; TWH, "Dickinson Letters," pp. 452–53.

not to live near her." She already had shown that she understood his feelings. When he took leave of her and followed the social convention of saying that he hoped to visit her again *"some time,"* she responded: "Say in a long time, that will be sooner. Some time is no time." [22]

The visit thoroughly obliterated the possibility created in their correspondence of a powerful male mentor leading a childlike woman poet. Gone now was any remaining chance that Higginson would try shaping either Emily Dickinson's life or poetry. After a second meeting, three years later, the distance widened; later in life the Dickinson family had to remind him that he ever had made a second visit. Higginson dropped any modicum of compassion and understanding for her behavior. He came to refer to his "eccentric poetess," and his reason for reading her poetry aloud to a Boston ladies' club (without her permission) was that it seemed weird and strange.[23] After his marriage to Minnie, he appeared ready to bring the correspondence to an end. But Emily Dickinson, remembering that their earliest letters possibly had saved her from insanity, responded to his silence with the pitiful plea: "Must I lose the Friend that saved my Life?" Higginson thereupon responded kindly and sent her a copy of his new book, *Short Studies of American Authors.*[24]

22. TWH to M. Higginson (Aug. 16, 1870), in Johnson, *Dickinson Letters, 2,* 476; TWH, "Dickinson Letters," p. 450. By far the most sympathetic account of the meeting and of Higginson's relationship with Emily Dickinson and her poetry is Anna Mary Wells, *Dear Preceptor: The Life and Times of Thomas Wentworth Higginson* (Boston, 1963), pp. 228–31. Because of the importance of Emily Dickinson, not because of her importance in Higginson's life, Mrs. Wells devotes about a third of her book to various aspects of their relationship. She omits, however, Higginson's revealing admission, after his visit to Amherst: "I am glad not to live near her." Also absent are Higginson's assertions that Emily Dickinson talked too much and made wanton overstatements. In sharp contrast to Mrs. Wells' account is Charles R. Anderson, "From a Window in Amherst: Emily Dickinson Looks at the American Scene," *New England Quarterly, 31* (1958), 147–71. Anderson does not give sufficient weight, in my opinion, to the view that Higginson might have been historically and philosophically justified—and not dense—for being critical of Emily Dickinson's statements.

23. TWH to A. Higginson, Dec. 9, 1873, in Johnson, *Dickinson Letters, 2,* 518–19; TWH to A. Higginson, Nov. 30, 1875, Higginson MSS; TWH to Mabel Loomis Todd, Sept. 12, 1890, quoted in Millicent Todd Bingham, *Ancestors' Brocades: The Literary Debut of Emily Dickinson* (New York, 1945), p. 63.

24. Emily Dickinson to TWH [1879], Dec. 1879, in Johnson, *Dickinson Letters, 2,* 649, 650.

A new relationship soon developed in which Emily Dickinson wrote to him more conventionally. The death of his first child and the birth of his second one prompted warm and understanding letters from the poet. Higginson and Miss Dickinson would never meet again, however, to test the new relationship. She died in 1886, and Higginson traveled to Amherst to be present at her funeral and to read aloud Emily Brontë's "Last Lines"—"a favorite with our friend who has now put on the Immortality which she seemed never to have laid off." In his diary he wrote about the death "of that rare & strange creature Emily Dickinson," and added: "How large a portion of people who have interested me have passed away." It has not been recognized that he soon composed a poem, "Astra Castra," published in 1889, about a woman in heaven, a "freed spirit, now transformed and taught/To move in orbits where the immortals are." [25] He noted her "instantaneous ways," and asked in language similar to that he usually employed when he wrote about her:

> Could we but reach and touch that wayward will
> On earth so hard to touch, would she be found
> Controlled or yet impetuous, free or bound,
> Tameless as ocean or serene and still?
> If in her heart one eager impulse stirs,
> Could heaven itself calm that wild mood of hers?

If Higginson, during the twenty-four years he corresponded with Emily Dickinson, bears the major responsibility for discouraging the publication of her poetry—though certainly she exerted some choice—he also deserves much of the credit, after her death, for bringing it to the world's attention. Mrs. Mabel Loomis Todd, the wife of the professor of astronomy at Amherst College and a friend of the Dickinson family, met with Higginson in early November 1889 to show him some two hundred Dickinson poems which Mrs. Todd had copied from the poet's manuscripts. Mrs. Todd, at the request of the Dickinson family, had come for his advice and help in editing and publishing them. After some hesitation because of his own ill-health, other literary projects, and the poet's "peculiarities of construction," Higginson consented to col-

25. TWH diary, May 17, 1886; TWH, *Afternoon Landscape*, p. 58.

laborate if Mrs. Todd would do the bulk of the editorial work. He
would be responsible for the final editing, the preface, publishing
arrangements, and publicity. It seemed unlikely that the volume,
its printing plates paid for by the Dickinson family, would succeed
in doing more than provide a modest memorial to Emily Dickinson.[26] But Higginson, who previously had received more than a
hundred poems during the poet's lifetime, examined those chosen
for the volume by Mrs. Todd and suddenly discovered that Emily
Dickinson was not just a private poet. With some incredulousness
he wrote to Mrs. Todd: "I can't tell you how much I am enjoying
these poems. There are many new to me which take my breath
away & which also have *form* beyond most of those I have seen
before. . . . My confidence in their *availability* is greatly increased." [27]

To recall that Emily Dickinson already had sent him many of
her best poems suggests that what most impressed Higginson with
the new ones indeed was the presence of *form*. Form meant maxi-
mum revision by the poet to conform to accepted literary standards. Neither of the two poems which Higginson judged to be of
the highest quality, it should be noted, was markedly unconventional in rhyme, meter, or imagery. And both poems had themes
common to New England verse.

> Glee! the great storm is over!
> Four have recovered the land;
> Forty gone down together
> Into the boiling sand . . .[28]

The other poem, which Higginson titled "The Lonely House,"
—"I know some lonely houses off the road . . ."—paralleled his
own poem, "The Dying House," previously published in a collection of his verse. For those Dickinson poems with more obscure
themes, Higginson sought to guide future readers by grafting on

26. M. T. Higginson, *Higginson*, p. 369; Bingham, *Ancestors' Brocades*, pp. 16–
18, 34, 53.

27. TWH to M. L. Todd, Nov. 25, 1889, in Bingham, *Ancestors' Brocades*, pp.
34–35.

28. TWH, "An Open Portfolio," *Christian Union*, 42 (1890), 392.

titles. Also titles like "Rouge et Noir," "Rouge Gagne," and "Astra Castra" were added to give the poems a learned weight.[29]

How to edit the body of the poetry, recent scholars have noted, was a complex matter, partly because it was difficult to know which poems had been considered final versions by Miss Dickinson. Although Higginson's own poetry employed standard rhyme, he conceded in his published criticism that the traditional roundel had been cloying. And while reading the Dickinson verse in December 1889, he wrote, unlike most critics of his day, that Thomas Bailey Aldrich's "most admired gems are really the mere resetting of what came first from someone else."[30] Still, Emily Dickinson's originality seemed to him very remarkable, though odd. So with an eye to public acceptance and standard grammar he sought to modify some of the oddity. Far too unorthodox for Higginson was "The grass so little has to do/I wish I were a hay." He asserted: "It cannot go in so, everybody would say that *hay* is a collective noun requiring the definite article. Nobody can call it *a* hay!" Therefore, he sent "the hay" to the printer along with the alteration of the line, "And what a Billow be," to "And what a wave must be." In other poems Higginson and Mrs. Todd eliminated unorthodox capitalization and added conventional punctuation.[31]

Perhaps the most important alteration of a major poem occurred in "Because I could not stop for death." Higginson titled it "The Chariot," changed some words, and omitted an entire stanza. His editing suggests that he interpreted the poem as only depicting the soul's ascension to heaven in a chariot. A birds-eye view of the ground, rather than the simultaneous existence of mortal remains and immortal soul, was the resulting emphasis. Thus he changed the last line from "The Cornice—in the Ground" (meant to be a coffin's cornice) to "The cornice but a mound" (a house's cornice viewed from above). The original stanza and Higginson's revisions are here illustrated:[32]

29. Mabel Loomis Todd and T. W. Higginson, eds., *Poems by Emily Dickinson* (Boston, 1891), pp. 15, 16, 112; TWH, *Afternoon Landscape*, pp. 34–36.

30. *Nation, 36* (1883), 336; *Nation, 48* (1889), 522.

31. TWH to A. Higginson, Aug. 28, 1890, Higginson MSS; Bingham, *Ancestors' Brocades*, p. 58; Thomas H. Johnson, *The Poems of Emily Dickinson* (Cambridge, 1955), 2, 742; Todd and TWH, *Dickinson Poems*, p. 26.

32. Ibid., pp. 138–39; Johnson, *Dickinson Poems*, 2, 546–47. To interpret the

We paused before a House that seemed	We paused before a house that seemed
A Swelling of the Ground—	A swelling of the ground;
The Roof was scarcely visible—	The roof was scarcely visible,
The Cornice—in the Ground—	The cornice but a mound.

Omission of the revealing fourth stanza further changed the poem's intent:

> Or rather—He passed Us—
> The Dews drew quivering and chill—
> For only Gossamer, my Gown—
> My Tippet—only Tulle—

Again, the coexistence of mortality and immortality is lost. Also the symbolic interchangeability of love with death is eliminated or obscured because the editor never displays the woman in her bridal dress traveling to her marriage with God. Here and elsewhere, Higginson missed the central fact of Emily Dickinson's symbolism. He, as has been said about Emerson, was "remote from the specific possibilities of the *literary* symbol." [33] But in "The Chariot," as well as in other poems, alterations were probably less drastic than would have been made by any other editors of the era—if indeed anybody else would have consented to associate his name with such poetry. Higginson, for example, accepted the unconventional rhyming of "pearl" with "alcohol," and "own" with "young." [34] (Tennyson, however, provided precedent for such assonance.) As editor, Higginson was torn by a personal obligation to Emily Dickinson's memory and a historical obligation to documentary truth as against his own conception of good poetry and the hostile reception expected from critics and public. Not only was this conflict reflected in the editorial results but also in his prefatory remarks which introduced Emily Dickinson to the world.

---

poem I have relied heavily upon Charles R. Anderson, *Emily Dickinson's Poetry: Stairway of Surprise* (New York, 1960), pp. 241–48.

33. Charles Feidelson, Jr., *Symbolism in American Literature* (Chicago, 1953), pp. 55, 122.

34. Bingham, *Ancestors' Brocades*, p. 58.

To publicize this forthcoming volume, Higginson wrote an article for the *Christian Union*. While similar to his subsequent preface to the poems, it was less guarded in discussing the poet's motives and the level of the poetry. Emily Dickinson, he suggested, was akin to those poets "who wrote for the relief of their own mind and without thought of publication." Granting that she had a standard of her own, he likened her verse to poetry plucked up by the roots, with earth, stones, and dew adhering—it was wayward and unconventional in the last degree; defiant of form, measure, rhyme, and even grammar. But he hoped that the faulty rhyme and defect of workmanship would be compensated by its power. He chose to publish, for the first time, fourteen of the poems she had sent to him during their many years of correspondence.[35]

To explain why no volume of her poetry had been printed during her lifetime, he wholly blamed the poet by asserting that she had been asked again and again for verses to be published. It should be recognized, however, that neither Higginson nor any of his defenders have produced any documentary evidence showing that he ever had asked her. And if the primary blame for altering Emily Dickinson's verse is Mrs. Todd's, as a recent Higginson biographer has argued, it also must be acknowledged that he was a willing accomplice, with a long-held conviction that much revision and criticism were prerequisites to publication. His marked antipathy to the other poetic innovators of his day makes even a circumstantial defense tenuous. On the eve of the first volume's appearance, Higginson conceded some misgiving in allowing its publication at all.[36]

In the preface to the first edition, Higginson neither admitted misgiving nor said that the verse was written for mental relief. Instead, he stressed that Emily Dickinson had absolutely no choice in the *way* she wrote and the way she received flashes of wholly original and profound insight into nature and life. Now praising this recluse woman for touching the "very crisis of physical or mental conflict," he confined his criticism to the uneven vigor and the lack of a sustained lyric strain. And he assured readers that the

35. TWH, "An Open Portfolio," pp. 392, 393.
36. Ibid., 392; TWH, "Letter to a Young Contributor," pp. 402, 404; TWH, *Atlantic Essays*, pp. 36, 41. Higginson is defended in Wells, *Dear Preceptor*, pp. 120, 226, 233–34, 278–79.

poems "are here published as they were written, with very few and superficial changes." [37]

On publication day, November 12, 1890, Higginson wrote to Mrs. Todd: "Books just arrived—bound. I am *astounded* in looking through. How could we have doubted them." No less astounding was the success of the public sale; the first edition of five hundred copies was quickly sold and followed by second, third, and fourth editions. The prestige of the printed word and the extent of the sale caused him to reconsider, once again, the meaning of Emily Dickinson's life and poetry. To Mrs. Todd, who was planning another collection of Dickinson poetry, Higginson suggested: "Let us alter as little as possible now that the public ear is opened." The second series received less editing than its predecessor.[38]

Just prior to its publication, Higginson promoted the collection by writing a revealing biographical essay for the *Atlantic* which outlined his meetings with Emily Dickinson and quoted extensively from her letters to him. He stressed the tension in her "abnormal life," but for the first time insisted that he had always known that she was a genius. And from then on, some thirty years after he first received her poems, the image of a raw genius characterized his comments about her work. Reviewing the second series in his unsigned column in the *Nation*, Higginson urged that the poems be read as "sketches, not [as] works of conscious completeness." Her work made it appear "as if she had been in at the very birth of her birds and flowers." [39] When a young man, Higginson had described in precisely these terms the romantic work of Jean Paul Richter. Now Emily Dickinson's work had incorrectly come to exemplify what Schiller had called the naïve and sentimental in poetry.

Mrs. Todd edited a third series of Dickinson poems without Higginson's assistance (he had been paid a very small sum by the Dickinson family for his past work), but he reviewed them in the *Nation*. He found that the poet had heeded Emerson's plea for a distinctive national literature in her representation of "the peculiarly American quality of the landscape, the birds, the flowers."

37. Todd and TWH, *Dickinson Poems*, pp. iii, v, vi.
38. Bingham, *Ancestors' Brocades*, pp. 72, 82, 83, 127.
39. TWH, "Dickinson Letters," pp. 445, 453; *Nation*, 54 (1891), 297.

Her poetry, he concluded, with all "its flagrant literary faults" could be appreciated only in terms of what "Ruskin describes as 'the perfection and precision of the instantaneous line.' " Once having said that Emily Dickinson would "wait many days for a word that satisfied," he increasingly turned to the opinion that her poetry lacked the traditional care of revision and was primarily the spontaneous expression of a "pitifully childlike poetic genius," who was strange, solitary, and morbidly sensitive. For him the obscure, inscrutable quality of her poetry with its fractured grammar and "defiance of form" could best be comprehended by believing that it "rests content with a first stroke" and therefore lacks the "proper control and chastening of literary expression." [40] Incredible as it may seem today, Emily Dickinson's poetry and her personality were being measured against Helen Hunt Jackson's.

It was "H. H." whom Higginson viewed as the best kind of "poet of passion," one who tempered her waywardness and controlled her poetic impulses by being always ready to revise and correct her verse at his suggestion. Aided by the openness and frankness Mrs. Jackson showed toward him, he had achieved the everyday comradeship lacking in his relationship with Emily Dickinson. Mrs. Jackson was also able to combine an ardent and impetuous nature with an ability to be pleasantly sociable and congenial. Her prejudices against Negroes and her lack of sympathy with the woman's rights cause were less important to him, he granted, than her personal generosity. At a time when he criticized Longfellow's poetry for being too easily and quickly comprehended, and Whittier's for having an obtrusive moral, Higginson found that Mrs. Jackson's best poetry contained just enough obscurity to compliment the intelligent reader. [41]

While obviously impressed that 30,000 copies of Miss Dickinson's poetry had been sold by 1895, Higginson privately noted that her work was not valued by the finest minds. Publicly he acknowledged its quality by ranking her with those women poets he es-

40. *Nation*, 53 (1896), 275; TWH, "An Open Portfolio," p. 392; TWH, *American Literature*, p. 130.

41. TWH to E. C. Stedman, Aug. 19, 1888, Stedman MSS; TWH, *Contemporaries*, pp. 143, 150, 164; Ruth Odell, *Helen Hunt Jackson* (New York, 1939), pp. 70, 72; TWH, "Helen Jackson," *The Critic*, 7 (1885), 86.

teemed most: Helen Hunt Jackson and Elizabeth Barrett Browning. He began to use her poetry as a standard with which to criticize other poets who were seeking a new means of expression. Mrs. Annie Fields' poetry was inferior to Mrs. Jackson's and Miss Dickinson's in "passion and originality." And when the Dickinson poems sold poorly in England he defended her work against the poetry that he most disdained: "Apparently the English polite cannot stand the unconventional except with a good coarse flavor as in Whitman." With the appearance of Stephen Crane's *The Black Rider and Other Lines*, Higginson noted that Crane grasped "thought as nakedly and simply as Emily Dickinson," but was an amplified Emily Dickinson. Here too was "poetry torn up by the roots." Apparently reconsidering, however, his own previous praise for Emily Dickinson in this regard, Higginson suggested that such a style was "always interesting to the botanist, yet bad for the blossoms." Edward Arlington Robinson, one of the most promising of our younger poets, he said, was also given credit for displaying an "obscurity that is often like that of Emily Dickinson when she piques your curiosity through half a dozen readings and suddenly makes all clear." But while Higginson acknowledged the poet's right to be obscure, Robinson sometimes came near the unintelligible. The cause of such a flaw was working too much alone —exactly his criticism of Emily Dickinson.[42]

Higginson's final estimate of American poets devoted a scant two pages to Emily Dickinson. He predicted that the poem most likely to bring her lasting fame was one he had titled "Vanished." [43] It ended:

> Her little figure at the gate
> The angels must have spied,
> Since I could never find her
> Upon the mortal side.

The paternal compassion and fascination that attracted Higginson to Emily Dickinson and her enigmatic poetry and personality

42. TWH to Brander Matthews, Mar. 6, 1896, Matthews MSS; *Nation*, 70 (1900), 265; *Nation*, 61 (1895), 296; *Nation*, 75 (1902), 465; TWH to Brander Matthews, Nov. 22, 1891, Matthews MSS.

43. TWH, *American Literature*, p. 264; T. W. Higginson and Mabel Loomis Todd, eds., *Poems by Emily Dickinson* (Boston, 1891), p. 216.

were wholly absent in his response to Whitman and his poetry.
This was true despite Higginson's willingness to be critical of the
renowned Aldrich, to label Bayard Taylor a "champion imitator,"
and to charge that Richard Henry Stoddard was "burnt out." He
suggested that writing *Leaves of Grass* was no discredit to Whitman—"only that he did not burn it and reserve himself for something better." Claiming to have read the poem in 1855, during his
rough sea voyage from the Azores, Higginson was uncertain about
which had more upset his stomach.[44] But when he reviewed the
Boston edition of *Leaves of Grass* in 1881 he was sure that its "nau-
seating quality remains in full force." Republication of the poem
only could provide satisfaction for those who feared the dominance
of "Anthony Comstock and his laws respecting obscene publications." According to Higginson, Whitman displayed the animal
impulse of the savage who knocks down the first woman he sees
and drags her to the cave. The savage, however, wrote no resound-
ing lines about it. Responding to an expurgated Boston edition of
Leaves of Grass in 1892, Higginson said that it may be left openly
about the house but its profuseness and wordiness remain.[45]

"Drum-Taps" was tasteless in a different manner. It was hypo-
critically hollow because Whitman, who had been trumpeted by his
admirers as having the finest physique in America, had avoided Civil
War battlefields and instead served in the hospital with the non-
combatants. Whitman's patriotism was the sheer bravado of thousands of Fourth of July orations. And similarly, the poet's celebration of the laborer rang false because he had never labored; Whitman tried to use folk language without having studied the localisms
of the day.[46]

The modicum of tolerance Higginson had exhibited toward
Emily Dickinson's poetic style was absent. In Whitman's verse the
reader was not pierced by the "rifle-bullet effect" of the instantaneous line, but instead was assaulted by the poet's "bird-shot," his
endless enumerations, and the ostentatious effort at cosmopolitanism exhibited in the sudden use of French words. Reminded of the

44. *Nation*, 59 (1894), 74; *Nation*, 53 (1891), 321; TWH, *Atlantic Essays*, p. 44;
Yesterdays, p. 230.

45. *Nation*, 31 (1881), 476; *Nation*, 55 (1892), 11, 12.

46. *Nation*, 31 (1881), 476; TWH, *Contemporaries*, p. 75; TWH, *Reader's History of American Literature* (Boston, 1903), p. 233.

long rambling lines and excessive romantic effusiveness of Martin Tupper, the English aphorist he had admired in his youth, Higginson concluded that Whitman lacked the stylistic control required of a poet.[47]

This virulence was unmatched in Higginson's many pieces of criticism except for his comment that Rudyard Kipling's poems have "that garlic flavor which makes a very little of them go a great way, and makes the reader himself soon wish to go a great way off." Whitman, and Kipling to a lesser extent, represented a repugnant kind of manliness. Holding to a chivalric conception, he believed that Whitman epitomized an exclusively muscular manliness. Higginson's views ranged close at times to an Anglo-Saxonism that looked upon the best American man as a transplanted Englishman transformed into a "type more high bred, more finely organized, and also more comprehensive and cosmopolitan." [48] Or in another way, Higginson conceived of himself in relation to the Greek ideal, relegating Whitman to the role of a Roman Bacchus. In his article "The Greek Goddesses," for example, Higginson equated Greece with high-minded purity, and derided both Ovid and Aristophanes for writing irreverent indecencies about women and for failing to recognize Aphrodite's essential modesty. He also was critical of writers who "find some indecency in every ancient symbol." [49]

With acuteness and venom, Higginson compared Whitman to Oscar Wilde by noting that they wrote about nudity in a way not comparable to the "sacred whiteness of an antique statue, but rather [to] the forcible unveiling of some insulted innocence." A real man would never read such literature aloud in the presence of ladies. True literature combined power with delicacy, and elevated mankind to a realization of its higher nature. What Whitman valued as "the sexual fibre of things," Higginson judged as animalism and a failure to understand love as an ideal emotion.[50] Defending a tradition infused with transcendentalism and puritanism

47. Ibid.; *Contemporaries*, pp. 77, 83, 84.

48. *Nation*, 53 (1891), 321; "American Physique," *Woman's Journal*, Oct. 7, 1876.

49. "The Greek Goddessess," *Atlantic Monthly*, 25 (1869), 98, 99; *Nation*, 28 (1879), 204.

50. "Unmanly Manhood," *Woman's Journal*, Feb. 4, 1882; *Contemporaries*, p. 80.

against a poet who believed that the absence of a significant American literary tradition made personal vision necessary, Higginson believed that Whitman was a sheer egoist. The poet's failure to distinguish between a goddess and a streetwalker showed only blindness to moral verities.

Whitman believed that Higginson was responsible for much of the hostility toward him in Boston. And only later in life did Higginson discover a spark of greatness in the poet's work. In reviewing a collection of Whitman's complete writings, he noted "occasional bursts of fine humility which are too rarely visible in the writings of this remarkable man," and which by their "manly modesty . . . atone for a multitude of sins." [51] But Higginson never forgave Whitman's failure to fight in the Civil War, nor forgot that this self-styled democratic poet received not one popular vote for the Hall of Fame of Immortals. There were only two poems Higginson ever praised. One was "My Captain," which came nearest to regularity of rhythm and proved the importance of adhering to recognized poetic method. It ranked, in his estimation, with some of the best American poems of the nineteenth century. "Joy, Shipmate, Joy," he praised for the "fine outburst" and "sunny spirit" in Whitman's conception of death and immortality; these lines, Higginson said at age eighty-two, could be a fitting inscription on his own memorial stone. But in assessing all of Whitman's poetry he agreed with Sidney Lanier's criticism: " 'A republic depends on the self-control of each member; you cannot make a republic out of muscles and prairies and rocky mountains; republics are made of the spirit.' " [52] For Higginson, restraint and spirit were the "austere virtues" that had been bequeathed to American literature by puritanism and transcendentalism.

Not until after Lanier's death in 1881 did Higginson appreciate this southern poet and rate him among the "master singers." In

51. Whitman to W. D. O'Connor, May 25, 1882, in *The Correspondence of Walt Whitman*, ed. Edwin H. Miller (New York, 1964), 3, 283; TWH to Wendell Phillips Garrison, Nov. 14, 1905, Misc. MSS, Library of Congress; TWH, review of *Complete Writings of Walt Whitman* by Richard Bucke, Thomas B. Harned, and Horace L. Traubel (New York, 1903) in *Nation*, 76 (1903), 401.

52. TWH, review of *Life of Walt Whitman* by Henry B. Binns, in *Nation*, 81 (1905), 469; TWH, *The New World and the New Book* (Boston, 1892), p. 101; *Contemporaries*, p. 79; *Nation*, 77 (1903), 487.

"Recent Minor Poetry" Higginson had previously reviewed the only volume of collected verse published in Lanier's lifetime; he found little of real poetic sentiment. Although "Corn" displayed a genuine feeling for nature, and "The Psalm of the West" had some moving passages, Higginson discovered "no symptom of relaxing that convulsive and startling mode of utterance" of the "Centennial Cantata." He concluded that the entire absence of simplicity spoiled everything.[53]

Lanier's death, and the subsequent publication of the tragic details of his life that accompanied a collection of his poetry, enabled Higginson to write about him again in the *Nation*. Responding, as he had repeatedly done with other poets, to personal character, he now called Lanier a man of genius whose fame would grow. If his verse was not simple, this must be excused and attributed to youth and ill health and "an almost morbid conscientiousness in the direction of certain theories of sound and phrase." "Sunrise" was declared to be his best poem, and Higginson recommended it to the young followers of Whitman, because it seemed to be constructed on Whitman's methods; but instead of "bald and formless iteration, it is everywhere suffused with music as with light; every stanza chants itself, instead of presenting a prosaic huddle of long lines." He viewed Lanier as the first distinctly southern poet—comparable in his lyricism to Poe.[54]

Now transformed from critic to advocate, Higginson noted in an article about Paul Hamilton Hayne that Lanier was "by far the most gifted of Southern bards." Comparing Lanier's manliness in life and poetry with Whitman's, he extolled this southerner's service in the Confederate Army in contrast to Whitman's hospital service for the North. There was "refined chivalry" in "The Symphony," but "fleshiness" in "Leaves of Grass." Lanier's poetry was always single-minded, noble, and pure. Higginson was as sympathetic to his portraits of southern scenes as he had been to Whittier's northern ones. (This appreciation for local color would cause him also to commend the Celtic scenes found in the early poetry of William Butler Yeats.) Higginson would never acknowledge that Lanier had praised Whitman, nor would he ever comment upon

53. *Nation*, 22 (1877), 16.
54. *Nation*, 39 (1884), 528.

Lanier's attacks on radical Reconstruction, but he did sympathetically quote the southerner: " 'with us of the younger generation in the South since the war, pretty much the whole of life has been merely not dying.' " Lanier, he concluded, was the "Sir Galahad among our American poets." [55]

Higginson's biographies of Fuller, Longfellow, and Whittier and his innumerable essays about other antebellum writers reveal his reliance upon the New England writers of the forties and fifties as a guide for developing postwar American literature. Although he was sympathetic to Emerson's plea for a distinctly American literature of insight, not tradition, he also agreed with a postwar critic, Horace Scudder, that half a dozen great writers before the war had provided a viable tradition. Higginson understood that Emerson had loosened American writers from their dependence upon European literature by having mastered a national idiom with distinctly American images. Emerson's condensed style packed each word with thought.[56]

Of lesser note, but important because its recognition in Europe gave American writers hope of ultimate acceptance, was Longfellow's work. Higginson suggested that though it lacked profundity it would survive for more homely qualities. Whittier, in contrast to Longfellow, he considered the poet of the people, the leading bard of the antislavery crusade, the Burns of the Merrimack Valley. If his poetry too often was marred by a superfluous moral, his skill in depicting American domestic life provided a tradition that united art and democracy.[57]

In praising Henry Thoreau and Margaret Fuller, Higginson was rare among postwar literary critics. He appreciated Thoreau's protest against worldly materialism which simultaneously stayed close to the world of labor and literature. Before the war, Higginson had been exceptional in praising *A Week on the Concord and Merrimack Rivers*; after the war he published sympathetic reviews

55. *The Chautauquan*, Jan. 1887, p. 230, April 1887, pp. 417, 418; *Nation, 51* (1895), 430.

56. *Henry Wadsworth Longfellow* (Boston, 1902); *John Greenleaf Whittier* (New York, 1902); *American Literature* pp. 134, 172–74.

57. TWH, *Longfellow*, p. 262; TWH, *Whittier*, pp. 3, 151, 152, 160; TWH, *Nation, 37* (1883), 515. Also see TWH "Longfellow's Poetry," *Nation, 34* (1882), 267–68, and "Whittier," *Nation, 60* (1892), 199–200.

of both *The Maine Woods* and *Cape Cod,* finding in them a lyrical strain superior to Emerson's. He also advocated the publication of Thoreau's journals. Margaret Fuller, he believed, stressed the ideal but still succeeded far more than Emerson in recognizing that thought and action were inseparable, that the best part of intellect was action. Higginson was her first sympathetic biographer, denying, unlike others, that egomania characterized her life.[58]

Higginson considered the work of Holmes and Lowell less admirable. He realized that recognition of Holmes' serious writing had been submerged by the popularity of his "delightful trifles," and yet Higginson failed to acknowledge the uniqueness of this writer's scientific orientation. Instead, he criticized the excessive stylistic self-consciousness and accepted the oversimplified view that Holmes should be remembered primarily because he epitomized the past ascendancy of Boston Brahminism. Higginson, to some degree, acknowledged his link to Holmes by recalling those antebellum *Atlantic* dinners at which Holmes' wit highlighted the proceedings, but he carefully noted little rapport with Holmes' conservatism regarding slavery.[59] Higginson did not recognize the similarity of his own literary style to that of Holmes. To follow Emerson was Higginson's desire, but he seldom emerged from Holmes' shadow.

Higginson found little in Lowell to commend except his odes commemorating Lincoln and Grant. He judged him personally disagreeable and his poetry lacking in finish. Also Lowell had arrogantly denigrated Thoreau and Fuller.[60]

Nathaniel Hawthorne was the greatest artist of the transcendental era, and indeed of American literature; Higginson judged him

58. TWH, review of *The Maine Woods* in *Atlantic Monthly, 14* (1864), 386–87; TWH, review of *Cape Cod* in *Atlantic Monthly, 15* (1865), 381; TWH, "Thoreau," *Atlantic Monthly, 16* (1865), 504–05; TWH, *Carlyle's Laugh and Other Surprises* (Boston, 1909), pp. 68–69; TWH, *Fuller,* pp. 303, 308–10.

59. TWH to E. C. Stedman, Nov. 16, 1873, Stedman MSS; TWH, *American Literature,* pp. 153–59; TWH, "Holmes' Emerson," *Nation, 26* (1878), 119, 120; *Nation, 39* (1885), 99.

60. TWH, *American Literature,* pp. 160–66, 193, 196; TWH to George Woodberry, Jan. 31, 1899, Woodberry MSS; TWH, review of *James Russell Lowell's Letters,* ed. C. E. Norton (New York, 1892) in *Nation, 47* (1893), 488; *Nation, 51* (1895), 297.

a writer who synthesized the two most important elements of the
American experience: the "spiritual subtlety" of transcendentalism
and the "moral earnestness" of puritanism. And Hawthorne was
a truly American writer because he chose his country's past for
literary themes. For Higginson, as for many other postwar writers,
Hawthorne served as model and inspiration. Higginson refrained
from criticizing either his denial of transcendental optimism or his
view about the central place of sin in human character. And he
uncritically accepted Hawthorne's assertion of having been an
Abolitionist in feeling but not in fact.[61]

Higginson, like most of his contemporaries, could find no value
in Melville. He was never aware of that author's literary worth.

About Edgar Allan Poe's work, he was uncertain. While conceding that Poe's place in "imaginative prose-writing is as unquestionable as Hawthorne's," Higginson suggested that he lacked
Hawthorne's philosophical profundity. Poe's failure to comprehend
Hawthorne's originality and his ferocious attack on Longfellow for
plagiarism convinced Higginson that no one had ever done more
in America to lower the tone of literary criticism. The "weird"
and lyric quality of Poe's verse—especially "Israfel"—attracted
Higginson despite the poet's excessive absorption "in his own
fantastic life of the mind." But he concluded that Poe's work was
a dangerous model to emulate and that the austere virtues, the
virtues of Emerson, Hawthorne, and Whittier, were more condu-
cive to quality.[62]

Higginson had confessed to Emerson that he was "lured by the
joy of expression itself." It accurately explained more than Higginson's literary interests, for much of his reform activity had
depended upon the desire to speak forcefully to people. Now he
called for a vigorous literary style, one which would appeal to
thirty million auditors who would reject stale pedantry. To attract
a mass audience through literature, the cultivated writer must
avoid mere ornamentation; he must make simplicity and freshness
his instruments of expression and be willing to revise his manu-

61. TWH, *American Literature*, pp. 185, 186; TWH, *Short Studies of American Authors* (Boston, 1880), pp. 6, 7; TWH, *Contemporaries*, p. 102.
62. TWH, *American Authors*, pp. 19, 20; TWH, *Nation*, 26 (1878), 328.

script thoroughly. He criticized Emerson for lacking freedom and "self-abandonment," but Higginson emphasized spontaneity far less than the need for culture. Unlike Emerson in the "American Scholar," he judged poise and proportion, not inspiration, to be the main ingredients of literary artistry. Learned and rational literary craftsmanship—with "one drop of nervous fluid" to distinguish it from the British product—was the formula bequeathed, in Higginson's view, by the antebellum New England writers.[63]

Higginson encouraged a didacticism and an ideological commitment in fiction which he had come to condemn in good poetry. Central to this concept was the role he envisioned for the postwar intellectual. Upon withdrawing active support for Reconstruction in 1867 he had said that American politics no longer needed the artist's skilled hand to do the plain work of politics. The writer's responsibility, however, should not be limited to mere felicity of expression: writers of romance should provide imaginative insights into American society and draw plans for shaping the nation's future. Men participating in politics were not able to do this and could not be expected to state the problem confronting the future. By utilizing and transcending the facts of daily life, and by using literary skill to convince his readers, the imaginative writer would be serving a major social function by illuminating society's problems and suggesting their solution. Such social consciousness was not demanded from the poet, who must seek the joy of expression and "fill the desires of the soul instead of subjecting the soul to external things." [64]

Higginson found in Hawthorne's fiction the best model of the writer as seer. Others like Charles Brokden Brown, Washington Irving, and James Fenimore Cooper, in their early portraits of America, lacked a larger insight, and too often they viewed America as merely a province of England. While Mrs. Stowe, in *Uncle Tom's Cabin*, had shown that Negroes, like Cooper's Indians, were a picturesque, heroic, and interesting race, her evangelical fervor and excessive melodrama hampered the credibility of the

---

63. TWH to Emerson, July 7, 1864, Higginson-Huntington MSS; TWH, *Atlantic Essays*, p. 19; "Literature as Art," *Atlantic Monthly*, 20 (1867), 746, 750; TWH, "Emerson," *Independent*, Oct. 29, 1868.
64. TWH, *American Authors*, p. 36.

tale. An American writer with Hawthorne's plastic imagination was needed to portray the variety of American character and explore the depths of individuals.[65]

Applying his criteria for good fiction to the work of Henry James, Higginson highly praised two early short stories—"Madonna of the Future" and "Madame de Mauve"—but he claimed that *Daisy Miller* and *The American* were ruined by "the conventional limits of a stage ending." These two books, like *Portrait of a Lady*, were chiefly objectionable to him because they stressed America's failure to prepare its people—depicted as rich and innocent—to deal with the immoral European aristocracy.[66]

James' attitude toward America was central to Higginson's criticism. Fleeing to Europe had a literary parallel in the author's indifference to accurate descriptions of American locales. James' care in describing European scenes and his failure to appreciate the cosmopolitan and cultured people living in America offended Higginson's national and personal pride. In response to James' assertion that a monarchical society is "more available for the novelist than any other," he argued that a republic develops "real individuality in proportion as it diminishes conventional distinctions." He concluded that James suffered from being out of touch with the mass of mankind. James, in turn, wished that "Higginsonian fangs" would stop "bespattering public periodicals with my gore." [67]

As James' reputation grew, Higginson, whose most critical comments predate *The Ambassador* and *The Golden Bowl*, came to appreciate his skill in character delineation. But he also became disdainful of the author's involved and often puzzling style; Higginson believed that James had rejected the standard of stylistic simplicity set by Thoreau, Hawthorne, and Emerson. And he would not forgive him for abandoning America and favoring everything that condemned America, nor for being like those writers who "become oblivious of the outer world altogether, and

65. TWH, *The New World and the New Book* (Boston, 1892), p. 64; Introduction to *Uncle Tom's Cabin* (New York, 1898), pp. vi, xii; *American Literature*, p. 127.

66. TWH, *American Authors*, pp. 53, 56, 58, 59.

67. Ibid., pp. 51, 53, 56: James quoted in Robert Falk, *The Victorian Mode in American Fiction 1865-1885* (East Lansing, 1965), pp. 92, 62.

entangle themselves more and more in intellectual subtleties of their own weaving." [68]

For a time it appeared to Higginson that Edward Bellamy would would become the American novelist as seer. In *Dr. Heidenhoff's Process* and *Miss Ludington's Sister*, romances running counter to the realism of James and Howells, he found imaginative conceptions unmatched since Hawthorne's work. But after the publication of his two most important novels of social analysis, *Looking Backward* and *Equality*, Higginson's sense of literary craftsmanship tempered his praise. He was enthusiastic about the author's ideas but felt that Bellamy lacked Hawthorne's technical skill. By the turn of the century, when Higginson reviewed American literary accomplishments, Bellamy was eliminated from his list of important writers.[69]

Higginson never accepted Mark Twain as more than a light humorist or *Huckleberry Finn* as more than regional literature. In his opinion, the best novelist of the postwar era was William Dean Howells. As early as 1862, in the same *Atlantic* article that attracted Emily Dickinson's attention, Higginson had become one of the first influential American critics to attack the dominant sentimental fiction of the day. Declaring that the familiar and commonplace should provide the material for fiction, he, like Howells, revered Jane Austen's treatment of everyday life with what Higginson called grace and Howells called an exquisite touch. In *Malbone*, Higginson had failed to follow his own advice about avoiding melodrama and an involved plot (in a later edition of the novel he complained that no one had believed that there actually had been a secret staircase in the home he had depicted), but he appreciated Howells' ability to do so. He recognized a skilled craftsman who sought to confront the "essential forces" of American society. He also liked his repugnance for the extravagant emotionalism of sentimental fiction and his allegiance, in the early books, to the imaginative romance. Assuring Higginson that he was aware of the moral function of the novel, Howells wrote to

68. TWH, review of *William Wetmore Story and His Friends* by Henry James in *Nation*, 77 (1903), 365, 366; *Nation*, 70 (1900), 361.
69. "The Return of the Ideal," *Woman's Journal*, July 19, 1884; TWH to E. C. Stedman, Feb. 10, 1888, Stedman MSS.

him of feeling "ashamed and sorry if my work did not teach a lenient, generous, and liberal life." Higginson, in 1879, responded favorably to *A Chance Acquaintance, Out of the Question,* and *The Lady of the Aroostook. Chance Acquaintance,* depicting a clash between an independent western woman and a Bostonian of caste and etiquette, contributed insights into the future of our society. "How is it to be stratified? How much weight is to be given to intellect, to character, to wealth, to antecedents, to inheritance?" Such questions again were posed to Higginson's satisfaction in Howells' farcical play, *Out of the Question,* where the natural gentleman confronts education, social standing, and wealth in Back Bay Boston.[70]

Higginson and Howells began to differ as early as the seventies. Higginson deplored Howells' declaration that *A Foregone Conclusion,* with its neurotic and hopeless characters, was his first genuine novel because neither lofty language nor idealized character was employed. Undersized characters dominated the book while full-sized humanity was absent, observed Higginson. Such devotion to the commonplace, if it meant omitting individuals with emotional or intellectual maturity, was not the new fiction he sought. Also *The Lady of the Aroostook,* which he largely approved, presented another objectionable part of Howells' early efforts at realism. "It was only necessary," Higginson suggested, "for a refined woman like the heroine to know the *fact* of the man's intoxication and not the facts." [71]

But when Howells, in *The Undiscovered Country,* wrote a romance, Higginson applauded and discerningly compared it to *The Blithedale Romance.* He also approved of its sweetness and wholesomeness. The publication of *The Rise of Silas Lapham* further pleased him. Judging that the characters, especially Irene Lapham, were sketched in full dimension, he wrote Howells: "You are trusting yourself in these deeper motives of human emotion in which I always wanted to see you—your place is with

70. TWH, *American Literature,* pp. 247-48; Everett Carter, *Howells and the Age of Realism* (New York, 1950), p. 44; Howells to TWH, Sept. 17, 1879, in *27th Annual Report of the Bibliophile Society,* ed. George Hellman (Cedar Rapids, 1929), p. 38; TWH, *American Authors,* pp. 36, 37.

71. Ibid.; Edwin Cady, *The Road to Realism* (New York, Syracuse, 1956), p. 185.

Tourganef & not with Trollope or even with James." Only
Turgenev, in Higginson's view, treated a variety of social classes.
Despite Howells' allegiance to the "photographic school" of realism, Higginson praised him for treating American social problems
in an optimistic way.[72]

Higginson thought that Howells' best book, despite the devotion
of the first six chapters to the hero's search for an apartment, was
A Hazard of New Fortunes. It appealed to the cultivated reformer
of principle who was interested in observing the variety of people
living in postwar urban America: the self-made capitalist, the
European-bred socialist, the aristocrat, the laborer. Confirmed
here also was Higginson's belief in the essential goodness of man
and in the eventual power of the ballot box to correct social evils.
Soon after reading the book, he wrote Howells: "If I could write
fiction as you do, I would leave criticisms to those who cannot
create." [73]

Higginson's response to *A Hazard of New Fortunes* marked the
height of rapport between the two men. Howells' increasing commitment, by the late eighties, to realistic fiction and to criticism of
American society began to trouble Higginson. Even their mutual
devotion to Turgenev became a source of difference. Higginson,
who had met Turgenev at a Paris meeting of the International
Literary Congress in 1878 and described him as uniting the "fine
benignant head of Longfellow with the figure of Thackeray,"
denied that the Russian was a truly realistic writer. Although at
first praising *Virgin Soil* (a reformist novel that advocated gradual
change, not revolution) as second only to *War and Peace,* he ultimately decided that Turgenev's greatness was best illustrated by
Poems in Prose, where allegory and aphorism abound. To Howells,
however, Turgenev was a model realist devoted to portraying the
common life without romantic plot and melodrama. And in
Howells' essays, *Criticism and Fiction,* the line that separated him
from Higginson was visible when he criticized those "pastured on
the literature of thirty or forty years ago . . . [who] preach
their favorite authors as all the law and prophets." Higginson, in

72. *Scribner's Monthly,* 20 (1880), 794; TWH to Howells, July 16, 1880, June
7, 1885, Howells MSS.

73. TWH diary, May 24, 1899; TWH to Howells, Jan. 30, 1891, Howells MSS.

response, called Howells a narrow critic: "It is not necessary, because one prefers apples, to condemn oranges." [74]

By comparing Howells to George Eliot, Higginson marked his position betwen the realists and their enemies. Eliot, unlike Howells, does not banish "the ideal side of life. . . . She only asserts the so-called little things of life to be equal in importance to the great, and does not claim for them a superior, much less an exclusive importance; . . . [she] does not deride the other half of art, and banish Raphael and Shakespeare to the domain of Jack the Giant-killer." [75]

Higginson also disagreed with some of Howells' social views. He did not support the anarchists convicted after the Haymarket riot and criticized Howells for doing so. He rejected the indictment of American society in *Traveler from Altruria*: to characterize America as a plutocracy ignored, in Higginson's view, the high degree of social democracy prevailing in America in the nineties.[76] Howells, he concluded, had become sad and morbid, and blinded to the noble and beautiful in life. Having lost sight of the basic theme of democratic literature—the dignity and inalienable value of the individual man—Howells had found in "altruism an entanglement as ineffectual as that met by Mr. James in introspection." Such social criticism further displayed by pessimistic determinists like Theodore Dreiser and Ellen Glasgow had brought American literature, Higginson complained, to a point where even Hawthorne's masterpieces were forgotten.[77]

Far worse, however, were the cynical writers who embraced the *fin de siècle* spirit and autocratically emphasized the stupidities of democratic government. "Better a thousand times to train a boy on Scott's novels or the Border ballads," argued Higginson, "than educate him, on the one side, that chivalry was a cheat and the troubadours imbeciles, and on the other hand, that universal suf-

74. Quoted in Abrahm Yarmolinsky, *Turgenev* (New York, 1926), p. 332; Howells, *Criticism and Fiction* (New York, 1891), p. 12; TWH, *New Book*, pp. 14, 219.

75. TWH, "George Eliot as Realist," *Harper's Bazar, 21* (1888), 198.

76. TWH to Howells, Feb. 22, 1895, Howells MSS; TWH to Brander Matthews, Oct. 31, 1892, Matthews MSS; *Nation, 51* (1895), 421; TWH, "A Social Revolution," *Harper's Bazar, 20* (1887), 774.

77. TWH, *New Book*, p. 11; *Nation, 70* (1900), 361; *Nation, 75* (1902), 290.

frage is an absurdity and the real need is to get rid of our voters." [78]

Insisting that a writer should be interested in more than the development of his own petty talent, he endeavored to separate himself from the reigning genteel writers and critics who sought to avoid major postwar social problems. In the tradition of his generation of Transcendentalists he still looked to experience as the microcosm of truth. Neither his allegiance to the ideal side of life nor to Scott's novels kept him from giving the highest praise to the "war photography" found in both *War and Peace* and *The Red Badge of Courage.* He fully appreciated Stephen Crane's ability to present "the real tumult and tatters of the thing itself." And he understood a part of Tolstoy's greatness when he wrote that *War and Peace* "reveals both the brilliancy of war and its tediousness and dreariness—its waste, aimlessness, and disconnection." [79]

But while he agreed with Howells by esteeming Crane and Tolstoy, Higginson remained a critic of America's realist and naturalist writers. They failed, in his opinion, to touch the essence of the American spirit by forsaking the optimism and faith in the individual; they failed to utilize, therefore, the basic reality of American society. At first he was hopeful that the triumph of the abolitionist crusade had returned the alienated intellectual to the center of American life, as a respected spokesman for society's problems and their solutions. Higginson came to fear, however, the result of fleeing democracy like Henry Adams and Henry James, disdaining it like Thomas Bailey Aldrich, or harshly criticizing it like either Howells or the naturalists. Such behavor, he believed, once again deprived America of intellectual leadership and alienated the intellectual. Higginson always rejected the idea that intellectual alienation might be, to a large degree, a permanent and even necessary thing.

Higginson so often reflected prevailing literary and social views that posterity has relegated him to anonymity and failed to recognize the degree of uniqueness that was his. His literary criticism, despite severe limitations, deserves attention because of his role

78. TWH, *American Literature,* p. 269.

79. TWH, "On Literary Tonics," *Independent,* Feb. 23, 1888; TWH, *Book and Heart: Essays on Literature and Life* (New York, 1897), pp. 41–46; TWH, "Recent Novels," *Harper's Bazar,* 21 (1888), 810.

in publishing Emily Dickinson and in praising Sidney Lanier's poetry, Thoreau's essays, and the work of Crane and Howells. His acute criticism of the day's most popular writers—Aldrich, Taylor, Stoddard, and Kipling—reveals a man who eludes the category of literary Brahmin.

20

The Man of Letters as Reformer

Higginson's dismal failure in fiction led him to other means of influencing society. To be recognized as an essayist and literary critic was insufficient. Somewhat defensively he reported that his nomination, in the fall of 1879, as the Republican representative from Cambridge to the Massachusetts legislature had been wholly unsought, but political office seemed worth trying. During the height of his abolitionist militancy he had said that men of principle could not participate in the compromises of politics. But now he distinguished himself from his Abolitionist ally, Abby Kelley Foster: "Probably I belong by temperament to the half-loaf party and she to that which will accept nothing short of the whole." Higginson's transformation was also reflected in his opposition to New Mexico's admission to the Union "because a vast majority of the population are of the most ignorant class of Spanish Americans, who cannot even speak the English language." And after his first term in the legislature he noted that "personal freedom is an absolute right, . . . suffrage is a relative right, belonging to a certain stage of human progress." [1]

Higginson's legislative record during two terms in office reveals the direction of his reform views in the early eighties. He supported political and economic rights for women by seeking to enfranchise them in town meetings and make them eligible for election to local school committees. A local law was enacted, but the legislature failed to provide the franchise or eligibility for state office to women.[2] His lifelong sympathy for the poor was shown

1. M. T. Higginson, *Higginson*, p. 298; Cambridge *Chronicle*, Nov. 8, 1879; TWH, "The Worcester Convention," *Woman's Journal*, Nov. 6, 1880.

2. Cambridge *Chronicle*, Nov. 6, 1880; *Journal of the House of Representatives of the Commonwealth of Massachusetts*, Feb. 2, 1880, p. 100, Feb. 19, 1880, p. 214, Apr. 4, 1881, p. 431, Feb. 4, 1880, p. 129, Feb. 5, 1880, p. 146.

in his vote with the majority to prevent the disfranchisement of veterans who were either tax delinquents or paupers; he was in the minority in opposing a bill to jail tramps and beggars. Bills requiring cities to pay their employees at intervals not exceeding seven days, and private employers to pay within fourteen days, passed with Higginson's support. But the Committee on Banks and Banking ruled "inexpedient" his motion to limit the interest rates savings banks charged on loans.[3]

Higginson voted against two reform measures during the two years in office. He joined the majority in defeating the extension to nonmanufacturing establishments of the ten-hour law for women and children. And again sympathetic to business he successfully supported the state's insurance companies in their fight against a bill which would have made them liable for the face value, rather than the depreciated value, of real property.[4]

Still interested in the religious pluralism that had attracted him to the Worcester Free Church and to the Free Religious Association, Higginson championed religious freedom. He led the unsuccessful legislative battle against banning the court testimony of witnesses who denied God's existence. His work on the legislature's Education Committee helped strengthen religious freedom in the Massachusetts public schools: instrumental in drafting and securing passage of a law limiting classroom Bible reading, Higginson approvingly witnessed the elimination of legislation which favored the "tenet of any particular sect of Christians." Classroom commentary on Biblical text also was prohibited, and parents, by written notice, could withdraw their children from participating in any Bible ceremony.[5]

What most impressed Higginson during his two years in the legislature was that a college man did not encounter prejudice and distrust from his less educated colleagues. In fact, undue respect, he observed, was given to the highly educated by those who knew

3. Ibid., Feb. 12, 1880, pp. 183–85, Apr. 20, 1880, pp. 485–86, Feb. 16, 1881, pp. 230–31, Mar. 23, 1880, pp. 368–69, Feb. 4, 1880, p. 130, Mar. 5, 1880, p. 298.

4. Ibid., Apr. 28, 1881, pp. 509–11, Mar. 4, 1880, pp. 292, 293.

5. Ibid., Jan. 22, 1880, p. 53; *House Document* No. 173, Feb. 27, 1880; *House Journal*, Feb. 27, 1880, p. 257; TWH, "After the Defeat," *The New Age*, Sept. 16, 1876.

far more than he did about the practical business which mainly occupies legislatures.[6]

Both in and out of office Higginson was one of America's most articulate spokesmen against the anti-Catholicism which swept New England in the last decades of the century. Denying Francis Parkman's allegation that Catholic women were so subservient to parish priests that the church would gain enormous power with the enfranchisement of women, he declared it absurd to believe that Catholicism endangered American institutions. The Catholic Church in this country was committed to religious liberty, he noted, and not only did not threaten the status quo but indeed opposed change and social reform.[7]

With President Charles W. Eliot and the Reverend Edward Everett Hale, Higginson defended the newly established Catholic parochial schools. Their rapid growth in the mid-eighties had been met by a counter-movement to force Catholic children into public schools, and in 1888 a School Inspection Bill (directed against parochial schools) was introduced in the legislature. Higginson returned to Beacon Hill to testify at the hearings. Citing past Protestant religious bigotry, exemplified by the burning of the Charlestown Ursuline Convent during his childhood and the anti-Catholic demonstrations of the "Know Nothing" movement during the fifties, he warned that the pending bill would renew such hate. To his listeners, a "howling audience of reactionaries," Higginson forthrightly asserted that if religious bigotry were revived then "it would not be necessary to go farther than this room to find those who would lead the mob." The bill's provisions, he argued, "would practically kill all experiments in the way of education, which are always made . . . in private and not in public schools.[8]

He preferred that the public schools seek to attract students by providing a better education than parochial schools. And when

6. TWH, "What Representative Government Means," *Woman's Journal*, June 19, 1880.

7. TWH, "The Roman Catholic Bugbear," *Woman's Journal*, Oct. 4, 1879; TWH to Marcus Conway, Feb. 13, 1881, Conway MSS; Arthur P. Stauffer, "Anti-Catholicism in American Politics, 1865–1900," Unpublished doctoral dissertation, Harvard University, 1933, p. 382.

8. TWH quoted in Katherine E. Conway and Mabel W. Cameron, *Charles Francis Donelly* (New York, 1909), p. 65; TWH diary, Mar. 27, 1888. See Barbara M. Solomon, *Ancestors and Immigrants* (Cambridge, 1956), pp. 42–58.

questioned, because of his experience as an author of history text-books, whether the state should interfere if private schools distorted historical material, he replied: "Heaven forbid!" The state merely should require attendance at a school which teaches reading and writing. Credit for the defeat of the 1888 bill was given to Higginson and Eliot. A school bill ultimately passed, but it was a victory for the friends of religious tolerance: it simply required that children annually attend any public or private school for twenty weeks.[9]

When anti-Catholicism combined with nativist sentiment in attacks against Irish and Italian immigrants during the nineties, Higginson defined Americanism from the public platform. Invited to speak at a memorial service in 1891 for John Boyle O'Reilly, poet and editor of the Catholic newspaper *The Pilot*, he maintained that America had failed "if it was only large enough to furnish a safe and convenient place for the descendants of Puritans and Anglo-Saxons, leaving Irishmen and Catholics outside." [10]

Although northern intellectuals like Eliot and Howells also defended immigration and decried intolerance toward Catholic immigrants, Higginson went beyond this. Facing the rising anti-Semitism in the nineties and the prejudice against Jewish immigrants, he neither echoed the anti-Semitic attitudes of Longfellow, Lowell, and Norton nor ignored anti-Semitism's existence as did Eliot, Howells, and other ordinarily reliable opponents of bigotry. Instead, he extolled the lack of drunkards among Jewish immigrants and suggested to the spokesmen of racial purity that "Jews from whatever quarter, have probably a less mingled descent than most of those who deprecate their arrival." [11]

When Thomas Bailey Aldrich expressed in verse the fear of America's "Unguarded Gates," a fear shared by many other intellectuals, Higginson replied:

> Of all nations this is the last where we can regard newcomers
> as anything but American in the making. . . . Those who

9. Conway, *Donelly*, p. 67; Stauffer, "Anti-Catholicism," p. 258; Robert W. Lord, *History of the Archdiocese of Boston*, 3 (Boston, 1945), 116, 118, 131.

10. *A Memorial to John Boyle O'Reilly* (Boston, 1891), p. 40.

11. Kermit Vanderbilt, "Howells Among the Brahmins," *New England Quarterly*, 35 (1962), 303, 306-07; TWH, *Book and Heart*, p. 155. For a discussion of

are appalled by the aspect of the latest arrivals are apt to forget the looks of some that preceded them. Those early squalid
crowds have simply vanished in their descendants. . . . No
race has ever yet submitted to privation merely for the love
of it.

But he believed that the new American, though transformed, would
always be distinguishable.[12]

Against the outspoken advocates of Anglo-Saxon superiority he
denied a monopoly of virtue by any race. For Higginson, as for
most of his contemporaries, "race" was confused with religious,
national, and ethnic groups.

The Irish race has its characteristic faults, partly the result
of temperament partly of oppression; but I maintain that a
due proportion of Irish admixture will help, not hinder American society: through the sunny nature of the race, its humor,
its physical courage, its warmth of heart, and its strong domestic affections.

Unique in rejecting both the Anglo-Saxon conformity and melting-
pot conceptions, he was some two decades ahead of his time in
advocating the goal of cultural pluralism. Higginson believed that
the American environment would bring harmony among diverse
groups to prevent anarchy, while innate temperamental characteristics peculiar to each "race" would assure a stimulating diversity.
"It is immigration," he said, "not natural increase which has made
the material greatness of this country." [13] By combining environ-
mentalism and racial views in his conception of cultural pluralism
Higginson could optimistically predict the future: he envisioned a
country with perpetual variety and increasing tolerance.

His continuing activity for woman's rights had similar assumptions. As an editor of the *Woman's Journal* from 1870 to 1884,
with Lucy Stone and Henry Blackwell, Higginson's articles in

anti-Semitism see Martin B. Duberman, *James Russell Lowell* (Boston, 1966), pp.
307–10.

12. *Book and Heart*, pp. 156–59, 163.

13. TWH, "The Physique of Irish Americans," *Woman's Journal*, June 21,
1884; Milton M. Gordon, *Assimilation in American Life* (Oxford, 1964), pp. 86,
136, 150.

this weekly newspaper of the Massachusetts Woman's Suffrage Association argued that women must be enfranchised in order to achieve self-respect and self-protection, not because their temperaments were the same as men. His negative response to the theme of Sarah Orne Jewett's novel about an unmarried woman physician, *A Country Doctor*, again reveals the emphasis that he placed upon the innate character of disadvantaged groups. Suggesting that *A Country Doctor* could be more accurately titled "The New Celibacy," because it held that nature by having produced more women than men had decreed the naturalness of celibacy for those women who remained unmarried, Higginson asserted that it was important to every man or woman to have the experience of love, marriage, and parentage. Although opposing self-supporting wives and believing in inherent physical and psychological limitations of women, he still denied that women existed only for producing and rearing children. Yet these responsibilities were foremost and brooked no exceptions.[14]

Higginson was no more equalitarian in championing woman's legal and political rights than in advocating Irish and Negro rights. Woman's innate domesticity—and here the childlike Negro and the strong domestic affections of Irishmen had a parallel—was among her natural qualities. He characterized women as deductive, instinctive, intuitive, and imaginative. And "as for tears, long may they flow! They are symbols of that mighty distinction of sex." Part of his advice to women pleading for political rights was an admonition against wearing eyeglasses because they were so unbecoming to a woman, disfiguring her face and depriving it of much of its power.[15]

During Reconstruction Higginson had found woman's rights agitation competing with the freedman's cause; in the eighties it vied with civil service reform for his support. In Massachusetts, in 1882, one Republican gubernatorial candidate favored woman's suffrage and the other stressed civil service reform. Unlike Lucy

14. Lois B. Merk, "Massachusetts and the Woman-suffrage Movement," Unpublished doctoral dissertation, Radcliffe College, 1956, pp. 16, 25; TWH, "Too Many Voters Already," *Woman's Journal*, Feb. 8, 1879; TWH, "The New Celibacy," *Woman's Journal*, Aug. 23, 1884; TWH, *Common Sense About Women* (Boston, 1881), pp. 40, 250.

15. Ibid., pp. 14, 17, 167; *Woman's Journal*, Feb. 28, 1880.

Stone, Henry Blackwell, and other prominent woman's rights reformers, Higginson supported Robert Bishop, the civil service advocate. After Bishop won the nomination and opposed Democrat Benjamin Butler, who ran on an equal rights plank, Higginson again differed with his woman's rights friends. When Butler was elected, the *Woman's Journal* contained another Higginson attack on him. By mutual agreement with the other editors he temporarily terminated connections with the newspaper.[16] But after returning, he opposed Butler's effort in 1883 for re-election, called him a thoroughly false and unscrupulous man, and suggested that the woman's suffrage movement "must be more matured in the public mind before it can wisely be submitted to an ordeal of battle." [17] It should not ally itself, he concluded, with any political party. Increased civil service reform must be foremost so that when women were enfranchised their votes would not be undermined by political corruption.

Higginson subsequently was ostracized from the Massachusetts woman's rights organization; his name was stricken from the society's long list of vice-presidents, and he was assailed by its leaders both at woman's rights meetings and in private letters. After a heavy public attack on him, Fanny Garrison Villard commented: that he seemed to want to go back on his record; she attributed his views to a "latter-day conservatism." And another advocate relished hearing "St. Thomas dealt with in such a manner." Hurt but undaunted, Higginson continued to contribute money to the Massachusetts organization, permanently left the *Woman's Journal*, and began writing for *Harper's Bazar*, the popular woman's magazine that had a circulation of 100,000.[18]

Higginson had become too sympathetic to the mugwump movement by 1876 to change his course on the priority of civil service reform. Because of bipartisan corruption it took a high-powered

16. Merk, "Woman-suffrage," pp. 84–96; TWH, "Women and Civil Service Reform," *Woman's Journal*, Nov. 12, 1881.

17. TWH, "On Butler's Message," *Woman's Journal*, Jan. 13, 1883; TWH, "Let Us Have Peace," *Woman's Journal*, Nov. 10, 1883; TWH, "Woman Suffrage and the Republican Party," *Woman's Journal*, Dec. 8, 1883.

18. William Lloyd Garrison, II to Ellen Garrison, Jan. 26, 31, 1887, Garrison Family MSS; Fanny Garrison Villard to Wm. L. Garrison, Jr., Jan. 31, 1887, Garrison MSS; TWH, "After Fifteen Years," *Woman's Journal*, Dec. 17, 1884.

microscope, he insisted, to distinguish the faint difference between Democrats and Republicans. He became a leader in 1884 of the Massachusetts Independent Republicans who bolted the party and urged the Democrats to nominate a worthier candidate than Republican James G. Blaine. At a Boston meeting prior to the Democratic convention, Higginson joined other mugwumps in urging the Democrats to nominate Grover Cleveland. Largely urban middle-class Protestants, the Massachusetts men were prominent lawyers, writers, journalists, and college professors and included the presidents of Amherst, Williams, and Harvard. Higginson offered a resolution asking other Republicans to oppose the ticket of Blaine and Logan because they had been nominated in "absolute disregard of the reform sentiment of the nation, and represent political methods and principles to which we are unalterably opposed." [19]

When Cleveland was nominated in mid-July, Higginson, a member of the national Independent Republican committee, met in New York City under Carl Schurz's direction to marshal support for the Democrat. Later, at a public rally in Boston, he was among the featured speakers. "The secret of this movement," Higginson announced, "is that it represents the future and not the past. It belongs to modern history, not ancient." [20] Also speaking in New York, New Jersey, and New England, he defined ancient history by suggesting that Republican efforts to "wave the bloody shirt" exaggerated accounts of current outrages against southern Negroes. He deplored having southern Negroes constantly used merely as pawns or dice in a game played by Republican political tricksters. He attributed the Negro's declining vote to lack of interest, not to the shot gun and tissue ballots. The Mississippi plan to disenfranchise them deserved no more criticism than the method by which the Republicans carried Louisiana in 1876, or Indiana in the 1880's. The major issue in the 1884 election, he said, was that the Republican party of Lincoln and Sumner was now controlled by

19. New York *Evening Post*, Oct. 4, 1884; Gordon S. Wood, "The Massachusetts Mugwumps," *New England Quarterly*, *33* (1960), 435; Geoffrey Blodgett, "The Mind of the Boston Mugwump," *Mississippi Valley Historical Review*, *44* (1962), 617; TWH quoted in Raymond L. Bridgman, *The Independents of Massachusetts in 1884* (Boston, 1885), pp. 8–9.

20. TWH diary, July 22, Oct. 1, 1884; quoted in Bridgman, *Independents*, pp. 36–37; Solomon Griffin, *People and Politics* (Boston, 1923), p. 292.

"Star route contractors and naval speculators." Higginson concluded that the "Civil War has long since ended and we must test
men by their fidelity to the great works of peace." This view especially appealed to his younger mugwump allies who had not experienced the antislavery and civil rights battles of the past.[21]

To those who could not support Cleveland when it was disclosed
that he had once sired a child out of wedlock, Higginson suggested
that political virtue, not chastity, was among the qualifications for
the presidency. He refused to cease supporting the candidate because of this sin of early manhood. Conceding that he would not
have supported Cleveland if he were being considered for the su-
perintendency of a girls' school, he said that even though sexual sins
of men are far greater than those of women, the latter cannot be ex-
onerated unless it is assumed that they are an "absolutely helpless
and irresponsible class of beings." [22] Again he differed from most
woman's rights advocates.

Just prior to the election, Higginson met Cleveland (who was a
cousin on his paternal grandmother's side) and judged him unpol-
ished, honest, frank, and strong. To the mugwumps, Cleveland was
a refreshing contrast to the wily corrupt politicians so successful
since the Civil War. Although Higginson and his friends would
have preferred one of their own men—honest *and* polished—they
understood that polished men did not win national elections.
Sharing the joy of Cleveland's victory, Higginson denied he was
seeking the rewards of presidential patronage. He wrote the President regarding the appointment of a certain Massachusetts man, "I
have neither endorsed him nor any one else for any office, but have
steadily refused all such requests." [23]

Having become chairman of the Cambridge Reform Club, he received the Democratic nomination for Congress in 1888. At first deciding to decline (he was 65 years old), he not only changed his

21. W. L. Garrison, II to Ellen Garrison, Oct. 29, 1884, Garrison Family MSS;
quoted in *Evening Post,* Oct. 4, 1884.

22. TWH, "Public and Private Virtue," *Woman's Journal,* Aug. 30, 1884; TWH
to Moncure Conway (Aug. 1884), Conway MSS; TWH, "To Tell the Truth,"
Woman's Journal, Aug. 9, 1884; TWH, "Justice to Men," *Woman's Journal,*
Sept. 13, 1884.

23. TWH diary, Nov. 7, 1884, June 25, 1888; TWH to Levi Thaxter, Oct. 30,
1884, Higginson MSS; TWH to Cleveland, July 18, 1885, Cleveland MSS, Library
of Congress.

mind, but wrote in his diary: "It seems to me very likely that I shall be elected, & must make my plans accordingly." Standing on a plank which called for civil service extension and judicious reduction of the tariff, he was opposed by General Nathaniel P. Banks. The National Association of Wool Manfacturers, the Home Market Club, the Chamber of Commerce, and various banking and brokerage companies supported Banks and high tariff. Banks sought to attract businessmen, Negroes, and laborers by opposing the forces of slavery and free trade—the latter labeled "slavery for the American laborer." Higginson, on the other hand, argued that tariff reduction would benefit both business and labor. To stress his antislavery record he publicized his colonelcy of the first Negro regiment and successfully sought the support of the Abolitionists Frank Sanborn, William Lloyd Garrison, Jr., and Lloyd McKim Garrison.[24]

But Sanborn, the Garrisons, and Higginson relied on past reputations, not on their present attitudes toward the Negro. Massachusetts Republicans had attacked Higginson for condoning the "murder and fraud" by which Mississippi Negroes were being disenfranchised. He had denied the presence of injustice, defended the complicated election laws designed to confuse Negro voters, and said that southern literacy tests were comparable to the ones in the North. "There is the same prejudice here against the colored man that is found in the South," Higginson declared. Republicans denounced him for believing that education should be paramount. The southern Negro, Higginson responded, had *voluntarily* decided to quit politics until he acquired education and property. Race riots were less indicative of southern conditions than that a generous amount of money had been spent to school former slaves, he said. Similarly, Higginson criticized George W. Williams' *History of the Negro Race in America* for its "lack of judicious spirit" on the race question, and for the black author's "curious feeling of petty hostility" toward Massachusetts to which he owed his education.[25]

24. TWH diary, Sept. 23, 24, Oct. 4, 1888; TWH to A. Higginson, Sept. 26, 1888, Higginson MSS; William F. Phelps to Nathaniel P. Banks, Sept. 25, 1888, Banks MSS.

25. TWH to Editor, Sept. 28, 1885, Oct. 1, 1885, Boston *Advertiser*, Sept. 29, 1885, Oct. 3, 1885; quoted in Boston *Globe* Oct. 24 1888; TWH, review of *The*

Looking back on the antislavery crusade, Higginson chided Abolitionists for their harsh judgments and suggested that

> In the mortgaged and deeply indebted plantations of Virginia, the most enlightened slaveholder rarely had the means of removing his slaves. . . . The more we dwell on this complicated situation . . . the more charitable we become toward those exceptional slaveholders who had opened their eyes to its evil, yet found themselves bound hand and foot.

Higginson's new fondness for the Democrats had heightened his desire for sectional reconciliation and his repugnance for "waving the bloody shirt." [26] He had lost his zeal for Negro rights (and even the memory of it), but maintained a noblesse oblige attitude. Those antebellum southerners who had seen slavery's evil and felt powerless to abolish it could evoke empathy now from a powerless mugwump reformer confronting the problems of his own era.

There was one former Abolitionist who refused to become charitable toward either slaveowners or those who had turned against radical Reconstruction. Frederick Douglass wielded a heavy blow to Higginson's election chances by issuing an open letter in support of Banks. Higginson and his allies by "having left the Republican party, are traitors, not only to that political organization, but to the cause of liberty itself," said Douglass. Conciliating the South was necessary, responded Higginson, because radical Reconstruction had proven that force had failed. "My friend Fred Douglass, who began his life by running away from a slaveowner," he told an election rally, "seems to have now convinced himself that he is a slaveowner, and everyone who differs from him must be brought back." [27]

Understandably, one of Higginson's supporters found Cambridge's Negro ward hostile to the Democratic candidate. "I admit," reported Lloyd McKim Garrison, "that my grandfather's sanguine expectations of the near triumph and glory of the negro

---

History of the Negro Race in America by George Williams (New York, 1883), *Atlantic Monthly*, *51* (1883), 564–69. See Stanley P. Hershson, *Farewell to the Bloody Shirt* (Indiana, 1962), pp. 129–33.

26. TWH, "William Lloyd Garrison," *Atlantic Monthly*, *57* (1886), 124.

27. Cambridge *Chronicle*, Oct. 27, 1888; Boston *Globe*, Oct. 24, 1888.

race seem to me to have little prospect of ultimate fulfillment. . . . I confess to the belief that the negro, beyond his sweet disposition and courtesy, has not the qualifications for a very useful citizen, though he may be a peaceful, industrious, and orderly one." [28]

Not only did Higginson fail to win traditional Negro support away from the Republicans but other flaws in his credentials alienated some normally Democratic voters. During the great labor strikes of 1877 he had remained silent, pleading lack of knowledge and the primacy of the woman's rights cause. But while serving in the Massachusetts legislature he had been no friend to labor. And in 1884 he had criticized Wendell Phillips for championing labor, arguing that unlike the antislavery movement—a great moral movement so logically simple—the proper relationship between capitalists and laborers was difficult to determine. Higginson made no comment in 1887 when 700 strikes occurred in Massachusetts, twice as many as the five previous years.[29] In the following year, however, during a major strike by conductors of Boston and Cambridge horsecars, he revealed his position with characteristic fanfare.

Affiliated with the Knights of Labor, the strikers declared their sympathy with striking coal handlers in New York and New Jersey against monopolistic corporations. Cambridge's mugwump Mayor, William E. Russell, who was a dependable ally of business but also cognizant of the political need to placate the large number of laborers in east Cambridge, initially supplied police protection to enable the streetcars to continue operating. But with the outbreak of violence he pleaded with the company to discontinue its service. Refusing to submit this dispute over the work schedule to the State Board of Arbitration, and succeeding in the recruitment of non-union men (many Harvard students volunteered), the company waited until the mayor summoned two companies of state militia, and the strike was broken.[30]

From the strike's outset, Higginson, like most mugwumps, had

28. Lloyd McKim Garrison to TWH, Nov. 15, 1888, Higginson-Barney MSS.

29. TWH, "Wendell Phillips," *Nation, 38* (1884), 118; Geoffrey Blodgett, "Massachusetts Democrats During the Cleveland Era," Unpublished doctoral dissertation, Harvard University, 1960, p. 179.

30. Boston *Evening Transcript*, Feb. 10, 1887; Blodgett, "Massachusetts Democrats," pp. 103, 127.

little sympathy for locked-out union men. Observing the physical clashes occurring between the strikers and the new nonunion men, and then between the strikers and the police, his antagonism to the union men grew. During a union solidarity parade Higginson purposely boarded one of the horsecars. Amid a fusilade of stones he rode through the picket line, ostentatiously standing on the car's open platform. After witnessing the battles between the strikers and policemen all around him, and being hit by a flying stone, he recalled that only his Anthony Burns efforts and army experiences had rivaled this confrontation with violence. "Find myself," he noted, "enjoying this little danger as of yore." [31]

Having supported labor in the Amesbury strike of 1852 and having criticized businessmen for taking no stand against slavery, Higginson had become sympathetic to the enlightened philanthropic businessman. During the seventies, eighties, and nineties his "Aristocracy of the Dollar" lecture repeatedly hailed the social responsibility of the businessman. Recognizing its similarity to his own Gospel of Wealth, Andrew Carnegie warmly praised it. And many other influential businessmen applauded and financed mugwump efforts. But labor reformers, Higginson admitted, were wholly unsympathetic to his position. Organized labor, in his view, threatened individualism, social peace, and the necessary harmony between capital and labor. Learning at this time that the Haymarket anarchists had been convicted of murder, he publicly supported the decision on the grounds that all of them, because of common design, were equally guilty of murder. It was wrong for others to petition to save their lives.[32]

Higginson's initial optimism about his chance for election was shattered by Cleveland's defeat and his own inability to win either Negro or labor support: a mugwump candidate's success depended upon winning the votes of both the men of Harvard College and

31. Ibid., pp. 625, 626; TWH diary, Feb. 2, 17, Mar. 4, 1887.

32. "Aristocracy of the Dollar," New York *Tribune*, April 18, 1876. Andrew Carnegie to TWH, Dec. 10, 1884, Higginson-Barney MSS; TWH diary, Jan. 19, Dec. 26, 1877; on Haymarket see *Independent*, Sept. 22, 1887, and *Nation*, 46 (1888), 18. The aristocracy theme is repeated by Higginson in "The Antidote to Wealth," *Woman's Journal*, Aug. 4, 1877; *The Word Philanthropy* (Boston, 1875); "The Antidote to Wealth," *Harper's Bazar*, 29 (1896), 16; "Aristocracy at Market Price," *Independent*, Dec. 8, 1898; Amherst *Student*, Feb. 4, 1893.

the slums. Without this, Higginson was just another "miserable mugwump" in a normally Republican congressional district. The Massachusetts law of 1887 which exempted veterans from needing civil service qualifications for public office, and now the defeat of Cleveland and the Democrats, profoundly discouraged Higginson and other mugwumps.[33] The fruits of nearly two decades of tariff and civil service agitation had been destroyed. It appeared that Higginson's past efforts for Negro rights, radical Republicanism, and mugwump reform had been rebuffed.

Soon after his election loss Higginson turned to the newly organized Boston Nationalist Club. He previously had heard the ideas of Edward Bellamy, Henry George, Richard Ely, and William P. Bliss during the meetings of the American Social Science Association and the Round Table Club. Bellamy, who had just published *Looking Backward*, wrote Higginson that free trade could become a reality only after the nationalization of industry. Civil service reform, he maintained, was an essential administrative step toward ultimate nationalization. This interest in mugwump reforms and Higginson's rejection at the polls helped move him to join Edward Everett Hale, Julia Ward Howe, Lucy Stone, and William Dean Howells as members of the Boston Nationalist Club. He was comfortable in an organization which termed itself of Brahmin caste and expressly sought members who commanded social respect and exhibited "the prestige of their social position and the force of their intellect." [34]

But he had reservations: he did not support the nationalization of all industries. In Bellamy's magazine, the *Nationalist*, Higginson granted the existence of an increasing number of persons who wanted government ownership of the telegraph, railroad, and gas industries. Believing that he was looking in the same direction as Bellamy, he declared: "I have made up my mind that the tendency of events is now towards Nationalism—or State Socialism, if you

33. Wood, "Massachusetts Mugwumps," p. 447; Fred H. Harrington, *Fighting Politician: Major General N. P. Banks* (Philadelphia, 1948), p. 211; Cambridge *Chronicle*, Nov. 10, 1888; TWH to A. Higginson, Nov. 7, 1888, Higginson MSS.

34. TWH diary, Jan. 10, Feb. 22, 1889; Bellamy to TWH, Jan. 1, 188[9], Higginson-Barney MSS; Arthur Morgan, *Edward Bellamy* (New York, 1944), p. 251; Cyrus F. Willard, "The Nationalist Club of Boston," *The Nationalist*, 1 (1889), 16–20.

please—and am prepared to go a few steps farther, at any rate, in that direction." [35] And to show his concern for the plight of the laborer, Higginson wrote "Heirs of Time" for the *Nationalist*, the poem which predicted that in the future, the patient armies of the poor would reap their just rewards.[36]

During an age of momentous farmer and labor protest, and of reform frustrations, the plea for patience in the present was more indicative than the talk of future socialism. Also revealing was the Nationalist Club's constitution: "We advocate no sudden or ill considered change; we make no war upon individuals; we do not censure those who have accumulated immense fortunes simply by carrying to a logical end the false principles on which business is now based." Even the radical nature of *Looking Backward* diminishes when it is recalled that it suggests that the labor strife of the nineteenth century had been subsidized by scheming capitalists and that it fails to mention the Negro. When a second Nationalist Club was organized in 1891, advocating immediate reforms like the eight-hour day and subsequently supporting the Populists in 1892 and 1894, Higginson no longer was a member.[37]

Besides ignoring the farmer's protests, Higginson viewed Henry George's analysis of the American land problem as excessively critical and pessimistic. George, he charged in 1889, had not proven that land monopolies existed. Granting the legal right of the state to equalize land, Higginson suggested the impossibility of such action unless some very great wrong could be shown to upset the "essential conservatism of a self-governing people in all that relates to property." He did not understand that George, unlike Bellamy, wanted a mixed economy. By 1895, amid economic depression, Higginson pronounced himself sixty per cent socialist but simultaneously deplored Socialists' desire to equalize and charged that they ignored the need for highly trained leaders and placed manual labor on a level with brain labor. Also there was danger of a latent tyranny in the discipline required by a full socialistic program. Rejecting, then, the equalitarian values of socialism, he argued that

35. TWH, "Step by Step," *Nationalist*, 1 (1889), 147; TWH to Editor, *Nation*, 48 (1889), 505–06.

36. *Nationalist*, 1 (1889), 5.

37. Ibid., p. 16; Arthur Mann, *Yankee Reformers in the Urban Age* (Cambridge, Mass., 1954), p. 158.

it was not the disparity of wealth that was wrong but rather the awful waste inherent in a system of unchecked competition.[38]

Eventually accepting George's assertion that large tracts of land were monopolized by big companies and a few individuals, Higginson still maintained that no new theory of property could essentially affect this situation, for, granted that the land belongs to the whole community, that was the way the community wished it to be used. And wealthy philanthropists, who might be swayed by Howells' *Traveler from Altruria*, could not be expected to act since Bellamy and George failed to reconcile their differences. At a time when the antitrust movement was gaining support, Higginson, in 1896, wrote: "Corporations do not pay salaries of twenty thousand dollars because it amuses them, but because the man whom they pay is worth that to them. . . . We have to deal with a world where certain men are born with certain gifts." [39]

The impact of socialist ideas, however limited, influenced Higginson's thought. He would join J. G. Phelps Stokes, Upton Sinclair, and Clarence Darrow in 1905 to support an Intercollegiate Socialist Society, not to develop but to foster study of a "great movement." Socialism, he suggested three years later, could be a remedy for many of the great existing ills of society, and had to be begun by municipal governments.[40] This "gas and water socialism" rather than the more systematic plans of George or Bellamy, attracted Higginson. Neither in the nineties nor during the Progressive era would he support third-party politics to initiate socialism.

He was as pleased with Cleveland's victory in 1892 as he had been in 1884. And when the Democrats repudiated the President's gold policy and nominated William Jennings Bryan in 1896, Higginson desired a narrow McKinley victory to punish the Democratic defectors to Bryan. Refusing, however, to support either McKinley or Bryan, he reluctantly voted for the Republican candidate despite a professed natural inclination for the underdog.[41]

38. TWH to Wm. Lloyd Garrison, Jr., Mar. 10, 1889, Garrison Family MSS; TWH, *Concerning All of Us* (New York, 1892), p. 195; Newspaper clipping, Mar. 18, May 15, 1895, Higginson MSS.

39. *Concerning All of Us*, pp. 72, 73; E. Bellamy to TWH, Jan. 21, 1890, Higginson-Barney MSS; TWH, *Book and Heart*, pp. 169–70, 176.

40. Boston *Post,* July 18, 1908.

41. TWH diary, Nov. 8, 1892; TWH to Brander Matthews, Aug. 30, 1896, Matthews MSS.

Cleveland's hard-money policy and low-tariff statements, in line with other mugwump sympathies, were not his only attractions. Higginson, having declared in 1892 that the American mission was not to conquer distant races, viewed him as an able opponent of growing imperialist sentiments. The President's protection of Hawaiian independence against American buccaneers like Sanford Dole was encouraging. During the Venezuelan boundary dispute with British Guiana in 1895, when the Monroe Doctrine was invoked and war threatened in order to stop British interference, Higginson (unlike Schurz, Eliot, and Godkin) had agreed with Cleveland's hard-policy line. "I hate jingoism and wholly deprecate war," Higginson declared; but he trusted the President and believed that if Britain were not checked she would threaten America's plans for an Isthmus canal. Touched for a time by the possibilities of an aggressive foreign policy, he had said that America "should look with sympathy on every [Latin] American colony's wish to detach itself from the parent Europe, even though the jingo spirit which I hate is mixed up in it." [42]

Higginson soon learned that stronger than the desire to give self-determination to small nations was his countrymen's love for imperialist domination. When most remained silent or joined in the jingoist chorus, he published an essay charging that "it is the trophies of Great Britain which will not allow Lodge and Roosevelt to sleep." The notion that Anglo-Saxons should control Latin America wrongly assumed that "self-government is unavailable for those who speak Spanish." When magazines glorified the Anglo-Saxon race and even Howells wrote of the unmorality of the Latin races, Higginson was an important minority voice. He remained unconvinced by Senator Henry Cabot Lodge's admonition to him that "we must make up our minds whether we are dominant in the Western hemisphere. . . . The old merchants of New England from whom you and I are descended," Lodge lectured, "would be pressing Congress to take vigorous action instead of trembling with fear lest we should do anything, as the present money power does." Neither was Higginson calmed by the appointment of Theodore

42. *Harper's Bazar*, 25 (1892), 163; TWH to Frank Higginson, Dec. 26, 1895, Higginson MSS; TWH to Wendell Phillips Garrison, Nov. 22, 1895, Garrison Family MSS; TWH to Editor, Boston *Transcript*, Dec. 23, 1895.

Roosevelt as Assistant Secretary of the Navy. With understatement, Secretary John D. Long admitted to Higginson that Roosevelt's energy sometimes made him uncomfortable. But he was certain that Roosevelt would not cause him the slightest trouble.[43]

The efforts of Roosevelt and other jingoists caused Long and Higginson more than just annoyance. When war over Cuba threatened in April 1898, Higginson noted in *Harper's Bazar* that "war is sweet to those who have never tried it." He called for a peaceful solution and claimed that the American Civil War had been fought only after many decades had proven that no peaceful solution was possible. But he realized that war fever had raged so out of control that the conflict was imminent.[44]

Once the news was received that the Spanish-American War had started, Higginson attended a rally of Harvard students held in the Yard. Called upon to speak he declared: "The war has begun, whether it be right or wrong, that is no longer our concern. It is our war, and we must finish it come what may." But in print he displayed sadness: although peace or war was "now beyond our personal control, we must only hope and fully believe that the new generation" will show its fathers' courage "with some added wisdom from being born in a later world." To the war enthusiasts he warned that it is "an added evil of war—which is in itself an unnatural and evil thing—that it becomes fascinating in the telling, whatever it was at the time." [45]

Momentarily excited by the "great news" of Admiral George Dewey's victory at Manila, he soon understood that only great resistance by moderates could keep the United States from global imperialism. If America succumbed, he warned, the traditional safeguards of the Monroe Doctrine would be lost because Latin America then would become open to European intervention. Here his views were representative of the small groups of articulate anti-

43. TWH, "The School of Jingoes," *Essays for the Chap-Book*, ed. Henry H. Boyeson (Chicago, 1896), p. 141; William Dean Howells, *My Literary Passions* (New York, 1895), p. 182; Lodge to TWH, Mar. 25, 1896, Long to TWH, Apr. 10, 1897, Higginson-Barney MSS.

44. *Harper's Bazar*, 31 (1898), 327; TWH to Moncure Conway, May 2, 1898, Conway MSS.

45. Newspaper clipping, May 4, 1898, Higginson MSS; *Harper's Bazar*, 31 (1898), 391.

expansionists.[46] Although fully qualified by family to adopt the prevailing Anglo-Saxon position, once again Higginson showed the same antipathy to reverence for all things English which he had displayed in supporting a distinctly American literature and in advocating non-English immigration. A fundamental belief in individualism, in the self-development of disadvantaged groups, always tempered his paternalistic and racial assumptions.

With American occupation of Wake Island and Puerto Rico, by July 1898, and the new demands for acquiring Hawaii, he had to concede that "strive as we may to withstand the perilous fear of imperialism, we can never again lead, as a nation, the detached and comparatively irresponsible life we used to lead." But to those who exulted at America's military might and the quick defeat of Spain, he recalled the quarterdeck admonition: "Don't cheer boys; don't you see the poor fellows are dying." And as the United States Senate prepared to consider the ratification of the peace treaty, at the end of 1898, Higginson joined in the formation of the Anti-Imperialist League.[47]

Bringing together Carnegie, Schurz, William Graham Sumner, William James, Mark Twain, and both Bryan and Cleveland, among others, the League primarily sought to marshal public opinion against further American involvement in the Pacific, especially in the Philippines. As the Filipino revolutionary Emilio Aguinaldo battled in his country against American control, Higginson, in articles and pamphlets, pleaded for Philippine independence. Claiming that America had always favored the underdog, he also suggested that the current view that the insurgents were incapable of self-government was no more valid than King George III's belief that no population was composed of worse men than Boston's. History also showed that because the United States had not seized chances to annex Mexico and Japan, these countries were prospering far more than India under British rule. "When a nation . . .

46. TWH diary, May 7, 1898; *Harper's Bazar, 31* (1898), 495; Leonard Lutwack, "The Dynamics of Conservative Criticism: Literary Criticism in American Magazines, 1880–1900," Unpublished doctoral dissertation, Ohio State University, 1950, pp. 326–27.

47. TWH, "The Casting of a Die," *Harper's Bazar, 31* (1898), 550; *Nation, 67* (1898), 449; Fred H. Harrington, "The Anti-Imperialist Movement in the United States, 1898–1900," *Mississippi Valley Historical Review, 22* (1935), 218.

once enters in the project of managing the affairs of its neighbors it is on the wrong track. . . . Freedom is freedom; and it is not for a nation born and reared on this theory to ignore it in judging the affairs of others." [48]

Speaking at Anti-Imperialist League meetings, Higginson assailed British intentions in the Boer War and, because of Bryan's opposition to imperialism, he actively supported him in the campaign of 1900. These meetings seemed like old mugwump gatherings, and he tried to assure former mugwumps, with their hard-money orientation, that Bryan was more interested in deflating the imperialists than in inflating the currency. In a campaign pamphlet, "Reasons for Voting for Bryan," Higginson argued that American policy in the Philippines "if unchecked can only end in vaster armies, ever increasing pension lists, higher and higher taxes, ending at last in an oligarchy of rich men and in the disappearance of the republic of Jefferson and Lincoln. Every vote for Bryan is a vote to avert this end." [49]

Striving to highlight the racial ramifications of imperialism for the American Negro, he convinced William Lloyd Garrison, Jr., and George Boutwell to join him in issuing the election pamphlet: "How Should a Colored Man Vote?" Just as in his own campaign for Congress in 1888, he now hoped to win Negro votes from the Republicans by calling upon names associated with antislavery. By this time, however, his attitude had changed again about the status of the southern Negro. Back in the seventies and eighties he had been convinced that the race problem was in responsible and humane white hands. And even in 1890, when he had visited the Gettysburg battlefield as state historian responsible for editing *Massachusetts in the Army and Navy*, he was a long way from militant abolitionism. Standing among some veterans of that battle, one of whom had been left deaf by the artillery's roar, Higginson for the first time viewed this silent scene from what seemed like a forgotten era. He observed a great Luna moth quietly reposing

48. Ibid., pp. 211–19; TWH diary, Jan. 6, Feb. 10, April 4, 1899; TWH, "Where Liberty is Not, There is My Country," *Harper's Bazar, 32* (1899), 671.

49. TWH diary, Jan. 16, 1900; TWH to (?), June 3, 1897, Higginson MSS; James Bryce to TWH, Feb. 10, 1899, Higginson-Barney MSS; TWH, "Reasons for Voting for Bryan," Springfield *Republican*, Sept. 1, 1900.

against a tree, and concluded that Gettysburg was a haunting place. When he also remembered the slavery issue in his introduction to a reprint of *Uncle Tom's Cabin*, he said:

> The time is past, fortunately, when "Uncle Tom's Cabin" need be read in any sectional spirit . . . [for slavery was] a mighty wrong, whose responsibility was shared by a whole nation and for which the whole nation paid the bitter price.[50]

Selfish profit had not perpetuated slavery, as he had charged in the antebellum era, rather habit, pride, and tenacious custom. The Republican party, said Higginson in "Anti-Slavery Days," failed to keep the promise of its youth, while the Abolitionists failed to admit that the slaveholder was legally prohibited from freeing his slaves. But it is very unlikely that the urbane Higginson literally shed tears, as Edward Channing mockingly claimed (and others have repeated) over the death of the slaveowner in Thomas Nelson Page's portrayal of kindly master and loyal slave in "Marse Chan." More likely Channing's disdain for Abolitionists explains this exaggeration.[51] It is true, however, that he had come to give greater credence to Page's account of slavery than Theodore Weld's or Mrs. Stowe's.

A change in Higginson's view was evident by 1899. His humanitarian and paternalistic conceptions were affronted by the triumph of jingoist race prejudice, the increase in Jim Crow legislation, and incidents of southern violence—the number of lynchings rose sharply after 1888. He was affected now by the adoption of the grandfather clause to restrict voting in Louisiana, and by McKinley's silence on the matter. Like some others in the North who had justified southern white supremacy as humane and sensible, he was shocked by the race riot in Wilmington, North Carolina, where a score or more of Negroes were killed. Presiding at a protest meeting in Boston, and joined on the platform by Massachusetts Governor J. Williams Brackett and former United States Consul Archibald Grimke, Higginson firmly denied that further patience was

50. "How Should a Colored Man Vote?" Boston *Herald*, Oct. 11, 1900; TWH to M. T. Higginson, April 19, 1890, Higginson MSS; *Massachusetts in the Army and Navy* (2 vols. Boston, 1896); *Uncle Tom's Cabin* (New York, 1898), p. xiii.
51. Ibid., pp. x, xii; TWH, "Anti-Slavery Days," *Outlook*, 60 (1898), 57.

the solution. Instead he urged public protest and economic sanctions against Georgia, the scene of the most recent atrocities. To him the gathering seemed like an "old Anti-Slavery meeting." [52]

Rejecting Negrophobe claims that the colored man had innate tendencies to a licentious self-indulgence, Higginson declared:

> These people have a right to the freedom of civilization, the freedom of political rights, the freedom not merely to escape being held as slaves, but to have a position as free men that is worth having. The trouble is that the freedom of these people in the South is the nominal, not the real freedom. [53]

Also displaying a new repugnance for Thomas Nelson Page's defense of the South, he lashed out in the *Nation*, at the southerner's *Red Rock: A Chronicle of Reconstruction*. Page did not comprehend that "negro suffrage was absolutely the only method by which negroes who had proved almost the sole Southern friends of the Union, could be protected in their most ordinary rights." Higginson now found it "unquestionable that the persons mainly responsible for the misdeeds of the so-called 'carpet-baggers' were the people of the South themselves." [54]

Bryan, therefore, as an opponent of racist imperialism overseas was the friend of the oppressed Negro American. Higginson admitted privately the difficulty in getting his message understood by the black voter, especially the more ignorant. And he was uncertain whether the Democratic party, with its Jim Crow southern wing, deserved the Negro's vote any more than the Republicans. [55]

Bryan's defeat and Roosevelt's eventual succession to the presidency provided another dilemma for Higginson. Roosevelt's White House luncheon invitation to Booker T. Washington not only provoked Bryan's criticism but also his refutation of precisely the arguments Higginson had raised to urge Negro support for the Democrat. Bryan judged it invalid to equate the treatment of Filipinos and Puerto Ricans under imperialist rule with the treatment of the

---

52. Rayford Logan, *The Negro in American Life and Thought* (New York, 1954), p. 89; TWH diary, May 9, 1899; Boston *Evening Transcript*, May 10, 1899.
53. Ibid.
54. TWH to Editor, *Nation*, 66 (1899), 22.
55. TWH to Wm. L. Garrison, Jr., Sept. 11, 14, 1900, Garrison Family MSS.

southern Negro. For the Negro, he argued, still had the Constitution's protection and merely experienced what was common in all civilized countries: "It is simply a question as to which race shall exert a controlling influence. . . . The more advanced race has always exercised the right to impose conditions upon those less advanced." Even Lincoln, he maintained, had understood the fallacy of advocating social equality. Booker T. Washington's efforts on behalf of his race "will be weakened rather than strengthened by any efforts on his part to desert those of his own color in order to shine in white society. . . . Race pride, like self-respect, is a valuable characteristic." [56]

Feeling betrayed, Higginson responded by canceling his subscription to Bryan's *Commoner*. "It is in my opinion an essential part of Democracy," he wrote Bryan, "that social distinctions should be merely individual, not racial. Character is character and education is education. What social gradations exist should be effaced as rapidly as possible." Heatedly denying that Abolitionists had been anti-equalitarian (Higginson would attack James Ford Rhodes on the same grounds), he avoided any further discussion of Bryan's justification of Negro disfranchisement. Nor is there any record that Higginson replied to Bryan's subsequent assertion that social equality leads to amalgamation of the races.[57]

Disenchanted with Bryan he turned to Booker T. Washington, who at least championed the Negro. This black spokesman for accommodation to southern racism told Higginson: "It gives me great pleasure to know that your own views coincided so fully with mine, and that you believe that education is a cure for most, if not all, of the evils from which we suffer." During the 1904 campaign, Higginson did not support either Roosevelt or Alton B. Parker. Roosevelt was an imperialist and Parker "must rely for support chiefly on the solid South [which] has taken up an attitude wholly inconsistent with our pledge to the negroes." Higginson's Phi Beta Kappa poem, which he read at Harvard in 1904, recalled the source of this pledge. Asking whether anything could be nobler than forgiving former southern foes, he responded that it would be even

56. Ibid., Sept. 15, 1900; *Commoner*, Nov. 1, 1900.
57. TWH to Bryan, Nov. 27, 1901, James Ford Rhodes to TWH, Oct. 24, 1905, Bryan to TWH, Dec. 3, 1901, Higginson MSS.

more noble to pardon Negroes from the onus of being black. Negro soldiers had heroically filled the depleted white ranks of the Union army, he noted. "You built Shaw's statue: can you calmly doubt that those who marched with him should vote, like you?" [58]

But these words were directed, of course, to an educated and predominantly white northern audience. He rejected civil rights agitation as a means to redeem the pledge to protect the southern Negro. "I constantly urge my colored friends," he assured Thomas Nelson Page, "to be peaceful & hopeful & leave the future to settle matters for itself, under the influence of higher education all around." [59]

From the public platform Higginson praised the important educational movement in the South. His goal for Negro education was the same as Booker T. Washington's—a chance to become self-supporting. Negroes eventually would move from old huts to comfortable homes if they sought vocational education and "did not expect to force providence." Having become reconciled to the deteriorating southern racial situation, Higginson had little to offer for justice. More revealing than he intended was his comment, after having attended a reception at a Boston home for aged Negroes: "It is a long time since I have been so close in relations with them & their hearts were as warm as ever." [60]

Higginson, at eighty-six, prepared an important statement about race relations for a meeting in June 1909. The meeting of the National Negro Conference, sponsored by John Dewey, Jane Addams, William Dean Howells, Oswald Garrison Villard, and W. E. B. DuBois demanded civil and political equality for the Negro. Incensed by the 1908 race riot in Springfield, Illinois, the delegates rejected Booker T. Washington's faith in patience and industrial education. Instead, they laid the foundation for the organization of the National Association for the Advancement of Colored People during the following year.[61]

58. B. T. Washington to TWH, June 20, 1904, Higginson MSS; TWH to William Roscoe Thayer, Oct. 18, 1904, Thayer MSS; *Harvard Graduates' Magazine*, *13* (1904), 47.

59. TWH to Thomas Nelson Page, May 3, 1905, Page MSS, Duke University.

60. Fitchburg *Daily Sentinel*, Nov. 9, 1905; TWH diary, Feb. 23, 1904.

61. Frederick L. Broderick, *W. E. B. DuBois* (Stanford, 1959), p. 90; Elliot M. Rudwick, *W. E. B. DuBois* (Philadelphia, 1960), pp. 120, 122.

Because of age Higginson was unable to attend this National Negro Conference meeting, but he forwarded his view:

> In 1868 and ever since I have regarded the indiscriminate extension of the suffrage to an entire class as class, whether negroes or others, to be politically inexpedient; that is not conducive to the general interest, which in this particular is more important than the interest of the individual.

Without explicitly admitting his support for Negro suffrage during Reconstruction, Higginson now said that having enfranchised him was "particularly unwise" inasmuch as it was

> a cause of great friction between the races and an injury to the negro himself. He would better turn himself to his industrial and educational development than to strive for the establishment of a civil and political status which . . . can never be effectually attained or if ever, only through a conflict of terrible consequences. . . . No white community will ever consent to the political supremacy of either the black man or the colored man or the yellow man. I make this declaration philosophically and as a result of observation and reflection and absolutely without feeling of prejudice, for I have none.[62]

In conclusion, he asked the convention to abandon its advocacy of Negro civil and political rights and to refrain from complicating and embarrassing the work of the new Taft administration, which could not overrule the action of the Supreme Court. The Negro's true friends instead should conciliate the more progressive class of southern white citizens and remember that "the first great step is to have public schools at all, either for whites or blacks." [63]

A year later, Higginson defended sectional conciliation against the criticism of one of the founders of the N.A.A.C.P., Albert Pillsbury: "It must be remembered that the Southerners were not fighting *primarily* for slavery, but for the states rights in which they had been bred & to which they were loyal." [64]

62. Boston *Evening Transcript*, June 1, 1909.
63. Ibid.
64. TWH to Pillsbury, Feb. 21, 1910, Higginson MSS.

Higginson outlived most of the reformers and literary figures whom he had known during his long life. He delivered an address at the funeral of the Reverend Samuel Johnson, his Divinity School friend, and at the memorial service for his Abolitionist ally Samuel Gridley Howe; he was among the large group which boarded the special train to Concord to attend Emerson's funeral. In later years he spoke at the burial of Lucy Stone and was present at those of Julia Ward Howe, Horace Scudder, Thomas Bailey Aldrich, and Edward Everett Hale. With the privilege of an old man who frequently attends the ceremonies accompanying death, he judged that Hale's funeral was "rather impressive but not to be compared with Aldrich's." And in newspaper obituaries and magazine reminiscences Higginson evaluated the lives of Parker, Bronson Alcott, Whittier, Garrison, Phillips, Grant, Sumner, R. H. Dana, G. W. Curtis, G. F. Hoar, Agassiz, Stedman, and Norton, among others. He frequently delivered a public address, "People I have Met." [65]

But neither nostalgia nor the tempo of old age satiated his interest in new American developments or in physical activity. At age sixty he had learned to ride a tricycle which brought back the pleasure of real exercise, though he was surprised that his legs tired from the effort. With his young daughter settled behind him he enjoyed cycling from his home on Buckingham Street down Brattle Street to the Harvard Yard. His health was so good at sixty-six that a life insurance company agreed to issue him a policy. [66]

His wife and daughter continued to provide the domestic pleasure lacking during his first marriage. Even when she was ill Minnie maintained her "sweet look" and congenial disposition. His diary indicates either that he spent more time with Margaret than with his wife, or that being with his daughter seemed especially worth recording. He found her full of "stuff and character" and was gratified that she had no wish to go to college, but was a good pianist and had a fine voice. The Higginsons presented their daughter at a coming-out party for six hundred guests at Brattle Hall. [67]

65. TWH to Moncure Conway, June 9, 1882, Conway MSS; TWH diary, Aug. 21, 1898, Feb. 15, 1901, April 3, 1902, June 10, 13, Oct. 16, 1909.

66. Ibid., Oct. 16, 1883, Sept. 1898, Jan. 1901, Feb. 15, 1901; Eva Moore, "Intimate Glimpses of Thomas Wentworth Higginson," MS, 1936, Harvard Archives; TWH to A. Higginson, Jan. 28, 1890, Higginson MSS.

67. TWH to Ellen Conway, Dec. 10, 1883, Oct. 12, 1885, Conway MSS; TWH

At times during the nineties, Higginson's health failed severely. A milk diet and extended rest were required to soothe what his doctor described as "neurosis of the stomach, a sort of nervous dyspepsia." At other times he suffered from eczema. But he was able to maintain an active voice in national affairs, give public lectures, write prodigiously (hiring a secretary and also learning to type at seventy-five), and to receive in person the honors bestowed upon a man of renown. When elected vice-president of the Harvard Phi Beta Kappa chapter he was both pleased and surprised: "I have had so little reason to think myself a favorite son of my Alma Mater." Later learning that Western Reserve University planned to give him an honorary degree he bitterly commented: "Harvard has certainly given the LL.D. to some whom I cannot regard as my superiors." Soon after, President Eliot sent him the traditional letter: "The Corporation and Overseers have an intention the execution of which would depend upon your presence at Sanders Theatre on Commencement Day." Higginson recorded, on June 28, 1898: "Received degree of LL.D. somewhat tardily, but glad of delay for the sake of applause from the audience. . . . It was wholly a surprise for me and was something to have lived for." [68]

Applause also came from other sources as he learned from Professor Brander Matthews of the Columbia University English Department that his *Atlantic Essays* were studied in class with essays by Franklin, Emerson, Thoreau, and Parkman. Higginson placed fourth among forty candidates in a public poll conducted by the magazine *Literary Life* to choose an Academy of Immortals from among living Americans. Only Edison, Twain, and Carnegie received more votes; he was chosen the leading essayist, John Burroughs was second. Twice invited to deliver the Lowell Institute Lectures in Boston, he spoke about American orators and oratory, and then about American literature. During four trips to Europe, in 1872, 1878, 1879, and 1901, he was cordially received by some of the world's famous literary figures.[69]

---

to Edmund C. Stedman, May 2, 1899, Aug. 22, 1905, Stedman MSS; TWH diary, Dec. 4, 1899.

68. TWH to Matthews, June 19, 1890, Matthews MSS; TWH diary, July 1, 1887, May 14, June 28, Sept. 1, 1898; Charles W. Eliot to TWH, May 24, 1898, Higginson-Barney MSS.

69. Brander Matthews to TWH, Dec. 18, 1892, Higginson-Barney MSS; Newspaper clipping, Feb. 1900, Higginson MSS; *Yesterdays*, pp. 270–325.

Although no longer belonging to twenty-six clubs, ranging from the Massachusetts Bicycle Club to the Dante Club, and no longer having to pay $100 in assorted annual dues, he still regularly attended meetings of the Boston Authors' Club, and he still gave money to needy college students and instructors and to the stranger seeking carfare home—but the latter risked being followed and asked to return the money if he headed for a saloon.[70]

Fascinated in his old age by the automobile, he also enjoyed a ride on the recently completed New York City subway: "went by admirable underground railroad to 42nd Street station in 10 minutes." Then, perhaps to get his bearings, this man, who had been born when Monroe was President, visited the more familiar surroundings of the New York Harvard Club. In Cambridge he described his enjoyment of a Harvard football game by characteristically noting: "When a young man attempts to kick a goal in such a game as today's, he has 36,000 pairs of eyes fastened with interest upon him. Is there any other such opportunity in life?"[71]

Higginson was the center of attention at a Harvard Commencement in 1906 when he led the Phi Beta Kappa procession and heard a Negro graduate deliver an address entitled: "Colonel Higginson and the First Colored Regiment." As one of three surviving members of the Class of 1841 his picture appeared in local newspapers: a tall and erect figure at the head of the line of Harvard alumni. During the annual meeting of the Phi Beta Kappa chapter, he proposed an amendment to the society's constitution to allow ladies from other chapters to attend anniversary dinners of the Harvard society. At his sixty-fifth reunion dinner, which he attended with Mrs. Higginson, two toasts were offered: "one to the survivors, drunk merrily, and the other to 'The Class of '41'—and that was drained in silence and an empty glass turned down."[72]

As Higginson became reconciled to the likely transcience of his literary reputation he began to realize that he had earned a noteworthy place in the history of American reform. Looking back at the causes that had succeeded and those that still remained, he

70. TWH diary, 1886; TWH to Julia Ward Howe, Feb. 5, 1907, Higginson-Barney MSS; Moore, "Glimpses of Thomas Wentworth Higginson."

71. TWH diary, Nov. 22, 1901, Dec. 11, 1905, May 19, 1906.

72. Ibid., June 8, 1906; Newspaper clipping, "Graduation Book," p. 127, MS, Harvard Archives; *Harvard Graduates' Magazine*, 15 (1906), 78; Boston *Herald*, June 28, 1906.

wrote in the Epilogue to his autobiography, *Cheerful Yesterdays:*

> Personally I should like to live to see international arbitration
> secured, civil service reform completed, free trade established;
> to find the legal and educational rights of the two sexes equal-
> ized; to know that all cities are honestly governed . . . ; to see
> natural monopolies owned by the public, not in private hands;
> to see drunkenness extirpated; to live under absolute as well
> as nominal religious freedom; to perceive American literature
> to be thoroughly emancipated from the habit of colonial def-
> erence.[73]

Conspicuously absent in this era of Jim Crow injustice was any
mention of Negro rights.

By forsaking his antebellum militancy Higginson largely had
avoided the alienated role of the radical reformer. Mugwumps and
Progressives, unlike Abolitionists, were seldom ostracized socially
or professionally nor were they charged with fanaticism. Higginson remained sympathetic with Philip Nolan's plight in *The Man
Without a Country*, but as a social critic and man of moral courage
in an age of imperialistic nationalism, he came to believe that Hale's
story had too much of the "My Country, right or wrong" spirit
about it. He had remained a reformer, therefore, although he had
abandoned radicalism. Having been more militant in his abolitionism than Sumner, Garrison, or Phillips, he had come to embrace
the compromising view of Booker T. Washington. Born when family still helped determine a man's status, growing up in a society
where wealth became the major source of power and vied with
the democratic process for political control, Higginson generally
had rejected the criteria of birth, wealth, and thoroughgoing equalitarianism. Instead he espoused the stewardship of the publicly active
man of education. "If all the scholar's education in a republic," he
wrote, "gives him no infallible advantage over the man who cannot
read or write," then the educated have failed.[74] Unlike many of his
educated contemporaries, however, Higginson would not denounce
democracy. "The glory of universal suffrage," he wrote, "is in the

73. TWH, *Yesterdays*, p. 363.
74. TWH to Eve Tappan, Mar. 20, 1903, Misc. MSS, Essex Institute; TWH,
"The Cowardice of Culture," *Atlantic Monthly, 96* (1905), 485.

power it gives to intellectual leaders; a man of trained intellect really throws not one vote only, but a thousand." [75] The means by which Higginson as an intellectual exerted such power varied, of course, with personal and public needs.

During his childhood and adolescence, an emphasis on manly self-assurance and paternalism had developed in a manner far surpassing his similarly inclined contemporaries. He displayed aggressive action primarily in the Negro's cause—through militant words and more conspicuously through physical feats. With an increased sense of personal fulfillment during his second marriage (and the fathering of a child), his need for physical dominance markedly diminished. He then strove to attain intellectual leadership through literature: even granting the literary fecundity of many nineteenth-century writers, Higginson's enormous amount of diverse publications suggest that writing became another way to prove his strength. He also sought to maintain a moral leadership by pursuing non-militant means to achieve reforms. Yet in the context of both the racism and economic changes of the late nineteenth century and early twentieth century, Higginson's very moderation excluded him from the vanguard of those fighting for the rights of Negroes, laborers, and farmers. Perennially an optimist, he now succumbed to the widespread liberal faith in "time." The sense of romantic immediacy that had been one of his motives for abolitionist radicalism had given way to compromise. [76]

While his psychological needs undoubtedly helped shape his conscious and unconscious choices in the public sphere, his society and its history also limited and shaped his choices, and indeed gave impetus to his personal needs. The contrast, therefore, of Higginson's antebellum militancy to his post-Reconstruction moderation must also be understood in relation to the historical changes in institutional alternatives, social issues, and radical values. Henry James reflected the opinion of many antebellum intellectuals in noting the relative absence of institutions in America." But by 1880 they were

75. Ibid.

76. An excellent discussion of the American concept of gradualism relative to abolitionism is Martin Duberman's, "The Northern Response to Slavery," in *The Antislavery Vanguard*, pp. 395–400.

77. For a seminal analysis of the anti-institutional aspects of antebellum life and thought, see Elkins, *Slavery*, pp. 142–43, 193–206. This theme is further developed

more clearly discernible and fully acknowledged. Universities, literature and art, government and business bureaucracies, and a class of writers and academics had become part of the national scene. That "anarchic individualism" which dominated the antebellum era now was only one of the paths open to reformers. No longer did a middle-class reformer have to join a maverick Free Soil party or an antipolitical Garrisonian organization, or have to advocate revolution to express moral opposition to the status quo. The Republican party, for a time, had become a powerful vehicle for reform. When it failed ultimately to fulfill its ideals, a moderate reformer could abandon it and seek to influence the Democrats with real hope of some accomplishments. Even during the great political miasma of the last twenty-five years of the nineteenth century, and certainly during the Progressive era, there was more hope to be found within the established parties than Abolitionists could have looked for from Garrison's rise in 1830 to the formation of the Republican party in 1854. And the new professional institutions provided channels for protest; it was those connected with these institutions who were the mugwump and Progressive leaders.

The legacy of the past was important too. Abolition for Higginson and his contemporaries had been based upon the simple moral issue that slavery was evil. Simple moral issues, however, were less evident to urban middle-class reformers in the new era unless one pointed to dishonesty in government and advocated civil service reform. The issues raised by labor and farm leaders were complex, and economic rather than moral. There was a certain continuity in premises, therefore, between radical Abolitionists and mugwump moderates.

Before the Civil War, and to some degree before the abandonment of radical Reconstruction, radical abolitionism did not require a thoroughgoing commitment to equalitarianism but rather to individual freedom. After the war, new forms of radicalism rested more heavily upon equalitarianism—a value which the paternalistic Hig-

in George H. Frederickson's important book, *The Inner Civil War* (New York, 1965), which, in my opinion, too exclusively emphasizes the organizational demands of the Civil War as the cause of the new faith in institutions. Also, Frederickson does not recognize the importance of the antebellum legacy in keeping many intellectuals close to pluralistic individualism and away from equalitarianism.

ginson had mainly rejected. Grover Cleveland and the mugwump program represented the cause of individual freedom to many humanitarian reformers. But individualism itself, now tied more tightly than ever to economic acquisitiveness, was losing its moral force. It is less true that Higginson moved away from antebellum radicalism than that radical assumptions had shifted. He remained convinced that only the few very well-educated men fathomed the basic needs of society: "Thus does every reform lie latent in the public mind until the public finds its leaders." [78] Eugene V. Debs and Tom Watson were not the appropriate leaders for him nor were his assumptions and goals the more equalitarian ones of the labor movement or the Populists. Higginson acted in the tradition of the educated Puritan ministry of Francis and John Higginson and followed the later, more secular Higginsons, who assumed their stewardship as cultivated public leaders. For a reformer whose life spanned abolitionism and progressivism, Higginson was remarkably consistent—history was less so.

Hopes to perpetuate his memory were raised by the marriage of his daughter to a Boston physician, J. Dellinger Barney, and the birth of a grandson, Wentworth Higginson Barney. He was pleased, of course, when his daughter published, under her maiden name, two short stories which reflected her father's belief in immortality and his love for children. But her baby pleased him most: "I have a living representative in the new generation after I am gone. . . . [He] makes immortality seem nearer and less improbable." While maintaining his belief in life after death, Higginson hated to accept the imminent, cruel end of communication "between the living and the so-called dead." Close to the end, he continued to keep his diary as he had done for seventy-six years. In April 1911 he grew too weak to write in it. And on May 9, seven months short of his eighty-eighth birthday, Mrs. Higginson recorded in its pages: "Passed from earth 11:30 P.M." [79]

Religious services were held in the First Parish Church of Cambridge, which he had attended as a boy. The Thomas Wentworth

---

78. TWH, "The Cowardice of Culture," pp. 485, 486.

79. Margaret Waldo Higginson, "A Little Story of a Child," *Outlook*, 84 (1906), 476–78, and "The Soul of Little Manuel, *Outlook*, 87 (1907), 75, 77; TWH diary, Aug. 13, 15, 1905, Oct. 22, 1906, April 29, 1911.

Higginson Loyal Legion Post conducted military honors and a group of black soldiers sounded muffled drums. The worn flag of the 1st South Carolina Volunteers draped the coffin. There was a reading from Aldrich's "Monody on the Death of Wendell Phillips." Two of Higginson's hymns, "Waiting for the Bugle" and "To Thine Eternal Arms, O God," were sung. His ashes were deposited in Mt. Auburn Cemetery in Cambridge.[80]

Two days after Higginson's death, Francis Jackson Garrison, president of the Boston branch of the N.A.A.C.P. wrote that his last communication from Higginson was a postcard expressing surprise that he had not been asked to join the general committee for the annual N.A.A.C.P. convention in Boston. "I replied that it was because he had refused to give his name two years ago when the Association was formed," noted Garrison. "But I was sorry that I had not given him a last chance." [81]

80. Cambridge *Chronicle*, May 13, 1911.
81. Francis Jackson Garrison to Ellen Wright Garrison, May 11, 1911, Villard MSS, Houghton Library.

Manuscripts Cited

The following list indicates the location of manuscript collections cited in the previous pages. It does not indicate the miscellaneous collections, the locations of which are given in the footnotes.

Andrew, John Albion, MSS, Massachusetts Historical Society
Atkinson, Edward, MSS, Massachusetts Historical Society
Banks, Nathaniel P., MSS, Essex Institute, Salem, Massachusetts
Brown, John, MSS, Massachusetts Historical Society
Carter, Robert, MSS, Houghton Library, Harvard University
Clarke, James Freeman, MSS, Houghton Library
Conway, Moncure, MSS, Columbia University
Dana, Richard Henry, Jr., MSS, Massachusetts Historical Society
Eliot, Charles William, MSS, Houghton Library
Ellis, George E., MSS, Massachusetts Historical Society
Fields, James T., MSS, Massachusetts Historical Society
Foster, Abby Kelley, MSS, Worcester Historical Society
Foster, Stephen S., MSS, American Antiquarian Society, Worcester, Massachusetts
Fuller Family MSS, Houghton Library
Galatea MSS, Boston Public Library
Garrison Family MSS, Smith College
Garrison, William Lloyd, MSS, Boston Public Library
Gay, Sydney, MSS, Columbia University
Harvard College Papers, Harvard University Archives
Harvard Corporation Papers, Harvard University Archives
Harvard Secretary File, Harvard University Archives
Harvard-Student MSS, Harvard University Archives
Higginson, Thomas Wentworth, MSS, Houghton Library
Higginson-Barney MSS, Houghton Library
Higginson-Brown MSS, Boston Public Library
Higginson-Burns MSS, Boston Public Library

Higginson-Duke MSS, Duke University
Higginson-Huntington MSS, Huntington Library
Higginson-Kansas MSS, Kansas State Historical Society
Higginson-Student MSS, Harvard University Archives
Hinton, Richard J., MSS, Kansas State Historical Society
Howells, William Dean, MSS, Houghton Library
Hutchinson, William, MSS, Kansas State Historical Society
Hyatt, Thaddeus, MSS, Kansas State Historical Society
Johnson, Samuel, MSS, Essex Institute
Knox, Henry, MSS, Massachusetts Historical Society
Lowell, James, Russell, MSS, Houghton Library
McKim, J. Miller, MSS, Cornell University
Matthews, Brander, MSS, Columbia University
May, Samuel J., Jr., MSS, Boston Public Library
Osgood, Samuel, MSS, New York Historical Society
Parish Records, First Religious Society of Newburyport, Newbury-
   port, Massachusetts
Parker, Theodore, MSS, Boston Public Library
Pierce, Edward L., MSS, Houghton Library
Siebert, William H., MSS, Houghton Library
Sparks, Jared, MSS, Houghton Library
Spooner, Lysander, MSS, Boston Public Library
Stedman, Edmund C., MSS, Columbia University
Sumner, Charles, MSS, Houghton Library
Villard, Oswald Garrison, MSS, Columbia University
Weston, Marie (Chapman), MSS, Boston Public Library
Whitney-Benjamin MSS, Boston Public Library
Whittier, John Greenleaf, MSS, Essex Institute
Woodberry, George, MSS, Columbia University

Books Published by Higginson

Winifred Mather's *A Bibliography of Thomas Wentworth Higginson* (Cambridge, 1906) and Mary Thacher Higginson's *Thomas Wentworth Higginson* (Boston, 1914) contain an incomplete list of Higginson's articles and books that includes some 500 titles. My footnotes and the indexes to the *Woman's Journal, Atlantic Monthly,* and the *Nation* expand this number considerably. The following are books written or edited by Higginson:

Thalatta, TWH and Samuel Longfellow, eds., Boston, 1853.
Out-door Papers, Boston, 1863.
Harvard Memorial Biographies, TWH ed., Cambridge, 1866, 2 volumes.
Malbone: An Oldport Romance, Boston, 1869.
Army Life in a Black Regiment, Boston, 1870.
Atlantic Essays, Boston, 1871.
Oldport Days, Boston, 1873.
English Statesmen, New York, 1875.
Young Folks' History of the United States, Boston, 1875.
A Book of American Explorers, Boston, 1877.
Short Studies of American Authors, Boston, 1880.
Common Sense About Women, Boston, 1881.
Margaret Fuller Ossoli, Boston, 1884.
Larger History of the United States, New York, 1885.
Hints on Writing and Speech-making, Boston, 1887.
Travellers and Outlaws, Boston, 1889.
Life and Times of Francis Higginson, New York, 1890.
Poems of Emily Dickinson, TWH and Mabel Loomis Todd, eds. Boston, 1890.
Poems by Emily Dickinson: Second Series, Mabel Loomis Todd and TWH, eds., Boston, 1891.
Concerning All of Us, New York, 1892.
The New World and the New Book, Boston, 1892.

Such as They Are: Poems, TWH and Mary T. Higginson, Boston, 1893.

English History for American Readers, TWH and Edward Channing, New York, 1893.

Massachusetts in the Army and Navy during the Civil War, TWH ed., Boston, 1895–96.

Cheerful Yesterdays, Boston, 1896.

Book and Heart: Essays on Literature and Life, New York, 1897.

Contemporaries, Boston, 1899.

Writings of Thomas Wentworth Higginson, Boston, 1900, 7 volumes.

Henry Wadsworth Longfellow, Boston, 1902.

John Greenleaf Whittier, New York, 1902.

Reader's History of American Literature, TWH and Henry H. Boynton, Boston, 1903.

Part of a Man's Life, Boston, 1905.

Life and Times of Stephen Higginson, Boston, 1907.

Carlyle's Laugh, and Other Surprises, Boston, 1909.

Descendants of the Reverend Francis Higginson, Boston, 1911.

Index

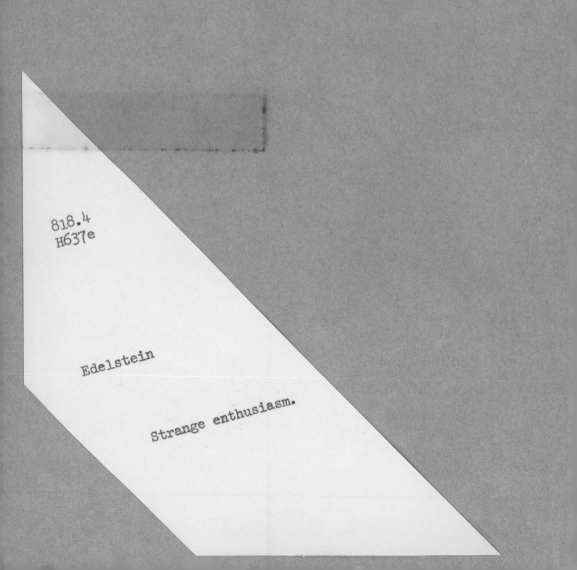